The Peoples of the British Isles

Also available from Lyceum Books, Inc.

The Peoples of the British Isles: A New History from Prehistoric Times to 1688, 3E by Stanford E. Lehmberg and Samantha A. Meigs
The Peoples of the British Isles: A New History from 1688 to 1870, 3E by Thomas William Heyck
The Peoples of the British Isles: A New History from 1870 to the Present, 3E by Thomas William Heyck
The New Nature of History by Arthur Marwick
The Middle Classes in Europe 1789–1914 France, Germany, Italy, and Russia by Pamela M. Pilbeam
The Transformation of Intellectual Life in Victorian England by Thomas William Heyck

The Peoples of the British Isles
A New History

From 1688 to 1870

Third Edition

Volume Two

Thomas William Heyck
Northwestern University

LYCEUM
BOOKS, INC.

5758 S. Blackstone Ave.
Chicago, Illinois 60637

For Hunter and Shannon, literally

© Lyceum Books, Inc., 2008
Published by

LYCEUM BOOKS, INC.
5758 S. Blackstone Ave.
Chicago, Illinois 60637
773+643-1903 (Fax)
773+643-1902 (Phone)
lyceum@lyceumbooks.com
http://www.lyceumbooks.com

12 11 10 09 08   1 2 3 4 5

ISBN: 978-1-933478-23-4

Library of Congress Cataloging-in-Publication Data

Lehmberg, Stanford E.
    Peoples of the British Isles : a new history / Stanford E. Lehmberg, Samantha A. Meigs. — 3rd ed.
        p. cm.
    Vols. 2–3 by Thomas William Heyck.
    Includes bibliographical references and index.
        ISBN 978-1-933478-01-2 (v. 1 : alk. paper) — ISBN 978-1-933478-23-4 (v. 2 : alk. paper) — ISBN 978-1-933478-24-1 (v. 3 : alk. paper)
    1. Great Britain—History. 2. Ethnology—Great Britain. 3. Ireland—History. 4. Ethnology—Ireland. I. Meigs, Samantha A., 1958– II. Heyck, Thomas William, 1938– III. Title.
DA30.L44 2008
941—dc22   2007047345

Contents

List of Illustrations ix
List of Maps xi
Preface xiii

Part I The Age of the Landed Oligarchy, 1688–1763 1

1 The Lands and Peoples of the British Isles at the End of the Seventeenth Century ... 3
England 5
Wales 12
Scotland 14
Ireland 18
Suggested Reading 22

2 The Revolution of 1688 and the Revolution Settlement 25
The Reign of Charles II, 1660–1685 25
Whigs and Tories Rebel, 1685–1688 28
William III and the Revolution in England 32
The Revolution in Ireland, 1688–1691 36
The Revolution in Scotland, 1688–1692 39
Foreign Wars, 1689–1713 41
The Hanoverian Succession, 1714 44
Suggested Reading 45

3 Society and Economy in England, 1715–1763 47
The Social Structure: An Open Hierarchy 47
Social Relations: Property, Patronage, and Deference 51
Land, Marriage, and the Family 53
The Agricultural System 57
Commerce 59
Custom Versus Contract 62
Suggested Reading 63

4 Political Structure and Politics in England, 1715–1760 65
Achieving Political Stability, 1700–1720 65
Local Government 68
The Structure of National Politics, 1715–1760 71
Walpole and the Robinocracy 73
William Pitt the Elder 76
Popular Politics 78
The Growth of the British State 80
Suggested Reading 81

5 High Culture and Popular Culture in Eighteenth-Century England 83
The Enlightenment in England 84
The Empiricist Tradition 84

Natural Religion and Deism 87
Literature 89
Religion and the Church 91
Architecture and Painting 94
Popular Culture: Facts of Life 98
Beliefs and Values 100
Recreations 101
Suggested Reading 102

6 Scotland in the Eighteenth Century **105**
The Union: 1707 105
The Jacobite Rebellion of 1715 107
The '45 109
The Destruction of the Clans 112
The Scottish Enlightenment 115
Suggested Reading 119

7 The Expansion of British Power and Empire, 1715–1763 .... **121**
The European State System 121
British Interests and Power 123
The Colonies 126
The War of Jenkins' Ear—King George's War (1739–1748) 131
The Seven Years' War (1756–1763) 132
The Prizes of Victory 135
Suggested Reading 136

Part II The Age of Revolutions, 1763–1815 .... **139**

8 The Crisis of Empire, 1763–1783 .... **141**
George III and the Politicians 141
John Wilkes and Popular Politics 144
Britons into Americans 146
Tightening the Empire 149
The War for Colonial Independence 152
The Aftermath 155
Suggested Reading 156

9 The Rise of the Protestant Nation in Ireland **159**
The Protestant Landlords and Their Culture 159
Economy, Land, and Potatoes 162
Rise of the Protestant Nation 166
Grattan's Parliament 169
Suggested Reading 172

10 The Triple Revolution, 1760–1815 .... **173**
The Agricultural Revolution 174
Enclosure 175
The Population Explosion 177
The Industrial Revolution 180
Key Industries: Iron, Coal, and Cotton 181
Geographical Specialization 186

Causes of Industrialization 187
Social Preconditions 188
Cultural Preconditions 189
Social Consequences of the Triple Revolution 190
Suggested Reading 196

11 The War Against the French Revolution, 1789–1815 .... **197**
William Pitt the Younger and National Revival 197
Origins of the War with France 200
War with France, 1793–1798 202
The War at Home 204
The Crisis of 1797–1798 205
War, 1798–1815 208
The Prizes and Costs of War, 1793–1815 211
Suggested Reading 213

12 Intellectual and Spiritual Revolutions, 1780–1815 .... **215**
Utilitarianism 215
Parson Malthus 217
John Wesley and the Theology of Revival 218
The Appeals of Methodism 221
The Evangelicals 223
Methodism in Wales 224
Romanticism 225
The English Romantic Poets 226
Romanticism in Wales and Scotland 228
British Romantic Architecture and Painting 231
Suggested Reading 232

Part III The Rise of Victorian Society, 1815–1870 .... **235**

13 Class Society, 1815–1850 .... **237**
British and Irish Populations, 1815–1850 238
The British Economy, 1815–1850 240
The Landed Class: Aristocracy and Gentry 243
The Middle Class 247
The Working Class 252
Suggested Reading 257

14 Politics and the State, 1815–1850 .... **259**
The Structure of Politics and the Scope of the State in 1815 259
Two Decades of Reform, 1815–1835 261
The Structure of Politics, 1832–1850 266
The Condition of England, 1832–1850 270
Class Politics: Anti-Corn Law League and Chartism 273
Suggested Reading 278

15 Ireland from the Union to the Famine **281**
The Irish Question 281
Daniel O'Connell and Catholic Emancipation 285
Repeal and Young Ireland 287

The Great Famine, 1845–1850 289
Young Ireland and 1848 293
Suggested Reading 295

16 Mid-Victorian Society and Culture, 1850–1870 .... **297**
Economic Stability 297
Muting of Social Conflict 299
The Crystal Palace, 1851 301
High Culture of the Victorian Period 303
Exemplars: Carlyle, Dickens, Tennyson, and Mill 304
Women Writers in the Victorian Period 308
Victorian Painting and Architecture 309
The Rise of Science 311
Natural Science and the Decline of Religion 313
Suggested Reading 316

17 The Overflow of Power—British Empire and Foreign Policy, 1815–1870 .... **319**
British Power and Interests 319
The Free Trade Empire 320
India 326
Foreign Policy, 1815–1850 329
The Crimean War 332
Splendid Isolation and an Imperial Culture 334
Suggested Reading 336

Appendixes **339**
A Kings and Queens of Great Britain, 1685–1901 339
B Chief Cabinet Ministers, 1721–1874 341

Index **345**

List of Illustrations

Chapter 1
London in the late seventeenth century 6
Highland clansmen of the late seventeenth century 16
Monea Castle, Ireland 22

Chapter 2
William of Orange landing at Torbay in 1688 33
The First Duke of Marlborough, by Adriaen van der Werff 43

Chapter 3
Mr and Mrs Andrews, by Thomas Gainsborough 48
Marriage à-la-Mode, by William Hogarth 55
The Warrener, by George Morland 58

Chapter 4
The Polling, by William Hogarth 67
Sir Robert Walpole as Ranger of Richmond Park, by John Wootton 74
William Pitt, First Earl of Chatham, by Richard Brompton 77

Chapter 5
John Locke, by M. Dahl 85
St. Martin's-in-the-Field 95
Mereworth Castle, Kent 96
Mrs. Siddons as the Tragic Muse, by Sir Joshua Reynolds 97

Chapter 6
The Battle of Culloden, by D. Morier 111
Adam Smith 117

Chapter 7
Britannia in Distress 125
The British Victory at Quebec 134

Chapter 8
George III in Coronation Robes, by Allan Ramsay 142
John Wilkes, by William Hogarth 145

Chapter 9
Irish Volunteers Firing a Salute in Lisburn, 1782, by John Carey 167
Parliament House, Dublin 170

Chapter 10
The Iron Bridge at Coalbrookdale, by William Williams 182
Boulton and Watt Steam Engine 183
Woman and child dragging a basket of coal in a mine 193
A threatening letter from General Ludd to the foreman of a Nottingham jury . . . 195

Chapter 11
Prime Minister William Pitt the Younger addressing the House of Commons ... 198
Admiral Horatio Nelson at the Battle of Trafalgar 209

Chapter 12
John Wesley Preaching in Cornwall, by Frank Dadd 219
The Royal Pavilion, Brighton 229
The Hay-Wain, by John Constable 230
A Fire at Sea, c.1835 231

Chapter 13
Over London by Rail, by Gustave Doré 239
Excavation of the Olive Mount on the Liverpool to Manchester Railway,
by Thomas Valentine Roberts 243
Queen Victoria, Prince Albert, and Their First Five Children,
by Franz Winterhalter 249

Chapter 14
Sir Robert Peel, by H. W. Pickersgill 268
Dear bread and cheap bread, a membership card of the
national Anti-Corn Law League 274
The last great Chartist demonstration, 1848 277

Chapter 15
Daniel O'Connell 288
The Great Famine in Ireland, 1846 290

Chapter 16
The Crystal Palace, 1851 302
The Ladies' Advocate. A *Punch* cartoon of John Stuart Mill 307
Past and Present, Number One, by Augustus Egg 309
The Houses of Parliament 310

Chapter 17
An imperial scene of the Indian Mutiny, 1857 328
Lord Palmerston 330

List of Maps

Historic counties of Great Britain and Ireland 2
Topography of the British Isles 11
The British Empire in 1689 127
The British Empire in 1815 128
Military campaigns against the American colonists during the
American Revolution 154
The advance of the Industrial Revolution from 1760 to 1848
    The Industrial Revolution in 1760 184
    The Industrial Revolution in 1848 185
The British Empire in 1870 323

Preface

The purpose of this book is to tell the story (or rather, stories) of the peoples of the British Isles in the first two centuries of the modern period. It is a great story, full of drama and relevance to the peoples of the former Empire and the United States. The book is meant to be different from the conventional English history textbooks in two ways. First, it covers *British and Irish*, not just English history. Second, it takes as its central focus the lives of all the peoples of the British Isles, not just those of the political elite. Because England has long been the largest and most powerful country in the British Isles, English history will receive the most coverage. Indeed, one of the main themes of British history in the modern period—that is, since the end of the seventeenth century—has been the expansion of English power and influence within the British Isles. But Wales, Scotland, and Ireland have in the last fifty years or so become the subjects of vital, growing, and fascinating historiographies that demand the attention of students of British history. The histories of the peoples of what came to be called "the Celtic fringe" often had much in common with the history of the English, but at times they diverged sharply. To study comparatively the development of the different societies in the British Isles often throws new light on seemingly well-known events. Moreover, the Welsh, Scots, and Irish were often "problems" for the English, but the English were problems for them as well. To treat the Celtic peoples as mere intrusions into the English story yields not only a deformed historical account of Wales, Scotland, and Ireland but also an incomplete history of the British Isles as a whole.

Economic and social history form the backbone of this account. The book thus follows the most exciting trends in recent historiography. When dealing with national politics, the book offers two things: (1) an account of the origin and development of the British state; and (2) analysis of the structure, functions, and impact of the political system as it evolved rather than a detailed narrative. It places "high politics" in the context of the whole way of life of the peoples of the British Isles. The focus, then, throughout is on the lives of "real" people—how they made a living, how they organized their society and institutions, how they related to each other individually and in groups, and how they understood themselves and their world. What was it like to be a farm laborer in the English Midlands in the 1730s or a Highland clansman in the 1760s? How did a handloom weaver experience the advent of steam-powered textile mills? How did middle-class men and women understand class and gender? What were the consequences of famine in Irish society? This book will attend to these kinds of questions.

Each of the historical eras spanned by the years 1688 to 1870 has its own character, its own special mix of economic arrangements, social structure, political style, and cultural expressions. The three parts of the book are meant to mark out for analysis these historical eras—the age of the landed oligarchy; the age of revolutions; and the rise of Victorian society. The flow of historical events is continuous, and certain themes tie the historical eras together. One is the expansion of English influence within the British Isles and the formation under English leadership of the multinational British state. Related to that is the development of separate national identities in the Celtic countries. A second theme is the rise of Great Britain to great power status and then its decline to the rank of an ordinary European power. A third is the remarkable economic expansion of the late eighteenth and nineteenth centuries, which made Britain the first industrial nation in the world and which has been followed by a long and painful relative industrial contraction and economy restructuring. Fourth, there is the theme of changing social structure and social relations—the origins and development of class society from the social hierarchy of preindustrial Britain. Finally, there is the theme of the evolving structure of the state and the political system, which involves not only the expansion of the role of the state in the British economy and society but also the development of democratic institutions.

If this book succeeds, it will be by helping students understand the peoples of the British Isles in the early twenty-first century—why they are the way they are. It should also help American students understand themselves and their own society a little better, for the British are enough like the Americans to make comparisons numerous and enough different to make contrasts revealing.

A NOTE ON TERMINOLOGY

Because Britain is a multinational state that does not now include all of the peoples of the British Isles, one should be very careful about using labels like "English" and "British." But this is an area in which it is difficult to be perfectly consistent and to avoid irritating nationalist sensibilities. Geographically speaking, "Britain" correctly denotes the whole island composed of England, Wales, and Scotland, but not Ireland. But "Britain" has also been used by people around the world to refer to the United Kingdom, which came to existence only in 1707, which included Ireland from 1801 to 1921, but which today includes only Northern Ireland as well as England, Wales, and Scotland. For much of the nineteenth century, "Britain" meant not only the United Kingdom but also the British Empire. At the same time, many people both within the British Isles and around the world said "England" when they meant "Britain," and by force of habit many people still do. Today, "Britain" technically means "the United Kingdom of Great Britain and Northern Ireland," but it would make no sense to apply that usage to any historical period before 1921.

I have done my best to refer to the English, Welsh, Scots, and Irish as the circumstances require, to be careful when speaking of "Britain," and to be accurate in distinguishing the political entity of England from that of Great Britain.

ACKNOWLEDGMENTS

I would like to thank a number of people for the help they have provided in the writing of this book. First and foremost are all the scholars of modern British and Irish history on whose work this volume depends. They are too numerous to name here, and even the Suggested Readings after each chapter give only a partial indication of my debt to them; but I hope that all will understand how much I appreciate their contributions even where I have given my own twist. I have learned a great deal over the years from Larry McCaffrey of Loyola University, Emmet Larkin of the University of Chicago, and from my colleagues and friends at Northwestern: Lacey Baldwin Smith, Tim Breen, and Harold Perkin. My undergraduate students at Northwestern have played a larger role in this book than they know, and I am grateful to them and to my energetic and resourceful research assistants: Kevin Mahler, Jill Marquis, Helen Harnett, and Suzette Lemrow. Thanks go to the scholars who have read and commented on all or parts of the book: Stewart J. Brown, James Cronin, Stanford Lehmberg, and Standish Meacham. Thanks also go to the reviewers—Nancy Fix Anderson, Loyola University, New Orleans; George L. Bernstein, Tulane University, New Orleans; Anna Clark, University of North Carolina, Charlotte; Kimberly K. Estep, Auburn University; Walter R. Johnson, Northwestern Oklahoma State University, Alva; Neil Rabitoy, California State University, Los Angeles; Karl Von den Steinen, California State University, Sacramento; and Meredith Veldman, Louisiana State University, Baton Rouge—for their helpful comments. David Follmer has been supportive at several stages of the work. Greatest thanks of all go to my wife, Denis Heyck, who willingly helped in countless ways since the inception of this project.

Part I

The Age of the Landed Oligarchy

1688–1763

Historic counties of Great Britain and Ireland

Chapter 1

The Lands and Peoples of the British Isles at the End of the Seventeenth Century

In the three centuries since 1688, life has changed almost totally for the peoples of the British Isles. Most people at the end of the seventeenth century were engaged in agriculture; at the end of the twentieth and the beginning of the twenty-first, most are involved in industry or allied services. In the seventeenth century, most people lived in rural villages; in the twenty-first, most live in dense metropolitan areas. Before 1700, the social structure generally took the form of an intricately graded hierarchy; by the 1900s, a class system prevailed. In the late seventeenth century, society was characterized by face-to-face relationships; today, social relations tend to be more impersonal and bureaucratic. Most women before 1700 lived in subordination to men; by the end of the twentieth first century, relations between men and women were more equal. Life expectancy in the seventeenth century was perhaps thirty-five years; today it stands at over seventy. The number of people living in the British Isles has increased more than fivefold. The scope as well as the pace of individual experiences has increased at a dizzying rate. In those three centuries Britain has solidified as a nation, has grown to great power status, and now has receded to a more normal position as an average European state. In short, since 1688 the British and Irish peoples have experienced as much change as any on earth, and more than most.

One of the most striking ways in which the British Isles of the late seventeenth century differed from that of the 2000s was the degree to which geography and climate dominated the life of people and contributed to sharp regional differences—differences not only in local customs but also in economy, politics, and culture. The British Isles are not spacious, containing approximately 121,000 square miles (slightly more than half the size of France). They include a remarkable variety of regional topographies, everything from rolling hills to craggy peaks, from watery bogs to storm-beaten rocky islands. The suddenness of changes in landscape can make Britain seem a large nation to the traveler. This fact was accentuated in the late seventeenth century by poor roads and slow means of travel. In 1700, it took more than two days to travel from London to Bath, four and one-half days from London to Manchester, and eleven days from London to Edinburgh. In bad weather, many roads became impassable and travel by sea impossible. In good conditions communications were slow and undependable; hence there was little central government control.

Great Britain as a political entity did not exist. It is true that Wales had been administratively absorbed by England in the sixteenth century, but Scotland and Ireland retained much of their ancient independent status. The Scots had resisted English encroachment since the thirteenth century. In 1603, an accident of inheritance made James VI of Scotland also James I of England, but this union of crowns did not unite the two countries. Scotland had its own Parliament, legal system (based on Roman law rather than Common Law), and established church. As for Ireland, Henry VIII of England had been designated king of Ireland by the Irish Parliament. But the English conquest of Ireland was far from complete at that point; indeed, it was not until the beginning of the nineteenth century that the English took the final step in eradicating Irish autonomy, only to find that autonomy successfully reasserted 120 years later.

In the late seventeenth century, then, there was no British state; nor was there a single national community. The English amounted to slightly more than one-half of the 9 to 9.5 million people in the British Isles toward the end of the seventeenth century, and their culture as well as power tended to spread outward into Wales, Scotland, and Ireland. Generally speaking, the closer any part of the British Isles was to England, more specifically London, the more strongly it felt English influence. But the peoples of the British Isles were (and are) a mixture of a variety of ethnic groups, and the various original cultures were still much in evidence. In England, the Celtic population had long since been submerged by successive invasions of Anglo-Saxons, Scandinavians, and Normans. Even so, Cornish was still spoken in the southwestern corner of England, and Welsh was spoken in Herefordshire. In Wales, Scotland, and Ireland, the Celtic heritage was very prominent. The vast majority of the people in Wales and Ireland spoke no English, nor did many clansmen in the Scottish Highlands. English Common Law was alien to these Celtic areas, though in Wales it had prevailed officially for a century. In Wales, the established church was the Church of England, but because the Scriptures and Prayer Book were available in Welsh, Anglicanism actually contributed to the preservation of Welshness. In Scotland, the church preferred by a majority of people was Presbyterian rather than Episcopalian, and this "kirk" was much more strongly influenced by Calvinism than by the Church of England. In Ireland, the Anglican church was also the official religion, but the overwhelming majority of the people were Roman Catholics. In sum, by neither political tradition, language, cultural heritage, nor religious affiliation was there yet a British nation. Many people, isolated and illiterate, probably identified with nothing larger than a county, a region, a village, or a clan; insofar as they felt any national allegiance it was as an Englishman, a Welshman, a Scot, or an Irishman. These allegiances have died hard, if at all. Over the centuries many people have retained their local loyalties even as their sense of being British matured.

ENGLAND

England is the largest and most geographically blessed of the countries in the British Isles. It encompasses 50,851 square miles, with nearly 2,000 miles of coastline. No point in England is more than 75 miles from the sea, and most of England is deeply etched by rivers and river mouths. Naturally, the proximity of the sea has had a great impact on English history and culture. For a long time, the seas provided relatively easy avenues of invasion for peoples from the Continent, and this remained a threat through the eighteenth century. But the sea also made the English enthusiastic sailors, turning their attention to fishing, to overseas trade, and eventually to oceanic empire. Out of their seafaring tradition the English developed the resources in ships and skilled men by which they converted their position as an offshore island of Europe into a great source of security. But in the late seventeenth century, the threat from the sea still seemed as great as the safety it offered.

England generally is characterized by rolling hills and valleys. Like the weather, the topography does not run to extremes. The land is highest in the North and West and gradually drops away to green undulating plains in the Midlands, South, and East. The North of England is dominated by the Pennine chain of low mountains, which run southward from Northumberland and Yorkshire to the Midland plain. Most of this hill country is too rough for tillage and is best for hill pasturage in its valleys and moorlands. Eventually, the Pennine hills would be the principal area of iron and coal mining. The Midland plain, including Cheshire, Staffordshire, Worcester, and Warwick, is extremely fertile rolling land, long the heart of rural England. To the south and east of the Midland plain, from the English Channel on the south to the eastern part of Yorkshire, is a wide belt of rich agricultural land, very productive of grain, vegetables, and cattle. In the Southwest lies a high plateau covering much of Devon and Cornwall. This corner of England has a dramatic, picturesque coast with excellent natural harbors, and inland it includes desolate, boggy moors—Exmoor, Bodmin Moor, and Dartmoor—on which even today a traveler can scarcely imagine that he or she is still in a densely populated island.

The English climate is moderate and well suited for farming. The prevailing wind is from the southwest, which means that the warm waters of the Gulf Stream tend to pull average temperatures upward. Consequently, although England lies as far north as Labrador, the temperature hovers between cold and warm: the coldest month has a mean temperature of 40°F, the warmest 62°F. Rainfall is plentiful everywhere in England, though heaviest in the western hills, where the rainfall averages 35 inches per year. Because of the moderate climate and the fertile soils, agriculture spread through most of England. The once dense forests, characterized

London in the late seventeenth century: a view from the River Thames at London Bridge. This engraving, completed in 1675, shows London as rebuilt after the Great Fire of 1666. Note the magnificent dome of the new St. Paul's Cathedral, designed by Sir Christopher Wren.

by oak, ash, and elm, had largely been cut by the last half of the seventeenth century, especially in the South and East. As early as Queen Elizabeth's reign, the English were concerned about a shortage of timber for fuel and shipbuilding—perhaps the earliest indication that the English population would put great pressure on natural resources.

The English population stood at about five million at the end of the seventeenth century. The Midlands and Southeast were relatively densely populated compared to the Uplands of the North and Northwest and the moors of the Southwest. Throughout England the population was distributed in nucleated villages in the valleys and river bottoms. About three-fifths of all English men and women lived in villages of three or four hundred people, and given the poor roads and lack of economic impetus, few ever moved outside their villages or local county market towns. Apart from London, only Bristol and Norwich had more than twenty thousand people. There were about eight hundred country market towns, but together they comprised less than 15 percent of the population.

London was the great exception to the rule of rural life in the seventeenth century. Its population was 550,000 in 1700, about 11 percent of the population of England, and it was growing rapidly, having doubled in size since 1600. London was the largest European city west of Constantinople. It was the center of national politics, the location of the high courts, the greatest port in England by far, the radiating nucleus of foreign trade, and the home of a growing financial interest. It was also the receptacle of thousands of unemployed from the provinces and teemed with street people of all sorts—vagrants, venders, cutpurses, confidence men, prostitutes, gamblers, and beggars. London was the focal point of fashion but was also regarded as an unhealthy influence on the nation, partly because it drained away wealth and population and partly because it housed the makings of a mob that might intimidate the government.

Important as it was, London was not England. The great majority of English men and women of the late seventeenth century spent their lives in the villages and fields of the countryside. To be sure, the elite of the social order—the families of the two hundred temporal and spiritual lords, plus those of the richest of the non-noble landowners—liked to spend several months a year enjoying the London "season." Yet even these wealthiest of families lived for most of the year in their great country houses. Maintenance of political power and social order demanded their presence in the country. The aristocracy (titled nobility) and gentry (large landown-ers)—a total of approximately fifteen thousand families—stood at the top of the social hierarchy, which ranged downward from the gentry through yeomen, tenant farmers, village tradesmen and craftsmen, farm laborers, cottagers, and paupers. Maintenance of social order, which was crucial to people who had lived through the turmoil of civil war in the 1640s and 1650s, required that the elite display their superiority in person, exact deference from their inferiors, and carry out local administration and justice. Moreover, many of the local squires were too poor and socially inept to venture into London.

Backwoods squires—coarse-mannered, rough-and-ready in dispensing justice, patriotic, independent, and suspicious of London monied interests—correctly regarded themselves as the heart of the nation. After the restoration of the Stuart line in 1660, the gentry reigned like little kings in the countryside. There was no police or standing army, and the gentry controlled the militia. As justices of the peace (J.P.s), the gentry took responsibility for law and order at the local level; as justices of the Quarter Sessions, teams of J.P.s ruled the counties. They were not paid for this work. As Sir William Petty said, "The honour of being trusted and the pleasure of being feared hath been thought a competent reward."

The populace over whom the aristocracy and gentry ruled was divided into a number of social orders. Some (perhaps 30 percent of the population) were small farmers, both owners and tenants, and their families; others (another 10–12 per-cent) were professionals, merchants, tradesmen, shopkeepers, and craftsmen (and craftswomen) and their families. Most of the rest—"the laboring poor"—led pre-carious lives of relentless work. The majority were farm laborers (men, women, and children) who worked the land for the farmers and landowners. The landowners took care to win for themselves absolute rights of private property during the sev-enteenth century, but they gave no such rights to tenants and laborers, who remained completely dependent on the landowners. The only restraints recognized by the big landlords were the documented rights of small owners, the goodwill aris-ing from immemorial custom, and the stubborn insistence by the poor on their tra-ditional rights. The customs of paternalism constituted the best hope for the poor.

Standards of living varied wildly in late seventeenth-century England. The wealthiest aristocrats and gentry enjoyed upward of several thousand pounds ster-ling a year, but most laborers earned twenty pounds a year or less. Some of the

Royalist aristocracy and gentry were overwhelmed by the fines and debts incurred during the Civil War, but on the whole the tendency was toward larger estates. The bulk of the population, however, lived at the margin of real hardship. Agricultural techniques had been very slowly improving, and by the late seventeenth century the English people were beginning to leave behind the subsistence crises that from time immemorial had periodically afflicted the population. Nevertheless, bad weather could still cause a poor harvest, high bread prices, and widespread hunger. Housing improved in the second half of the century, many of the traditional hovels being replaced by stone or brick houses.

Compared to the rest of the British Isles, England in the late 1600s was a prosperous nation. Agriculture was the main source of wealth as well as the principal occupation. The medieval system of agriculture had long been in decline in England, being replaced by more commercially oriented farming, and most crops were produced for the market rather than for subsistence. Further, much land had been enclosed (that is, fenced in) for pasturage since the sixteenth century. However, a majority of English farming went forward according to time-honored custom, most notably in the Midlands, where the old open-field system still prevailed. Very little English farming was specialized, except in a few areas such as the environs of London, where market gardening for the ever expanding London population prospered. Grains were the main crops—a variety of wheat, plus some barleys and oats. A new style, progressive agriculture, was introduced in Norfolk by aggressive landlords interested in turning a profit, but the extent of this progress in the seventeenth century should not be exaggerated. Harvests were generally good in the 1680s, and England even began to export surplus wheat. But this progress was due mainly to incremental improvements in farming techniques and additions to arable land, not to any full-blown agricultural revolution.

England already had a bustling manufacturing sector. The principal industry of the late seventeenth century was wool. England had long been known for the production of wool. Much land had already been enclosed for sheep pasturage, as the landlords did not care whether their profits came from sheep raising or wheat farming. In the seventeenth century, the government prohibited the exportation of unfinished woolen fabric in order to encourage the various English industries involved in producing finished woolens. Between 1660 and 1700 the value of finished woolen cloth exported probably doubled. Woolens were produced everywhere, but principally in the west country between Exeter and Bristol, in East Anglia, and in Yorkshire. Its production was entirely a domestic industry—that is, the wool was "put out" by a merchant to craftsmen in their cottages and carried through the various stages of hand production: carding, spinning, weaving, fulling, and dying. Most of the laborers were farmers and their families, who supplemented their agricultural income by producing the woolens. Hence even this key industry remained highly seasonal and deeply attached to country life.

Woolens were not the only source of England's industrial strength. Although wool production increased in the last decades of the century, its share of industrial exports fell. Assisted by the aggressive English foreign and colonial policy, and by the immigration into England of French Huguenot skilled craftsmen, a number of industries rose in the last part of the century: other textiles such as silk and linen, plus paper, glass, and cheap housewares. Brewing and soap making became major enterprises, as did tin, copper, lead, and coal mining. There was as yet no significant change in the organization of industry, for most production was still carried out in households by nuclear families and apprentices and laborers. Wages were kept low, since it was widely thought that the pinch of poverty alone made the common people work. It is clear in retrospect that England was moving beyond the usual European level in manufacturing and far beyond most of the rest of the British Isles.

The commercial expansion of England was even more impressive. As Professor Charles Wilson wrote: "England was becoming a world entrepôt, serving not only Europe, but the extra-European world, and was herself served by a growing fleet of merchant shipping, a growing equipment of docks, shipyards, wharves and warehouses, a growing community of merchants and tradesmen." Again assisted by an aggressive trade policy of the government, and building on the fact that England was the largest free-trade area in Europe, England's foreign trade expanded in both volume and variety. Exports went up by about 50 percent between 1660 and 1700 and imports by more than 30 percent. Most important in this remarkable expansion of trade were reexports: English merchants imported raw materials and food (like sugar, cotton, and tobacco) as well as slaves from colonial areas and reexported them all over the world. Every transaction brought profits to Englishmen and encouraged the development of comparatively sophisticated financial institutions. Merchants, shipowners, and shipbuilders needed to borrow, and their needs brought into existence a new set of middlemen between lenders and borrowers, principally in London. Scriveners and goldsmiths, with whom lenders could deposit their money, as well as lending merchants, thus became protobankers. By the 1670s, a highly unpopular but very important group of men in the city of London were carrying out the essentials of banking: taking deposits, discounting bills of credit, and issuing notes. The commercial revolution was producing a "financial interest," a sign of the unique (except for Holland) commercialization of the English economy.

The merchants and financiers of England were often associated with religious nonconformity (non-Anglican Protestantism) and so played an important role in the shifting religious composition of the country. Religion was crucial to the English people in the seventeenth century; it was capable of arousing strong emotions and radical political action. Most people still thought that eternal life and death were at stake in matters of church polity and doctrine. Moreover, most people thought that without an established, unified religion, the nation would splinter and the social order would crumble. "Religion it is that keeps the subject in obedience," Sir John Eliot had said. The experience of the Civil War years only confirmed this truth in the minds of the landowners. The great iceberg of English society had turned over for a decade. With the restoration of Charles II in 1660, the iceberg had been righted, the common people resubmerged. Landowners wanted to make sure the great overturning could never happen again. They believed that an established Church of England on the episcopal model (that is, with bishops ruling dioceses) was a main instrument of social order.

The English had long adhered to the tradition that church and state are two parts of one organism. Thus, even though many varieties of Christianity grew up after the Reformation, most believed in a uniform established church, to which all the English people should belong. By the 1660s the form of that church had been in dispute for more than a century. Queen Elizabeth's settlement of the church issue had taken the form of a compromise between the Anglo-Catholicism of her father, Henry VIII, and the more extreme Protestantism advocated by Continental reformers. Thus in Elizabeth's time, the Church of England recognized the monarch as its "supreme governor" and maintained the traditional episcopal ecclesiastical structure. The Church of England retained much of the old Roman Catholic liturgy and a modified sacramental doctrine: the Church was regarded as the true institution established by Jesus to be the necessary intermediary between God and the individual.

Such views had come under attack by the Puritans of the late sixteenth and seventeenth centuries. Puritanism was a general belief in individual judgment based on reading the scriptures firsthand, which downplayed the Church as a divinely established intermediary. Puritanism also denoted a preference for a simpler liturgy and for strictness in the conduct of life. It was a force for reform within the Church of England, appearing in both the English Presbyterian movement and the Independent (Congregationalist) movement of the seventeenth century. Presbyterians would have substituted councils (or presbyteries) of ministers and lay elders for the bishops, whereas independents sought to place ultimate church power in the individual congregations. During the Civil War, Parliament abolished the episcopacy and installed a Presbyterian structure, but the army's belief in independence and toleration soon led to an anarchy of competing sects. Because a majority of the aristocracy and gentry associated these religious reform movements with turmoil and insecurity in state and society, they were determined in 1660 to restore the Church of England on episcopal lines.

One thing the various brands of Protestants agreed on was their opposition—perhaps *fear* and *loathing* are more accurate words—to Roman Catholics. Although the Anglican church was not far removed from Catholicism in doctrine or church structure, it had long been strongly anti-Catholic. The Puritans were ever more militantly anti-Catholic, and for many years they had demanded strict enforcement of the laws against the remaining English Catholics (known as recusants), of whom there were very few, mainly some landed families in the North and Northwest.

When Charles II was invited in 1660 to return to England, he promised "liberty to tender consciences," but Parliament was in no mood to encourage religious pluralism. The Church of England was therefore restored as firmly as the Stuart line. The Act of Uniformity of 1662 required all clergymen to use the Anglican Book of Common Prayer and to subscribe to the Thirty-Nine Articles, the defining creed of

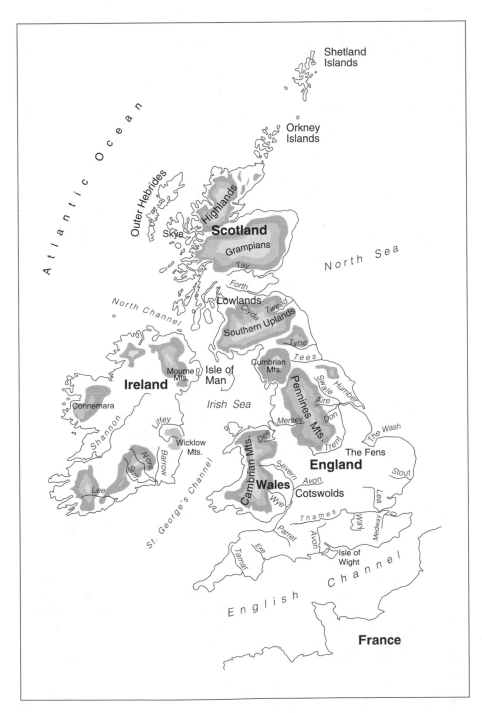

Topography of the British Isles

Anglicanism. The Act also reestablished the authority of the bishops and removed from their livings all clergymen who would not submit. About a thousand clergymen (out of nine thousand total) were thus ejected from the Church of England; they constituted the formal foundation of English nonconformity (or dissent). Subsequent parliamentary acts suppressed any unauthorized religious meeting, whether non-conformist or Roman Catholic. Actually, these acts (collectively known as the Clarendon Code) succeeded only in dividing Protestantism in England. Nonconformists became highly politicized in their efforts to win toleration. Yet Puritans offered surprisingly little resistance to the reimposition of Anglicanism. Perhaps the Puritans had been demoralized and discredited by their association with sedition, or perhaps Puritanism's emotional power was being eroded by the growing atmosphere of rationalism and scientific revolution. In any case, Puritanism in a general sense undoubtedly survived in many English families, both within the Church of England and without, and stood ready to catch fire again in the evangelical movement of the eighteenth century as well as to express its unbending anti-Catholicism.

WALES

Unlike England, Wales is almost entirely mountainous. Nearly all of its area (7,467 square miles, about one-sixth the size of England) is covered by a series of mountains extending roughly from north to south and dominating the whole of the interior. The mountains are highest in the North and South, the central section being a high, broken plateau. There are narrow coastal plains to the south and west, but even these are hilly. The mountainous interior is deeply cut by a number of rivers, which fan down and out from the central ridges toward the Lowland areas. The rivers that rush down steep slopes into broader valleys are especially numerous in South Wales, where great deposits of iron and coal were eventually found.

The Welsh people settled in the valleys of their rugged country. The difficulty of the terrain kept the population sparse: there were not more than 400,000 Welsh people at the end of the seventeenth century. The deep valleys with their steep slopes had long made invasion difficult and enabled the Welsh to preserve much of their ancient Celtic culture. The isolation of individual settlements and the vestiges of Celtic tribalism exaggerated the importance of certain great families, whose aggressive assertion of family rights and pride earned for Wales in the minds of Englishmen a reputation for turbulence. An English member of Parliament in the seventeenth century declared that the Welsh are "an ydolatrous nation and worshippers of divells . . . thrust out into the mountains where they lived long like thiefs and robbers and are to this day the most base, peasantly, perfidious peoples of the world."

Of course, the English themselves had much to do with turbulence in Wales. Land-hungry Norman barons based in England had conquered Wales, often by a process of allying themselves with locally powerful Welsh families. Welsh language and literature, as well as many prominent Welsh families, survived; Norman law and order prevailed only in their baronies. Two subsequent major wars of independence by the Welsh—most notably that of Owen Glendower in the early fifteenth century—encouraged a strong sense of Welsh separateness from Anglo-Norman England. But Welsh attachment to England was strengthened and order spread in the countryside by the fact that Henry Tudor (Henry VII of England) was partly of Welsh blood. By the famous Acts of Union of 1536 and 1542, Henry VIII's eminent civil servant, Thomas Cromwell, redefined the Welsh border, extended the English system of shires and Common Law to Wales, and incorporated Welsh representatives into the English Parliament at Westminster.

The Acts of Union did not integrate the Welsh and English cultures, but they did begin a long process of separating the Welsh ruling order from the mass of the people. In Wales, the aristocracy did not amount to much, and the country was in the hands of the gentry families, most of them Welsh in origin. During the sixteenth and seventeenth centuries, many of the men in these gentry families were attracted by the economic and political opportunities in London; many became pensioners of the English Crown; some married English heiresses. As a result, the Welsh gentry became steadily more anglicized in language, tastes, and style of life. By the latter 1600s, many gentry were losing their ability to speak Welsh, which, however, remained the language of the overwhelming majority of the common people.

Under these conditions, both geographic and cultural, Welsh agriculture in the seventeenth century was comparatively backward. The soil on the whole was poor, and the topography encouraged isolated farms rather than village settlements. Many estates were in the hands of either anglicized Welsh gentry living in England or absentee English landlords. Roads were extremely bad, maintained if at all by forced labor commanded by the local vestry (parish ruling council). Local loyalties remained very strong, as each community was virtually self-supporting. The internal market was weak, and improved farming techniques spread very slowly; even the scythe was uncommon outside the richest wheat-growing valleys. Arable land was scattered in the valleys and river bottoms throughout the Highland interior, but it was always combined with pasturage. Even in the more easily farmed vales of the South and East, only about one-third of the land was arable, the rest being meadows for hay. Hence Welsh agriculture was predominantly pastoral, with sheep and cattle being the most important products. By the late seventeenth century, Welsh drovers herded cattle along eight or nine main roads eastward into the Midlands and South of England.

The conditions of agriculture kept standards of living in Wales very low for the great bulk of the population, lower than that of all but the poorest English men and women. The income of the laboring poor was almost totally dependent on farming. Most lived constantly on the starvation line, eating at the best of times milk and bread but almost no meat. Housing for most people was squalid: huts with mud floors and rush-thatched roofs, heated by peat fires. The vast majority of people were illiterate. Their lives revolved around the seasons and offered little leisure except for Christmas season and saints days. Wandering bards, a relic of Celtic culture, could still spin fantasies of the heroic past, but bardic culture was in decline. Farm activities like harvesting and threshing were done in groups, and these occasions were seized on for singing and dancing—practically the only bright spots in otherwise drab lives.

As is usual in such premodern societies, religion was the main consolation of life. The Reformation of Henry VIII was accepted in Wales without much trouble. As in England, Welsh monasteries were dissolved, churches plundered, and clerical land sold. The gentry benefited; the poor were indifferent. What mattered most to the Welsh was that Elizabeth appointed Welshmen to vacant Welsh bishoprics and had the Bible and Prayer Book translated into Welsh. These translations were required in Welsh-speaking parishes. These steps were important both because they helped preserve Welsh as a living language and because they kept Wales attached to Protestantism. No religious divide appeared between Wales and England such as would poison Anglo-Irish relations.

During the Civil War, Wales remained largely Anglican and Royalist. Only during the reign of Parliament did Puritanism make headway in Wales, and it was on the surface swept away at the Restoration of 1660. But the restored Church of England in Wales stood unreformed. Its dioceses and parishes were too big, allowing nonconformity to thrive at their peripheries. There was a shortage of trained clergymen. Welsh bishops regarded their appointments as stepping-stones to the richer dioceses of England and furthermore had to spend a good part of each year attending the House of Lords in London. Hence, though the Church tried to stamp out nonconformity in Wales, it failed. The nonconformists, rising mainly from the lesser gentry, substantial freeholders, tenants, and townsmen, were not numerous but had strong attachment to the Welsh language. They took an adversarial role against Anglicanism, the religion of the anglicized gentry and magistrates. Eventually, this would produce a severe tension in Welsh society.

SCOTLAND

Nowhere in the British Isles has geography had a more striking effect than in Scotland. The nearly 30,000 square miles of Scotland (about three-fifths the size of England) break into three distinct physical regions: (1) the Highlands; (2) the central plain; and (3) the Southern Uplands, just north of the English border. By long tradition, the latter two regions are referred to as "the Lowlands." Here is found the most fertile land, especially in a broad crescent extending from the central plain around to the eastern and northern coastal areas. But even the fertile crescent is fairly hilly, with much moorland and boggy fields. In the seventeenth century, no natural or manmade borders broke the vista into compact patches. The Lowlands were relatively treeless, a succession of windy moors, fields, and pastures.

The Highlands—about two-thirds of the total land area of Scotland—are much less hospitable than the Lowlands, though Highland scenery is often dramatic and beautiful. The Highlands are defined by the famous "Highland Line," a geological fault that runs from southwest to northeast, from the Firth of Clyde to Stonehaven. Behind the Highland Line—that is, to its north and west—the mountains of the Highlands spring up abruptly in a succession of parallel ridges to the west coast. Off the coast are more than 750 rugged, stony islands; to the far northeast are the islands of Orkney and Shetland. The Highlands and islands have a rugged terrain. Ben Nevis, at 4,500 feet the highest mountain in the British Isles, is in the Scottish Highlands. The mountain ridges are both separated and cut by deep valleys, called straths and glens; travel between these is often difficult. The mountains affect all of Scottish weather, since they receive heavy rainfall (60 inches a year in the West) while protecting eastern Scotland, which is comparatively dry. The Highlands therefore are considerably wetter and colder than the Lowlands—a tough terrain for a tough people.

The isolated straths and glens of the Highlands served as a haven for ancient cultures: Scandinavian in Orkney, Shetland, and Caithness (the northernmost county), and Celtic in the mainland. Celtic peoples once dominated all of Scotland but had been pushed into the Highlands by Anglo-Saxon invasions from the Southeast. In the seventeenth century, Norn, a variety of old Norse, was still spoken in the northern isles. Gaelic alone was spoken in most of the Highlands, and Scots, a derivative of Anglo-Saxon, was spoken in the Midland valleys. English was the language of the Southern Uplands, gradually spreading north and west.

The population of Scotland in the late seventeenth century stood at about one million, and was distributed very differently from today. About half lived in the Highlands and half in the Lowlands, with most of the latter in the central plain. Scotland generally was much more sparsely settled than England. There were about 275 towns ("burghs"), but most were tiny, with a hundred people or fewer. Only Edinburgh (with thirty thousand inhabitants) and Glasgow, Aberdeen, and Dundee (with about ten thousand each) were burghs of significant size. Over 80 percent of all Scots lived in the countryside, usually in hamlets (or "farmtouns"), consisting of a farm large enough to support a plow team. The arable land was too dispersed to support English-style nucleated villages. In the Highlands and Lowlands alike, people clustered on the slopes of strath and glen near the scattered arable land. Most of these country people were peasants, either tenant farmers, subtenants called "crofters" and "cottars," or farm laborers and servants. The upper social orders alone owned land—the nobility, the substantial nonnoble landowners (the "lairds"), and the petty landlords (the "bonnet lairds").

Law and custom alike retained much more of the feudal system in Scotland than in England. The most unusual feature of Scottish society in the seventeenth century was the Highland clans. The clans had originated in the Middle Ages when feudal social and economic relations were grafted onto the old Celtic tribal system. Kinship—real or mythical—was the key to the clans. Every member of a clan, from chieftain to shepherd, was thought to be related by common ancestry to the clan chief; hence a bond of kin loyalty underlay the connection between landlord and tenant. Traditionally, clan bards celebrated the heroism of the tribal ancestors and kept the folkloric genealogy of the clan. Because the primary function of the clan

Highland clansmen of the late seventeenth century. Notice that the clan soldiers are dressed in belted plaids, woolen stockings, and brogues. One carries the characteristic targe (shield) and broadsword.

was military, the clan chief had the right to call to battle all the men of his clan. In fact, most clansmen held land by a form of tenure called "ward-holding," which obliged the tenant to military service as well as rent.

The clans were quite warlike. Succession to clan leadership was by primogeniture, but the new chief was supposed to prove his bravery and honor by leading raids on other clans or on the long-suffering Lowlanders. Further, a crime against a clansman was to be punished not by the national government but by retaliation on the part of the victim's clan. Therefore, the Highlands were the scene of almost constant feuding—raiding and counterraiding as the debts of blood feuds were collected. The fighting often centered around the theft of cattle, since the wealth of a clansman was measured in cattle, the main product of Highland agriculture. The feuding often escalated to near civil war by shifting alliances among the clans, and especially by a long struggle between the Campbells and the Macdonalds for leadership of Highland culture.

This state of society in the Highlands, and its contrast with Lowland society, must be understood if Scottish politics in the late seventeenth and early eighteenth centuries is to be unraveled. Much of the bloodshed that characterized those years was a matter of one clan taking revenge on another. In particular, the expansion of the power of the Campbells in the Southwest was crucial because it set the Campbells at loggerheads with the MacLeans and the Macdonalds. Moreover, the Lowlanders and the Scottish government for many decades sought to end what they saw as lawlessness in the Highlands, as well as frequent eruptions of Highlanders into the Lowlands. The sight of a Highland clan on a raid, dressed in their belted plaids and armed with broadswords, shields, and dirks, was enough to turn any peaceful man's bowels to water—and to call forth repressive edicts known as "Letters of Fire and Sword" from the government. By the late seventeenth century, the clans were under severe pressure and believed that their way of life was at stake.

The standard of living in the Highlands was noticeably lower than in the Lowlands, but it was precarious everywhere. Scottish agriculture was devoted to raising barley, oats, and cattle. Most Scots ate little other than oatmeal, plus some milk, cheese, and butter. They ate oatmeal mixed with milk as porridge, or mixed with water as gruel, or baked as oatbread and bannocks. If the oat crop failed—as it did in the mid-1670s and later 1690s—peasants starved. They wore mainly coarse linen shirts and the blanketlike plaids (the kilt was not worn until the eighteenth century), both woven by the family at home. The nobility lived in substantial homes, more like castles than like country manors, but the peasantry lived in miserable huts. The usual peasant cottage had stone and turf walls, a turf-thatched roof, a mud floor, no glass in the windows, and no chimney. Most were heated by peat fires. Farm animals lived in the cottage with the family, though usually confined by a partition to one end of the single room. The most valuable parts of the cottage in that treeless country were the roof beams, which a family took with them, if allowed, when forced to move.

The Scottish economy suffered from both the harsh natural environment and the political instability of the country. The Lowlands generally were more prosperous than the Highlands. In the central plain, grain growing was fairly successful, though the techniques were almost wholly customary and unimproved. The Highland clans grew as much grain as the land allowed, but almost always needed to import it from the Lowlands. They paid for their grain imports with exports of black cattle. Scottish trade was recovering from the terrible years of war, disease, and confiscation of the 1640s and 1650s, but it could not match the volume or sophistication of the English mercantile sector. The Scots traded agricultural products (hides, skins, fish, wool) to northern Europe and France in return for timber, iron, and manufactured articles. The most important development in Scottish trade was an increase in the regular export of black cattle to England. The London market reached all the way to the Highlands and made cattle droving southward a major enterprise. Close to twenty thousand head of cattle a year were passing through Carlisle in the 1660s. Eventually, this trade would be a crucial link between England and Scotland, sufficient even to overcome centuries of hostility.

The Highland-Lowland division of Scotland had as great an effect on religion as on social structure and standards of living. Broadly speaking, the Highlands in the seventeenth century were too remote for the people to be deeply attached to any branch of religion, whereas the Lowlands were profoundly committed to reformed

Christianity. In the Highlands, a few clans—most notably the Macdonalds—remained Roman Catholic, whereas most of the others were loosely Episcopalian (that is, they believed in a church ruled by bishops). In the Lowlands, Calvinism in Presbyterian form prevailed. The intensity of Lowland Presbyterianism is worthy of note. The Reformation in Scotland had not been led by the Crown but by a broad alliance drawn from the nobility, gentry, and burghers. These people sought to return spiritual care to the mass of the people, whose needs had long been neglected by the Catholic church. Out of a desire to prevent a return to clerical corruption, the Scottish reformers had adopted a system of church government allowing the laity to share power: elected "kirk sessions" (church councils) at the parish level and presbyteries (representative bodies) instead of bishops at the diocesan level. An attempt by Charles I (king of both England and Scotland from 1625 to 1649) to crush Presbyterianism had radicalized the Scottish reformers and put the Scottish church in the hands of the Covenanters—militant Puritans who would brook no compromise with either bishops or an undisciplined populace.

The Covenanting tradition remained a vital part of Scottish life for centuries, especially in the Lowlands. There, the aim of the reformers to establish schools as well as kirk sessions in every locality had largely been met. Presbyterianism penetrated deep into the social structure, and literacy spread much more widely than in any other part of the British Isles. Hence, when Charles II was restored to the Scottish as well as the English throne in 1660, his determination to bring the episcopacy back to Scotland was decidedly unpopular in the Lowlands. Approximately three hundred Scottish clergymen refused to accept the bishops and were ejected from the Church of Scotland. Many of these were extreme Covenanters, as were many of the common people. The government tried in the 1660s and 1670s to stop by force all nonconformist meetings but failed. Violence flared, notably in a Covenanter rising in the Southwest of Scotland, which the government put down with the assistance of Highland troops. The Highlanders seized the occasion to pay back with savage ferocity the grudge they bore from earlier Covenanter persecution. By the 1680s, then, Lowland Scotland was Calvinist and Presbyterian, and the Highlands were at least nominally Episcopalian and Catholic—another dimension to the clash of cultures between Lowlanders and Highlanders.

IRELAND

Everywhere in the British Isles of the seventeenth century, land and religion were vital to the lives of the people, but nowhere were they of such significance, nor their intertwining so explosive and tragic, as in Ireland. The peculiar way that issues of landownership and religious affiliation became tightly bonded would make for extraordinary political violence and economic backwardness in Ireland as well as for strained constitutional relations with England for more than two hundred years.

It seems doubly tragic that Ireland should suffer so, because the Emerald Isle by nature should be a bountiful country. Ireland is the westernmost of the British Isles, situated about 13 miles from Lowland Scotland and 70 miles from England.

It consists of 32,000 square miles; hence it is slightly larger than Scotland and about three-fifths the size of England. Unlike Scotland and Wales, Ireland has no central spine of mountains. The central region of Ireland is a broad, gently rolling plain, surrounded by low mountains. These mountains come in clusters, and routes between them offer easy access to the central plain. No part of Ireland is wholly cut off from the rest, although the mountainous areas of the North and West are remote as well as barren. Further, the northeastern province, Ulster, is fairly clearly defined by a chain of mountains and lakes. The Celtic culture held on longest in the North and West. Indeed, Ulster was the last of the four provinces (the others being Leinster, Munster, and Connacht) to fall to English conquest.

For the most part, the soil of Ireland is good and the climate equable. As the westernmost European offshore island, Ireland is the most subject to the influence of the Atlantic. The weather is consistently cool and damp and does not go to extremes in any direction. Ireland is neither as warm and dry as southeastern England nor as cold and wet as Wales and the Scottish Highlands. A typical day is cloudy and rainy: rain falls 250 days a year in the West and 180 days in the East. A fairly warm drizzle causes the Irish to say, "It's a fine soft day, thanks be to God." The island is green all year long, with lush pastures, meadows, and fields, but the wet climate makes for numerous bogs, heaths, lakes, and streams. Peat bogs even today cover one-seventh of Ireland.

The population of Ireland in the 1680s was about two million. It had increased significantly since midcentury, for the population was recovering from the destructive wars of English conquest in the late sixteenth century and the civil wars of the 1640s and early 1650s. The population was almost entirely rural. As in Scotland and Wales, Celtic culture had never held towns to be of great importance, and even in the late seventeenth century, there were few Irish towns of any size. Dublin, the capital and center of trade, had a population of sixty thousand in 1675. Only a few other port and trading towns had more than five thousand inhabitants—most notably, Cork, Limerick, Waterford, and Galway.

The Irish population was deeply divided over religion. About 75 or 80 percent of the people in Ireland were Roman Catholic; the rest were Anglican and Presbyterian. In Leinster, Munster, and Connacht, the Protestants were a tiny minority among the Catholics, who were about 95 percent of the total. In those three provinces, the Protestants were a thin veneer laid over a vast block of rough Catholic wood. Not so in Ulster, where Protestants amounted to about half of the population, and most of them were concentrated in the six northeastern counties. Everywhere, most Catholics were native Irish, whereas most Protestants were of English or Scottish descent.

To aggravate matters, most landowners by the late seventeenth century were Protestants, and most tenants and farm laborers were Catholics. This startling and dangerous socioreligious alignment developed because the Reformation did not "take" in Ireland. The Irish did not object to Henry VIII's substituting himself for the pope as head of the Church of England, but they resisted when more enthusiastic Protestants tried to impose significant doctrinal reforms on Ireland. The religious dispute in Ireland soon was superimposed on a much older struggle between the English Crown and the Irish Celtic nobility for power in Ireland, a clash reaching back to 1169. That struggle was not finished even at the accession of Queen Elizabeth (1558), and Ireland became the entrepôt for attempts by Catholic powers to win the British Isles back to the papacy. Just as the defense of Anglicanism became a principal ingredient in early English nationalism, so Catholicism became identified with Irish patriotism.

Early in the seventeenth century, Elizabeth's successor, James I of England and VI of Scotland, sought to bring an end to Irish disorder and the threat to English security by the policy of plantation. According to this scheme, land confiscated by the Crown from Irish rebels was redistributed to English and Scottish Protestant "planters," in return for which they were to colonize Ireland with loyal and trustworthy Protestants. This policy had been attempted on a smaller scale in the previous century. Now James had an opportunity to implement it on a large scale in Ulster, where two of the last great Celtic chiefs had fled the country. Between 1610 and 1625 Ulster was "planted" by adventurers who were willing to undertake colonization. Their plantations were more successful than earlier attempts because they were able to bring from England and Scotland colonists at all levels of society—tradesmen, artisans, and tenants as well as landowners. Most of these colonists were in fact Scottish Presbyterians, who from that day to this have given Ulster much of its uniquely hard-working but grim character.

Additional transfers of land were yet to come in the seventeenth century. In 1641, the Catholic aristocracy and gentry, many of whom were native Irish but some of whom were descendants of the Anglo-Norman families who had begun the conquest of Ireland, still owned about 58 percent of all Irish land. But the Civil War, which was more confused and bloody in Ireland than anywhere else in the British Isles, resulted in the confiscation of more Catholic land. The Catholic people of Ireland had precipitated a furious rebellion in 1641 with an outburst of pent-up frustration against Protestant colonists. This alleged massacre eventually brought down on Ireland the wrath of Oliver Cromwell and his Puritan army. The New Model Army crushed the Catholic rebels and opened the way for a massive transfer of land ownership. In order to repay English entrepreneurs who had financed the expedition, to pay off the soldiers of his army, and to plant in Ireland Protestant veterans who might bring order to the countryside, Cromwell expropriated large numbers of Catholic landowners—essentially, all who could not prove their "constant good affection to the commonwealth of England" during the Civil War. Thousands were simply moved into the barren and sparsely settled land west of the Shannon in Connacht; others were packed off into servitude in the West Indies. When it was all over, an additional 35 percent of Irish land was taken from Catholics and given to English Protestants, who were now the landlords of a mass of Gaelic-speaking Irish tenants and farm laborers.

The expropriated Irish Catholic landlords never accepted their fate. Those who could pursued every legal and political means to recover their estates. Some became tenants and laborers—understandably sullen and uncooperative—of the

Anglo-Protestants. Others became bandits who roamed the countryside, half rebel and half thieves—men called "Tories" who assuaged their family pride by stealing from the colonialists. All of the dispossessed hoped that a restoration of the Stuarts to the throne would bring return of their lands.

When Charles II was restored in 1660, the moment of vindication for the expropriated Catholics seemed at hand. But their dreams were not to be realized. Charles II politically could not remove the Cromwellians from their new estates. He arranged a compromise that returned one-third of the Cromwellian estates to Irish landlords, Catholic or not, who had not been guilty of rebellion against the Crown. Nevertheless, English and Scottish landlords planted in Ireland now owned nearly four-fifths of the land, whereas Irish Catholics owned only slightly more than one-fifth.

Under these circumstances, it is remarkable how well the Irish economy performed in the late seventeenth century. The wars had been devastating, the transfer of landownership disruptive, and the social and religious divisions debilitating. Yet the Irish economy made a significant if gradual recovery in the second half of the century. In particular, Ulster prospered, for the plantation policy established new towns, revived old ones, and invigorated farming. The new landlords everywhere in Ireland felt unrestricted by custom, and by hard work and a commercial outlook they increased the output of the hard-pressed agricultural sector. Apart from the domestic production of woolens and linen, iron smelting and the cutting of barrel staves were the most important industries. Both tended to disappear locally when the deposits of iron ore and the stands of trees were exhausted. Cattle constituted the main export, and Irish cattle exporters did so well after the 1650s that English cattle breeders brought pressure on Parliament at Westminster to stop the importation of Irish cattle into England.

By the 1680s, Ireland was probably marginally more productive than Scotland. Nevertheless, it must be emphasized that Ireland remained a backward country, even by premodern standards. The landlords could live in comfort, but as their castlelike fortified houses showed, they were never free from the fear of raids by "Tories" or of a general uprising by the Catholic populace, whose Gaelic tongue they could not understand. Living in isolation, the landlords developed a fortress mentality. Many of them were upstarts—ex-soldiers and "men on the make." Hence the squires and squireens of back-country Ireland were known in England as an exceptionally rough lot—hard drinking, hard riding, heavy gambling swaggerers.

The bulk of the population lived on the brink of starvation and in the midst of unrelenting hardship. Most lived on milk, oatcakes, and potatoes—the last having become common in Ireland by the 1650s. Potatoes and grains alike are vulnerable to wet weather; thus, when the summer growing season was cold and wet, the Irish people had nothing to fall back on. Good weather and bad, most Irish men and women lived out their lives in miserable huts, usually of wattle and mud, sometimes of whitewashed stone, but rarely with floors, chimneys, or even the most primitive furniture. They toiled in their landlords' fields, cut their own peat for fuel, and grew potatoes on small plots with only the simplest tools.

Monea Castle in County Fermanagh, Ireland. This fortified house, built in the early seventeenth century, shows how concerned the inhabitants of Ireland were about security.

For comfort, the majority of Irishmen turned to traditional folkways. One was simple hospitality: sitting around a peat fire in a dark cabin gossiping and telling stories of superstition and the heroes of legend. Sometimes they could welcome one of Ireland's wandering poets, the vestiges of the bardic tradition in which great Celtic families had retained poets and harpers to celebrate clan genealogy and glory. Another folkway was Catholicism, brought to them by hard-pressed priests, most of whom were on the run (for it was the Catholic clergy who suffered most from persecution in Ireland during the Restoration period). Finally, the Irish peasantry enjoyed occasions, such as weddings and wakes, when they could come together with singing, eating, and drinking. The peasants had no education and no books. For news they depended on traveling peddlers. All of these were highly oral activities, which under the circumstances encouraged the telling, retelling, and embroidering of Celtic myths, the manufacture of martyrs, and the fantasizing about the day when the "army of the Gael" would again rise to restore the land to the Irish people. For them, Restoration had not occurred in 1660; it lay in the future.

Suggested Reading

Beckett, J. C., *The Making of Ireland, 1603–1922* (Boston: Faber & Faber, 1987).

Bingham, Caroline, *Beyond the Highland Line: Highland History and Culture* (London: Constable, 1991).

Bottigheimer, Karl S., *Ireland and the Irish: A Short History* (New York: Columbia University Press, 1982).

Canny, Nicholas, *Kingdom and Colony: Ireland in the Atlantic World, 1560–1800* (Baltimore: Johns Hopkins University Press, 1988).

Cullen, L. M., *An Economic History of Ireland Since 1660* (New York: Barnes & Noble, 1972).

Davies, Norman, *The Isles: A History* (New York: Oxford University Press, 1999).

De Paor, Liam, *The Peoples of Ireland, from Prehistory to Modern Times* (Notre Dame, Ind.: University of Notre Dame Press, 1986).

Devine, T.M., *The Scottish Nation: A History, 1700–2000* (New York: Viking, 1999).

Dodd, A. H., *A Short History of Wales* (London: Batsford, 1972).

Dodgshon, R. A., and R. A. Butlin, eds., *An Historical Geography of England and Wales* (New York: Academic Press, 1978).

Evans, E. D., *A History of Wales, 1660–1815* (Cardiff: University of Wales Press, 1976).

Evans, E. Estyn, *Irish Folk Ways* (London: Routledge & Kegan Paul, 1957).

Foster, R. F., *Modern Ireland, 1600–1972* (New York: Allen Lane, 1988).

Grant, I. F., *Highland Folk Ways* (London: Routledge & Kegan Paul, 1957).

Hill, Christopher, *Reformation to Industrial Revolution* (Harmondsworth, England: Penguin, 1969).

Hill, James Michael, *Celtic Warfare, 1595–1763* (Edinburgh: J. Donald, 1986).

Jenkins, Geraint, *The Foundations of Modern Wales: Wales, 1642–1780* (New York: Oxford University Press, 1988).

Kearney, Hugh, *The British Isles: A History of Four Nations* (Cambridge: Cambridge University Press, 1989).

Lenman, Bruce, *An Economic History of Modern Scotland, 1660–1976* (Hamden, Conn.: Archon Books, 1977).

Ohlmeyer, Jane H., ed., *Political Thought in Seventeenth-Century Ireland: Kingdom or Colony* (Cambridge: Cambridge University Press, 2000).

Smout, T. C., *A History of the Scottish People, 1560–1830*, 2nd ed. (London: Collins, 1970).

Tompson, Richard S., *The Atlantic Archipelago* (Lewiston, N .Y.: E. Mellen Press, 1986).

Williams, David, *A History of Modern Wales*, 2nd ed. (London: J. Murray, 1977).

Wilson, Charles, *England's Apprenticeship, 1603–1763*, 2nd ed. (London: Longman, 1984).

Withers, Charles, *Gaelic Scotland: The Transformation of a Cultural Region* (London: Routledge, Chapman, & Hall, 1988).

Wrightson, Keith, *English Society, 1580–1680* (New Brunswick: Rutgers University Press, 1982).

Chapter 2

The Revolution of 1688 and the Revolution Settlement

In the standard interpretation, the modern period in English political and constitutional history is thought of as beginning in 1688. In the so-called Revolution of 1688 and in the Revolution Settlement of the following twenty-five years, the English resolved many of the constitutional issues between Crown and Parliament that had been contested since early in the seventeenth century. These dramatic events laid the groundwork for the remarkable constitutional stability of Britain for the next three centuries. The events of 1688 and the Revolution Settlement asserted the supremacy of Parliament, the liberties of the individual, the security of property, and the rule of law against the arbitrary power of the Crown—and all without bloodshed, in England at least. Not surprisingly, the English have long thought of the developments of 1688 and after as the "Glorious Revolution."

There are, however, problems with this simple interpretation. For one thing, the events of 1688 themselves were not revolutionary but rather were a preemptive act by the English political elite to *avoid* a revolution. For another, there was no social upheaval in 1688 or in the two decades afterward. The revolutionary developments in England came in the years of the Revolution Settlement and were political and constitutional, not social. Moreover, many of these crucial changes in politics and constitution derived from the international conflict in which the English found themselves after 1688. The Revolution of 1688 was not an exclusively *English* event: it was part of European power politics, and it affected all of the British Isles, and its consequences were very different in Scotland and Ireland than in England. Between 1688 and 1715, the English advanced their power in the British Isles, and England became a great power in Europe. The political turmoil of 1688 necessarily involved England in two major European wars, during which the English asserted their influence on a new scale. These processes—the successful rebellion of 1688, the constitutional settlement, and the expansion of English power—were three sides of the same triangle.

THE REIGN OF CHARLES II, 1660–1685

To understand the events of 1688 and after, we must look briefly at the two previous decades. On May 8, 1660, Charles Stuart, who had been invited back from exile, was proclaimed king of England, as well as of Scotland and Ireland, ending eleven years of rule by Parliament and its army. Despite the joyous celebration that greeted his return from exile, many of the constitutional issues that had torn England apart since the early years of the century remained unresolved. Charles II survived the conflict implicit in the unresolved constitutional issues partly by personal qualities and partly by exploiting the fear of civil war. The "Merry Monarch" was a splendid politician, determined not to "go on his travels" again and therefore prepared to give way before a crisis on most issues. He was also a man of few principles and a master of dissimulation. Although an indolent man, Charles possessed grace and wit. Because of the widespread relief of being out from under the bony thumb of Puritanism, the political nation was more than ready to forgive, even to appreciate, his many mistresses, his lusty appetites, and his hearty enjoyment of sport with his rakish young friends. Ever the pragmatist and shrewd tactician, Charles held dear only one principle: the legitimate succession to the throne.

Not even religious belief was vitally important to him. Charles was the cousin of Louis XIV and had spent much of his exile in France; consequently, many Englishmen suspected that Charles was a Catholic. But Charles remained a regular communicant in the Anglican church, converting to Catholicism only on his deathbed. In public policy, Charles preferred toleration; hence, the Clarendon Code, with its penal laws against Catholics and Protestant dissenters, did not originate with him. In 1672, Charles suspended the penal laws by his Declaration of Indulgence, an act of the royal prerogative (arbitrary power). But when Parliament pressured him to cancel the Declaration of Indulgence, he bent to their wish, and the next year, when Parliament passed the Test Act (1673), requiring all Crown officeholders to take the sacraments in the Anglican church, swear the oath of supremacy, and deny the Catholic doctrine of transubstantiation, Charles signed it. Throughout his reign, Charles took care never to appear as an enemy of Protestantism, nor to alienate the Anglican establishment and its supporters.

In another potentially dangerous matter—royal finances—Charles again avoided ultimate confrontation with the English parliament and the country even though he never thought he had enough money. His first Parliament granted him for life far greater revenues than his predecessors had ever enjoyed. Charles was supposed to "live of his own"—that is, conduct the affairs of government on these revenues. But he was expected to return to Parliament to seek money for extraordinary expenses, such as he incurred in the two Dutch wars (1665–1667 and 1672–1674). By keeping Charles on a short leash, Parliament meant to retain some control over his conduct of affairs. In fact, however, the short leash made Charles partially dependent on Louis XIV, monarch of the richest and most powerful nation in Europe, and put Crown and Parliament on a collision course.

The issue over which Charles clashed with Parliament most fiercely was the proposed exclusion from the throne of the rightful heir, Charles's brother James, duke of York. Much to Charles's annoyance, James had converted to Catholicism in 1668. James tended thereafter to display all the zeal characteristic of converts.

Where Charles was clever and flexible, James was slow witted and rigid. From the early 1670s, the desire grew among many Protestants to keep James from succeeding to his inheritance. In 1679, the House of Commons passed a bill that would have excluded James from the succession. This Charles could not accept, and he defeated the measure with one of the strongest weapons still in the monarch's political arsenal: he dissolved Parliament. In 1680, a new House of Commons passed a second Exclusion Bill, and the exclusion of James remained such a threat that Charles dissolved Parliament twice more in 1681. It did not meet again in his lifetime.

The Exclusion Crisis of 1679–1681 brought about the formation of political parties in England, which were restricted to the tiny "political nation" consisting of the aristocracy and gentry plus perhaps 250,000 voters. Those who proposed to exclude James became known as the "Whigs," a derisive label worn theretofore by the ultra-Protestant Covenanter rebels of Scotland. The Whigs were neither republicans nor democrats, but were opponents of royal absolutism, advocates of limited monarchy, and defenders of individual "liberties," which in that day meant not only personal freedom but also the untrammeled right to exploit private property. The Whigs were also fierce defenders of Protestantism, which they equated with the rule of law and free Parliaments. To them, popery necessarily led to absolutism, particularly since James, in their eyes, had so alienated the Protestant people of England that he inevitably must try to rule absolutely.

The Tories—their label taken from expropriated Irish rebels—were devoted to divine right monarchy, though not necessarily to rule by royal prerogative. They were concerned with maintaining order in the state, which implied protection of the divinely established social hierarchy with the king at the top. They felt especially strongly about maintaining the power of society's "natural" rulers—the aristocracy and gentry—in local matters. The Tories saw themselves as defenders of societal peace and harmony and regarded the Whigs as proponents of demogogy, faction, and rebellion. The Tories believed the Whigs were a party of self-interest, whereas they themselves were the party of unity in church and state. In short, the Tories took the Crown and the Anglican church as the twin pillars of social order and peace.

Charles resisted depending on either party, for while in exile he had learned to trust no man or set of advisers. As one official wrote, "He lived with his ministers as he did with his mistresses; he used them, but he was not in love with them." The parties as yet had no means of forcing the king to accept a particular group of advisers for any length of time. Nor could the Crown control Parliament, even with the liberal application of government bribery. The inability of Charles to command the Commons during the Exclusion Crisis proved that from the king's point of view a more certain means of control was mandatory.

Charles chose to do without Parliament altogether until he could alter the constituencies so as to assure himself of a majority of members of Parliament (M.P.s). Louis XIV's financial support helped free him temporarily from dependency on Parliament. Then, from 1681 to his death in 1685, Charles used his prerogative powers to alter the composition of borough (town) constituencies in order to make them politically favorable. Similarly, he tried to win control over the militia and local government by purging Whigs from the ranks of the lords lieutenant, sheriffs, and justices of the peace. His policies, however, threatened the liberties, rights, and property of *all* the local elites, not just those of the Whigs. Local elites had won more power during the Civil War and did not want to give it up. But Charles was saved from confrontation with a united class of landowners by the extraordinary Tory fear of a recurrence of civil war. The Tories hastened to support the monarchy. Charles was also fortunate in dying in 1685: he had failed to bring about toleration of Catholics, but he had throttled his opponents and then died at the peak of the Tory reaction.

WHIGS AND TORIES REBEL, 1685–1688

His brother James was to be far less fortunate. Given the opposition to him during the Exclusion Crisis, James succeeded his brother with surprising ease in 1685. Certainly *he* was surprised, for James expected his accession to be greeted by rebellion. This attitude was characteristic of James, who was not only narrow and rigid but also apprehensive and suspicious. No doubt this is one reason he was so intolerant of opposition. To be sure, James took from his father, Charles I, the idea of a divinely anointed monarchy. But that elevated idea of his status as a king gave James no sense of security. He feared what he knew of the English—their inclination toward faction and obstreperous opposition, not to mention regicide. He regarded concession and compromise as signs of weakness and independent opinion as a badge of disloyalty. In his anxiety, James assumed any opposition was a harbinger of rebellion. Never in English history was there such a clear case of a self-fulfilling prophecy.

Even James's religious policies bore the marks of his apprehensiveness. In his own time, James was thought of as a king who would destroy the Church of England and return the nation to Roman Catholicism. But his motives were much more problematic than that. He was indeed an ardent Catholic and insisted on attending mass in public. He tended to trust only Catholic advisers and to view all Protestants as heretics. He frequently spoke of "establishing" the Catholic church in England, yet it is not clear what he meant. James was not misguided enough to think he could make Catholicism the state church in his own lifetime. He was keenly aware that at the time of his accession the heirs to the throne—his daughters (by his first wife) Mary and Anne—were both Protestants. Apparently he reasoned that if Catholicism in England was to be protected, he would have to move swiftly to establish it on a more secure basis—that is, free from the penalties of the Clarendon Code. He imagined that once Catholicism was free from the penal code, converts would multiply. Thus, despite the obvious difficulties, James was determined to execute his Catholic policy. As he admitted, if he had just kept his religion a private matter, he would have had a successful reign, "but, having been called by Almighty God to rule these kingdoms, he would think of nothing but the propagation of the Catholic religion . . . for which he had been and always would be willing to sacrifice everything, regardless of any mere temporal situation."

James's trouble was that the English Parliament refused to cooperate with him in his Catholic policy. That meant he had to operate by the royal prerogative, which only roused opposition on a second front—defense of parliamentary liberties. Other events had the same effect. The Parliament he summoned immediately after his accession was almost uniformly Tory and eager to please him, for the constituencies had been well prepared by Charles II. Parliament granted James for life almost twice as much in annual revenues as Charles II had enjoyed. But when James asked for repeal of the Test Act, Parliament refused. This request was important to James because he believed he needed to have Catholic officers in the army, which was prohibited by the Test Act. Hardly three months after his accession, the earl of Argyll led a rebellion in Scotland, and a month later, the duke of Monmouth, Charles II's bastard son, invaded the West of England. James's paranoia seemed well founded, and though Parliament granted him the finances he needed to put down the rebellions, he found himself in the end sharply divided from his legislature over the Catholic officers and the continued presence of the army.

The first of these rebellions—that led by Argyll—was largely the result of James's activities in Scotland before he succeeded to the throne. Charles had sent James to Scotland to keep him out of the way during the Exclusion Crisis. James had obtained a Test Act from the Scottish Parliament in 1681, which required all officeholders and parliamentary electors to swear to uphold the royal supremacy in the Scottish state and church and to give up any interest in altering the state or church. This was an oath the ninth earl of Argyll, the son of a Covenanter and a Whig, could not take. Argyll was head of the Campbell family of Argyllshire, a clan that had been expanding their local power at the expense of other clans, particularly the MacLeans and the MacDonalds. While in Scotland, James had tried to curry favor with the Highland clans and knew that he could advance this strategy by using the Test Act to bring down Argyll. In 1681, Argyll fled to the Continent but returned in May 1685 to lead a rebellion against James. His rebellion was a complete fiasco, for the Scottish government staged a preemptive strike against the Argyll Whigs. The earl himself was captured and beheaded.

Monmouth's rebellion was a more serious affair. The duke of Monmouth was a favorite of his father, Charles II, as well as a handsome young man of considerable physical prowess and charm. He was also a Protestant; thus the Whigs hoped to have him legitimized as Charles's successor during the Exclusion Crisis. Although Charles doted on Monmouth, he would not allow James to be supplanted. In June 1685, Monmouth landed in Dorset with a small force, claiming that James had usurped the throne and now threatened the Protestant religion and the rights of Englishmen. Later, Monmouth actually claimed the crown for himself. Monmouth was attractive to the remnants of Puritanism and radicalism found among the artisans and small farmers of the West Country. In a final manifestation of support for the "good old cause," about six thousand men joined Monmouth. But the crucial Whig and Tory gentry did not, nor did radicals in the rest of England. The king's army defeated Monmouth's ragtag and pathetic rebels at Sedgemoor in July, and Monmouth was seized and executed.

James quickly threw away the advantages presented by the defeat of Monmouth's rebellion. In the autumn, Judge George Jeffreys carried out a savage judicial repression of the rebels of the West Country. Jeffreys was later to claim that James encouraged him in his "Bloody Assizes," which he may well have done; in any case Jeffreys felt strongly enough to act on his own. He wrote: "Good God! That we should live in such an age, when men call God to protect them in a rebellion." The landed elite were inclined to think that the rebels got what they deserved and little complained that more than three hundred men were hanged, their corpses left dangling until they rotted. When, however, James sought to maintain his army of twenty thousand men and to keep the ninety Catholic officers he had appointed in defiance of the Test Act, the political nation—Tories included—felt that their liberties and their power were being threatened: Parliament had been defied and a standing army established.

James needed to proceed with utmost caution; instead, he now pursued his "Catholicizing" aims aggressively. He encouraged Catholic priests to return to England, allowed them to proselytize by education and propaganda, exchanged representatives with the Vatican, accepted a Vicar Apostolic (bishop) from Rome, and even took two Jesuits into his intimate circle. In 1686, he began the tactic of "closeting" members of Parliament—canvasing and pressuring them to repeal the Test Act and the Clarendon Code against Catholics. He issued numerous dispensations from the Test Act to enable Catholics to take office. He appointed a Catholic, Richard Talbot, earl of Tyrconnell, lord deputy of Ireland. All of these acts, coming as they did in the wake of Louis XIV's revocation of the Edict of Nantes (which had protected French Protestants), deeply disturbed the English Protestant elite, who believed that James was undermining the laws, the constitution, and the Church of England.

James's policies destroyed any chance he had of maintaining an alliance with the Church of England, which had been a bulwark of royal legitimacy and had adopted a posture of "passive obedience" to the king's will. James aggravated his relations with the Church by reestablishing in new form the old prerogative Court of High Commission, by which he would discipline recalcitrant clergymen. Next, in the winter of 1686–1687, James sought to break the Anglican monopoly over higher education by opening Oxford and Cambridge to Catholics. He successfully appointed Catholics as head of Christ Church, Oxford, and Sidney Sussex College, Cambridge. But when he attempted to catholicize Magdalen College, Oxford, the fellows (all of whom, as at the other Oxbridge colleges, were clergymen in the Church of England) resisted. James then removed the fellows from their posts, which struck English Protestants not only as a blow to Protestantism but also as a threat to the rights of private property. The climax of James's campaign came in April 1687, when he issued a Declaration of Indulgence, suspending by royal edict the Test Act and penal laws against Catholics and dissenters alike.

By then, James had decided that his best hope of support lay with the Protestant dissenters (nonconformists) rather than with the Anglicans. His strategy put the dissenters in a quandry. As the descendants of the Puritans, the dissenters had long been more hostile to Romanism than had the Anglicans; yet their treatment at the hands of the Anglican-dominated Parliament since 1660 and their persecution since the Exclusion Crisis made it hard for them to warm up to the Anglicans, who now reached out to the dissenters in an attempt to form an Anglican-dissenter alliance against the king's popery. The dissenters welcomed toleration but did not trust its author, James. As the marquis of Halifax warned them, James's policy was mere politics: "This alliance, between liberty and infallibility, is bringing together the two most contrary things that are in the world." On the whole, the dissenters agreed, and opted for alliance with Anglicanism. By the spring of 1688, this alliance was maturing. In the end, the dissenters' decision was to win them toleration.

James, however, pressed on doggedly with his plan of establishing toleration for Catholics in order to secure *their* freedom and *his* crown. He extended with a vengeance Charles II's efforts to purge the boroughs, the lord lieutenancies, and the magistracy of his opponents. But now the purged individuals were Tories. He and his agents subjected parliamentary candidates to an inquisition, to determine whether they would repeal the Test Act and Clarendon Code. In April 1688, James reissued the Declaration of Indulgence, and in May ordered the Church of England to have it read aloud in all its parish churches. This was too much even for the most passive Anglicans, for it required them to participate in propagating what they regarded as religious error.

Seven Anglican bishops, including the archbishop of Canterbury, petitioned James on grounds that his prerogative powers gave him no right to force the clergy to read the Declaration. James was surprised and outraged by the petition. He had the seven tried for seditious libel but was unable to win a verdict of guilty. Dissenters rallied round the bishops, and London crowds cheered them when they were acquitted.

Thus in only three years James had succeeded in alienating Whigs and Tories, Anglicans and dissenters, all largely on grounds of a seemingly commendable policy—religious toleration. No doubt Protestant bigotry must share some of the blame, but James's haughty insensitivity and rigidity played a vital role.

Also, luck was against James. One of the reasons that Protestants had accepted him was that his heirs were Protestant. James was fifty-one when he acceded to the throne, and his second wife, the Catholic Mary of Modena, had proved to be infertile. But in November 1687, she announced to a surprised and skeptical world that she was pregnant. Many Protestants assumed that her pregnancy was a fake, a scheme to produce a Catholic heir. On June 10, 1688, Mary gave birth to a son, which meant that James's Catholic goals would be continued. Frantic Protestant propaganda suggested that the baby was not the queen's child but had been smuggled into the royal bedchamber in a warming pan. Hence the atmosphere in which the seven bishops were tried was full of hysteria and intrigue. Therefore, it is not surprising that on the evening of June 30, the same day the bishops were acquitted, seven men—six English nobles and one bishop, three of them Tories and four

Whigs—wrote William of Orange, the Protestant stadtholder of Holland and husband of James's eldest daughter Mary, to come to England with an army to assist them (and the 95 percent of the English population they claimed to represent) to resolve their problems with James.

WILLIAM III AND THE REVOLUTION IN ENGLAND

William, in fact, already had made up his mind to intervene in England. The invitation from the "Immortal Seven" had been written at his request. William had been carefully watching English affairs for years, and his agents were in frequent contact with English political leaders. Yet it would be wrong to say that William originated the plot to overthrow James. William was a cautious, shrewd opportunist, who sought to take advantage of the English opposition to James in order to fulfill the great goal of his life: to block the expansion of Louis XIV's France.

William of Orange accomplished much in his strenuous life (1650–1702), but he was a strange man and would become an unpopular king of England. He was a silent, reserved, moody Calvinist, hawk-nosed, thin, and chronically ill. He was not a brilliant politician or soldier, but he had a dogged tenacity that served him well. As prince of the House of Orange, William was distrusted by many leaders in the Dutch Republic, who suspected that he aimed to be the absolute ruler of the United Provinces. Actually, William sought only to use whatever power he might gain, in Holland and in England, to play the role he believed God had assigned him—to defeat the Catholic France of the Sun King. His design on England was simply to commit England against France, or at worst to keep it neutral. A grandson of Charles I and husband of Mary Stuart, eldest daughter and heiress presumptive to James II, William harbored no desire to diminish the power of the English Crown. From his point of view, the ideal would be for England to escape civil war with the monarchy intact for Mary to inherit, meanwhile allying with the Dutch against France. Alas, James was destroying any chance for the ideal to become real.

The decisive event for William was the birth of an heir to James and Mary of Modena—which William was all too ready to consider as a fraud perpetrated by the Jesuits. Fed by biased and even hysterical information from English and Scottish exiles in Holland, William by 1688 feared that England would be torn apart by civil war. One way or another, his wife Mary was being deprived of her inheritance. In April 1688, William decided to invade England, if, as the Whig Gilbert Burnet wrote, "invited by some men of the best interest to . . . come and rescue the nation and the religion." His agents in England told him that most of the Whig and Tory aristocracy had become disaffected from James and that the royal army would not fight. An invasion in sufficient strength would succeed.

Still, an invasion would be a great risk, and William could not move unless and until the European military situation allowed. For him, the descent on England was part of a mighty struggle for power in Europe. Unless Louis XIV's armies were otherwise occupied, they stood as a threat to William's army in Holland. Fortune favored William, because in 1688 Louis saw an opportunity—one that had to be

William of Orange landing at Torbay in 1688. William landed with about 15,000 troops in southwestern England and met no opposition.

seized quickly—to advance his long-standing interests in the Rhineland. The great Continental rival to France, the Holy Roman Empire, was winning decisively over the Turks in Eastern Europe, which would free imperial troops for service in the West. The emperor would then be able to throw major support to his brother for the archbishopric of Cologne, a post of great importance because it carried a vote in the imperial electoral college. Louis had already nominated his own candidate. Feeling the urgency of the situation, Louis began his military operations in the Rhineland in September 1688. His enemy thus occupied, William was freed to move on England.

William's fleet of 275 ships, carrying a carefully prepared army of fifteen thousand men, sailed on October 30, taking advantage of an unusual wind blowing from the east. This "Protestant wind," coupled with indecision in the English navy, stranded James's fleet in the mouth of the Thames. William's army landed unopposed near Exeter, his banner proclaiming "The Protestant Religion and the Liberties of England." The manifesto William circulated cleverly stated the purposes of his invasion: it rehearsed the long list of complaints about James's attack on the Church, the parliamentary boroughs, and the privileges of the county elite; it asserted the rights of Parliament as against James's unlawful use of the prerogative; and it promised election of a free Parliament and investigation of the birth of the Prince of Wales.

If the people or the landed orders had rallied to James, William would have been thrown back into the sea. But the people at large were not consulted: the rebellion of 1688 was of, for, and by the landed magnates. The Whigs threw their support to William, and it was uncertain whether the Tory landlords would remain loyal to James and legitimacy. James hastily reversed his recent policies in order to appeal to the Tories, reinstating, for example, the fellows of Magdalen College. But the Tories no longer trusted James, who in early 1688 had horrified English Protestants by importing three thousand Catholic troops from Ireland. James forced the Tories to choose between the Church and their local power on the one hand and the principle of monarchical legitimacy on the other. They chose the Church and their local power. A curious apathy settled on most of England as William began his slow, deliberate march from Exeter to London. Most people stood aside, fearing civil war. Meanwhile, there was a steady bleeding of support among the elite from James to William. James could not even depend on his army. Although it was far larger than William's, it was weakened by a stream of desertions, the most important of which was that by John Churchill, the greatest soldier in England.

As his army retreated toward London without fighting, James lost his nerve—and then his crown. On December 8, he sent the queen and the Prince of Wales to France and fled himself two days later. He did not abdicate, but he apparently sought to bring all government to a halt, because he disbanded the royal army and threw the Great Seal into the Thames. Fearing chaos, a sign of which erupted in anti-Catholic riots in London, nearly all the aristocracy and gentry now looked to William to keep public order. William could not have hoped for a better chain of events, which was spoiled only by some Kentish fishermen who captured James and returned him to London. William had no intention of making a martyr of James; hence, he arranged for James to escape again, this time successfully.

With the administration of the nation already effectively in his hands, William summoned a "Convention" Parliament in January 1689 to settle affairs. By then the aristocracy and gentry had assumed their normal positions at the head of county society, so the elections proceeded without unusual disturbances. But the Convention Parliament faced a complicated question: Who was now the monarch and by what right? All agreed that William should run the country, but not necessarily as king. The Whigs argued, as they had done in the Exclusion Crisis, that the monarchy existed for the utility of its subjects. If the king broke the original "social contract" by which civil society had been initially formed, then the people, through their representatives, had the right to depose him and select a new monarch. This view received its clearest statement by John Locke in his *Two Treatises of Government*, which he wrote during the Exclusion Crisis but published first in 1689. The Whigs, therefore, did not hesitate to interrupt the strict line of succession and to have Parliament act as the source of the royal title. Under Whig influence, the House of Commons resolved that James had broken the original contract and by fleeing the country had abdicated the throne.

The Tories, however, remained reluctant to abandon their adherence to the legitimate succession. They abhorred the notion of an elected monarchy, to which they believed Whig logic inexorably led. Few had resisted William's invasion but none was happy about taking arms against the king, which contradicted their deep-seated patriarchal view of social and political order. In short, the Tories were confused. As one gentleman wrote, "How these risings and associations can be justified, I see not; but yet it is very apparent had not the Prince come and these persons thus appeared, our religion had been rooted out." Hence the Tories, who had considerable power in the House of Lords, insisted that the throne was not and never could be vacant, and preferred to make William and Mary regents for James.

William settled the argument—and in characteristically abrupt fashion. He refused to act as regent for James or to serve as mere consort to Mary. As the contemporary historian Gilbert Burnet wrote, William "said no man could esteem a woman more than he did the Princess; but he was so made that he could not think of holding anything by apron strings; nor did he think it reasonable to have any share in the government unless it was put in his person and that for term of life; if they did think to settle it otherwise . . . he would go back to Holland and meddle no more in their affairs." Mary, ever the submissive wife, agreed. In the face of William's firm stand, the Lords gave way. William and Mary received the crown jointly. William now had a firm grip on the reins of English policy, following an invasion that resulted in almost no bloodshed and a settlement of the throne that defied logic.

This change of rulers was no revolution. It was a rebellion instigated by one section of the English ruling order, the Whigs, and more or less reluctantly accepted by another, the Tories, for the purpose of preventing the aggrandizement of royal power and the "establishment" of Catholicism. The real revolution came in events subsequent to the change of rulers—the alteration of the English constitution known as the "Revolution Settlement." First, along with the crown, Parliament presented William and Mary with the Declaration of Rights (enacted in 1689 as the Bill of Rights). This famous act was mostly negative, preventing the monarchy from continuing certain of James's objectionable practices. It declared the royal power of dispensing with and suspending laws illegal; abolished all prerogative courts; forbade taxation without parliamentary approval; prohibited the raising of an army without parliamentary consent; and asserted that parliamentary elections should be free. Further, the Bill of Rights declared that the monarch could neither be a Catholic nor marry one. In general, the Bill of Rights helped establish the rule of law, free speech for Parliament, and the power of the landed oligarchy. Second, a new coronation oath required the monarch to govern England according to the laws agreed to by Parliament. Third, William voluntarily pledged that judges would serve on good behavior rather than at the king's pleasure. Fourth, in 1694, Parliament provided for frequent elections by passing the Triennial Act.

All this represented a significant expansion of parliamentary power and judicial independence vis à vis the Crown. That power was further extended by the Mutiny Act (1689), which was passed for a year only. Thereafter, the monarch could maintain discipline in the military services only if Parliament met annually and renewed the Mutiny Act. Of even greater consequence was the financial settlement that evolved during William's lifetime. Parliament refused to grant William revenues for life, thereby forcing him to consult Parliament frequently for funds. As one M.P. said, "Secure this House, that parliaments be duly chosen and not kicked out at pleasure, which never could be done without such an extravagant revenue that they might never stand in need of parliaments."

The financial restriction became all the more important in that from 1689 almost to his death in 1702, William was at war with the French. The revenues required were enormous, and only Parliament could grant them. William's need to seek funding regularly from Parliament gave M.P.s the opportunity to inquire about how the funds were being expended, a powerful means of oversight on executive activities. The king still functioned as first minister, but with the power of the purse in hand, Parliament (especially the House of Commons) had won a much more powerful role in the workings of the constitution.

The Parliament of 1689 also settled the religious issue, and in a way that was to last for nearly 150 years. Given the alliance between Anglicans and nonconformists that had emerged in 1688, some kind of religious freedom for the nonconformists was inevitable. Inclusion of nonconformists within the Church of England was discussed but abandoned. Thus the toleration the nonconformists won in 1689 was narrow. It simply exempted from the penalties of the Clarendon Code all who would swear allegiance to the Crown and deny Catholic doctrines of the mass. Henceforward, dissenters—but not Catholics or Jews—could worship freely in their own chapels (provided the doors were unlocked), but they remained second-class citizens. They were still excluded from Oxford and Cambridge; they had to pay tithes to the Church of England; they could not hold national or municipal offices; or sit in parliament without taking communion according to Anglican rites.

The final step in the Revolution Settlement came in 1701, when the Act of Settlement was passed. The Bill of Rights had declared that Mary's sister, Anne, would succeed after William and Mary both died. Anne was a strong Anglican, and it was expected that her eldest son would succeed her, thus keeping the crown on a Protestant brow. But though the unfortunate Anne had seventeen pregnancies between 1683 and 1700, none of her children survived childhood. Parliament felt compelled to pass the succession to the Electress Sophia of Hanover, the nearest Protestant relation. The Act of Settlement did this, along with insisting that all English monarchs be Anglicans, and that no monarch could leave the country without the permission of Parliament. In this way, the last vestige of strict legitimacy in the succession disappeared; Parliament clearly affirmed its authority over the succession and limited the power of the Crown.

THE REVOLUTION IN IRELAND, 1688–1691

The Revolution Settlement in England formed an important package of constitutional change, but it neither arose from nor inspired social upheaval. The situation, however, was far different in Ireland and Scotland. In Ireland, the events of 1688 brought about large-scale warfare that was of great significance both in the European-wide struggle between William's grand alliance and France and in the century-long struggle between native Catholics and Protestant planters in Ireland.

James II made his stand in Ireland, and even though he had no sympathy for Irish patriotism, he became the focal point of a national uprising against the English.

During the reign of Charles II, two issues dominated Irish public affairs: land and religion. The expropriated Catholic landowners had been disappointed that Charles did not restore their estates. and they strove ceaselessly to reclaim them. The English and Scottish planters and the new Cromwellian landlords had benefited from the Restoration and dominated the Irish Parliament on the rare occasions when it met. but they lived in fear that the Catholics might recover their land. The Protestant nonconformists in Ireland were equally nervous about the Restoration Religious Settlement, which reimposed the Episcopalian Church of Ireland. Catholics were subject to penal legislation but were relatively free from persecution. The Protestant nonconformists, especially the Ulster Presbyterians, were deeply disturbed about the situation. They had supported the Restoration in hopes of having Presbyterianism established throughout Ireland, but it brought instead public burning of the Covenant. When the Scottish Covenanters revolted, their Presbyterian cousins in Ulster nearly caught the fever. And when the "popish plot" (a bogus claim in 1678 that Jesuits were plotting to put James on the throne, which caused an outbreak of Protestant paranoia) caught fire in England, the Irish Protestants feared that the moment had come for Catholic rebellion. Charles's rule was maintained only by the firmness and moderation of his viceroy, the duke of Ormond, head of one of Ireland's oldest and most loyal Protestant families.

When James succeeded Charles, he was determined to pursue an aggressive "Catholicizing" policy in Ireland. He relieved Ormond of his office and began promoting in power the Irish Catholic Richard Talbot. A swaggering adventurer and incorrigible liar, Talbot was a member of James's household and one of the principal agents of the Catholic ex-landowners. Raised to the peerage in 1685 as the earl of Tyrconnell, Talbot succeeded as lord lieutenant of Ireland in 1687, much to the delight of Catholics and the horror of Protestants. As one Englishman wrote, "Lord Tyrconnell has gone to succeed the lord lieutenant in Ireland, to the astonishment of all sober men, and to the evident ruin of the protestants in that kingdom." Tyrconnell increased the size of the Irish army with Catholic recruits and staffed it with Catholic officers. Catholics were appointed sheriffs in the counties, and borough charters were reissued to put Catholics on the ruling corporations—the same sort of policies that James followed in England but much more dangerous in Ireland, from the Protestant point of view, because of the vast sea of Irish Catholics.

When William invaded the West of England, Tyrconnell held Ireland for James. But the Ulster Protestants quickly raised troops for William; seized control of several walled towns, including Derry (always called Londonderry by the Protestant settlers); and proclaimed William and Mary king and queen. Civil war in Ireland began, characterized by the pitiless brutality that religious conflict often inspires. In March 1689 James himself arrived in Ireland from France, intending not to make Ireland independent but with French assistance to defeat the Irish Protestants and then lead a Catholic army on England. He laid siege to Derry, which held out in the face of overwhelming strength and terrible hardship. Thousands starved before William's ships could lift the siege of Derry at the end of July—one of the great moments in Ulster Protestant historical mythology.

The desperate urgency with which the Irish Protestants fought in this war was accentuated by the actions of a new Irish Parliament (the "Patriot Parliament"), which sat in the early summer of 1689. Overwhelmingly Catholic, this Parliament expressed the land hunger and the nationalism of the native Irish—sentiments that the thoroughly English James disliked but could not resist. The Patriot Parliament asserted the exclusive right of Irish Parliaments to legislate for Ireland, enacted toleration for all sects, and repealed the Cromwellian and Restoration land settlements. Further, the estates of nearly 2,500 Protestants were seized. Together, these acts would have meant the end of Protestant domination of Ireland.

William heeded the pleas for help from the Anglo-Irish Protestants. He landed in June 1690 with a large and experienced army made up of Dutch, French, Huguenot, English, Anglo-Irish, and Danish troops. On July 12, William's army met and defeated James's army of French regulars and ill-trained Irish peasants on the river Boyne, north of Dublin. It was *the* decisive battle in modern Irish history and one of the most important in the larger struggle between William and Louis XIV. It is still commemorated by the Protestants of Northern Ireland in patriotic parades. James fled to France again, this time for good. William was able to return to England, though the war in Ireland lasted another year. The French and Irish were defeated in an awful bloodletting at Aughrim and then were penned up in the town of Limerick. Despite the inspired leadership of Patrick Sarsfield, the Irish rebels were forced to surrender in October 1691.

The Treaty of Limerick (1691), which ended the war in Ireland, gave honorable terms to the Irish but was soon tragically undone. The treaty allowed Irish troops to take service in France if they wished; about eleven thousand did so. It also secured a degree of toleration for Catholics in Ireland, plus protection of property for James's supporters (called "Jacobites," after *Jacobus*, the Latin for James) who chose to remain in Ireland. William and Mary ratified the Treaty, but the Irish Parliament, once again completely dominated by Protestants, refused to accept its civil articles. This Parliament, bent on revenge, ignored the provisions for toleration and passed instead a series of penal laws against Catholics, a stringent code that was extended and strengthened in the early eighteenth century. The penal laws were aimed at crushing the Catholic gentry. They prohibited Catholics from buying land or acquiring land from a Protestant by inheritance or marriage. On the death of a Catholic landowner, his land would be divided equally among his sons, unless the eldest converted to the Protestant Church of Ireland, in which case he got it all. Catholics could not send their children abroad for education or open schools in Ireland. Catholics could not enter the professions or (after 1727) vote. Catholic bishops were banished, and Catholic priests were required to register and take an oath against the Stuarts.

The penal laws came on top of yet another confiscation of Irish Catholic land— this time the estates of about 270 rebels. By 1700, only one-seventh of all Irish land remained in the hands of Catholics, and the penal laws would further reduce that proportion. In Ireland, therefore, the rebellion of 1688 did not bring law and liberty for the mass of the people but rather brought a great extension of the power of the English garrison. The Protestant landlords were known thereafter as "the Protestant Ascendancy."

THE REVOLUTION IN SCOTLAND, 1688–1692

James II and VII had advantages in Scotland that he did not have in England. As nominal head of clan Stewart, James had a unique claim on the loyalty of the Highlanders. The Stuarts were a Scottish dynasty (they Anglicized the spelling of their clan name) and therefore touched the patriotism of all Scotsmen. The Scots displayed their support by giving James an enthusiastic welcome when he, as duke of York, first visited Scotland in 1679. Furthermore, the tradition of the Scottish Crown was more autocratic than the English and the power of the Scottish Parliament correspondingly weaker. But the turbulence of the Highlands and the gravity of Scottish religious disputes caused difficulties for James, no less than for any other monarch.

The biggest problem for the Scottish government in the 1670s and 1680s was that the established Church of Scotland was Episcopalian, whereas the religion of the most forceful section of the Lowland Scots was Presbyterian. The conflict between Episcopalians and Presbyterians was becoming very disruptive in both the Highlands and the Lowlands. The Presbyterians, fortified by their Covenanting tradition, could not abide prelacy. The Covenanting tradition was especially prevalent in the Southwest of Scotland, where extreme Presbyterians formed a militant movement known as the Cameronians. These enthusiasts had rebelled in 1679, and though defeated at Bothwell Brig by a combination of Highland and English troops, they continued to erupt in the early 1680s. The Episcopal Church of Scotland thus depended wholly on royal authority. Nevertheless, when James succeeded to the throne of Scotland, the government seemed to be consolidating its power, and James's prospects looked good.

Some leading Scots, however, could not accept a Catholic king and looked to their fellow Calvinist, William, as their savior. Scottish Whig refugees joined English exiles in Holland after 1685 in encouraging William to invade. James, meanwhile, busied himself in throwing away the advantages he enjoyed in Scotland, largely by precipitating a dispute with the Scottish Parliament. He appointed as his chief ministers two men who promptly forfeited public support by converting to Catholicism. Next, James asked Parliament to repeal the penal laws against Catholics, but not (at first) those against Presbyterians. Parliament refused, and in 1687 James used his prerogative powers to extend toleration to Catholics. When in June 1688 he also granted indulgence to the Presbyterians, it was too late. To make matters worse, James began rearranging parliamentary boroughs in the same way that had seemed threatening to Englishmen. Still, Scotland remained quiet when William landed in England. James even moved his Scottish troops south to help fend off William—a major mistake, for with them went the ultimate source of royal power in Scotland.

James's flight to France in the face of William's invasion left the Royalist party in Scotland in disarray. Many a canny Scottish politician, not wishing to be left out in the cold, hurried to London to make his peace with William. Jacobite power in Scotland was still potentially as great as that of the Williamites, but when William called a Scottish Convention Parliament, the confusion of the Royalists allowed the Whigs and Presbyterians to dominate it. Consequently, the Scottish Convention Parliament, and its successor, pushed through a more extreme Revolution Settlement than that in England. The convention declared that James had "forefaulted" his crown; invited William and Mary to rule jointly; and abolished Episcopalianism in favor of an established Presbyterian church—one shaped by its militants at that. William would have preferred not to be so dependent on one party in Scotland but could not avoid it. His inclination toward toleration found only a faint echo in Scotland.

Seeing the flow of power to their Whig and Presbyterian opponents, the Scottish Jacobites (mostly Episcopalians) abandoned Parliament and took up arms against William. Led by John Graham, Viscount Dundee, some of the Highland clans—the Macdonalds, Camerons, Appin Stewarts, MacNaughtons, and MacLeans—rallied to the Stuart cause, partly because of their sense of loyalty to their sworn king but more significantly because of their hostility to the Campbells (including the new earl of Argyll), who were prominent Whigs. In July 1689, Dundee's Highland host of perhaps three thousand men swept down the slopes of the Pass of Killiecrankie and overwhelmed a royal army. But Dundee himself was killed, and no one else was able to thwart the natural tendency of clansmen to drift back to their glens after a fight. James meanwhile sent little assistance, though the Highland leaders declared "We will all dy with our swords in our hands before we fail in our loyaltie and sworn allegiance." At the little town of Dunkeld, the remaining Highlanders were broken by a disciplined force of Covenanters. The clansmen retired to their remote lairs, beaten for the moment but not reconciled to William's regime.

The problem remained for William and his government to pacify the Highlands. One step was to build a fort in the heart of the Highlands—Fort William. Another was to bribe the clan chiefs into loyalty. The key figure behind this scheme was the unscrupulous Sir John Dalrymple, the master of Stair, who loathed the Highland clans, some of whom had ransacked his estates in the 1670s. He coupled the bribes with a strict requirement for an oath of allegiance to William, hoping that if some chief missed the deadline of January 1, 1692, that clan might be punished as an example to all the others. Ideally, the clan so punished would be the Macdonalds of Glencoe, widely thought to be Catholic.

The Jacobite clan chiefs were reluctant to take the oath until James released them from their prior oath to him. He was slow in giving permission. Among the few chiefs who failed to make the deadline was MacIan, chief of the Glencoe Macdonalds, who came in five days late after slogging through a blizzard. Stair, probably with William's knowledge, sought to annihilate the Glencoe Macdonalds by a dishonorable plan. A company of troops (Campbells) were sent to Glencoe, where they claimed traditional Highland hospitality. This was granted, but after spending almost two weeks in the homes of the Macdonalds, the troops in February 1692 rose before dawn and slaughtered all of the clan they could lay their hands on, men, women, and children. About forty Macdonalds were butchered, but most escaped, much to the anger of the master of Stair.

The massacre of Glencoe discredited William's government. It became the object of a parliamentary investigation and deep indignation by the Scots. Stair was forced out of office, but other officials were protected, and the conspiracy was covered up. In the short run, Glencoe helped quell the clans. But beneath their temporarily lawful behavior, many of the clans harbored strong Jacobite feelings. The Revolution Settlement in Scotland remained precarious for the rest of William's reign.

FOREIGN WARS, 1689–1713

The fighting in Ireland and Scotland was part of a European-wide conflagration between the forces led by William III and the armies of Louis XIV. The war that began for England in 1689 was to last even past William's death in 1702—in fact, it continued (except for a brief respite) until 1713. It had two phases: the War of the League of Augsburg (1689–1697) and the War of the Spanish Succession (1701–1713). By the end of this protracted and exhausting struggle, England (by then, as we will see, properly known as Britain) had emerged as a great power in Europe.

The League of Augsburg—the Dutch Republic, Spain, Sweden, Savoy, the Holy Roman Empire, and some smaller German states—had gone to war against Louis' vainglorious aggression in 1688, and French support for James brought the English into it. Thus, for the English the war was primarily a matter of defending William III and deposing James II. In addition, some English mercantile interests felt threatened by the expansion of French commercial strength, for France had become the greatest power in Europe by far. Given the mercantilist theories prevalent at the time, this English concern was rational: trade was thought of in terms of warfare, every transaction bringing a winner and a loser. William himself was mainly concerned to defend Dutch interests and above all to keep France out of the Spanish Netherlands (roughly, modern Belgium). "Dutch William" used English resources to subsidize his allies, buy mercenaries, and supplement the Dutch navy with the English. Though he was not a great general, he was an able diplomatist. With English cash he kept the Grand Alliance together and put pressure on the French, which helped him to achieve his objectives.

The war soon became a war of attrition. Once the Dutch and English navies had defeated the French fleet at La Hogue (1692), the British Isles were safe from another French invasion. But William's determination to confront the French on land became extremely unpopular with the English "Country" opposition, who preferred a cheaper maritime strategy of choking off the imperial and seaborne trade of the French. Though William persisted, the English by 1697 grew as weary of war as the French. In the Peace of Ryswick, Louis recognized William as king of England, allowed the Dutch to garrison forts in the Spanish Netherlands, and ceded Newfoundland and the Hudson Bay territories to England.

William's impressive achievement was made possible by the mobilization of English financial resources. Like all of the European states of the late seventeenth century, England was inefficient in making war: ships and men were regularly wasted; only the poor were dragooned into the army or impressed into the navy; and the officer corps of the army was corrupt. But in the institution of Parliament, William had a unique instrument of financial power. Through Parliament William was able to win, by consent of the social and political elite, access to England's wealth. He levied taxes at a level undreamed of by his predecessors—an annual average more than twice the revenues of James II. The land tax was the key, raising almost one-half of total revenues. Taxes paid two-thirds of the cost of war, a sure sign of the landowners' willingness to pay for their revolution. Moreover, Parliament authorized William to borrow to pay for the other one-third of war expenditures and voted taxes to pay the interest on the loans. In 1694, Parliament created the Bank of England to help mobilize credit for the government and to manage the new and rapidly expanding public debt. The bank brought great profits to the Whig financiers who composed it, but served a crucial public function in financing the war and issuing reliable paper bank notes. The entire "monied interest" had a stake in continuing the war and was hated by the Tories. However, this greedy financial clique played an important role in making England a great power.

The resources of England were strained to the limit in the second phase of the conflict, the War of the Spanish Succession. This complex struggle taught the English to think for the first time in terms of supporting a balance of power in Europe. For the Continental states, the great issue was whether a Bourbon or a Hapsburg would succeed to the Spanish throne and to the Spanish possessions, Charles II of Spain being childless. For Louis, to wear, or to have a relative wear, the Spanish crown would be the culmination of his quest for glory as well as confirmation of French domination of the treasures of the Spanish-American Empire. For the Dutch, such an augmentation of French power would spell the end of Dutch independence. For the English, French success would threaten anew to restore the Catholic Stuarts, to do grave damage to English commerce with the Continent, and to end their own hopes of feasting on the Spanish Empire. For all these various reasons, the opponents of France formed a new Grand Alliance and went to war when Louis claimed the Spanish throne for his grandson in 1701.

Any hesitation the English might have felt was set aside when, on the death of James II in September 1701, Louis recognized James's son ("the Old Pretender") as James III. William died in 1702 and was succeeded by Queen Anne, who, though possessing some ability, was not capable of conducting the war. Overall direction of the allied war effort fell to John Churchill, duke of Marlborough, incomparably the greatest soldier in Europe. Marlborough was immensely charming and good-

The First Duke of Marl-
borough, *by Adriaen
van der Werff. John
Churchill was granted
the title duke of Marl-
borough for his tri-
umphs over the armies
of Louis XIV. Here he is
shown in ducal splendor
at his magnificent
home, Blenheim Palace,
near Oxford.*

looking, as well as none too fastidious in furthering his own career. Anne was very fond of him and was thoroughly dominated by his wife Sarah, duchess of Marlborough. For nearly ten years, Marlborough was the effective ruler of England.

Marlborough was not only a great battlefield commander but also a supreme strategist and diplomatist. His task was to keep the Grand Alliance together while leading its armies in another war of attrition against France. Between 1702 and 1709, Marlborough directed the allied army to an unprecedented series of victories in set-piece battles: Blenheim (1704), Ramillies (1706), Oudenarde (1708), and Malplaquet (1709). He was rewarded with the highest honors England could bestow, including his famous house, Blenheim Palace. He failed, however, to take advantage of the allies' strong position to settle with France in 1708, and as the war dragged on, Tory opposition to it grew stronger. To the backwoods Tory gentry, Marlborough was making unreasonable demands on the French and thereby unnecessarily continuing a bloody and expensive war. In 1710, a general election put a Tory peace ministry in office; a year later, Marlborough was dismissed. The Tories, led by Robert Harley (the earl of Oxford) and Henry St. John (Viscount Bolingbroke), succeeded in negotiating the Treaty of Utrecht in 1713, leaving the allies to settle with France as best they could.

England benefited from the war. By the Treaty of Utrecht, the English (now formally the British) recognized Louis' grandson as king of Spain, but on condition that the crowns of France and Spain never be joined. The English saw to it that the Spanish Netherlands were divorced from Spain and garrisoned by the Dutch, who had become clients of England. Further, the English acquired or were confirmed in important colonial holdings: Newfoundland, Nova Scotia, St. Kitts, Gibraltar, and Minorca. Finally, they won the *Asiento*, the right to trade in the Spanish Empire and the symbol of England's displacement of France as the chief predator in the Spanish Empire. The English had defended their successful rebellion of 1688 and the Revolution Settlement, developed strong public financial institutions, and successfully pursued a balance of power. In so doing they had become a great power in Europe.

THE HANOVERIAN SUCCESSION, 1714

The Treaty of Utrecht was very unpopular in some English circles, for it did not seem to bring value equal to the costs of war. The Whigs believed that the war effort had been sold out by the Tory ministry. Moreover, the treaty infuriated Prince George, elector of Hanover, Queen Anne's heir presumptive. Hanover had participated in the Grand Alliance against the French, and George thought that the English had left him in the lurch in 1713. But his hostility to the Tories was equaled by theirs to him, for they abhorred the idea of a German Lutheran on the English throne. The Tories even began to think that James III might be preferable.

This high-Tory Jacobitism had been growing ever since the accession of Queen Anne and was inflamed by the prolongation of the war. Besides opposition to the war, there were two elements in the Jacobite mind. One was their longing for the principle of hereditary divine right, which made them hope William III's kingship was a one-time-only aberration. The other was the high-flying ecclesiastical views of Tory Anglicans, who disliked what they regarded as the subordination of the Church to the state, and especially the toleration of nonconformists. The Tories believed the Church was in danger, not least because of the practice of "occasional conformity," which had grown since 1688. In the spirit of toleration, nonconformists had been allowed to hold municipal and state offices in violation of the Clarendon Code and the Test Act, provided they communicated once a year in the established Church. In a series of bills after 1702, the Tories tried to abolish occasional conformity, finally succeeding in 1711. They recognized, however, that if the elector of Hanover, with his Whig prejudices, became king, occasional conformity would resume, and the Church would be endangered again.

A number of high Tories began conspiring to deny the throne to George and to restore it to James III; how many were involved and how far they went is not clear. Oxford and Bolingbroke certainly flirted with Jacobitism. They tried to persuade the Old Pretender to convert to Anglicanism, which would have solved their central problem, but to James, England was not worth renouncing his religion, and he flatly refused to convert. Bolingbroke might have risked a Jacobite restoration even at that point, but he could not be sure of the army's support. When Anne died on August 1, 1714, the Privy Council proclaimed George I king; his accession met no resistance. The last Stuart (Anne) had died, and the Hanoverian line was installed. The Revolution Settlement was thereby saved, and England entered a period of remarkable stability and expansion of power.

Suggested Reading

Barnett, Corelli, *Britain and Her Army, 1509–1970* (London: Allen Lane, 1970).

———, *Marlborough* (London: Eyre Methuen, 1974).

Beckett, J. C., *The Making of Modern Ireland, 1603–1923* (Boston: Faber & Faber, 1981).

Clark, J. C. D., *English Society, 1688–1832* 2nd ed. (Cambridge University Press, 2000).

Claydon, Tony, *William III and the Godly Revolution* (Cambridge University Press, 2004).

Ferguson, William, *Scotland, 1689 to the Present* (London: Oliver & Boyd, 1968).

Gray, Tony, *No Surrender! The Siege of Londonderry, 1689* (London: Macdonald and Janes, 1975).

Harris, Tim, *Politics under the Later Stuarts: Party Politics in a Divided Society, 1660–1715* (New York: Longman, 1993).

———, *Revolution: The Great Crisis of the British Monarchy: 1685–1720* (London: Allen Lane, 2006).

Holmes, Geoffrey, *British Politics in the Age of Anne* (London: Macmillan, 1967).

———, *The Making of a Great Power: Later Stuart and Early Georgian Britain, 1660–1722* (New York: Longman, 1993).

Hopkins, Paul, *Glencoe and the End of the Highland War* (London: John Donald, 1986).

Jenkins, Geraint H., *The Foundations of Modern Wales, 1642–1780* (New York: Oxford University Press, 1987).

Jones, D. W., *War and Economy in the Age of William and Marlborough* (Oxford: Blackwell, 1988).

Jones, J. R., *Country and Court: England, 1658–1714* (Cambridge, Mass.: Harvard University Press, 1978).

———, *The Revolution of 1688 in England* (London: Weidenfeld & Nicolson, 1972).

Kenyon, J. P., *Stuart England* (London: Allen Lane, 1978).

Kishlansky, Mark, *Parliamentary Selection: Social and Political Choice in Early Modern England* (Cambridge: Cambridge University Press, 1986).

MacCurtain, Margaret, *Tudor and Stuart Ireland* (Dublin: Gill & Macmillan, 1972).

Miller, John, *The Glorious Revolution* (London: Longman, 1983).

Ogg, David, *England in the Reigns of James II and William III* (Oxford: Clarendon Press, 1955).

O'Gorman, Frank, *The Long Eighteenth Century: British Political and Social History, 1688–1832* (London: Arnold, 1997).

Ohlmeyer, Jane E., eds., *Political Thought in Seventeenth-century Ireland: Kingdom or Colony* (Cambridge: Cambridge University Press, 2000).

Pocock, J. G. A., ed. *Three British Revolutions: 1641, 1688, 1776* (Princeton: Princeton University Press, 1980).

Schwoerer, Lois G., *The Declaration of Rights, 1689* (Baltimore: Johns Hopkins University Press, 1981).

Speck, W. A., *Reluctant Revolutionaries* (New York: Oxford University Press, 1988).

Chapter 3

Society and Economy in England, 1715–1763

The rebellion of 1688 and the subsequent Revolution Settlement set the stage for the golden age of the English landlords. As we will see, the landlords still had to bring stability to the party system and to fend off further resurrections of Jacobitism; nevertheless, the foundations for their preeminence were laid. Having secured the rule of law (which they wrote and enforced), the rights of property (which they defined and enjoyed), and the power of Parliament (which they monopolized and wielded), the English landed magnates surveyed Britain from a pinnacle of wealth and power. The society over which they ruled by all appearances seemed one of stability and cohesiveness, whether viewed in terms of the culture, the social order, or the economy. The landed elite's serene domination of the nation resembled Caesar Augustus' rule of the early Roman Empire; hence, eighteenth-century England has long been labeled "the Augustan Age."

In fact, however, the eighteenth century was a time of contrast and paradox—between the majestic stability of the social hierarchy and the unseemly scramble of people for higher rungs on the social ladder; between the warmth of paternalist social relations and the naked lust for power; between the breathtaking wealth of a few and the heartbreaking poverty of the many; between the rituals of deference given by inferiors to superiors and the startling frequency of riots; and above all between the stately calm of agricultural England and the bustling aggressiveness of towns and commerce. The problem for the historian of eighteenth-century England is not to find "the truth that lies in between" these contrasts but to see how all of them can have been true at once.

THE SOCIAL STRUCTURE: AN OPEN HIERARCHY

The key feature of eighteenth-century English society was that it was arranged as a status hierarchy, not as a class society. In the sense that a historian or sociologist can assign the people he or she is studying to predetermined pigeonholes called "classes," then all societies are and have been class societies. But in the historically more important sense of how people actually related to each other and identified themselves in their social order, then eighteenth-century English men

Mr and Mrs Andrews, *by Thomas Gainsborough (1748). This painting reflects the comfortable self-assurance of the English country gentry in the eighteenth century.*

and women ordered themselves in a status hierarchy. The basic sets of relationships should be envisioned as vertical, not horizontal. Each person was thought to have been ascribed at birth a position in the natural—indeed, divinely established—pecking order, and each felt that his or her loyalty was to social superiors, not to fellow workers. Hence the social structure was like a status ladder, or rather a number of parallel ladders, each rung being a status gradation with its own generally accepted duties and privileges. If a person moved up or down the ladder, it was off one rung and onto another, the ladder itself remaining unchanged. Dr. Samuel Johnson, the great wit and man of letters, remarked that the English people were set in their hierarchical places "by the fixed, invariable rules of distinction of rank, which create no jealousy, since they are held to be accidental." Thus, when the English talked about social position, they spoke in terms of "degrees," "order," and "ranks"—gradations of status, not of class.

"Mankind," Dr. Johnson observed, "are happier in a state of inequality and subordination." Such was the view unanimously held by those at the top of the hierarchy and ceaselessly preached to those below them. This is not surprising, since the distance in wealth and prestige from top to bottom was enormous. On the highest rung of the hierarchy stood the titled nobility, consisting of fewer than two hundred families. All the nobles were great landlords who dominated their counties in near-majestic splendor. They lived in palatial country homes, often gigantic edifices of close to one hundred rooms, and enjoyed on average £8,000 a year. A few, like the duke of Bedford and the duke of Devonshire, raked in more than £30,000 a year from rentals alone—the equivalent of many millions of dollars today. Just below the nobility came the ranks of the big landlords—baronets, knights, esquires, and gentlemen—more than fifteen thousand families, each enjoying upward of £1,000 a year and each living in a stately country house. Together, these landlords and their families—the nobility and the gentry—amounted to less than 3 percent of the population, but they enjoyed 15 percent of the national income. All also enjoyed the vitally important status of "gentleman"—a position of honor, to be fought for if necessary, assigned to the lucky few born into "good" families, and displayed by badges of status like genteel education, graceful deportment, and conspicuous consumption. Gentle status was defined as the ability to live well without working for a living, or, as the novelist Daniel Defoe put it, gentlemen were "such who live on estates, and without the mechanism of employment."

In the countryside, below the gentlemen (and ladies) came those who actually worked the land—freeholders, tenant farmers, and farm laborers. Freeholders were owner-occupiers, distinguished from the gentry in that they managed their farms themselves. Freeholders still claimed the traditional label of "yeomen," but this was a dwindling order. Most farms were worked by tenants, some of them well-off, others struggling, all of whom leased land from the landlords for cash. Their access to a tenancy and the terms of their leases were normally set by custom, though some landlords simply rented to the highest bidder. Together, the freeholders and farmers of England numbered about 350,000 families, most earning between £40 and £150 a year. They employed large numbers of farm laborers and domestic servants, who were themselves ranked in distinct hierarchies—husbandmen, stableboys, milkmaids, housekeepers, cooks, butlers, gardeners, and scullery girls.

Some of the farm laborers and domestics were hired on a yearly basis and "lived in" the farmer's household. Most worked on a daily or seasonal hiring, having offered their labor for sale at a local market. The latter were the "cottagers," who rented a cottage and a scrap of land on which to grow vegetables, who usually had customary rights to the use of village commons and waste lands, and who with their wives undertook some craft like weaving, glove making, or straw plaiting in slack times. In good years, cottagers and their families could scrape together a meager living; in bad years, they had to look to the parish for assistance. The leading statistician of the day made no distinction between "cottagers" and "paupers"—400,000 families with an average of only six or seven pounds a year. In rural England, the laborers ranked above only those with no claim on the society at all—vagrants, beggars, thieves, and the like.

The rural laborers formed part of the "laboring poor"—the base of the social hierarchy that comprised almost a quarter of the population. The other segment of the laboring poor lived in the towns. The urban laboring poor, like those in the countryside, were often in need of assistance from the Poor Law or private charity; they included vagrants, beggars, criminals, soldiers, sailors, and unskilled male and female workers.

Above the urban laboring poor came the wide range of the "middling sort," who constituted a dynamic and growing element in English society, amounting to about 15 percent of the English and Welsh population in the early seventeen hundreds. The middling sort did not fit neatly into the traditional social hierarchy. At the lower end of the middling scale stood artisans, shopkeepers, tradesmen, and their families, earning perhaps £50 a year. Artisans had their own hierarchies: apprentices, journeymen, and masters, most of whom were male, though women sometimes did become apprentices and learned the trades. Some master artisans owned their own shops and employed apprentices and journeymen. The *London Tradesman* in 1747 listed more than 350 different crafts and trades: butchers, bakers, and candlestickmakers; but also jewelers, goldsmiths, shipwights, carpenters, joiners, shoemakers, saddlers, harnessmakers, tailors, lacemakers, weavers, cutlers, printers, chainmakers, spurriers, gunsmiths, hatters, clockmakers, and all the rest of a world of manufacturing now largely gone.

Above the artisans and shopkeepers in incomes and standards of living were the merchants and professional people. Rich businessmen could earn anything from hundreds to thousands of pounds a year. Professional men—women could not enter any of the professions until the late nineteenth century—included clergymen, lawyers, and doctors; they earned a wide range of incomes and improved their status throughout the century. At the beginning of the century, professional men were regarded, like tradesmen and merchants, as overly ambitious and therefore not genteel. By the end of the century, however, they had gained considerable respectability and were even thought of as satellites of the landed orders. The middling sorts would eventually form the germ of the middle class, but in the eighteenth century their main desire was to make enough money to buy an estate and join the elite circle of landed society.

Eighteenth-century society, then, was a finely graded hierarchy in which status distinctions were carefully defined, observed, and protected. Yet England was not a caste society. While there was little movement at the top level, the titled aristocracy, none of the rungs on the social ladder was legally closed to outsiders. Landowners enjoyed privileges, but the privileges defined by the law were surprisingly few in number: the titled nobility sat in the House of Lords and were entitled to trial by their peers; otherwise, nobility and gentry were subject to the same body of law as everyone else and theoretically opened their ranks to newcomers. These concessions composed the social price that the landowners paid for the preeminence they won in 1688. In eighteenth-century England, property determined status, and property could be purchased. In medieval society, property followed status, but this rule had now been reversed. It was possible for a person to acquire a fortune, buy property, and move up to the appropriate rung on the social ladder. At the same time, it was possible for a family to squander its fortune and its estates and thus to find itself reduced in status. Rich businessmen tried to marry daughters of the gentry so as to acquire status; younger sons of landed families often had to marry mercantile wealth or to find positions in the professions. In sum, there were numerous opportunities for social mobility in eighteenth-century England.

There was also an often unseemly scramble as people jostled for positions in the social hierarchy. Barons sought to become earls, squires to become knights, farmers to become squires, merchants to become gentlemen, and shopkeepers to become merchants. Money was the key, and Englishmen impressed foreigners with their love of money. The most significant aspect of the upward scramble was for wealthy merchants and financiers to buy estates and so cross the all-important line into gentle status. The society was full of men who had achieved privileged status: Sir George Dashwood, a London brewer; Sir Josiah Child, a banker; and Sir George Wombwell, a merchant of the East India Company. The most famous example was Thomas ("Diamond") Pitt, the son of an Anglican clergyman who became a sea captain, an interloper in the trade of the East India Company, and finally a merchant and governor in the Company—a poacher turned gamekeeper. Pitt made so much money in Indian trade that he was eventually able to buy more than ten estates in England and set himself up as a member of Parliament. His grandson William became earl of Chatham. (Pitt also brought home from India a diamond of 410 carats, which he later sold for £135,000.) Such businessmen usually lacked the social graces to be fully accepted by landed society, but one or two generations later the family passed as the genuine article. As Defoe put it, "After a generation or two, the tradesmen's children, or at least their grandchildren, come to be as good gentlemen, statesmen, parliament men . . . bishops and noblemen as those of the highest and most ancient families."

The upward and downward flow of people did not destroy the status hierarchy but rather preserved it. Each person and family assumed the style, the duties, and the privileges of their new position as they moved up the rungs. Social mobility thus provided a safety valve for the economic dynamism of the country. It marked off England as very different from Wales, Ireland, and even Scotland, where the social hierarchies were comparatively petrified. In England, as long as everyone recognized and accepted the hierarchy itself and behaved according to the prescribed forms and standards at each level, then the structure itself was stable.

SOCIAL RELATIONS: PROPERTY, PATRONAGE, AND DEFERENCE

Property was one of the pillars of eighteenth-century society because it provided a person or family with the means of survival, because it formed the basis of power, and most of all because it determined social status. "The great and chief end . . . of men uniting into commonwealths, and putting themselves under government," John Locke had written, "is the preservation of their property." The central features of social relationships were closely related to property: *patronage* and *deference*. Property enabled a person to disburse patronage—gifts, jobs, appointments, contracts, favors—and the ability to act as a patron was the crucial measure of property and status. To be a great man or lady was to be able to dispense patronage to clients, called in that day one's "friends" or "interest." From the recipient's point of view, to have a niche in life, a means of survival and advancement, required being within the circle of some patron's friends. According to the essayist Joseph Addison, "To an honest mind the best perquisites of place are the advantages it gives a man of doing good"; by "doing good" he meant being helpful to one's friends.

Patronage played in eighteenth-century England the role that merit and achievement play in modern societies. Almost all government offices, clerical (that is, church) appointments, tenancies on landed estates, jobs for laborers, apprenticeships for boys, commissions for artists and architects, assignments for writers, military and naval posts, and the vast array of positions in domestic service were distributed by patronage. No one took entrance or civil service exams or had to show certificates of qualification. Furthermore, few looked on patronage as corruption, for it was simply the way that the political (as we will see), economic, and social systems worked. Nor did English men and women believe that seeking help from a patron was degrading or that receiving such help was unfair. Here is a prime example of an unashamed request for patronage: the archbishop of Tuam in the 1740s wrote the duke of Newcastle on the death of the archbishop of Armagh: "The death of our late primate happening when I was at Dublin, I am later than others in my application upon that event; but as the race is not to the swift . . . I hope it will not be too late for me to lay my small pretentions . . . before yr. Grace." From the patron's side, we have the word of Sir Robert Walpole, great landowner and politician, who declared that "while he was in employment, he had endeavoured to serve his friends and relations; than which, in his opinion, nothing was more reasonable, or more just."

In return for their patronage, patrons demanded deference, which included postures of gratitude, loyalty, service, and obedience. If a man felt entitled to claim assistance from his superior, he also felt it right to defer to that patron's opinions and wishes. Laborers were expected to move aside and pull their forelocks when the landlord or members of his family rode by; tenant farmers to vote the way the landowner wished; sons and daughters to defer to their parents; artists to render their patrons (or even their patrons' prize animals) beautiful in portraits; and clergymen to preach on the lines preferred by their patrons. Deference was not regarded as servile, but as honorable. As one late seventeenth-century guide for husbandmen put it: "A just fear and respect he must have for his landlord, or the gentleman his neighbour, because God hath placed them above him, and he hath learnt [in the Fifth Commandment] that by the father he ought to honour is meant all his superiors."

There were plenty of occasions, as we will see, when deference broke down in the eighteenth century, for people, even the common folk, also had a strong sense of traditional rights and privileges, and sometimes the sense of rights clashed with that of obligations. Nevertheless, patronage and deference, more than force, held the society together. This was made possible by the fact that people were connected to each other by face-to-face relationships up and down the social hierarchy. It would be a mistake to think of those personal relationships as necessarily loving or friendly. The relationship was harsh if the patron was unfair or abusive, a situation for which there was no end of opportunities. The connection between patron and client was always unequal, and exploitation was an inevitable feature of such an inequalitarian society. To see the inegalitarian attitudes, one need only to look at the prevailing view toward the poor. As one observer wrote toward the end of the century, "Poverty is . . . a most necessary and indispensable ingredient in society, without which nations and communities could not exist in a state of civilization."

When, however, a patron was moved, like the novelist Henry Fielding's Squire All-worthy, by decency and generosity, and above all when a patron allowed himself or herself to be regulated by custom, then the face-to-face connections took on something of the warmth and trust of paternal relationships.

The face-to-face relationships could exist only because the "scale of life," as Professor Harold Perkin called it, was small. As late as 1760, 75 to 80 percent of the 6.5 million people in England lived in villages or small towns. It remained true that few people outside the elite ever traveled beyond the parish or the nearest market town. Few people ever saw more than several hundred others gathered at one time—church services, markets, fairs, and traditional celebrations at the manor house being the main occasions. Each of these moments reinforced the local community. In rural England, everyone knew everyone else. Even the units of production were small. The greatest noble households may have numbered a hundred servants and laborers, but most farm households were much smaller. Even in the towns, most work was done in households by the master or journeyman, his wife and family, and his apprentices and laborers. A large shop consisted of fifteen to twenty people. Peter Laslett has written: "Time was when the whole of life went forward in the family, in a circle of loved, familiar faces, known and fondled objects all to human size."* This observation perhaps sentimentalizes the small scale of life, but it touches on the very different quality of human relationships in preindustral England from those of the modern world.

LAND, MARRIAGE, PATRIARCHY, AND THE FAMILY

Landed property was the foundation of the social hierarchy. Land produced much of the nation's wealth and gave employment to most of the laboring force. Land was the source of prestige and therefore the key to status. To own an estate placed a man at the top of the social ladder and gave him political power. But the size of estates grew throughout the century, and the number of estates was small; hence land was expensive, and increasingly so during the century. Two features of the society followed from these facts: (1) there was severe competition among the wealthy to buy (or to add to) estates; and (2) the object of all landowners was to keep their estates intact.

The landowners used several devices for these purposes. The first was the principle of *primogeniture*, or inheritance of the property by the eldest son. Younger sons and daughters might be given a lump sum of money or an annuity, but the estate as a whole passed to the eldest son, or in the absence of a son, to the designated heir. Landowners did everything possible to avoid and prevent sale of an estate or parts of it. Primogeniture was largely a matter of custom and operated in law only when a property owner died without a will, which no competent landowner would ever allow to happen. Hence the most important device for ensuring the passage of an estate intact was the *strict settlement*. These settlements, wills

---

*Peter Laslett, *The World We Have Lost*, 3rd ed. (New York: Scribner's, 1965), p. 21.

carefully drawn up and defended by the law, provided that each inheritor got the land under severe restrictions: he must not alienate (sell) any of it; it was thus *entailed*. By the principle of entailment, therefore, strict settlements turned the owner of an estate into a sort of life tenant. A squire might settle his land on his son, but on legal condition that the son in turn pass the estate to the grandson. And the son, by powerful social custom, resettled the estate on his son by making the same sort of will, and so on down the generations.

This desire to keep estates intact had heavy consequences for other sons in the family and for all daughters. Because only the eldest son would inherit, different means of support had to be found for all the other offspring. Here is where patronage, "friendship," and "interest" came into play. With proper connections, younger sons could be sent into the professions—the clergy, army, navy, or medicine. Entry into business was much less favored, since work of a self-interested sort was thought to be tainted by "trade" and therefore to some degree was dishonorable and thus ungentlemanly. But no landlord opposed money itself; hence the typical landlord would be delighted if his sons married wealthy heiresses, regardless of the source of their fortunes. Marriage to a rich banker's or merchant's daughter might provide a financial base for a second or third son from which he might launch an effort to buy an estate. In this way, there was an important flow of noninheriting sons downward into the professions, which over time helped to elevate the professions in status and which raised the status of mercantile daughters upward into landed society. This upward and downward mobility helped bond landed and commercial wealth together.

Daughters provided a major problem for landowning families, for they had to be married off well, without loss of status; yet the daughters rarely brought an estate with them. Women could own landed property, and a significant number (mainly widows) did; but the custom in landed families generally was to keep the estates in men's hands. Thus to find and secure suitable marriages for their daughters was a matter of ceaseless calculating and campaigning for the landowner and his wife. To make his daughter attractive on the marriage market, a landowner customarily bestowed a dowry on his daughter at the time of her marriage. These dowries might amount to thousands of pounds, and everyone thought it perfectly proper if the prospective groom (or rather his family) bargained to get the dowry increased. Thus, having a bevy of daughters was a serious drain on a family's resources and was regarded by most landlords as at best a mixed blessing.

These circumstances made marriage arrangements within the landowning orders a matter of delicate negotiations and bargaining between families, not unlike diplomatic negotiations between countries. Family fortunes and the status of the lineage were at stake, so parents played a major role in choosing partners for their children. The precise weight assumed by parental opinion varied from family to family, depending on the particular mix of personalities involved. Moreover, the balance between parental choice and the young person's preference was shifting during the century, as individualism, reason, and eventually romantic sensibility grew in cultural importance. As the decades passed, young people expected to play a bigger role in their own matchmaking and the parents a lesser role. In the sev-

Marriage à-la-Mode, *by William Hogarth (1743). Here the great satirical English painter depicts mercenary negotiations held by the heads of two wealthy families and their lawyers, while the prospective bride and groom wait, unconsulted, at the side.*

enteenth century, the parents largely arranged the marriages; in the eighteenth century their role slowly moved toward one of exercising a veto over their children's choices.

Nowhere are these familial tensions better shown than in Henry Fielding's great comic novel, *Tom Jones.* In it, the dashing, handsome Tom and the lovely, maidenly Sophia Western love each other. Alas, Tom is illegitimate and thus an unsuitable match for Sophia, whose aunt expresses to her the traditional view:

> So far, madam, from your being concerned alone [in your marriage], your concern is the least, or surely the least important. It is the honor of your family which is concerned in this alliance; you are only the instrument. Do you conceive, mistress, that in an intermarriage between kingdoms . . . the princess herself is alone considered in the match? No, it is a match between two kingdoms rather than between two persons. The same happens in great families such as ours. The alliance between the families is the principal matter.

But Mr. Allworthy, Tom's excellent guardian, has a more modern view: young people should marry if they love one another, provided that their families are consulted and have the right of refusal. This is also the honorable Sophia's view and clearly that of Fielding: Sophia vows never to marry without her father's consent, but she also refuses to marry *his* choice (in this case the sniveling Mr. Blifil), since she does not love him.

Such issues reached to the heart of marriage and family life themselves. What was the nature of the relationship between husband and wife, or between parents and children, in eighteenth-century England? The surviving evidence sheds most light on the families of the landowners and the well-to-do people of the middling sorts. The law was clear: as the famous legal philosopher Sir William Blackstone put it, "In marriage husband and wife are one person and that person is the husband." In the gentry and aristocracy, a woman was supposed to be under the care (and the control) of a man all her life—first her father, then her husband. But here, too, actual behavior was changing. Family life, like the social structure itself, had long been authoritarian and patriarchal. For many centuries, the father had ruled the roost; the husband demanded absolute obedience from his wife; the parents together demanded obedience from the children; and the lineage itself was more important than the individuals of any one generation. In the seventeenth century, Puritanism had accentuated patriarchal control in the family and had intensified the parental desire to subordinate the will of the children to their own, as well as to close the nuclear family to the claims of the lineage as a whole. That peculiar Puritan intensity tended to diminish during the eighteenth century. The reasonableness and tolerance advocated in late seventeenth- and early eighteenth-century thought mitigated some of the harsh intensity of the Puritan-style family and led to more companionable relations between husbands and wives as well as to more affectionate concern by parents for their children. For this reason, toys and children's books emphasizing fun and pleasure became important consumer items for the first time in the eighteenth century.

Of course, not all English families became warm and affectionate. Among the wealthiest landed families, the great fortunes still allowed parents to neglect their children. In the eighteenth century, the English custom emerged of sending the children away to school as early as possible. For example, Robert Walpole, who was later to become prime minister, was sent away at age six to boarding schools and later to Cambridge, and he returned only at age twenty-two, rarely having spent more than a few weeks at home. Among the poorest families, poverty ensured that parental attitudes toward children remained erratic and unpredictable, alternating among warmth, cruelty, and indifference. Young men and women among the lowest levels of the laboring poor could marry without fearing that their parents would punish them through disinheritance, because there was no property to be inherited. They also found all too often that they could not feed all the children they produced. Among these families, brutality born of ignorance and frustration sometimes stood at a high level. Finally, Puritanism kept its hold on many families. Cotton Mather, the colonial Puritan divine, wrote of childrearing:

> First I beget in them a high opinion of their father's love to them and of
> his being able to judge what shall be good for them. Then I make them sen-
> sible 'tis folly for them to pretend unto any wit or will of their own; they

must resign all to me, who will be sure to do what is best; my word must be their law.

THE AGRICULTURAL SYSTEM

The social hierarchy, the village community, and the patriarchal family were central features of a world we have lost. The agricultural system was another feature of this world. It is clear, as we have already noted, that English agriculture had been changing at least since the sixteenth century and that the estates had been integrated into a market economy. Some landlords from the late 1600s on had been enclosing fields, planting improved crops, and adopting new techniques of cultivation. However, because the most intense period of innovation in England came after 1760, this chapter will focus on the more traditional sector of the agricultural system. This sector remained significant to the English economy as a whole: agriculture was still the largest industry in England, the income of landlords and tenants alone composing half of the national income. Farming directly or indirectly employed more than half of the English people. Over 25 million acres were cultivated, of which about half—including the rich grain-producing land of the Midlands—were farmed using the traditional methods.

This traditional system originated in medieval agriculture, though it had become much altered by the eighteenth century. Instead of lords of manors who held their land from their feudal superiors in return for military service, and who farmed the land by both free and unfree labor, eighteenth-century England was dominated by estate owners, who leased parcels of land to tenant farmers, all of whom were legally free. The tenants and their wives worked the land with the assistance of hired farm laborers, both male and female. Feudal duties and labor services had long disappeared, but certain elements remained from the medieval system: (1) the three-field (or "open-field" system); (2) common rights; (3) cooperative management; and (4) relatively low yields. Estates in the traditionally farmed areas normally included a manor house and one or more villages, surrounded by several kinds of fields: first, the small "home farm," near the manor house, farmed directly by the landlord's steward; second, large unfenced ("open") fields divided into strips; and third, common land (or wastes). Each of the large fields was allowed to lie fallow every third year so that it could restore itself naturally; therefore, an estate typically had one-third of the fields in wheat, one-third in barley, and one-third in natural grasses. Each small owner and each tenant farmer held strips—the number depending on the size of the ownership or tenancy—in each of the three fields, and with his hired laborers went out each day from the village to work his strips. Because not all small owners and tenants could afford an expensive plow team, plowing usually had to be cooperative among tenants. Similarly, certain seasonal activities like haymaking and harvesting required a communal effort.

The common land or waste was an important part of the system, especially to the cottagers. By custom, tenants and cottagers had certain rights to the common land: to pick up fallen branches or to cut peat for fuel; to turn a few pigs and geese

The Warrener, *by George Morland. In this drawing we have a glimpse of the rural labor-ing poor—in this case a rabbit hunter and his family.*

onto the common to forage; to graze cows and sheep; or to dig clay for making bricks. Such rights often were decisive for cottagers and their families between survival and starvation; thus, the customary rights governing the common or waste land were carefully defined and zealously defended.

The system as a whole was inefficient. Not only did millions of acres lie fallow each year but also tenants and laborers had to go long distances from strip to strip. One Buckinghamshire farmer, for example, held 2 1/2 acres, which were divided into twenty-four strips scattered among different fields. It was difficult to experiment with new crops or techniques, to carry out systematic fertilizing of the fields, or to improve the quality of the livestock. Indeed, it was difficult to keep the cattle out of the fields or to keep a large number of livestock alive over the winter. Yields were therefore low—perhaps two bushels per acre in wheat. Nevertheless, agricultural production increased during the first half of the century, partly because of advances in the more modern sector of farming (see Chapter 10) and partly because of two decades of excellent harvests in the 1730s and 1740s. England for a time had a surplus of wheat for export. Food prices thus were relatively low, and this fact left thousands of British consumers with money after their food purchases to spend on other goods. This happy circumstance would eventually prove to be of enormous significance. Meanwhile, to most observers, the green fields of England seemed unusually prosperous and productive. As the novelist Tobias Smollett wrote: "I see the country of England smiling with cultivation: the grounds exhibiting all the perfection of agriculture, parceled into beautiful enclosures, corn fields, hay pasture, woodland and commons."

COMMERCE

Successful as agriculture was, commerce composed the growth sector of the English economy. By the early eighteenth century, England was well into the commercial revolution. Dr. Johnson observed: "There never was from earliest ages a time in which trade so much engaged the attention of mankind, or commercial gain was sought with such general emulation." This was an age of *commercial capitalism*, for capitalist practices (rational investment of money in commercial enterprises for the purpose of increasing profits) had emerged in the 1600s, a century before industrialization began. The middling sorts provided a substantial number of men with the rational outlook and the commercial skills to direct the expansion of trade and take the necessary risks. As the historian Roy Porter wrote, "England teemed with practical men of enterprise, weather-eye open, from tycoons to humble master craftsmen."* Hence, although official policy remained that of mercantilism, the state did not plan or direct English commercial expansion. It did, however, respond to the needs of powerful commercial interests in promoting and protecting foreign trade (by war if necessary), in chartering exclusive commercial and financial companies, and in avoiding both the heavy taxation and the internal tariffs that would have dampened trade. The state tried to protect manufacturing by tariffs and other regulations. But mercantile houses, banks, shipping firms, turnpike trusts, woolens companies, and countless shops across the country all were established by individual initiative.

Commercial expansion could be seen in both domestic consumption and foreign trade. England enjoyed what has been called a "consumer revolution" during the eighteenth century. Landlords, tenant farmers, and people of the middling sort all indulged their desire for luxury, fashion, and convenience by consuming goods of all kinds. Shops providing the consumer goods sprang up in even the small cities and towns. Not only did the landlords build, reconstruct, and redecorate their great houses with marvelous furniture and objects of art, but also professional and other middling sorts with less ostentatious wealth enjoyed consumer products like textiles, tablecloths, china services, pottery, cutlery, ceramics, prints, books, and newspapers to a degree that was entirely new in any European society. Refinement of manners usually accompanied the goods. Some aristocrats became anxious about the consumer pretensions of their social inferiors; and many traditional moralists denounced society's growing taste for luxury. But the desire for consumer goods could not be quashed, for the intent of the landlords to impress each other and overawe those below them in the hierarchy only inspired the desire among the less wealthy to emulate them.

---

*Roy Porter, *English Society in the Eighteenth Century* (Harmondsworth, Middlesex: Penguin, 1982), p. 95.

Foreign trade continued to grow in all its branches—exports, imports, and reexports. The "new trades," such as the importing and reexporting of tobacco, sugar, linens, calicoes, and slaves, grew steadily in comparison to the old staple export, finished woolens. The basic pattern of English trade was shifting, for while the proportion of English imports from northern Europe still stood at over 30 percent in 1750, the English over time imported less from Europe and more from the East Indies, the West Indies, and North America. Similarly, exports and reexports to Europe (especially to Spain and Portugal) remained of great importance, but shipping to North America and the East Indies won a larger share. Overall, English overseas trade doubled between 1700 and 1760, accelerating from a growth rate of about 1 percent a year in 1700 to 2 percent a year in 1760—a remarkable performance for a preindustrial society. England in the early eighteenth century was no Third World economy.

This foreign trade, as well as the coastal trade in coal and foodstuffs, made shipping a formidable business. In the 1740s, for instance, more than two hundred ships (most of them English) worked the tobacco trade alone. Because of the Navigation Acts, more than four-fifths of all ships calling at British ports were British owned; and British shipping tonnage more than doubled between 1700 and 1770. London continued to be the largest port by far and to grow in size—to more than 700,000 people in 1760, probably a quarter of whom worked in the port trades. London's insatiable demand drew in goods from most of the British Isles: cattle from Wales and Scotland, fruits and vegetables from the Thames Valley and the West Country, grains from the Midlands and East Anglia, coal from Newcastle, and iron from Sussex, the western Midlands, and eastern Wales. The new trades also stimulated the expansion of other cities, Liverpool, Bristol, and Glasgow in particular. Liverpool, the center of the slave trade, grew from about five thousand people in 1700 to thirty thousand in 1750. Thus, London's *share* of England's expanding trade declined as provincial wealth grew.

London was the hub of an internal market that incorporated most of the regions of England, as well as parts of Ireland, Wales, and Scotland. This market was to be a key force in integrating the economies of the British Isles. The degree of commercialization in England and the average Englishman's love of cash and profits must not be underestimated. This was true of landowners and farmers as well as townsmen. The sinews of England's market economy were becoming tougher. London's financial institutions grew in size and number: in addition to the Bank of England, the East India Company (1709) and the South Sea Company (1711) were chartered in part to finance the national debt. A craze for joint-stock companies and speculation in their stock soared until 1720, when the South Sea Company's inflated stock collapsed. Thereafter, laws severely restricted joint-stock company foundation, but the commercial sector found its own ways of raising capital and facilitating transactions, as private merchants and attorneys in growing numbers performed banking functions. The notoriously poor roads began to be improved by means of private turnpike trusts that financed their construction and maintenance by tolls. Water transport—slower but cheaper than road haulage—

improved as well, again by private efforts that added to the mileage of navigable rivers and began in the 1750s to construct a system of canals.

To get a sense of commercial development in the first half of the century, one can look at the example of Abraham Dent, who ran a general store in the small town of Kirkby Stephen in Westmorland. In the 1750s and 1760s, Dent sold a remarkable variety of items to customers from the town and nearby villages; tea, sugar, wine, beer, cider, barley, soap, candles, tobacco, lemons, vinegar, silk, cottons, woolens, needles, pins, books, magazines, paper, ink, and a great many other goods as well. Eggs, butter, and cheese he left to the village markets. His supplies came from a surprisingly wide area, including Halifax, Leeds, and Manchester in the North, Newcastle in the Northeast, Coventry in the Midlands, and Norwich and London in the East. He financed his operation in a sophisticated way—by handling bills of exchange and by extending credit to his customers and receiving it from his suppliers. He bought stockings knitted locally for retail to his customers and soon was having thousands made on order. Increasingly, then, he became a small capitalist, ordering goods made to sell to large-scale buyers, usually wholesalers in London. Almost inevitably, as he dealt in more complex financial transactions, Dent became a banker.

Not all shopkeepers were as successful as Abraham Dent, but his case illustrates the integration of the market economy and the connections between commerce and industry. Most manufacturing continued to be done by the "domestic" or "putting out" system. By this system, manufacturing remained decentralized, located in the cottages of hundreds of villages and small towns and devoted to processing native raw materials like wool and iron. An individual capitalist, often a merchant like Abraham Dent, bought raw materials and supplied them to the village craftspersons, paying each a piece-rate for his or her work in finishing the product; then the capitalist collected and sold the product himself. Such was the mode of production in woolens, the metal trades, nailmaking, watchmaking, leather goods, and many others. This system was of great advantage to the capitalist, whose investment was limited to the raw materials. Little initial investment was required. Further, when demand declined, the supplier reduced production simply by laying off workers: none of his own machines or tools stood idle. Finally, the system left problems of labor relations and work discipline to the laborers themselves.

The domestic system provided no golden age for its laborers. True, the nailers, weavers, and other craftsmen and craftswomen worked in their own cottages, alongside their families, and usually on machines they had purchased themselves. In many instances, there was a strong pride in independence that was later to be remembered with powerful longing. Many, however, went into debt to buy their looms or other tools and in effect had nothing to sell but their labor itself. In any case, while many farm families supplemented their incomes by doing one of the steps in the production process, other families found that poor soil in their locality or the increasing demand for textiles drew them, and their whole villages, into full-time spinning or weaving. In such areas, like the Northwest or the Pennines, the laborers left their work to help in the fields only at harvest time. The domestic workers were able to control the rhythm of labor themselves—typically slow early in the week and rapid toward the end—but they worked very long hours and were subject to abrupt layoffs as the market demanded. Many habitually were indebted to the master; if so, the domestic worker may have been an artisan but he had to struggle to maintain his independence. Most domestic workers depended as heavily on the merchant capitalist as the tenant or farm laborer depended on the landlord.

CUSTOM VERSUS CONTRACT

The commercial sector and the commercial spirit were principal factors making the eighteenth century in England an age of contrasts. They were like fast-running streams relentlessly eroding the massive hills of traditional England. In traditional English society, the hierarchical social structure, the face-to-face relations, the ideal of paternalism, and the power of custom combined to make a world very different from our own. The impersonal, hurried, bureaucratic, and competitive qualities of modern life were much less important then. Everyone except the very poorest had a place in the social system, with privileges and duties attached. Face-to-face relations meant that people lived their lives amid known, if not loved, faces. Paternalism may have been abused, but its claims were not easily ignored, and it provided that members of the elite felt a personal responsibility for those within their circle of clients. Custom was stultifying for the ambitious man, as it was for many women, but it taught rich and poor, landlord and tenant, farmer and laborer, journeyman and apprentice what their rights and responsibilities were.

During the eighteenth century, however, all these features of an earlier way of life were slowly being altered by commercial attitudes: the "cash nexus" or the relations of "contract" conflicted with custom in countless ways and in a myriad of localities. The commercialization of English life was not uniform in its effects in every place or in every set of relationships, nor was its work complete by the end of the century. Nevertheless, the desire for profit and for maximizing the return from every parcel of property unceasingly worked to shift the basis of relationships from customary arrangements to contractual bargains. This shift was as true for the agricultural world as for the commercial. Landlords enjoyed luxurious consumption and the requisite making of money just as much as the merchant or banker. Everyone among the propertied elite maneuvered to improve or consolidate his or her position on the status ladder. Given the power of the landlords and rich merchants, the customary rights of the poor came under constant pressure—a tenancy taken from the customary family and rented to the highest bidder; or rights of foraging on the wastes denied by new landowners; or customary prices for an artisan's work rejected in favor of a market price.

The inner social history of eighteenth-century England can be written in terms of this sporadic but often desperate struggle. One example, eloquently described by the historian E. P. Thompson, will have to suffice.* In about 1720, in the Windsor

---

*E. P. Thompson, *Whigs and Hunters* (New York; Pantheon, 1975).

Forest area on the border of Hampshire and Berkshire, a continuing conflict of such ferocity occurred that a stringent law called the Waltham Black Act was passed in 1723. This act added about fifty items to the already long list of capital crimes on the books, including such offenses as deer poaching, going about the forest at night with face blacked for disguise, and breaking the dams of landlords' fish ponds. The origins of the conflict that occasioned the act lay in the desire of new landlords in the area to exploit the economic opportunities of the forest more efficiently; in the enthusiasm of the "forest bureaucracy" (rangers and gamekeepers) to carry out the landlords' will; and in the efforts of the small owners, tenants, and laborers of the forest to maintain their traditional means of survival in the forest ecology. Thus, the customary "use rights" of property were disputed. The common people of the forest could eke out a living only if they could supplement their earnings from farm or craft by taking a deer occasionally, fishing in the streams, collecting "lops and tops" of felled timber, and cutting turf for fuel. None of these customary use rights squared with either the landlords' newly established absolute rights of private property or their lust for money. Paternalism in this case meant that the landlords tried to force the ordinary people to give up their customary sense of right. The landlords naturally had the power of both Parliament and king at their disposal, but the Forest people had resources of their own—secrecy, stealth, intimidation, and violence. In the short run, at least, the struggle was a standoff.

It seems clear that the fight in Windsor Forest was exceptionally dramatic. After all, there was only one Waltham Black Act during the eighteenth century. Yet this episode also seems representative in that it pointed to the main trend in eighteenth-century social history—the shift from an old to a new kind of society, from one based on custom to one based on contract.

Suggested Reading

Ashton, T. S., *An Economic History of England: The Eighteenth Century* (London: Methuen, 1966).

Beckett, J. V., *The Aristocracy in England, 1600–1914* (Oxford: Blackwell, 1986).

Berg, Maxine, *The Age of Manufactures: Industry, Innovation and Work in Britain 1700–1820* (Totowa, N.J.: Barnes & Noble, 1985).

Brewer, John, Neil McKendrick, and J. H. Plumb, *The Birth of a Consumer Society* (Bloomington: Indiana University Press, 1982).

Cannon, John, *Aristocratic Century: The Peerage of Eighteenth-Century England* (Cambridge: Cambridge University Press, 1984).

Fletcher, Anthony, *Gender, Sex, and Subordination in England 1500–1800* (New Haven: Yale University Press, 1996).

Habakkuk, H. J., *"England,"* in A. Goodwin, ed., *The European Nobility in the Eighteenth Century* (New York: Harper & Row, 1967).

Hay, Douglas, and Nicholas Rogers, *Eighteenth-Century English Society* (New York: Oxford University Press, 1997).

Hill, Bridget, *Women, Work, and Sexual Politics in Eighteenth-Century* (Montreal: McGill-Queen's University Press, 1994).

Hoskins, W. G., *The Midland Peasant* (London: Macmillan, 1957).

Hunt, Margaret R., *The Middling Sort: Commerce, Gender, and the Family in England, 1680–1780* (Berkeley: University of California Press, 1996).

Langford, Paul, *A Polite and Commercial People: England, 1727–1783* (New York: Oxford University Press, 1989).

Laslett, Peter, *The World We Have Lost* (London: Methuen, 1965).

Laurence, Anne, *Women in England. 1500–1760* (New York: St. Martin's Press, 1994).

Malcolmson, Robert W., *Life and Labour in England, 1700–1780* (New York: St. Martin's Press, 1981).

Mingay, G. E., *English Landed Society in the Eighteenth Century* (London: Routledge & Kegan Paul, 1963).

———, *The Gentry* (London: Longman, 1976).

Perkin, Harold, *Origins of Modern English Society, 1780–1880* (Toronto: University of Toronto Press, 1969).

Porter, Roy, *English Society in the Eighteenth Century* (London: Allen Lane, 1983).

Rule, John, *Albion's People: English Society. 1714–1815* (New York: Longman, 1992).

Sharpe, J. A., *Early Modern England: A Social History 1550–1760* (Baltimore: Edward Arnold, 1987).

Shoemaker, Robert B., *Gender in English Society, 1650–1850: The Emergence of the Separate Spheres?* (London: Longman: 1998).

Smail, John, *The Origins of Middle-Class Culture: Halifax, Yorkshire, 1660–1780* (Ithaca: Cornell University Press, 1994).

Snell, K. D. M., *Annals of the Labouring Poor: Social Change and Agrarian England, 1660–1900* (New York: Cambridge University Press, 1985).

Speck, W. A., *Stability and Strife: England, 1714–1760* (London: E. Arnold, 1977).

Stone, Lawrence, *The Family, Sex and Marriage in England, 1500–1800* (London: Weidenfeld & Nicolson, 1977).

Tadmor, Naomi, *Family and Friends in Eighteenth Century England: Household, Kinship, and Patronage* (Cambridge: Cambridge University Press, 2001).

Thompson, E. P., *Whigs and Hunters* (New York: Pantheon Books, 1975).

Vickery, Amanda, *The Gentleman's Daughter: Women's Lives in Georgian England* (New Haven: Yale University Press, 1998).

Wilson, Charles, *England's Apprenticeship, 1603–1763* (London: Longman, 1965).

Chapter 4

Political Structure and Politics in England, 1715–1760

Sharp contrasts marked the politics of eighteenth-century England. First, there was a strong contrast between the political violence and the "rage of party" of the first twenty years of the century and the political peace and stability of the middle four decades. Second, there was a distinct contrast between political theory and practice—between the theory of a "mixed constitution" of king, Lords, and Commons, the whole resting on the consent of the governed—and the reality of a narrow oligarchy. By the 1730s, England had nearly become in effect a one-party state, its apparent Augustan calm resting not so much on the support of a majority of the people as on the clear reflection by the political structure of the economic and social power of the Whig property owners. Third, there was a contrast between the liberty and cheap government praised by the English and the growth of a powerful English state. Finally, there was a profound contrast between the sedate world of parliamentary maneuvering that came into existence and the raucous and riotous world of popular politics. These contrasts give a sense of the rich flavor of the Augustan political system and serve as reminders that English politics and government in the eighteenth century were very different entities from those of the present.

ACHIEVING POLITICAL STABILITY, 1700–1720

As Professor J. H. Plumb wrote, the twenty-five or thirty years after 1688 composed an unstable and dangerous period in British politics: "Governments teetered on the edge of chaos, and party strife was as violent as anything England had known since the Civil War."* The first decades of the eighteenth century were afflicted by a "rage of party" as Whigs and Tories clashed at both the national and local levels. At stake were different ideologies as well as personal and family disputes. General elections were frequent, and the number of constituencies contested in each election was high. Yet by 1750, general elections had become

---

*J. H. Plumb, *The Growth of Political Stability in England. 1675–1725* (Harmondsworth, Middlesex: Penguin Books, 1969), p. 74.

infrequent and electoral contests rare. By then the Tories had been reduced to a small group in permanent opposition, and the Whigs dominated Parliament and alone formed governments. What the Tory prime minister Benjamin Disraeli was later to call the "Venetian Oligarchy" was firmly in place.

The reasons for the growth of this peculiar kind of stability lay partly in institutional changes, partly in the dissolving of divisive issues, and partly in certain long-term social trends. The institutional factors were influenced by the growing costliness of elections. The electorate of England and Wales was very small by modern standards, but it was growing to unprecedented size; there were perhaps 300,000 voters in 1700. Voters regarded their franchise as an office from which they were entitled to some benefit. Thus, rival candidates in a constituency had to ply the electors with copious servings of food and beer, as well as to patronize local tradesmen. The price of entertainment went up throughout the century: the Grosvenors, for instance, spent £8,500 on food and drink for the electors of Chester in 1784. Candidates also had to pay the fees of election officials and make donations to local charities—town halls, churches, almshouses, and so on. In some boroughs, bribery was a major expense. Voters in Weobly, for example, got twenty pounds apiece from the candidate of their choice. Also, patronage being the grease that lubricated the social system, candidates were expected to find offices for their supporters.

Soaring expenses led to a widespread desire among the ruling elite to hold down the growth of the electorate, to reduce the number of contested seats, and to cut the frequency of general elections. Many men opted not to stand for Parliament or simply were not wealthy enough to do so. Further, in numerous boroughs, aldermen found ways to stop the increase in the electorate, such as by raising the admission expenses of becoming a freeman of the borough. By 1715, the electorate was distinctly narrower than twenty years before. In addition, Parliament in 1716 passed the Septennial Act, which required general elections only every seven years instead of every three. Consequently, whereas there were twelve general elections between 1689 and 1715, there were only thirteen between 1715 and 1800.

Another institutional change contributing to stability was the concentration of government patronage. While the number of men who could afford a candidacy was dwindling, patronage was being centralized in the hands of the government, as opposed to the court. Together, these two trends contributed to the perpetuation of an oligarchy of the wealthiest families. Largely because of the demands of war, and because of the need to collect taxes and conduct complex foreign relations thereafter, the machinery of the British state grew. The number of government offices increased, particularly in the Treasury and the military services. Tax-collecting posts multiplied especially quickly: in 1714, nearly four hundred men collected salt taxes alone. All such jobs were doled out by the government as patronage. Under the control of Robert Walpole, Whig prime minister between 1721 and 1742, thousands of government appointments were used to build and maintain a massive structure of government support.

Such institutional changes, however, would not have sufficed to reduce political conflict if the political nation had been violently divided on the issues. Before

The Polling, *by William Hogarth. In this painting, Hogarth gives a clear picture of the somewhat chaotic and public quality of voting, complete with bribery and influence during the eighteenth century.*

1715, Whigs and Tories, as we have seen, had differed radically on a number of crucial issues—the legitimacy of and the succession to the Crown, the Treaty of Utrecht, and the Church of England. The Tories of the early eighteenth century took as their slogan, "Peace and the Church in danger," and the Whigs countered with "Trade and the Protestant succession." The intensity of these issues dimmed over time, however. The succession of George I and the Hanoverian line proceeded fairly smoothly. Religious fervor gave way to reasonableness, and property owners lost interest in theological controversy. Under Whig rule, nonconformists suffered no additional harassment, but neither did they win repeal of the Test and Corporation Acts: the compromise of occasional conformity (restored in 1718) remained in place. By this practice a man still had to be at least nominally Anglican to serve in public office, but he might qualify by occasionally (actually no more than once a year) taking communion in the Church of England. Likewise, war and its attendant taxation disappeared temporarily from the political agenda. The great Whig leader, Walpole, pursued a pacific foreign policy, with a view to reducing the land tax; indeed, his slogan for all policy was *quieta non movere* ("let sleeping dogs lie").

Perhaps most significant to their decline in political importance, the Tories were discredited by their association with the Jacobite cause. To most politically active Englishmen (and Lowland Scots, as we will see), Jacobitism sought to upset the settlement constructed in 1688 and after to restore tyranny and Catholicism to Britain. The precise extent of Jacobite support in England is not clear. Not only did the Tory leader Bolingbroke conspire with the Old Pretender in 1714 and flee to France in 1715, but many Tories continued to give allegiance to the Stuarts thereafter. The Jacobite threat broke out with drama and danger in 1715, when some Highland chiefs raised the Stuart banner in Scotland (see Chapter 6). Jacobitism proved to be of durable popularity in Scotland, but the rising in England was limited to a few thousand Catholics at most. English Anglicans, including most Tories, remained loyal to the new Hanoverian regime, and the English Jacobites were put down with ease. Jacobitism faded as a force in England, though enough Tories retained their sentimental attachment to the Stuarts to allow Walpole to exploit the issue by accusing all the Tories of harboring Jacobite sympathies. Some Jacobites tried to make a case for custom and paternalism against Whigish contract and commerce, but in actuality, as one Jacobite put it, the English Tories "are never right hearty for the cause, till they are mellow as they call it, over a bottle or two."

The Whig and Tory parties continued to exist through the 1760s, but until the last decade of the century, Whigs alone enjoyed the perquisites of power. Increasingly, the Whigs became the "Court" party, enjoying the ear of the monarch and speaking for the aristocracy, the financiers, and the most aggressive commercial captains. It is hard to determine what the Whigs after 1715 stood for, besides the "Glorious Revolution" itself, the privileges of the landowning elite, the expansion of trade, and the exploitation of state patronage. The Tories more and more adopted an "opposition" mentality. Along with some opposition (or "Country") Whigs, the Tories opposed the corruption attendant on the Whig oligarchy's wallowing in the spoils of politics. They argued for restoring the purity of the constitutional balance among king, Lords, and Commons established in 1688. The balance, they believed, was being eroded by Walpole's corrupt use of patronage, by which the House of Commons was being subjugated by the executive. Government officeholders ("placemen") should be barred from the House of Commons, elections held frequently, and boroughs in the pocket of some landlord disfranchised, so that members of Parliament could maintain their independence against the government.

The opposition philosophy of the Tories and the Country Whigs was unable to compete effectively against the very real attractions of power. Most oppositional critics of the ruling Whigs did not themselves oppose the principle of patronage, only what they regarded as the abuse of it. On the whole, the interests of all property owners, Whig and Tory alike, in eighteenth-century England were similar enough to dull the edge of political divisions. In the end, the prosperity, security, and self-interest of the propertied elite—and above all, of the landowners—brought political stability to England.

LOCAL GOVERNMENT

The landed oligarchy's power was firmly based in local government. Landlords in the counties and propertied men of commerce in the towns ruled without much control from either the central government above them or, usually, the populace below. The magnates, after all, had won their struggle with the Crown about who would rule in the localities. The power they exercised was of great importance, partly because it was bound up with the structure of social authority and partly because other than paying taxes most people had direct contact with government and law *only* on the local level, unless they were taken into the armed services. One must remember that the functions of the national government were severely limited: maintenance of law and order, conduct of foreign affairs in war and peace, protection of the rights of property, and a minimum of economic control, the most important aspect of which was taxation. At the local level, the nation ruled itself, in the sense that the "natural leaders" of society, acting as local officials, ruled the country—enforcing the laws, repairing the roads, caring for the poor, regulating fairs and markets, maintaining churches, and the like.

The institutions of local government composed a patchwork quilt sewn from swatches of historical accident, many of them reaching back to medieval times. But the presence of local autonomy, the variety of local governing institutions, and the rowdiness of the age did not mean that England was an ungoverned or frontier society. The system was unified not by central government direction but by the social homogeneity of local officials. All of them were men of property, not elected but self-perpetuating by means of cooptation. Men in positions of local power selected others for county and parish offices. This social solidarity was buttressed by the face-to-face relations of rural and small-town England. Except in the big cities—and above all in London, where anonymity was a fact of life—and some remote districts, men of property controlled everything.

The basic unit of government was the parish, of which there were about ten thousand. Four parish officers did most of the work: the church warden, the surveyor of the highways, the constable, and the overseer of the poor. All were unpaid amateurs, selected by the substantial property owners of the parish: the warden was selected by the church vestry and the others by the local justices of the peace. The warden took responsibility for the buildings of the church and for collecting the church rate (a local tax to maintain the churches buildings). The surveyor of the highways was responsible to the justices of the peace for maintenance of the roads. The constable and his deputies acted as the local policemen (there being no national or even county police force), apprehending criminals, settling domestic uproar, dealing with drunks, and so on.

The overseer of the poor had perhaps the most onerous duties: relieving paupers and coping with vagrants according to the regulations of the Poor Law of 1662. By this statute, every pauper in England had a right to economic assistance from his or her parish of settlement (that is, the parish of birth or residence) but *only* from that parish. The overseer thus provided from a parish rate assistance to his parish's poor, either in a workhouse or in the form of "outdoor relief" (that is, payment to a person outside a workhouse). He also had to remove to their own parishes the paupers, vagrants, and beggars who did not belong. These grew to be enormous tasks. In the first half of the century, paternalist attitudes provided relatively generous assistance. But gradually, attitudes toward the poor hardened, as the "cash nexus" spread through social relations, and administration of poor relief became more stringent. Parishes increasingly resorted to poorhouses, in the hopes that they would be cheaper for the ratepayers as well as sufficiently unpleasant to drive paupers back to work.

The work of these parish officers was supervised by the justices of the peace (J.P.s), who were by far the key figures in eighteenth-century English local government. Appointed by the county's lord lieutenant (usually the greatest nobleman of the county), the J.P. was a member of the gentry whose estate was worth at least one hundred pounds a year. Tories were purged from the lists of J.P.s early in the century, but as the landed oligarchy solidified, the appointments became nonpolitical: a man became a J.P. by dint of his local standing. To serve as J.P. was a heavy and expensive responsibility but also one of great social prestige. These unpaid officials held broad executive and judicial powers. A single J. P. exercised summary justice over petty criminals: the power to arrest, try, and punish drunks, game poachers, gamblers, and so on. Two or more J.P.s in "petty sessions" could try minor offenders as well as hold parish officials to their duties. In "Quarter Sessions," the J. P. s of a county together tried all criminal cases below capital crimes and administered the growing burden of laws put on their shoulders by Parliament—laws governing wages and prices (more and more ignored), roads, bridges, jails, and licensing of tradesmen, to name only a few. Britain, then, unlike many Continental countries, was ruled not by royal agents sent from the capital to the provinces but by volunteers from the landed orders, whose social and economic roots lay in the districts they governed.

The boroughs were as oligarchical as the counties. In most of them, the ruling corporation consisted of a mayor, a dozen aldermen, and two or three dozen councilmen. In a few boroughs, these officials were elected by the freemen, and in the city of London such elections were hotly disputed. In most boroughs, however, the aldermen and councillors selected themselves by "cooptation"—that is, they chose their own members. In any case, power increasingly flowed to the relatively small number who were ex officio J.P.s. These municipal J.P.s had the same powers as their rural brethren, but as the towns grew, the face-to-face relations tended to crumble, and the J.P.s were less and less able to cope with urban problems.

The events of 1688 and the subsequent Revolution Settlement had established the rule of law, and this fact distinguished England from the rest of Europe. In the eighteenth century, it was already England's pride and joy, and it remains so to this day. Nevertheless, the oligarchy managed to make the law work for themselves. Two important trends in the way that the law affected the people followed from the establishment of oligarchy. First, the penal code became increasingly severe over time: in 1689, for example, there were fifty capital crimes on the books; in 1800, there were more than two hundred. Second, laws protecting property became more obtrusive. Picking pockets of more than one shilling and shoplifting items worth five shillings both became capital crimes, as did destroying turnpike gates, forgery, or theft from a master by a servant. Most people who were hanged were executed for theft, not murder. Executions were staged as public events so as to symbolize to the common folk the necessity of maintaining the social order. As the novelist Oliver Goldsmith put it, "Laws grind the poor, and rich men rule the law."

THE STRUCTURE OF NATIONAL POLITICS, 1715–1760

The purposes of national politics, if limited in range, were of great importance to the propertied elite. Given the need to protect the rights of private property, to promote trade and imperial expansion, to conduct foreign policy, and to set taxes in the light of their interests, men of standing found it important to participate in parliamentary politics. Not only was Britain at war with scarcely an interruption between 1689 and 1713, but also war began again in 1739 and as we will see went on continually thereafter. The logistical requirements of this so-called Second Hundred Years War raised taxes, increased the national debt, and swelled the state bureaucracy, especially in the revenue departments. The landed oligarchy needed to control this burgeoning state apparatus and limit the negative influence of war-related taxes. Above all, they recognized the vital importance of winning through political influence a share of the succulent outpouring of state patronage: government contracts, military and naval commissions, posts in the civil service or tax-collecting agencies, clerical appointments, sinecures in the court, and many other juicy morsels. The way to get a seat at this prodigious banquet table was political clout. To cite only one example, Horace Walpole, the son of Sir Robert Walpole, enjoyed for fifty-nine years three sinecures—clerk of the estreats, usher of the Exchequer, and comptroller of the Pipe. Thus he was able to indulge his taste for art by means of state salaries, in return for which he delivered his vote for the government in the House of Commons.

These purposes of politics shaped the way the constitution worked. Theoretically, England had a mixed constitution of king, Lords, and Commons, in which each element checked and balanced the others—the monarchical element checked the aristocratic and democratic, and so on. The king remained the nation's chief executive officer, shorn of many of his former prerogatives but still retaining the right to appoint and dismiss his ministers. No one could serve in the government for long without the confidence of the king. But if those ministers were to carry on the king's government, they had to have the confidence of Parliament as well. Inevitably, eighteenth-century kings often had to struggle to sustain their favorites in office at times when they lacked the support of the House of Commons. Given the power of the Commons, this was a struggle that in the long run the kings could not win.

The difficulties of the Crown were aggravated by the unfortunate personalities of the first two Hanoverian kings. George I and II both were block-headed German princes (George I spoke very little English), not incompetent but stubborn, unimaginative, and unattractive. George I (1714–1727) was shy and indolent;

George II (1727–1760) was opinionated but could be bullied. Moreover, they detested each other. As Horace Walpole dryly observed, "It ran a little in the blood of the family to hate the eldest son." Partly for this reason, George I absented himself from group meetings of his ministers, where he would have had to meet his son, then Prince of Wales. This inadvertently contributed to the development of the cabinet system. In any case, neither king was capable of forging parliamentary alliances; hence, both were dependent on their parliamentary leaders. Yet they disliked having ministers forced on them by Parliament. "Ministers are the Kings in this country," George II complained.

In fact, however, the Georgian ministers stood in a constitutionally precarious position. The principle of the collective responsibility of the cabinet to the House of Commons did not yet exist. Ministers were responsible as individuals to the Crown. The institution of the cabinet did begin to emerge before 1760, but its evolution was sporadic and unplanned. In the late seventeenth century, a "cabinet council" had replaced the privy council as the effective organ of the king's advisers, simply because the privy council had become too large. In the first half of the eighteenth century, a smaller, secret cabinet tended to supplant this cabinet council, which itself had proved to be cumbersome. This effective cabinet, consisting of the five or six key ministers, slowly assumed a corporate identity, meeting in the king's private closet. The Hanoverians retained the right to meet with ministers individually, however, and only reluctantly gave up the right of consulting political advisors who were *not* in the cabinet. The cabinet did not function consistently as a corporate entity until after the end of the eighteenth century.

What drove the kings to deal with a cabinet collectively was their continuing need to have as ministers men who could command a majority in Parliament and, above all, in the House of Commons. The House of Lords was much under the sway of royal influence and so rarely presented problems, but the House of Commons was different. There was as yet in the Commons nothing like the well-disciplined parties of modern times. Hence ministers did not ride to power readily as the pre-chosen spokesmen of a majority party in the Commons; nor did they, once in office, dictate votes to an organized, obedient party. The House of Commons had 558 members, of whom about 100 were active politicians (all Whigs) seeking ministerial office, plus about 100 to 150 "placemen" who depended on the court and government for their livelihood, and about 250 "Independents." Some of the Independents were normally inclined to support the king's government, but others were permanently attached to the opposition mentality. The ministers of the day could count on the votes of the placemen but had to win the support of sufficient numbers of the active politicians and Independents as well to make up a majority.

Patronage was the means to this end. Not all M.P.s were vulnerable to political patronage: Tories and Country Whigs loudly opposed its use to build government majorities. But many could be bought by offices and favors—if not for themselves, then for relatives, friends, and other clients in their interests. Including military officers, the number of officeholders usually stood at between one-third and one-half of all M.P.s. Opponents among the active politicians were especially susceptible to influence. Indeed, the normal pattern of parliamentary politics was for some person outside the cabinet to make such a nuisance of himself by his opposition that a place would have to be found for him in the government and his clients pacified by patronage. This was known as "storming the closet," a game played to perfection by the two leading politicians of the period, Sir Robert Walpole and William Pitt (the Elder).

Outside the House of Commons, patronage was used to win elections and even to buy seats in the House of Commons. The power of patronage depended on the curiously variegated nature of the constituencies and the small size of the electorate in many of them. The major categories of constituencies were the counties and the boroughs. In the fifty-two English and Welsh counties, all males possessing freeholds worth at least forty shillings (two pounds) a year could vote. This qualification could be met by many thousands of small landowners and by tenants who owned some property. The county electorates, therefore, varied from several hundred to over ten thousand. Most county elections were dominated by aristocratic or leading gentry families. The borough franchise was much more irregular. In some boroughs, owners of particular houses voted; in others, just the members of the corporation voted. In still others, all males who paid the local tax voted, but in some the franchise went to "pot wallopers"—self-sufficient holders of hearth and home. In a few boroughs, all male householders held the franchise. As a result, several boroughs had upward of four thousand voters, but more than half had fewer than five hundred; Old Sarum, a parliamentary borough in southwestern England, had three or four. The government could control some boroughs where there were military installations, shipyards, or large concentrations of civilian officials. Many of the other small ones were controlled by wealthy patrons who had the voters in their pockets and whose loyalty could be purchased by government favors or cold cash.

The essence of the parliamentary game, consequently, was for the king to appoint as ministers men who could win a working majority in the House of Commons by force of personality and by judicious use of "influence" (patronage), and for ambitious members of the opposition to force the government to buy them off. Electoral promises and party platforms—developments of the future—were not factors, though voters usually did demand that their M.P.s meet their expectations of proper paternalist behavior. Except for some backwoods opposition radicals, M.P.s all regarded themselves as independent representatives, not as delegates from their constituencies. Public legislation did not much occupy them, for the vast bulk of legislation was private—that is, local and particularized enabling acts. Men went into politics not to legislate platforms, but to exercise their judgment on issues as they arose, to protect their interests, to win their share of the spoils, and to act out the political dimension of social authority.

WALPOLE AND THE ROBINOCRACY

Sir Robert Walpole (1676–1745) was the consummate master of the oligarchical system. The son of a Norfolk squire and himself the image of the blunt, coarse

Sir Robert Walpole as Ranger of Richmond Park, *by John Wootton. Walpole liked to present himself as the rugged English country squire.*

country gentleman, Walpole was the most brilliant political operator of the century. Short, fat, and red-faced, he exuded rustic power. He liked to munch Norfolk apples during parliamentary debate and to claim that his gamekeeper's letters took precedence over official dispatches. But he was no backwoods bumpkin. Walpole was an efficient administrator, a tireless manipulator of patronage, a formidable debater, and a master of national finance. Most important, he was a genius in understanding ordinary human motives. He could deftly detect and exploit the weaknesses of royalty and country M.P.s alike.

Walpole rose to power from a sound basis. As a loyal Whig M.P. from 1700 to 1721, Walpole served in a number of administrative posts that gave him an unmatched understanding of government operations and finance. He won the friendship and influence of the Prince and Princess of Wales. His great opportunity came in 1720, with the bursting of the South Sea "bubble." The South Sea Company had taken over a part of the national debt, on the basis of which it raised huge sums through inflated stock. The company bribed a number of politicians in order to win privileges, and when the collapse of its stock ruined thousands of investors, they angrily demanded that *someone* be punished. Walpole had escaped corruption when many national political leaders had discredited themselves; furthermore, he stepped forward with practical measures to restore public credit. Most important, he screened ministers from attack, limited the political damage, and won the gratitude of George I. In 1721 he was made first lord of the Treasury (the top ministerial post) and within a year had made himself in effect prime minister—the first in English history.

Walpole ruled from 1721 to 1742, his domination of court and Parliament earning the epithet of "the Robinocracy." With the assistance of his brother-in-law, Lord Townshend, an expert in European affairs, Walpole took control of every aspect of government policy. He systematically rooted out opponents from government departments, the royal household, the army, the navy, and the Church and replaced them with his own supporters, many of them relatives and friends. With painstaking attention to patronage, he molded a dependable majority in the Lords and the Commons alike. The Tory newspaper, the *Craftsman*, called Walpole's House of Commons a monster "who had above 500 mouths . . . fed on gold and silver." The ease with which Walpole was able to get the king's business done, not to mention his adroit handling of the royal mistresses, made George I dependent on him. When George I died in 1727, many politicians thought that Walpole was finished, but they reckoned without his shrewd human insight. Walpole recognized that the new king depended more on his queen, Caroline of Anspach, than on his mistresses, and Walpole got on famously with Caroline. Walpole influenced George II through her; as he put it, he "took the right sow by the ear."

The king's support enabled Walpole to survive the first crisis of his regime—a furor over an excise tax scheme in 1733. Walpole's policy in general was nonactivist: peace, trade, and tax reduction. By his excise plan, which would have extended the existing system of excise taxes to wine and tobacco, Walpole hoped to reduce or even end land taxes. Much to his surprise, the proposal caused a great public outcry, for the opposition was able to play on popular fears of an army of excise officers who would threaten every Englishman's liberty. Walpole was forced to withdraw his plan, but his rule was sustained by his retention of the king's confidence.

Queen Caroline died in 1737, and Walpole's grip on power slowly loosened; hence he was unable to withstand the opposition during the second crisis of his regime. This arose over his ineffective conduct of war with Spain. The war (the War of Jenkins' Ear) had been forced on him. For years, the eagerness of English merchants to milk the Spanish Empire, and the piratical efforts of the Spanish coast guard in the West Indies to stop them, had soured relations between England and Spain. Walpole preferred negotiations to war, but patriotic English merchants and squires thought he was too meek in asserting English interests. In 1739, he reluctantly agreed to war: "It is your war," he told Newcastle, "and I wish you joy of it." As we will see in Chapter 7, the conflict with Spain soon merged with a general conflict on the Continent called the War of Austrian Succession, which was to last through 1748. Because he opposed Britain's involvement, Walpole conducted the war effort ineffectually. His support in the Commons dwindled, as Independents withdrew their support and as holders of place and pensions sensed that a new source of patronage would soon hold office. Despite the king's support, Walpole resigned in 1742.

WILLIAM PITT THE ELDER

Walpole may have fallen in 1742, but his system did not. His principal critic in the House of Commons had been a young man of sweeping vision and rhetorical power, William Pitt (1708–1778). However, George II thought that Pitt had overstepped the boundaries of legitimate opposition and refused to have him as a minister of state. The government that succeeded Walpole was headed by Henry Pelham, an unprepossessing but efficient House of Commons manager, and his brother, the duke of Newcastle, an eccentric, incredibly wealthy, anxiety-ridden master of patronage. Together, the Pelhams managed to hold in harness a fractious ministry of Walpole Whigs and some of their former opponents until 1754, when Henry Pelham died. In 1746, they even succeeded in forcing George II to accept Pitt as paymaster general of the forces, which neatly bought off their most troublesome critic.

Pitt, however, could not be silenced for good. A manic depressive, Pitt was a man of insatiable ambition. He had inherited the uncontrollable temper of his grandfather, "Diamond" Pitt, and his moods swung violently from depression and lethargy to demonic energy. In his manic phases, Pitt had the self-assurance and the broad designs of a global statesman. He was also the most brilliant orator of the century, capable of making his listeners believe that they—and England—were walking with destiny. Pitt was not a good political operator, but his grandiose theatricality and inspirational rhetoric gave him power of a different sort—the emotional support of independent M.P.s and makers of public opinion. This was not a recipe that the oligarchy swallowed easily.

As we will see in Chapter 7, Pitt inspired the English to seize world power status. He couched the ruthless pursuit of English commercial interests around the world in terms of the highest principles. He began his political career in 1735 as a member of the opposition, passionately believing that Walpole was corrupting English politics at home and betraying English interests abroad. His first speeches were so threatening that Walpole had him dismissed from his army commission: "We must muzzle this terrible cornet of the horse." But Pitt was not to be muzzled. In 1739, he spoke for war with Spain: "When trade is at stake, you must defend it or perish. . . . You throw out general terrors of war. Spain knows the consequences of war in America, but she sees England dare not make it." Pitt *would* dare make it, for he pictured England's destiny to be one of commercial empire. Denied office in 1742 and then harnessed by office in 1746, Pitt was relatively quiet when new fighting with the French began in 1755. But his imperial vision and the lure of higher office finally led Pitt into opposition, and his debating power opened the way to the prime ministership. As the duke of Newcastle told the king, no one could rule without Pitt: "No one will have a majority at present, against Mr. Pitt. No man, Sir, will in the present conjecture set his face against Mr. Pitt in the House of Commons."

We will examine in Chapter 7 the objectives and the course of the war of 1756–1763. The point here is to understand how Pitt operated within the political system.

William Pitt, First Earl of
Chatham, *by Richard Brompton.*
Here Pitt the Elder, who had
become a great national hero for
his imperial leadership, is shown
in his noble's robes in 1772.

He stormed the closet in grand style by making himself the voice of outraged patriotism among both commercial interests and independent country gentlemen. His argument that England should contain France on the Continent while defeating them overseas spoke to their prejudices. Eventually Pitt forced his way into office on his own terms. However, he was a poor parliamentary manipulator, and for this task he needed the duke of Newcastle to manage the patronage. Newcastle had the votes of the "Old Corps" of Walpolean Whigs, and Pitt supplied the support of independent country squires—a potent combination that expressed the unity of the ruling oligarchy. Yet the significance of the king as a factor in the equation showed itself in 1760, when George III succeeded to the throne. George III hated Pitt and dreamed of reigning above "party." Even the "Great Commoner" could not retain office without the king's confidence; hence, Pitt resigned and went into opposition. He rose from his sick bed to attack the treaty that ended the war in 1763. By then, the oligarchical system was in disarray because George III did not accept the one-party structure of politics.

POPULAR POLITICS

The excise crisis of 1733 and the surge of patriotism in 1755–1757 show that despite the power of patronage, public opinion had a part to play in the political drama. Parliamentary politicians sometimes tried to drum up popular opinion for their own purposes, by patronizing journalists, manipulating the press, or stirring up crowd demonstrations. They found, however, that public opinion was a dangerous weapon, and on the whole the oligarchy felt threatened by public opinion and tried to control it. They were not always successful. Both voters and nonvoters typically played active roles in the often lively and boisterous politics of the constituencies, and parliamentary candidates had to placate them. Thus, outside the politics of the elite, outside the maneuverings of Parliament and the great country houses, there existed an "alternative structure of politics"—the politics of newspapers, coffeehouses, crowds, and "rough music." Especially at the local level, these activities played an important part in the way that the English people were governed.

Much of this alternative political world depended on written matter. Literacy in Georgian England was limited to perhaps 50 percent of the adult population (significantly more men than women), and even that figure includes many whose reading ability was elementary. Literacy was significantly higher in urban centers, and especially in London, where it may have reached 80 percent. This urban reading public supported an energetic and growing newspaper, magazine, and pamphlet press that was highly politicized. Moreover, improvements in communications such as the turnpike roads and the postal service made widespread distribution of publications possible. By 1760, there were a dozen newspapers in London and thirty-five in provincial towns. These newspapers, and the accompanying flood of pamphlets and broadsides, were intensively read and debated, most notably in the coffeehouses that enlivened public life in all the cities. In 1740 there were 550 coffeehouses in London and at least one in each of the larger market towns. Politicians tried to channel this obstreperous press toward their own views and to control it by means of the Stamp Tax, but without much effect. Public opinion as seen in the newspaper and pamphlet press remained staunchly patriotic and oppositional, except for papers such as *Lloyd's Evening Post*, which were controlled by the government.

An even more active role in popular politics was played by crowds. Demonstrations in London and elsewhere expressed support for the Tory priest Henry Sacheverell and his cry of "the Church in danger" in 1710; they helped force Walpole to withdraw the excise in 1733; and they caused repeal of an act allowing for the naturalization of Jews in 1753. But their targets extended far beyond national issues. Foreigners and Englishmen alike believed that crowds and riots were endemic in English life. Benjamin Franklin wrote in 1769: "I have seen, within a year, riots in the country, about coin; riots about elections; riots about workhouses; riots of colliers, riots of weavers, riots of coal-heavers. . . ."

The ruling elite wanted deference and subordination from the public, but insubordination and riot was often what they got. London was the worst afflicted, but the forest regions were also notorious for riotous behavior; riots could break out in any village or town where squire and parson either lacked authority or transgressed the popular sense of just rule.

Riots occurred over a wide variety of issues—the game laws (which prevented anyone but landlords from hunting), turnpike tolls, efforts by customs officers to stop smugglers, conditions of labor, denial of traditional rights to common land, and high food prices. These riots were not blind, aimless protests; still less were they the simple brimming over of energy in a lawless society. Riots in preindustrial England had clear, limited objectives and conformed to a popular consensus about moral principles and acceptable social practice—to a sense of a traditional "moral economy." Rioters were essentially traditionalists, not revolutionaries, for they ordinarily sought to get the natural leaders of the community—the squire and the J.P.—to enforce the law and to restore customary practices and standards.

The food riot was the most common form of crowd action. It is easy to see why, since a rise in food prices in any locality confronted many families with hunger and destitution. For example, food riots spread through sixteen counties in 1740 and twenty-four in 1766. In 1756–1757, there were more than one hundred food riots in thirty counties. The pattern in each of these was the same: rioters intervened in the local market system by intimidation or violence to restore what they regarded as a just price. They got J.P.s to enforce a just price for wheat or to prevent the export of foodstuffs from the region; they forced bakers to reduce the price of bread; or they evicted middlemen from the market. In 1757, for instance, laborers in a small town in Yorkshire:

> forcibly rung the Corn [wheat] Bell, and their Ringleader proclaimed the Price of Corn . . . ; which done, they seized the Sacks of the Farmers, and insisted upon having the Corn at the Price by them set, some of them paying, and others taking it without paying any Thing. Others of the Rioters set the price on Oatmeal, Potatoes, etc.

The outcome of this riot was typical in that the rioters succeeded. The magistrates could, of course, call in the army to put down any riot, but they did not like to do so. The gentleman J.P.s did not want to show their weakness by calling in outside forces, for that would have destroyed the aura of their social authority. The rioters normally were appealing to the local officials' sense of paternalist duties, which was in the interest of everyone to maintain. Thus the governing authority at the local level was exercised by the established landed rulers but was ultimately subject to the consent of the populace. Deference and obedience were given to the propertied, but often only on condition that they ruled through traditional moral wisdom.

Finally, the people participated in ruling themselves through the rituals of "rough music." These traditional expressions of popular opinion took different forms in different areas, but all consisted of stylized means of regulating behavior that was regarded as immoral or unnatural. A journeyman who took less than the trade's customary price could be ducked in a river or ridden out of town on a rail.

A man who beat his wife, or a man who was bullied by his wife, or a wife who beat her husband could be hung in effigy. A parish officer could be subjected to an elaborate, stylized drama on his doorstep. Usually these popular rituals, the form of which was handed down by local custom, included a procession in which the offender was caricatured and ridiculed to the accompaniment of raucous "music" on cow bells, tin pots, warming pans, and the like.

Only rarely did "rough music" or "skimmingtons" lead to physical violence. Their object was to express public disapproval in away calculated to humiliate the offender. Rough music seems to have been effective, for in each case it signified to all that the offender had stepped outside the moral boundaries of the community. By this public rebuke and the ostracism that followed, rough music sometimes drove its culprit to flight or even suicide. Like popular riots, rough music could not operate on behalf of a legislative platform or form the base of a sustained political movement. It worked where the established local authorities either could not or would not function in the customary way, as in popular marital issues. It was a form of "law" that came from within the community and lasted as long as the popular culture of a region was oral rather than literate, customary rather than rational; in some localities rough music lasted well into the nineteenth century.

THE GROWTH OF THE BRITISH STATE

The realities of this informal and customary world of popular local "politics" contrasted sharply with the great game of parliamentary politics played by the masters of the grand country houses. Until the last decade of the century, however, popular politics did not seriously threaten the landowners' regime; nor did the oligarchy establish repressive rule—not in England and Wales, at least. Compared to the heavy-handed and in some cases militarized states on the Continent, the English landowners in the eighteenth century provided comparatively light and unburdensome government for the English if not the Scottish and Irish people. The landed oligarchy was narrow and self-interested, but they made England a bastion of law, liberty, and localism.

Paradoxically, however, the size and power of the British state grew during the eighteenth century. The reason for its growth was the almost constant state of war. Britain was involved in major wars from 1689 to 1713, 1739 to 1748, 1755 to 1763, 1775 to 1784, and 1792 to 1815. Thus, although the government did not take on itself much in the way of social legislation, it nevertheless expanded its machinery in order to supply the logistical support for the army and navy and to subsidize the military forces of its allies. It was typical for Britain to have more than 120,000 men under arms during war-time. To raise and supply such forces cost huge sums of money. Governmental expenditures more than tripled between 1689 and 1763, and almost three-quarters of these expenditures went to support the army and the navy. To pay the bills, the British state increased taxes by about 300 percent over the same period and raised the national debt by about 800 percent. The British state in the eighteenth century had its biggest impact on the ordinary subject by recruitment of soldiers and sailors and by taxation. Except for a few examples, all having to do with Jacobitism, battles were not fought on the soil of the British Isles, but everyone paid taxes. The excise tax became the principal form of national revenue, and because it was a tax on the sale of certain products, it affected the price of consumer goods and the cost of living.

To collect the taxes and manage the swollen expenditures, the British had to increase the number of state officials. The number of employees in the central administrative departments went up by almost 700 percent to nearly one thousand men in the first half of the eighteenth century. In addition, the number of officials in the revenue bureaucracy tripled (to about 7,500 employees) during the same period; those in the excise office quadrupled. Tax collectors ranged throughout the country. Although all of these offices were filled by patronage, the level of professional competence and honesty was fairly high. It was partly because the offices were staffed through patronage that the new bureaucracy did not become alienated from the traditional ruling elite: the landowners wanted to put their friends and relatives in the jobs, not to destroy the bureaucracy. At the same time, the acute sense of liberty and property that had been affirmed in 1688 and in the Revolution Settlement made the political public alert to potential abuses by the state. British political rhetoric thus was filled with the vocabulary of law and liberty, and most real government occurred at the local level, but politics became intensely focused on the central government. This was one of the clearest examples of the contrasts so characteristic of eighteenth-century British politics and government.

Suggested Reading

Ayling, Stanley, *The Elder Pitt* (London: Collins, 1976).

Black, Jeremy, *Walpole in Power* (Stroud: Sutton, 2001).

Bradley, James E., *Religion, Revolution, and English Radicalism: Nonconformity in Eighteenth-Century English Politics and Society* (New York: Cambridge University Press, 1991).

Brewer, John, *Party Ideology and Popular Politics at the Accession of George III* (Cambridge: Cambridge University Press, 1976).

———, *The Sinews of Power: War, Money, and the English State, 1688–1783* (New York: Knopf, 1989).

Brown, Peter Douglas, *William Pitt, Earl of Chatham: The Great Commoner* (London: Allen & Unwin, 1978).

Colley, Linda, *Britons: Forging the Nation. 1707–1837* (New Haven: Yale University Press, 1992).

———, *In Defiance of Oligarchy: The Tory Party, 1720–1760* (Cambridge: Cambridge University Press, 1982).

Harris, Bob, *Politics and the Nation: Britain in the Mid-Eighteenth Century* (New York: Oxford University Press, 2002).

Hill, Brian, *The Early Parties and Politics in Britain. 1688–1832* (New York: St. Martin's Press, 1996).

Jenkins, Philip, *The Making of a Ruling Class: The Glamorgan Gentry, 1640–1790* (Cambridge: Cambridge University Press, 1983).

Kemp, Betty, *King and Commons, 1660–1832* (New York: St. Martins Press, 1957).

Kramnick, Isaac, *Bolingbroke and His Circle* (Cambridge, Mass.: Harvard University Press, 1968).

O'Gorman, Frank, *The Long Eighteenth Century: British Social and Political History, 1688–1832 (London: Arnold, 1997).*

————, *Voters. Patrons. and Parties: the Unreformed Electoral System of Hanoverian England, 1734–1832* (Oxford: Clarendon Press, 1989).

Plumb, J. H., *The First Four Georges* (New York: Hamlyn, 1956).

————, *The Growth of Political Stability in England, 1675–1725* (London: Macmillan, 1967).

————, *Sir Robert Walpole, 2 vols.* (Boston: Houghton Mifflin, 1956–1960).

Rogers, Nicholas, *Whigs and Cities: Popular Politics in the Age of Walpole and Pitt* (Oxford: Clarendon Press, 1990).

Rude, George, *The Crowd in History: A Study of Popular Disturbances in France and England, 1730–1848* (London: Lawrence & Wighart, 1964).

Speck, W. A., *Stability and Strife: England, 1714–1760* (London: E. Arnold, 1977).

Thompson, E. P., *Customs in Common* (New York: W. W. Norton, 1991).

Williams, E. N., *The Eighteenth-Century Constitution* (Cambridge: Cambridge University Press, 1965).

Chapter 5

High Culture and Popular Culture in Eighteenth-Century England

The high culture of eighteenth-century England was dominated by the needs and values of the landowners and their families, and by the interests and sensibility of the wealthiest levels of the middling sorts, with whom the gentry often socialized. Scholars today generally agree that the high culture produced by and for the English elite was one of the great achievements of Western civilization. Its stately and dignified houses, its superbly serene and well-crafted paintings, and its realistic but cheerful literature all reflected a highly civilized life. In culture as in politics, it is appropriate to think of eighteenth-century England as "the Augustan Age." Just as Caesar Augustus had ended a period of civil war and brought peace and expansion to the Roman Empire, so the propertied elite had ended a century of constitutional and religious strife and sponsored an era of stability and expansion in England. The landlords were keenly aware of the similarities between their own time and Augustan Rome, and they naturally took Rome as their model, adopting its standards and styles of thought in literature and the arts. The justly famous "English phlegm"— an approach to life reflecting calm deportment and the stiff upper lip—was an invention of the eighteenth century, much under the influence of Roman stoicism. Important also was the notion of "politeness," a cultural style combining civility, decorum, and propriety that was particularly attractive to the better-off middling sorts and set the wealthy property owners apart from those they regarded as the vulgar populace.

Great as achievements were, however, the Augustan and polite styles were not dominant in eighteenth-century popular culture. The mass of the English people shared little of them. The culture of the populace displayed little of the Augustan serenity and nothing of its classical values. Indeed, high culture in eighteenth-century England was in part the result of the elite's desire to display a consensus that would legitimate and solidify the social hierarchy and shore up their rule. Popular culture, on the other hand, was sometimes rebellious, often brutal, and always reflective of popular belief in traditional, custom-oriented standards and values.

THE ENLIGHTENMENT IN ENGLAND

The philosophy and theology of the Augustan Age reflected the landed property owners' view of the world. For this reason, the power and security of the English landowners made the English version of the Enlightenment more moderate and less corrosive than that on the Continent. In England, as elsewhere, the principal themes of enlightened thought were *nature* and *reason*. It was generally agreed that God had designed both the natural and the social orders and had endowed humanity with the faculty of reason as a perfectly adequate means of understanding them. "Nature" to the Augustan elite thus implied a divine plan, not a wild refuge for the sensitive imagination but an elegantly crafted machine operating according to natural laws. "Wilderness" was not something to be admired but to be tamed and made productive. Because nature moved according to a divine plan and because the deity is benevolent, then whatever is, is right. In this sense, the Augustan view of the world was essentially conservative. Similarly, the divine plan was thought to entail a static "great chain of being," a graded hierarchy of all living things from lowest to highest in which all beings had their proper place. Within that great chain stood the human social hierarchy, with the aristocracy and gentry near the top: English gentlemen enjoyed a cosmic status just below the angels. The word *natural* meant whatever was comfortable to gentlemen.

Reason held the key to decoding natural laws. Reason has often connoted a purely rational or speculative quality of thought, the special capacity that allows humanity to transcend worldly limitations. But in the eighteenth century, reason referred to more humble powers—the logical, calculating faculty and the *reasonableness* of cool common sense and restraint. Men and women in the propertied elite disliked extremism, or what they called "enthusiasm." Bishop Joseph Butler, for instance, said that enthusiasm is "a horrid thing, a very horrid thing." Englishmen had learned from their experience of civil war and revolution in the seventeenth century that extremism in politics and religion leads to conflict, war, and social turmoil. Just as they sought stability in the political structure, so they would have moderation preached in philosophy and theology. Alexander Pope, the greatest of the Augustan poets, wrote:

> For forms of Government let fools contest;
> Whate'er is best administered is best;
> For Modes of Faith, let graceless zealots fight;
> His can't be wrong whose life is in the right.

THE EMPIRICIST TRADITION

The themes of nature and reason received their clearest treatment by the empiricist philosophers of the late seventeenth and eighteenth centuries. They established a tradition that remains perhaps the greatest British contribution to philosophy—"British empiricism." The key figures in the tradition were Isaac Newton and John Locke. Newton (1642–1727) was the towering figure in the Scientific

John Locke, *by M. Dahl (1696).*
Locke, fashionably dressed and
coiffed in this portrait, was the
great philosopher of the Whigs
and of the events of 1688.

Revolution of the late seventeenth century. Building on the earlier work of Galileo, Copernicus, and Kepler, Newton set out universal laws of astronomy, mechanics, and physics that seemed to show God's creation to be an exquisite but comprehensible machine. In *Principia Mathematica* (1687), Newton combined experimental science with sophisticated mathematics to reveal that the law of gravity (that is, the attraction of one object to another varies inversely as the square of the distance between them) explains even the movements of the planets. Reason in the form of science seemed to banish mystery and open all the secrets of the world and the heavens. Pope wrote:

> Nature and Nature's laws lay hid in night:
> God said, *Let Newton* be! and all was light!

Newton's achievement, widely popularized, gave tremendous impetus to the belief in the scientific method—careful observation, rigorous inference, and meticulous experimentation. British empiricism thus held as its principal tenet that all knowledge comes through observation and fact. For the next two centuries, many a scientist and intellectual sought to become the Newton of his or her own field by reducing scientifically gathered data to one or a few elegant laws. Great as Newton's influence on philosophy was, however, that of John Locke was perhaps even greater. Locke (1632–1704) provided fundamental expression to three themes of central importance to eighteenth-century English thought: (1) empiricism, (2) civil government, and (3) religious toleration. In Locke's thought, and in that of most of the later empiricists, these three themes were tightly bound together. They shared the notion, crucial to individual liberty, that there are natural limits to the proper claims of human thought and endeavor.

A friend of Newton and other late seventeenth-century English scientists, Locke served the Whig earl of Shaftesbury in the 1670s and 1680s. Locke was forced to flee to Holland with his patron in 1683, returning to England only in 1688 after the deposition of James II. He soon became known as the leading philosopher of the Whig cause. The basis of his philosophy of political moderation and religious toleration lay in his empiricist epistemology—his philosophy of how knowledge originates. Like so many other Englishmen of the time, Locke wanted to find absolutely certain answers to any number of fundamental questions. He came to think, however, that the human understanding was not capable of absolute certainty in most realms of thought because all knowledge derives from experience, the basis of which is sense perception. By reason, we are able to combine simple sensory data into complex ideas, and we are able to reflect on our own mental operations. But because all knowledge originates in sensations, we are not able to go beyond experience except in a few limited areas. Hence the boundaries of *certain* knowledge are very narrow, whereas the boundaries of *probable* knowledge are quite wide.

Locke and his followers found it unreasonable to persecute others on the basis of probable knowledge. Consequently, he disliked absolutism in politics and enthusiasm in religion. In his second *Treatise of Civil Government* (1690), Locke set out a theory of limited government. He argued that men in the state of nature are essentially reasonable and obey the basic natural law of society—that "no one ought to harm another in his life, liberty or possessions." This was the English property owners' social ideal. Unfortunately, not everyone obeys natural law, so in order to protect their property, people form a civil society by agreeing among themselves to a "social compact." They give up certain of their powers to a government, but they do not give up their natural right of liberty and independence, nor do they surrender their sovereignty. A government therefore rules only by consent of the governed, and absolutism is incompatible with natural law and the social compact.

Obviously, Locke was justifying the outlook of his Whig patrons—individualism, rights of property, and constitutional monarchy. He did the same with his ideas on religion. Locke believed that the existence of God is demonstrable and that divine revelation of truths is possible. But he also contended that reason is the proper test of revelation and that people should beware of religious extremism. Consequently, he argued for toleration (except for Catholics, Muslims, and atheists). A church, he wrote, is a purely voluntary body and should have no compulsive authority; nor should the state try to enforce a particular religious view. A person's religious opinions necessarily are a matter for his or her own reasoning; furthermore, the alliance of church and state normally leads to oppression.

The empiricist tradition did not remain stagnant in the positions that Newton and Locke set out. For example, the most able empirical philosopher of the next generation, George Berkeley (1685–1753), used empiricist reasoning to refute the assumed materialism (that is, that matter exists) underlying Locke's philosophy.

One generation further along, the Scotsman David Hume (1711–1776), perhaps the most acute thinker among the British empiricists, used reason to defeat reason itself and to arrive at a position of skepticism concerning the nature and existence of material objects and causal relations among them. Berkeley sought to prove the existence of God, whereas Hume hovered on the edge of atheism. Both, however, were typical empiricists in insisting on the value of the ordinary reasoning individual's common sense. On the whole, eighteenth-century empiricists supported the assumptions and conclusions of Newton and Locke—that nature is orderly and operates by laws accessible to reason; that reason is largely a matter of manipulating the data of the senses and of restraining the passions; that reason, though limited, is perfectly adequate for human purposes; that civil society exists for the convenience of the individuals who make it up; and that as a practical matter the members of society who count are restricted to the propertied stratum.

NATURAL RELIGION AND DEISM

Hume's religious skepticism may seem like the logical consequence of the Newtonian view of the universe as a machine and of the Lockean emphasis on empiricism and reason. In fact, however, Hume's position was unusual in eighteenth-century England. The more typical Augustan view was that reason and Christian revelation were entirely compatible; indeed, this religiosity was the most clear-cut difference between the Enlightenment in England and that in France. Newton and Locke themselves remained Christians. According to Newton, God not only created the universe and its laws but also intervenes constantly to keep the cosmic machine moving. For his part, Locke believed that the very order of nature reveals the existence of God. "The works of Nature," he said, "everywhere evidence a Deity."

Locke's view expressed the essence of a central position of Augustan thinkers—namely, *natural theology*. Nature was thought to be another book of revelation: the study of nature by science and reason reveals that God exists and that He is good. Reason supports revelation, and revelation reason. The study of nature shows its providential design—that is, that the world was planned for the benefit of humanity. The world, including its human inhabitants, is no ruin reflecting the fall of Adam; rather, it is the product of divine wisdom and benevolence. Every thing and every person has its proper place; hence the social ideal arising from natural theology was, in the words of the theologian William Law, "each man walking in Godly wise in his state of wealth and poverty." Even poverty and ignorance have their appropriate roles to play. Poverty is beneficial because it calls forth the charity of the rich. Ignorance, said the Reverend Soames Jenyns, "is the opiate of the poor, a cordial administered by the gracious hand of providence."

To be sure, the eighteenth-century focus on nature tended to shift attention away from the Scriptures, just as the orderly whirl of the universal machine seemed to deemphasize the need for an intervening God. Thus, for some Augustan thinkers, reason constituted the *sole* authority in intellectual matters, to the point that they dispensed with both revelation and the teachings of the church. Such men, like John Toland and Viscount Bolingbroke, were *deists*. They believed that reason and nature teach that God exists, but not a personalized or active God. The deity, they contended, created the universe according to natural law and then let it operate on its own. Insofar as Christianity taught a morality consistent with reason, then Christianity is useful; but insofar as it rested its claims to authority on miracle stories (for which there can be no good evidence), then Christianity is merely a superstition. Deism remained the religion of a relatively small number of people and never had the influence in England that it had elsewhere. The French *philosophes* Voltaire and Diderot were deists, as was the American Benjamin Franklin. But deism struck orthodox theologians as the great danger of the day and thus called forth one of the most influential books of the century—Joseph Butler's *Analogy of Religion*. Bishop Butler wanted to show that acceptance of Christianity was perfectly reasonable. Everyone agrees, he argued, that scientific truths are only probable and leave many questions unexplained; yet devotees of reason like the deists unhesitatingly accept scientific findings as natural laws. By the same token, Butler wrote, we should have no qualms in believing religious truths, which, if ultimately mysterious, are also probable.

Butler also contended that it is probable our behavior in this world determines our happiness in the next. By this argument, Butler was setting out an ethics based on *reason*, which was characteristic of eighteenth-century England. Because the educated elite were shifting their attention from speculation about the supernatural to more mundane concerns, moral philosophy was of great interest to them. They wanted to know how to lead virtuous lives (as long as virtue did not disturb their pursuit of happiness), and they liked to think their ethics was based on reason. The interests of the property owners made *utilitarian* ethics popular. Utilitarianism holds that behavior should be based on a calculation of pleasures and pains. Although the pleasures and pains Butler had in mind would come in heaven or hell, other eighteenth-century utilitarians were more worldly: if we pursue our individual pleasure and avoid pain on this earth, we will in fact be pursuing virtue and avoiding vice. This was Locke's view, and a very convenient one it was for the Whig oligarchy. As we will see, an extreme form of utilitarianism later articulated by Jeremy Bentham became a theme in British radicalism.

Some other eighteenth-century English moralists contended that people have an *innate* moral sense. To know how to act, all one has to do is look within the conscience. Yet whether moralists were of the "moral sense" or the "reason" school, all agreed that in the refined and reasonable English gentleman would be found the proper standard of behavior. Lord Shaftesbury, the son of Locke's patron, put it this way: "The Taste of Beauty, and the Relish of what is decent, just, and amiable, perfects the Character of the Gentleman and the Philosopher."

The problem with such a morality is that it could lead to complacency in men and women of refinement, for it tended to confuse superficial attributes with genuine morals, and those failings in turn sometimes encouraged dissimulation and cynicism. The qualities were perfectly displayed by the career diplomat and politician Lord Chesterfield, in his justly famous *Letters to His Son* (1774). By these charming epistles of advice, Chesterfield tried to sculpt his son into the epitome of the courtly gentleman—reserved while seeming frank, mannered while seeming natural. The essence of his message was the *utility* of moral virtue and social graces, to the point that they became almost identical. "Pleasure is now, and ought to be, your business," Chesterfield advised. To get ahead in the gentlemanly world, one should bring pleasure to others by an artful cultivation of speech, deportment, fashion, and flattery. By this cultivation of refinement, Augustan empiricism and worldliness were put to good use: "Every man is to be had one way or another, and every woman almost any way."

LITERATURE

Given the values and beliefs of the propertied elite, it is not surprising that eighteenth-century taste inclined toward good sense and reasonableness. Certainly these qualities characterized the literature of the period. On the whole, writers in eighteenth-century England reflected the interests of their public—comparatively small but rapidly growing as it was—by focusing on straightforward issues of humanity in society and by opting for a basically worldly, cheerful outlook. For these reasons, the 1700s in England were a great age of prose. Poetry suffered as interest in the profound and the tragic dwindled, and poets were keenly aware of their situation. Furthermore, the different fortunes of prose and poetry were accentuated by changes in the way that literature was supported. Poetry had long found its support in patronage, which was now aristocratic rather than courtly, and insofar as poetry remained bound to patronage rather than a commercial market, it was confined to a small readership and to rigid literary conventions. Meanwhile, a new kind of reading public began to develop that was of larger size and middling social status and that expressed itself through market mechanisms. Here is where prose flourished.

In poetry, the central feature was the dominance of classical standards. Poetry of the Augustan Age—at least until the beginnings of romanticism toward the end of the century—emphasized *correctness* of feeling and expression, that sense of correctness derived from rules laid out by classical authors. Just as Horace and Virgil had written for an aristocratic sensibility, so did Augustan poets like Alexander Pope. Each poetic genre was thought to have its appropriate kind of diction, meter, and versification. At the same time, poetry was supposed to conform to nature, in the sense of the permanent, universal attributes of *human* nature. Classical poets were thought to have expressed these eternal qualities best. As Pope wrote:

> Those RULES of old *discovr'd*, not devis'd
> Are Nature still, but *Nature Methodized*;
> *Nature*, like *Liberty*, is but restrain'd
> By the same Laws which first *herself* ordained.

As a result of the prosperity and expansion of the economy, the reading public grew steadily throughout the eighteenth century. Most prominent among the new readers were women of propertied families, and men as well as women of the middling sorts. Such readers wanted two things: first, entertainment for their leisure hours, and second, information and guidance about every aspect of life and thought. The readers' voracious appetite for these two things generated a market for prose materials and called into being a new occupation, professional writing. Many of these writers were hacks who were totally dependent on entrepreneurial booksellers; they churned out pages for miserable pay in conditions known as "Grub Street."

The new reading public found prose more accessible than poetry and felt much less concern than did the patrician patrons for classical rules. Hence a popular press flourished, producing books of sermons, dictionaries, encyclopedias, histories, and periodicals like *The Spectator* (whose contributors included Joseph Addison and Richard Steele) and the *Gentleman's Magazine*. By mid century, the leading periodicals sold perhaps ten thousand copies per issue—not a huge number by twentieth-century standards but unprecedented for the time. Such periodicals featured superbly clear prose and clever satire, the two literary tools most suitable for social instruction and for moderate social criticism.

The most important response to the new reading public was the novel, which was for all practical purposes invented in the eighteenth century. With its focus on the individual, its freedom from classical rules, and its capacity to combine entertainment, instruction, and moral guidance, the novel was the perfect format for the age. The novelists of the eighteenth century, of whom the greatest were Daniel Defoe, Samuel Richardson, and Henry Fielding, depicted not heroic figures but believable people in real situations. Realism allowed them to be effective teachers. Defoe in *Robinson Crusoe* (1719) and *Moll Flanders* (1722) advocated the virtues of economic individualism. Richardson in *Pamela* (1740) and *Clarissa* (1747) explored with great psychological subtlety the difficulties of maintaining virtue in the paternalist, aristocratic social structure. In Richardson's novels one sees the growing importance of "sentiment": sentimental fiction celebrated the faculty of sentiment (refined pity and delicate emotion) as a central aspect of human nature. Fielding in *Joseph Andrews* (1742) and *Tom Jones* (1749) entertained with riotous satire while teaching the best values to be found in the gentry: natural high spirits and spontaneous generosity, tempered by loyalty and prudence.

One other great piece of Augustan prose literature worth noting is Edward Gibbon's *Decline and Fall of the Roman Empire*. Like two other monumental works published in the same year (1776)—Adam Smith's *The Wealth of Nations* and Thomas Jefferson's *Declaration of Independence*—Gibbon's work expressed many of the themes of the Enlightenment in England. Gibbon was a man of reason and balance, an admirer of the humanism and tolerance of classical civilization. Like his fellow Augustan historians, Gibbon regarded history as philosophy teaching by examples. To him the fall of Rome was a disaster for Europe and an object lesson for the English. From its height in the second century A.D., the Roman Empire collapsed under its own weight, the erosion of its moral fiber, the pressure of the barbarian tribes, and not least the expansion of Christianity. Gibbon's treatment of Christianity as one among many Oriental religions and his depiction of early Christians as intolerant zealots may have been a little extreme for eighteenth-century Englishmen, but they reflected the prevailing skepticism and rationality of high culture. "My book," he recalled, "was on every table, and on almost every toilette; the historian was crowned by the taste or fashion of the day."

Given the subordination of women to men in the eighteenth century, it is remarkable that a significant number of women distinguished themselves as writers. For women to publish their ideas and observations, or others to take a public role in intellectual life, was regarded as unladylike and even unchaste. Still, the Enlightenment across Europe encouraged women in the upper social strata to participate in intellectual life, including scientific work; and in England, some women managed to gain an education, establish connections with other men and women writers, and attain success in the literary marketplace. For instance, Mary Delariviere Manley (1663–1724) wrote a number of immensely popular and scandalous novels. Lady Mary Wortley Montagu (1689–1782), a friend and correspondent of Alexander Pope, won fame as a poet and especially as a letter writer. Charlotte Lennox (1729–1804) overcame poverty and the struggles of literary journalism to become one of England's best-known novelists and literary editors. Fanny Burney (1752–1840), a friend of Dr. Johnson, published several widely read novels, including *Evelina*, which comically depicted a broad range of society characters. Finally, the famous "bluestocking circle" of female intellectuals like Elizabeth Carter, Elizabeth Montagu, and Hester Chapone not only sponsored well-known salons but also asserted women's rights to intellectual interests in their poetry, fiction, and essays of the mid- and late eighteenth century.

RELIGION AND THE CHURCH

Because the preference of propertied folk was for balance and moderation and for matters of this world, the fires of religion burned low in eighteenth-century England. The elite felt confidence in divine providence, but their religiosity tended to be unenthusiastic. (John Wesley was to react strongly against this religious somnolence, but because the impact of his teachings came late in the century, it will be discussed in Chapter 12.) The dissenters had been scarred by the anti-Puritan reaction of the late seventeenth century and were content for the time to protect the toleration they had been granted and to work quietly for full political rights. Their numbers dwindled to about 250,000 in 1760. Roman Catholics remained a tiny and passive element in England, growing slightly after 1780 because of Irish immigration but still numbering only about eighty thousand in 1760. Almost everyone else was at least nominally an Anglican. Hence the Church of England was by far the largest denomination in England, and it was the one most profoundly affected by the hierarchical social structure and the preeminence of reason.

The two most important facts shaping the Church of England were (1) that it was of, for, and by the landed oligarchy and (2) that it was established as the national church. By the Test and Corporation Acts, Anglicans enjoyed a monopoly in national and local government. Even though the Toleration Act allowed dissenters to worship in their own congregations and the practice of occasional conformity allowed them to take public office, the Church of England enjoyed a privileged position. Many of the activities of churchmen were devoted to maintaining that position. They believed, therefore, that the Church had to be politically oriented. Anglicans disagreed about the best tactics for this aim. So-called High Churchmen thought that the toleration of dissenters should cease, for they believed that the Church of England as a divine institution ought to be recognized by the state as the only means of salvation. High Churchmen got Tory support, but as Toryism declined, the High Church position lost out to the Low Church. Many country parsons remained Tories and High Churchmen; but Low Churchmen were more numerous among the bishops. Their view was *Erastian*—that is, they believed that the church is properly subject to the dictates of the state because it is essentially a voluntary association of believers, not a uniquely divine institution. The Low Church view prevailed at the upper levels of the Anglican hierarchy partly because of the general cultural trend toward moderation and toleration and partly because pressure from the Crown and the Whigs favored the Low Churchmen. Hence, the triumph of Whiggery threw the weight of patronage behind the Low Church position.

The Church of England at the higher levels became deeply enmeshed in Whig politics. The twenty-six bishops, for example, as members of the House of Lords were crucial to Whig control of the upper chamber. Walpole and later Whig wire-pullers made sure that no one except politically sound men were appointed to the episcopal bench, and they made it clear to every bishop or lower church appointee what political behavior was expected. Any clergyman hoping for promotion had to be loyal to the government; thus a clergyman's political opinions became more important than his religious commitment. This situation affected the behavior of ambitious clergymen, for their careers often revolved around jostling for places and safe political maneuvering. The death of the holder of a desirable church office started an unseemly scramble for the vacancy. It was not unusual to see anxious candidates waiting in an anteroom, while inside a bishop breathed his last. Sometimes a candidate could not wait. One Thomas Newton wrote the duke of Newcastle this: "I think it my duty to acquaint yr. grace that the Archbishop of York lies a-dying, and, as all here think, cannot possibly live beyond tomorrow morning, if so long; upon this occasion of two vacancies, I beg, I hope, I trust your Grace's kindness and goodness will be shown to one who has long solicited your favour."

Once appointed, such people often devoted themselves to matters that were not religious. Bishop Hoadly, the most outspoken Low Churchman and a favorite of the Whigs, was made bishop of Bangor in 1715 and was promoted to Hereford in 1721, having only once gone to Bangor. In 1723, he was promoted from Hereford, never having traveled there at all. He occupied himself with politics and was finally raised to the wealthy See of Winchester in 1734. Some bishops attended to their duties in the House of Lords, at least, but at other times conducted themselves like wealthy landowners. Bishop Watson, bishop of Llandaff for thirty-four years, spent most of his time on Lake Windermere in the beautiful Lake District. He described his life's work there:

> I have now spent above 20 years in this delightful country but my time has
> *not* been spent in field diversions . . . no, it has been spent, partly in sup-

porting the religion and constitution of the country by seasonable publications; and principally in building farm-houses, blasting rocks, enclosing
wastes, in making bad land good, in planting larches, and in planting in the
hearts of my children principles of piety, benevolence, and self-government.

Such behavior was bound to affect the performance of the ordinary clergy of
the parishes. They typically behaved as what they were, members of the gentry, for
the clergy became a respectable and undemanding livelihood for younger sons of
the landed orders. An increasing number served alongside the squires as J.P.s. It
was frequently noted that the country clergy were more concerned to keep up in
the swirl of society and politics in the great country houses of the oligarchy than to
tend to their parishes. The Anglican clergy justifiably won the reputation of eating
well, hunting foxes, and drinking port. One foreign observer noted

> . . . the air of health and prosperity of the greatest part of them; and it is
> pleasant to see how fat and fair these parsons are. They are charged with
> being somewhat lazy, and their usual plumpness makes it suspected that
> there's some truth in it. It is common to see them in coffee houses, and even
> in taverns, with pipes in their mouths.

Of course, there was many a kindly and caring parson, a brother to the squire
and father to the laborers in the parish. At their best, the parsons helped maintain
the wholeness, not the holiness, of society. But the economics of clerical arrangements often made performance of their duties difficult. Most parish priests were
paid by endowments ("livings") established years before by individual landlords,
whose descendants still held the right of appointment. In many cases, inflation had
made the salary criminally low—fifteen or twenty pounds a year. Further, many
parsons, once appointed to a "living," had no intention of going there. Such a rector would hire a curate to do his duties. Of course, since the holder of the living
paid the curate out of his own stipend, he would keep it as low as possible. Whereas
the rector of Warton parish enjoyed £700 a year, one of his curates got only £5.
Other clergymen, in order to make ends meet or simply to maximize their incomes,
took more than one parish. As a consequence, pluralism and nonresidence were
grave problems. As late as 1809, 7,358 clergy out of 11,194 were nonresident. Moreover, as towns grew, ancient parish divisions no longer coincided with the real distribution of the population. Few new churches were built, so large towns—Manchester, for example, with a population of twenty thousand—had only one church.
Many clergymen were badly overworked and underpaid; others blessed by the
scramble for preferment were overpaid and underworked.

Many of the backwoods parsons were rabid Tories, even Jacobites, and therefore High Churchmen. Most others, however, took a more politic view of the world.
They held a position in between the individualism of Puritanism and the authori-
tative centralism of Catholicism. This position, called *latitudinarianism*, combined
elements of natural religion with belief in revelation. Latitudinarians held that
human reason was sufficient to deal with most issues; for the rest, revelation was
necessary—revelation as interpreted by the one true church, the Church of England. In any case, most clergymen in their teachings shied away from theological

principles and concerned themselves with everyday ethics and morals. Their message inevitably reflected the outlook of their patrician patrons, tempered by reasonableness and benevolence: charity for the rich and obedience for the poor. The point of the established church, after all, was to give liturgical expression to the existing social order.

ARCHITECTURE AND PAINTING

Like most aspects of eighteenth-century society, the visual arts reflected a shift from traditional patronage to more market-oriented arrangements. Architecture and painting throughout the century were heavily shaped by the values and wishes of their patrician consumers. Hence they usually expressed symbolically the hierarchical social order and the sensibility of the ruling elite. At the same time, however, the growing wealth of England generated a booming market in art objects—paintings, sculpture, furnishings, and the like. This market, associated as it was with the consumer revolution, went a long way towards commodifying high culture.

The main achievement of late seventeenth-century architecture was in ecclesiastical building. One influential figure was Sir Christopher Wren (1652–1725), the friend and colleague in the Royal Society of Newton and Locke. After the Great Fire of London (1666), Wren rebuilt fifty-five city churches, plus St. Paul's Cathedral. His main themes were compromise, moderation, and harmony. He managed to merge the Italian Catholic baroque style (with its ornate decoration, classical forms, and sensual rhythms of concave and convex lines) with the Dutch Calvinist preaching hall (with its plain rectangular shape and severe decoration). In the work of his successors, like James Gibbs (1682–1754), who designed St. Martins-in-the-Fields, the compromise shifted more to classical style, combining a single steeple (a Gothic element) with a rectangular hall fronted by classical columns and a hexastyle (triangular) portico. These serene churches expressed perfectly the Anglican compromise between Catholicism and Calvinism and appealed immediately to reason as well. The style spread widely in Protestant Britain and to America also, where it became the standard form of Protestant architecture.

In the eighteenth century, however, the great architectural monuments were the homes of the landed magnates. According to one French traveler, "The multitude of gentlemen's houses, scattered over the country, is a feature quite peculiar to the English landscape; the thing is unknown in France." English patricians thought it important to live most of the year on their estates so as to play the social and governmental roles they had claimed for themselves. Those who could afford it moved to London for the spring "season" and rotated through spas like Tunbridge Wells and Bath. But their country houses composed the focal points of high culture, set as they were in pleasing parks and filled with rich furnishings and fine paintings. The gentleman's country "seat" was the principal means by which he showed his taste and refinement and served as the base of operations for his beloved hunting sports. Thus the great country houses were the setting for endless enter-

St. Martin's-in-the-Field, designed by Sir James Gibbs (early eighteenth century). This beautiful church, a favorite with tourists, is perhaps the best example of neoclassical church architecture in England.

taining, for local estate and governmental business, for partisan political talk, and not least for sheer enjoyment of the fat of the land. Lord Hervey recalled of his visits to Houghton, Walpole's estate in Norfolk: "We used to sit down to dinner a snug little party of about thirty odd, up to the chin in beef, venison, geese, turkeys, etc.; and generally over the chin in claret, strong beer, and punch."

The design of the great country houses reflected these functions. Typically, they were magnificent and elegant on the interior, so as to display the wealth and connoisseurship of the owner to others of the same social stratum, and stately and grave on the exterior, so as to overawe the common folk. *Symmetry* was the pervasive theme. In the late seventeenth and early eighteenth centuries, the taste for the Baroque produced symmetrical but monumentally heavy piles, of which the great representative was (and is) the duke of Marlborough's Blenheim Palace. But as the eighteenth century advanced, the Whig preference for the appearance of moderation made the country houses less formal. The surrounding parks, designed by landscape architects like Capability Brown, shifted away from geometrical formality toward the "natural"—nature tamed by reasonableness. The houses themselves, by architects such as Lord Burlington (1694–1753), Colen Campbell (1676–1729),

Mereworth Castle, Kent, designed by Colen Campbell (1723). Mereworth Castle is a fine example of the Palladian house. Notice the perfect symmetry.

and William Kent (1685–1748), retained the symmetry of baroque but now stressed simplicity and proportion. The new style was called "Palladian," after the sixteenth-century architect Andrea Palladio, who was thought to have derived perfect formulas from Roman buildings. The typical Palladian house, an example of which is Mereworth Castle, began with a main rectangular block of several stories flanked on either side by precisely matched wings, fronted by rows of classical windows, and topped by a hexastyle portico over the main entrance. Inside, the design separated the business rooms and servants' areas "below stairs" from the elegant halls, drawing rooms, and chambers of the family "above stairs."

It seems almost inevitable that portraiture was the characteristic mode of English painting. The patricians were, after all, deeply interested in the individual—and above all, in themselves. Yet portraits under their influence became less heroic and grandiose than in the seventeenth century, for the landlords intended to have themselves depicted as at ease in the world they had won. Of the many great Augustan portrait painters, the two leading ones were Sir Joshua Reynolds (1723–1792) and Thomas Gainsborough (1727–1788). Reynolds became famous for his theory of the "Grand Style"—painting by the classical rules established by the old masters, concern for the general and ideal, and strict proportion—even at the expense of taking liberties with the actual features of the subject. Gainsborough was a less for-

Mrs. Siddons as the Tragic Muse, *by Sir Joshua Reynolds (1784). Reynolds painted in the grand style, striving for classical proportions and the ennoblement of his subjects through their pose or costume.*

malized painter, but he too portrayed his ladies and gentlemen in such a way as to express an ideal of ease, dignity, and grace.

One eighteenth-century painter stands out as a maverick genius—William Hogarth (1697–1764). Hogarth, a Londoner of middling social standing, had a keen eye for the hypocrisy and corruption of the day. He hated what he called "phizmongering"—idealized portraiture to please the rich—and sought to give a broad view of social life in the mode of dramatic narrative paintings. Each of these is as delightfully satirical, instructive, and morally didactic as a Fielding novel. The moral decay of an aristocratic rake, the marriage customs of the elite, the rowdiness of electioneering all fell subject to his brush. In such paintings, Hogarth revealed the greed, vanity, and turmoil that the veneer of Augustan high culture covered.

That turmoil was reflected also in the growing commercial market in art objects. In the prosperous English towns and cities, and above all in London, well-to-do commercial people—men and women alike—joined the landed elite in pursuing and purchasing paintings, sculpture, tapestries, drapes, furniture, and decorative items, as well as in attending concerts, operas, plays, and pleasure gardens. This cultural elite were intent on equipping their grand country homes and town houses so as to impress each other, and on distinguishing themselves by their refined taste—their "politeness"—from the common public. The demand for "old masters" resulted in the importation from the continent of some 50,000 paintings between 1720 and 1770, and ten times that many etchings and engravings. Galleries and auction houses were established in London, and the Royal Academy was founded in 1768 to help define and control high standards of taste. As an unintended consequence of this process of commodification, the very notion of "the fine arts" as a distinct (and superior) realm of human activity came into being.

POPULAR CULTURE: FACTS OF LIFE

The sources for the history of high culture are plentiful, and our knowledge of high culture is correspondingly deep. The sources for the cultural history of the common people are scarce, however, and our conclusions must be tentative. Some significant aspects of English popular culture have already been noted: the importance of custom in allowing the laboring poor to make ends meet; the effectiveness of popular politics in the form of crowd behavior; and the pervasiveness of rough music in the moral self-government of local communities. We need to turn now to other matters central to the lives of the poor—matters of living and surviving and of beliefs and values.

Life was difficult and brief, and death and pain were constant presences for most of the English people in the eighteenth century. No census was taken until 1801, but surviving records make it clear that life expectancy was short—perhaps thirty-five years. People were old by age fifty. Medical care that helped rather than harmed its recipients was practically nonexistent. Neither villages nor cities had any sewerage system except open gutters; refuse was dumped into the streets to rot and pollute water supplies. The stench was staggering and the health hazards grim. Diseases like smallpox, typhus, and influenza repeatedly swept through the population. The poor had no defenses against the cold and damp of winter. One physician watched the poor in his district die from an epidemic in 1727: "Nor did any other method which art could afford relieve them; insomuch that many of the little country towns and villages were almost stripped of their poor people." Death was frequent for women giving birth, and infant mortality was especially high: about one-fifth of all babies died before they were one year old. Given this high mortality rate of children, some historians believe, it is likely that parents among the laboring poor avoided investing heavy emotional commitment in their offspring. Prudence dictated a certain reserve until the parent was fairly sure the child would survive.

The decision of a couple to marry depended on their ability to set up a household and make a living. The number of opportunities to do so was growing slowly, but the society was relatively stingy in the niches it made available. Young men had to finish apprenticeships or wait for a cottage or tenancy to open up; young women often had to spend time in domestic service or as a farm girl. Thus the average age at marriage was relatively high—about twenty-seven years for men and twenty-five for women. Further, although marriage among the common people did not entail the diplomatic negotiations of the rich, it was nevertheless a calculated decision. After marriage a couple were together for a comparatively short time, during which they were capable of having children, but children were helpful to the family economy. On average, then, each couple had five children, but only three survived to age twenty. Large families were rare, and extended families (with more than one generation of adults living together under the same roof) were rarer still.

Work was a central part of family life. Most work in eighteenth-century England went on in households, and the family functioned as an economic unit. In farming households the division of specific tasks between men and women was not rigid, and women worked outside as well as inside the home. Women rarely did the plowing, but they participated in sowing, cultivating, and harvesting the crops; and they normally took care of the animals and the cottage garden, while also doing the dairying, brewing, cooking, and cleaning. In urban households, women worked alongside their husbands, whether in preparing the raw materials or in polishing or waxing the finished products. Artisanal households were different: while male craftsmen like shoemakers and carpenters needed their wives to produce income, they liked to keep their shops separate from the homes and to keep women out of them. Theirs was a culture of male solidarity born during their years of preparing as apprentices and journeymen and maintained by male bonding in alehouses and in craft guilds. In such families, wives generally were relegated to traditionally women's occupations like needlework, laundry work, and street selling.

Work was unrelenting for all, since the family economy required each member to contribute and since there were no provisions for hard times or retirement other than prudence and the Poor Law. Employment was seasonal and casual for most people. Moreover, pay for women amounted to only about half that for men. Thus a slump in demand, a poor harvest, or the death of a husband usually threw families onto the meager mercy of the Poor Law. About 20 percent of the population were in receipt of poor relief at any one time, the great majority of them women and children.

"Dogged determination," as one historian has called it, was probably the resulting relationship of husband and wife. Divorce was legally possible only by private act of Parliament and so was available only to the ruling elite. But there is some evidence that the practice of "wife sale," a ritualized form of ending a marriage in which a man took his wife to a fair and sold her by prearrangement, sometimes occurred in rural areas. Desertion was appallingly common. In any case, children were put to work very early, perhaps at six or seven years, scaring crows and picking rocks from the fields or helping with carding and spinning. Boys and girls between eleven and fourteen received the training by formal and informal apprenticeship in the trade that would occupy them the rest of their lives.

It must not be assumed that the work of the laboring poor demanded no skills or knowledge. Although work-related skills were normally taught informally in households and in the fields and not in schools, the amount of knowledge required was significant. A husbandman, for instance, had to know about the soil, the weather, and the crops; about feeding and caring for animals; about plowing, cultivating, draining, hedging, thatching, brickmaking, and woodworking; and about spinning or weaving for the slack season. A woman had to know about dairying, brewing, and gardening; and about spinning, sewing, lacemaking. Even more impressive were the skills, often carefully guarded "mysteries," of particular crafts.

A wheelwright, for instance, had to know which wood was best for spokes (oak), hubs (willow or elm), and felloes (ash). He had to cut and season the wood properly, then saw and plane it with great precision so that the wheel was perfectly round and the spokes chamfered out at the right degree. He, or a blacksmith, had to be able to forge an iron rim (or "tyre") of exact measurement, to heat it so it would drop exactly over the wheel without damaging it, and then to cool it to a tight fit and a smooth roll. The improper fitting of a spoke would make a wheel uneven and weak; a mistake in dropping a red-hot iron rim on the wheel would ruin a week's work. All such knowledge was passed on during years of hands-on experience by oral tradition.

BELIEFS AND VALUES

Schooling and literacy, then, had comparatively little to do with how common people made a living, nor did they contribute a great deal to the common folk's understanding of themselves and their world. This was particularly true in the countryside, where the literacy rate was lowest: in rural districts, probably less than half the men and a quarter of the women possessed even a rudimentary ability to read and write. Schooling, after all, was a haphazard proposition. There was no national school system. There were two universities in England (Oxford and Cambridge), but they were primarily seminaries for the Church of England and secondarily finishing schools for the sons of the property owners. Such secondary schools as existed were also out of the reach of the laboring poor: the handful of expensive "public" (that is, private boarding) schools like Eton and Harrow; a somewhat larger number of fee-paying "grammar" schools frequented by less wealthy gentry and professional boys; and the dissenting academies for the sons of the urban commercial nonconformists. Even in the propertied ranks, secondary schooling was for males only. Schools available to the laboring people consisted of some charity schools, a growing number of Sunday schools, and a larger number of tiny, ephemeral "schools" run by individuals on a private-enterprise basis. The teachers in this last category of schools often hung out their teaching shingle simply because they could find no other way to make a living. Probably a majority of the laboring poor who could read learned from their parents or taught themselves.

What ordinary villagers knew about themselves and their world we can only guess. It seems highly probable that their understanding of matters beyond the work place came from an amalgam of custom, oral traditions, and religion. Nursery rhymes, legends, folk tales, popular songs, and other oral traditions all taught traditional wisdom. Traveling peddlers brought information about politics and public events from outside the parish. It may be that in particular parishes the weekly sermons in the parish church provided a conceptual framework as well as moral guidance for a substantial number of people, including the laboring poor. Yet the Anglican church did not play the role that in theory it ought to have. In theory, a parson in every parish would teach essentially the same view of the world to practically all of the people. In practice, as we have seen, clergymen sometimes were negligent of their pastoral responsibilities. The evidence is shaky, but probably no more than 10 to 15 percent of the adult population were practicing Anglicans by midcentury.

No doubt the laboring people had powerful spiritual and intellectual needs, because their lives were full of mysteries and uncertainties—sudden illness and death, the failure of crops, downturns of the economy, inexplicable natural phenomena. As a result, many people in the rural areas did have a strong belief in the supernatural, but often in non-Christian or vaguely Christian terms. The local clergyman married, baptized, and buried people, but common folk often attributed their own meanings to these rituals. It was sometimes thought, for instance, that baptism would make a child physically strong. Superstition and magic gave the laboring poor, especially in the countryside, some sense of control over their environment. Thus they frequently believed in ghosts and witchcraft and resorted to magical folk medicine for healing the sick and to village wise men for foretelling the future or finding lost articles. There is some evidence that popular Protestantism inherited from the seventeenth century held sway in some households, particularly among town craftsmen who remembered ideals of "the freeborn Englishman" and who cherished two books—the Bible and John Bunyan's *The Pilgrim's Progress*, the seventeenth-century Puritan allegory of a Christian's progress through temptation and despair. There is also reason to believe that this popular Puritanism was in decline and that to a significant degree religious teachings were mixed with traditional pagan beliefs in the mind of the populace.

Popular consciousness, therefore, was largely dependent in the countryside on an oral culture. Consequently, people were very parochial and intensely suspicious of strangers. This localism obviously was under attack from the expanding network of trade and consumer goods, but it remained of real importance well into the nineteenth century. Only in the cities (and especially in London) among the skilled craftsmen and shopkeepers did literacy penetrate very far and a popular political consciousness develop. This contrasted with Scotland, where the kirk established schools in many localities. In rural England, people learned by oral transmission of beliefs and values from generation to generation. Although they seem to have imbibed a strong sense of collective behavior and common moral standards, and a community orientation hostile to the breaking of custom by property and contract, they had no means of articulating class identity or political programs.

RECREATIONS

The poor found relief from the harsh realities of life in a wide variety of recreations, many of which have now disappeared. There were routine enjoyments like telling stories over domestic work, singing in the fields or at the loom, or behaving playfully on trips to the market. The more public recreations often took a more ritualized form and sprang from the traditional calendar of holidays—a combination of Christian holy days and significant moments in the agricultural year. Almost every parish held annual festivals, or "wakes." For instance, in Claybrook at the parish wake, it was observed, "The cousins assemble from all quarters, fill the church on Sunday, and celebrate the Monday with feasting, with music, and with dancing." Annual fairs for hiring laborers or for selling horses, cattle, leather goods, and the like gave opportunities for mixing business with pleasure. Christmas, Easter, and Whitsuntide were the occasions for holidays and festivities, as were plow and harvest times. Many such festivals mixed the secular and the sacred calendars; all of them gave the populace a chance to play games, eat heartily, get drunk, and flirt with the opposite sex—in short, to escape the rules of everyday life.

Many of the popular recreations were purely of and for the laboring people. Varieties of soccer, for example, matched the men of one village against those of another. Drinking and games of quoits and bowling in the omnipresent public houses were strictly for the populace. Yet many of the popular recreations were approved, and even sponsored, by the gentry. Some recreations were exclusively for the gentry—most notably fox hunting, whereby the rich displayed their finery, horsemanship, boldness, and power. Other recreations allowed for social mixing, like horse racing, which was staged by the rich (and indeed became a fetish among them, which it remains) but which attracted large numbers of ordinary spectators, as did cock fights and boxing. Further, the gentry customarily entertained the local folk at important moments in the great family's life—the birth, coming of age, and marriage of a son. On such occasions, the landowners incorporated the laboring poor into rustic celebrations of the continuity of the lineage. Similarly, the gentry typically treated the common people to food and drink at harvest home and parish feast days. Tradition and the need to preserve the loyalty of the laborers dictated the squire's generosity. As Sir Joseph Banks noted ruefully in 1783: "This is the day of our fair when according to immemorial custom I am to feed and make drunk everyone who wishes to come which cost me in beef and ale near 20 pounds." In a more bloodthirsty line, gentlemen usually provided the unfortunate animal for bull baiting, which was a popular activity, not least because it normally ended with the slaughter of the bull for the poor to eat. Like the squires' typical willingness to negotiate with food rioters, their cooperation with popular recreations helped preserve the coherence of the local community and the deference on which their rule stood.

Suggested Reading

Barker-Benfield, G. J., *The Culture of Sensibility: Sex and Society in Eighteenth-Century Britain* (Chicago: University of Chicago Press, 1992).

Brewer, John, *The Pleasures of the Imagination: English Culture in the Eighteenth Century* (New York: Farrar, Straus & Giroux, 1997).

Black, Jeremy, ed., *Culture and Society in Britain, 1660–1800* (Manchester: Manchester University Press, 1997).

Carpenter, S. C., *Eighteenth Century Church and People* (London: Murray, 1959).

Chamberlain, Jeffrey, *Accommodating High Churchmen: The Clergy of Sussex, 1700–1741* (Urbana: University of Illinois Press, 1997).

Christie, Christopher, *The British Country House in the Eighteenth Century* (Manchester: Manchester University Press, 1999).

Colley, Linda, *Britons: Forging the Nation. 1707–1837* (New Haven: Yale University Press, 1992).

Cragg, G. R., *Reason and Authority in the Eighteenth Century* (Cambridge: Cambridge University Press, 1964).

Gaunt, William, *A Concise History of English Painting* (London: Thames & Hudson, 1964)

Gibson, William, *The Church of England, 1688–1832: Unity and Accord* (London: Routledge, 2001).

Girouard, Mark, *Life in the English Country House* (New Haven: Yale University Press, 1978).

Harris, R. W., *Reason and Nature in the Eighteenth Century* (London: Blandford, 1968).

Harris, Tim, ed., *Popular Culture in England, c. 1500–1850* (New York: St. Martin's Press, 1995).

Hartley, Dorothy, *Made in England* (London: Eyre Methuen, 1939).

Kidson, Peter, Peter Murray, and Paul Thompson, *A History of English Architecture* (Harmondsworth, Middlesex: Penguin, 1962).

Lipking, Lawrence, *The Ordering of the Arts in Eighteenth-Century England* (Princeton: Princeton University Press, 1970).

Malcolmson, R. W., *Life and Labour in England, 1700–1780* (New York: St. Martin's Press, 1981).

———, *Popular Recreations in English Society, 1700–1850* (Cambridge: Cambridge University Press, 1973).

Myers, Sylvia Harcstark, *The Blustocking Circle: Women. Friendship, and the Life of the Mind in Eighteenth-Century England* (New York: Oxford University Press, 1990).

Newman, Gerald, *The Rise of English Nationalism, 1740–1830* (New York: St. Martin's Press, 1987).

Rivers, Isabel, ed., *Books and Their Readers in Eighteenth-Century England: New Essays* (Leicester: Leicester University Press, 2002).

Rupp, Gordon, *Religion in England, 1688–1791* (Oxford: Clarendon Press, 1986).

Spaeth, Donald, *The Church in an Age of Danger: Parsons and Parishioners, 1660–1740* (Cambridge, Cambridge University Press, 2000).

Thomas, Keith, *Man and the Natural World* (New York: Pantheon Press, 1983).

Vincent, David, *Literacy and Popular Culture: England, 1750–1914* (New York: Cambridge University Press, 1989).

Virgin, Peter, *The Church in an Age of Negligence* (Cambridge: James Clarke, 1989).

Watt, Ian, *The Rise of the Novel* (London: Chatto & Windus, 1957).

Willey, Basil, *The Eighteenth Century Background* (New York: Columbia University Press, 1940).

Chapter 6

Scotland in the Eighteenth Century

Scottish history in the eighteenth century was even more strongly driven than English history by the tension between custom and contract. In Scotland, the clash between the commercial or "improving" sector of society and the traditional, customary sector was heightened dramatically by the conflict between Lowlands and Highlands. In the eighteenth century, the Highland culture, the most coherent and complete stronghold of Gaelic life in the British Isles, was eradicated, and the economy and the society of the Highlands began to be made over in the English image. In retrospect, it seems that the process was inevitable, because one can hardly imagine a feudal clan system surviving into the industrial age within a vibrant, commercial, modern state. Indeed, there is plenty of evidence that the clan aristocrats, irresistibly attracted as they were to the wealth and power of their English counterparts, might well have brought about the change themselves. In historical actuality, Highland culture was destroyed largely because many clan chiefs gave their allegiance to Jacobitism, which invited destruction by the British regime. Ironically, the triumph of contract and its Whig proponents in Scotland set the stage for a wonderful flowering of enlightened high culture in the cities of the Lowlands during the latter half of the century.

THE UNION: 1707

The stability sought by both the English and Scottish makers of the rebellion of 1688 was even harder to achieve in Scotland than in England. Though he wore the Scottish as well as the English crown, William III found it extremely difficult to deal with two different Parliaments. He stood in an impossible constitutional situation, for the Scottish Parliament frequently disagreed with his English ministers. Committed to a long war against France, William and his ministers wanted Scotland simply to supply money and troops; instead, Scotland supplied trouble. For instance, the Scottish Parliament insisted on the right to control Scottish trade, even when the trade ran counter to English interests, as did Scottish trade with France. Moreover, the Scottish Parliament in 1696 passed an Act of Security (reaffirmed in 1704) asserting the right to choose a monarch independently from England, should there be no Protestant heir to William. Finally, the Scottish Parliament in 1695 sanctioned a colonizing effort in "Darien" (modern Panama), which contravened English policy. William was at the time trying to placate the

Spanish, who had long claimed Darien; thus he opposed the Scottish Darien scheme on behalf of English interests, contributing thereby to the disastrous collapse of the colony and infuriating the Scottish investors. Persuaded of the impossibility of continuing the monarchy's relationship with two Parliaments, William on his deathbed advised his ministers to unite the Parliaments of England and Scotland.

Meanwhile, opinion among the Scottish ruling elite was also moving toward the view that the existing relations between England and Scotland could not continue: either the union of crowns must be broken and Scotland be completely independent or the two Parliaments must be merged. The Darien fiasco, which swallowed perhaps half of Scotland's capital, taught that lesson, as did a major famine that afflicted Scotland from 1695 to 1699. Thousands of people starved or died from diseases related to malnutrition. Obviously, the Scottish economy needed bolstering. The commercial elements prominent in the Lowland economy found themselves hampered by trade restrictions imposed on them by England on the one hand and by Continental nations on the other. By 1700, England had imposed tariffs on three of Scotland's leading export products—coal, salt, and linen. The Scots tried to retaliate by insisting on free trade with England and England's colonies. For instance, in reaffirming the Act of Security in 1704, the Scottish Parliament declared that they would exercise their right to select their own successor to Queen Anne if Scotland were not granted free trade in England's empire.

England, however, was too large and too wealthy to be bullied by the Scottish threat; moreover, the English ministers had decided that nothing less than a union of Parliaments was tolerable. Their patience, never in long supply, had run out. The immediate issue was to force Scotland to acknowledge the House of Hanover as the successors to Queen Anne. In 1705, the English passed an act threatening to treat all Scots in England as aliens if Scotland did not negotiate a union and accept the Hanover succession. This struck at Scottish aristocrats and merchants alike, and the English in addition promised to ban the trade in black cattle so crucial to Scotland. Consequently, Scottish political leaders agreed to negotiations, which were completed early in 1707. A treaty was drawn up uniting the two countries and creating a new state—Great Britain.

The Treaty of Union passed through the English Parliament quickly but met impassioned opposition in Scotland. Scottish patriots in the Scottish Parliament and a majority of public opinion in the towns thought that the treaty was a betrayal of Scottish interests and nationality. In fact, the English did get their way in the negotiations: the Scots won the free trade they sought, they protected their Presbyterian establishment and their own legal system, and they kept the heritable jurisdictions by which landlords in Scotland exercised judicial power, but they did not get a genuine merger of Parliaments. Instead, the treaty of 1707 abolished the Scottish Parliament and provided only that Scotland would be represented in the essentially English Parliament at Westminster by sixteen nobles in the House of Lords and forty-five M.P.s in the House of Commons. Proponents of the treaty contended that this was equitable and that the union was necessary for

Scotland's economic survival. "This nation," one argued, "being poor, and without force to protect its commerce, cannot reap great advantage by it, till it partake of the trade and protection of some powerful neighbour nation." Pro-union propagandists like the Englishman Daniel Defoe forecast a period of great prosperity for Scotland. These arguments, plus a liberal application of patronage and some outright bribery, won a majority, and the Scottish Parliament voted itself out of existence and the British state into life. The union of 1707 was a marriage of convenience, not affection. The Scottish and English peoples retained their separate national identities. The new kingdom, Great Britain, was a state, but in the sense of having a unified, integrated people it was not a nation. Yet a sense of "Britishness" would grow among the peoples of Scotland, Wales, and England over the course of the next century.

THE JACOBITE REBELLION OF 1715

The predicted economic benefits of union eventually came true, but not in the short run. Scottish goods proved to be of too low quality to compete well in the vast market the Scots had joined, and goods such as linen met official English discrimination. The trade in cattle flourished, but most others languished. The Scottish representatives in Parliament could offer little help because they were too few in number to be effective and were soon coopted by patronage into the Whig political system. The English had no regard for creating a union of hearts with the Scots. They proceeded to administer a series of blows that further alienated Scottish opinion. In 1712, Parliament restored the right of laypatrons to appoint ministers to parish livings in the Church of Scotland, an extension of patronage that violated the very principle of Presbyterianism. In 1713, Parliament attempted to extend the English malt tax to Scotland, which would have raised the price of beer and whiskey. Scots regarded this as the last straw, and the Scottish M.P.s in London actually moved for dissolution of the union—to no avail, of course.

All of this discontent in Scotland fed the fires of Jacobitism. Scottish Jacobitism amounted to more than ceremonial toasts to "the King over the water"; it had strong roots in the Catholic and Episcopalian populations, especially in the Highland clans, which had never taken to Presbyterianism. Furthermore, the Highland tradition of loyalty to one's chief made the Jacobite principle of hereditary right to the monarchy ring true. The massacre of Glencoe, connived at by William III and carried out by troops of the arch-Whig clan Campbell, had planted resentment deep in the heart of many a Highland chief. In addition, the Jacobites persuasively branded the disasters to the Scottish economy and polity from the 1690s to the 1710s (famine, financial fiasco, and commercial failures) as divine retribution for the deposition of the rightful king. The Treaty of Union, intensely unpopular in its own right, made the Jacobites the heirs of Scottish patriotism, because the union had been closely tied to recognition of the Hanoverian succession. For all these reasons, Jacobitism was a more formidable force in Scotland than in England, and by 1714 Scotland stood on the verge of a major rebellion.

The weaknesses that Jacobitism faced at the time were the same that hobbled the movement throughout its history. First, there was the obstinacy and political clumsiness of the Stuart line. James II had died and had been succeeded in exile by his son, James Edward (the Old Pretender), a melancholy and reserved man of the same rigidity as his father and a pretender to the throne incapable of inspirational leadership. Second, the Stuarts in exile were completely dependent on the French, whose support for the Jacobite cause waxed and waned as French interests dictated. Third, there was a fundamental confusion in Jacobitism between loyalty to the Stuarts, who considered themselves to be kings of England and Ireland as well as Scotland, and a simple desire for Scottish independence. The strength of the movement was in Scotland, where it was rooted in Scottish patriotism, but the Stuarts from James II through his grandson, Charles Edward (Bonnie Prince Charlie, "the Young Pretender"), wanted to restore the union of the crowns. These were far from identical objectives.

In any case, the Jacobite blow fell after Anne died and was succeeded by George I. Influenced by Whig slander, George snubbed one of his secretaries of state, the Scotsman John Erskine, earl of Mar, who had in fact helped to bring about the union. Mar fled to Scotland and raised the standard of "James VIII" (the Old Pretender) in August 1715. Partly on the basis of false claims of French support, Mar rapidly assembled a force of about twelve thousand men, mainly Episcopalians from the Northeast of Scotland plus elements of many Highland clans, including the MacLeans, Macdonalds, Macintoshes, Camerons, Mackenzies, and MacLeods. Not all of the Highland clans came out, for the decision whether to rebel or support the Hanoverians often depended on the position of a clan chief in local feuds and local politics. The Campbells, for instance, supported the Whig regime, as did some great northern clans like the Sutherlands and the Mackays. Simon Fraser of Beaufort wished to win recognition as chief of clan Fraser; despite the fact that he had spent much time at the Jacobite court in France, he gambled—successfully, as it turned out—on the Hanoverian side in 1715.

The ordinary clan member, who was the footsoldier of the Highland host, had nothing to do with the decision of his clan to join the fray. The decision was strictly a matter for the clan chief and his immediate family. In the Highland clans, the chief leased land at a low rent to his principal lieutenants, called "tacksmen," who were often kinsmen of the chief. In return for his land, the tacksman pledged military service to the chief and in turn subleased his land in small portions to the clansmen who served as the clan troops. Bound by the closest ties of blood, land tenure, and military duty, the tacksmen of a clan had to respond unquestioningly to the call of the chief to go to war, as did the ordinary subtenant soldiers. In relatively short bursts, this clan army would fight with great elan, mobility, and offensive striking power, but it was not suited to long campaigns or defensive warfare.

Mar failed to understand either the opportunities or the limits offered by the Highland army. He should have moved quickly to the attack, since the Hanoverian forces in Scotland were very weak. He might well have consolidated Scotland for James Edward and then moved to gather whatever strength Jacobitism had in England. Certainly the Jacobite army needed quick successes in order to prove to waverers that joining the rebellion was the politically astute thing to do. But Mar was an indecisive commander; he failed to take Edinburgh and chose to wait in Perth for James Edward to arrive from France. Finally, the duke of Argyll, sent by the British with a small army to defend the Lowlands, drew Mar into battle at Sheriffmuir in November. Sheriffmuir made a significant difference in Scottish national history. The bloody battle was a draw, but Argyll's troops held the field. Mar's Highlanders began to drift back to their mountain glens.

At this point James Edward arrived. He had been given no help by the French government, who were in a cautious mood after the death of Louis XIV earlier in 1715. James Edward was a brave man, but his perpetual gloominess was hindrance to his cause. On his arrival in December, he announced to his officers: "For me, it is no new thing to be unfortunate, since my whole life from my cradle has been a constant series of misfortunes." This was no speech to inspire dispirited men. The dwindling of Mar's army continued. Argyll received reinforcements, and in February 1716, James Edward and Mar left for France. Thus ended what was probably the best chance the Scots had of restoring their independence by force.

THE '45

The Stuarts did not stop trying to promote their cause after 1715. They were forever involved in intrigue in European courts against the Hanoverian regime, and in 1719 they even managed to get Spanish support for an armed expedition to Britain. In this case, as in so many others, the winds blew against the Jacobites, and a storm destroyed much of the Spanish fleet off Corunna. Only a few hundred Spanish troops reached Scotland, and they were soon defeated and their meager clan allies scattered.

The rebellion of 1715 and the abortive invasion of 1719 were of great help to the Whigs in establishing their preeminence in England. They could claim that the Tories were unsafe because of their Jacobite associations and that Whig rule was the only alternative to popery and foreign invasion. Meanwhile, the Whigs' policy in Scotland was from their point of view a sensible one, though it was unpopular and poorly executed—integration of the Highlands with the already anglicized Lowlands and incorporation of both in the British state. Laws were passed in 1716 disarming the clans, but these laws were ignored by the Jacobite clans. Titles of about nineteen leading Jacobites were suppressed, and a few estates were seized, yet most of the leading clan chiefs were able to avoid serious punishment. Of greater importance was a system of roads meant to break the isolation of the Highlands and open them to military patrols. Under General George Wade, the British army built approximately 260 miles of roadway, penetrating the central Highlands and connecting the British outposts on the Great Glen, Fort William and Fort Augustus, to Inverness. Finally, Wade instituted a system of policing the main Highland routes against Jacobites and clan cattle rustlers by recruiting Whig clansmen into independent army units (later organized as the famous Black Watch Regiment).

At the same time, a semi-official educational movement undertaken by the Lowland gentry increased the pressure on Highland society. This was the Scottish Society for the Propagation of Christian Knowledge (SSPCK), founded in 1709 after the model of the English SPCK to establish in the Highlands schools that would teach "religion and virtue." The founders believed that Highland culture was barbaric and superstitious and that its unlawful ways stemmed from three mutually supportive factors—Jacobitism, Catholicism, and the Gaelic language. The SSPCK would establish Presbyterian schools, confident that Calvinism and the English language would break the clan system and integrate the Highlanders into the mainstream of Anglo-Scottish life. The Church of Scotland, which had experienced great difficulty in penetrating the Gaelic-speaking areas, supported the SSPCK. By 1758, the SSPCK had founded 176 schools, most of them in the Highlands. This was cultural imperialism of a deliberate sort. Ironically, although popular culture in the Highlands proved to be highly resistant to being "improved" in this way, the Highland aristocracy and gentry, who increasingly had to live in both the Gaelic and the anglicized worlds, slowly began to accept the manners and speech of "polite"—that is, English—culture.

These forces, as well as the beginnings of a trend among some clan chiefs toward a more profit-oriented view of their land and tenantry, show that the Jacobite revolt of 1745 was not the outburst of a vigorous Gaelic society but the last stand of traditional Highland culture against the forces causing its decline—commercialism, anglicization, and governmental pressure from England and Lowland Scotland. This fact was not grasped by the English politicians until the 1780s, for they continued to fear Scottish rebellion during every war down to the French Revolution. Meanwhile, the prosperity and stability of Walpole's long rule had made the 1720s and 1730s relatively peaceful in Scotland. Jacobitism went into a period of somnolence. But when Britain went to war with Spain in 1739, and with France soon after, the opportunity again rose for a Jacobite rebellion in Britain, this time with French help. The opportunity was seized by one of the few charismatic figures produced by the Stuarts, Charles Edward, son of the Old Pretender.

Charles Edward, the Young Pretender, or Bonnie Prince Charlie as the Scots called him, was then in his early twenties, none too intelligent but tall, good-looking, graceful, and chivalrous. Born and reared in the Jacobite court in Rome, Charles was energetic and ambitious. Early in 1744, Charles went to France in order to persuade the French government to assist the Jacobite enterprise. The French, as usual were interested in using the Stuarts to further their own policies, though not in helping them otherwise. As it happened, the French in 1744 were planning an invasion of England, but a storm destroyed the invasion fleet. The French abandoned their invasion plans, turned their attention to the Continent, and left Charles on his own. In 1745, with little help from the French, Charles had two ships fitted out for an expedition to Scotland. The larger of the two ships, carrying most of Charles's troops, was intercepted and driven off by the British navy. Charles, however, persevered and landed in the Outer Hebrides, leading a grand total of seven men.

The Battle of Culloden, *by D. Morier (April 1746). This painting shows the desperation of the struggle when the Highland charge met the British lines. The Jacobite clans suffered total defeat.*

For some time, Charles had been in contact with the Jacobite clans, but most of them were discouraged by the absence of French troops. Only by an emotional appeal to the Highlanders' sense of personal loyalty was Charles initially able to win any support at all, and that predictably came from the Macdonalds and the Camerons. He boldly set out for the central Highlands and Edinburgh with no more than one thousand men. Luckily for him, the British had stripped Scotland of almost all of its forces, including the new Black Watch regiment. Moreover, the few troops remaining, inexperienced and untrained, were commanded by Sir John Cope, an incompetent officer who threw away what advantages he had by embarking on a long and pointless march to Inverness. Gathering support as he went, Charles moved directly to Edinburgh, which to a degree had been alienated from the union by earlier high-handed treatment on the part of the London government and which now saw no effective means of resistance. Edinburgh opened its gate to the Jacobites without a fight. Cope shipped his men back to Edinburgh but arrived too late. Shortly afterward, Charles's forces attacked Cope's army at Prestonpans (just east of Edinburgh) and routed them with a furious Highland charge.

Charles now held all of Scotland except for Glasgow and the Southwest, and he announced the revocation of the Treaty of Union. Yet Charles's army never numbered more than about five thousand Highlanders, and he had no means of actually administering the country. Perhaps he might have held Scotland for the Stuarts if he had been content to win Scottish independence, but maybe not: Jacobite sentiment simply was not as strong in 1745 as it had been in 1715, because the economic benefits of the union had slowly begun to make themselves felt. In any case, Charles held true to the Stuart aim of reclaiming *both* crowns; hence, with his small and restless Highland army, he invaded England. In a dramatic march he moved through Carlisle and Manchester as far south as Derby, only 130 miles from London. The British government panicked, and George II prepared to return to Hanover. In fact, however, Charles's advance had not brought out any significant *English* Jacobite support. After a heated argument with his commanders, Charles was prevailed on to retreat to Scotland.

The long retreat was disastrous for the Jacobite army because the Highlanders' morale dwindled and desertions increased. Until they were out of England, Charles's army was followed by a large, well-supplied, and methodical army led by William, duke of Cumberland ("Butcher Billy"), George II's enormously fat but capable son. Charles retreated all the way to Inverness, his troops exhausted and hungry. Cumberland was sent after him with about ten thousand men. At last the two forces met at Culloden, near Inverness, on a boggy field ill-suited to the impetuous Highlanders' mode of combat. The miserably cold and starving High-landers were forced to undergo a fearful pounding by the British artillery before they could stand no more and charged. This time the British troops knew what to expect from a Highland attack. The result was a complete defeat for the Jacobite army and the slaughter of about one thousand Highlanders. Charles was led from the field and left only the words, "Let every man seek his own safety the best way he can." For five months Charles was on the run from British forces in the High-lands. He was sheltered by loyal clansmen, and his adventures gave rise to many a romantic legend, but the Jacobite movement was shattered. Charles returned to France in September 1746 and spent the rest of his life in futile attempts to revive the Jacobite cause. He died in Rome in 1788; by then the British had ceased to worry about Jacobitism.

THE DESTRUCTION OF THE CLANS

The Battle of Culloden itself was a severe blow to the Highland clans, but British policies after Culloden did even more lasting damage. The Jacobite clans were in no condition to continue the struggles even by guerrilla war, and the duke of Cumberland pursued the remnants of the clan army with ruthless persistence. This pursuit, which earned Cumberland the nickname "Butcher," was a matter of official policy. The aim was to reduce the power of the Highlanders so that they could never again sponsor a Jacobite rebellion. Lord Chesterfield, the elegant expo-nent of worldly manners who at the time was lord lieutenant of Ireland, in fact urged a policy of genocide on Cumberland—the chiefs were to be captured and the peasantry massacred. Cumberland and his successors did not go quite that far, but their activities were thorough enough. British troops deliberately ravaged clan estates all through 1746, burning crops, destroying cottages, driving off cattle, and smashing tools. Any rebel captured with weapons was shot outright. Most ordinary clan soldiers who surrendered were transported to the colonies as indentured workers. About 120 Scottish Jacobite officers were executed.

These acts of rational brutality were only the opening efforts at destroying the Highland way of life. The British forts in the Highlands were strengthened, Wade's system of military roads vastly expanded, and military patrols extended and increased. Law and order came to the Highlands with a naked iron hand. Next, in 1746 Parliament passed the Disarming Act, forbidding the Highlanders to carry or possess arms or to wear Highland dress—that is, the tartan and plaid. Even the bagpipe was banned as a warlike instrument. A substantial number of estates belonging to clan chiefs were seized, and this time (unlike 1715) no legalistic evasion of forfeiture was allowed. Most important, the claims of the chiefs over their tenants that had made the clans such potent military units were broken. Military tenures were abolished, so the landlord-tenant relationship in the Highlands came to resemble that prevailing in England. Heritable jurisdictions were also eliminated throughout Scotland. Now the chief was no longer prosecutor, judge, and jury in his territory, and Scottish gentry and tenantry had access to courts established by the central government. Legal administration in Scotland was brought into line with English policies, though Scottish law itself remained separate.

The British government also hoped to deflect Highland energy from lawlessness and rebellion toward English-style efficiency and industriousness. Thousands of Highland clansmen were recruited for new regiments in the British army. These troops were to play a vital role in the expansion of the Empire. Moreover, the British attempted to use the forfeited Jacobite estates as models of improved farming, building a corridor of land 30 to 40 miles wide from Stirling to Inverness on which all rents would be used for "Civilising the Inhabitants upon the said Estates and other Parts of the Highlands and Islands of Scotland, thus promoting amongst them the Protestant religion, good Government, Industry and Manufactures, and the Principles of Duty and Loyalty to his Majesty, his Heirs and Successors." Gradually, however, the government lost interest in the scheme as their fear of Jacobitism died out, and by 1784 they had returned the estates to private hands.

Yet the landlords of the Scottish Highlands largely accomplished the British goal of completing the destruction of the clans. In increasing numbers since the beginning of the eighteenth century, Highland chiefs had sent their sons to be educated in the Lowlands, so that they could acquire the polish (and the language) of the "polite" world. Inevitably, some of the values of that world rubbed off on them. After Culloden, these semi-anglicized chiefs faced a choice of trying to sustain the traditional Highland culture against overwhelming odds or converting themselves into more-or-less English or Lowland-style landlords. During the three-quarters of a century after 1750, most clan chiefs opted for the latter route, sometimes reluctantly, often intermittently, but inexorably nonetheless. By this slow trend, pursued mainly for the increased rents and profits that would enable them gain recognition in the new Scottish world, the great landlords eradicated the close personal and patriarchal bonds that had knitted the clans together.

"Improvement," as it was called, had begun in the Highlands on the Argyll estates. There, the second duke of Argyll tried to increase his income by eliminating the tacksmen as intermediary tenants and letting the parcels of land directly to the tenants at higher rents. In the short run, this policy had hurt the military power of clan Campbell and in part accounted for Bonnie Prince Charlie's amazing early success. But after Culloden, many other Highland chiefs also elected to sacrifice military strength for enhanced rent in the same way—by eliminating tacksmen and offering leases to the highest bidder. They also consolidated the holdings on their estates, as was being done in England and in the Lowlands, thereby reducing the number of tenants required to farm the land. These policies destroyed not only the military basis of clan society but also the ancient cooperative farming practices of the Highlands. The "improving" policies drove hundreds of tacksmen to emigration, mostly to America. The tacksmen ordinarily organized the substantial tenant families on the estate to emigrate with them, leaving the poorest peasants to stay on. In the late 1760s and early 1770s, about twenty thousand Scotsmen left for America, most of them Highlanders.

In many cases, Highland landlords simply cleared their land of people to make room for sheep pasturage. From the 1760s through the early decades of the nineteenth century, hundreds of thousands of acres in the Highlands were turned over to the raising of Lowland black-face and cheviot sheep, for sheep brought profits. In some instances, the landlords tried to provide other occupations for their tenants—linen weaving, kelp burning (to make alkalai), and fishing, for example. In other cases, however, the tenants were simply evicted amid scenes of acute suffering and violent protest. The most notorious of these cases of the "Highland Clearances" occurred in Sutherland between 1807 and 1821, when agents of the countess of Sutherland expelled about ten thousand people to make room for sheep, destroying and burning peasant cottages, in some instances with people still in them. It is safe to say that many Highlanders have never forgotten or forgiven the Highland Clearances.

More emigration resulted from the Clearances, this time of people from a lower social and economic order. But because the population of Scotland was increasing as part of the general population explosion of late eighteenth- and early nineteenth-century Europe (see Chapter 10), the fringe areas around the sheep-raising districts, especially in the northwest Highlands and the western islands remained congested and impoverished. Here it remained the custom for a tenant to subdivide his holding, no matter how small it was, to provide tiny tenancies for his sons. The landlords believed they could do nothing to help, for the only alternative to congestion that they could think of was eviction. Thus the destruction of the clans was compete by 1830; indeed, the signs were clear for Dr. Johnson to read when he visited the Highlands in the 1770s:

> There was perhaps never any change of national manners so quick, so great, and so general, as that which has operated in the Highlands by the last conquest and subsequent laws. We came hither too late to see what we expected—a people of peculiar appearance and a system of antiquated life.

The clans retain little now of their original character: their ferocity of temper is softened, their military ardour is extinguished, their dignity of independence is depressed, their contempt of government, subdued, and their reverence for their chiefs abated. Of what they had before the late conquest of their country there remains only their language and their poverty.

THE SCOTTISH ENLIGHTENMENT

Considering its record of rebellion, war, and destruction of an ancient way of life, eighteenth-century Scotland hardly seems like a country capable of giving rise to a renaissance in high culture. Yet that is precisely what happened. In the second half of the century, Scotland produced a galaxy of intellectuals and artists to equal any in the European world. Social philosophers like Francis Hutcheson, Adam Ferguson, David Hume, and Adam Smith; scientists like Joseph Black; architects like William and Robert Adam; and painters like Allan Ramsay and Henry Raeburn were at least as brilliant and influential as their English and French colleagues. In short, Georgian Scotland—or more accurately, urban, Lowland Scotland—took a distinguished place in the age of Enlightenment.

How can we explain this remarkable cultural efflorescence in a time of such national difficulty and indeed political extinction? What was the connection of the cultural renaissance to the union with England and the destruction of the clans? Such questions are not easy to answer and to a degree at least must remain a matter of speculation. Nevertheless, it seems reasonable to say that this particular cultural flowering was the result of not any nationalistic reaction *against* the union or of a nostalgic defense of Highland values but a solid *joining* of the Lowlands to the wider English economy and culture. Enlightened thought in Scotland, as elsewhere, was urbane, cosmopolitan, and secular. It drew on old cultural connections between Scotland and Continental Europe. One of the preconditions that had to exist before the Enlightenment could take root anywhere was an end to isolation and the forging of links to the wider cultural world. The union helped to create this for Scotland. Similarly, enlightened ideas could flourish only in conditions of political stability. Here, too, the union with England was important, because English power ended the incessant strife between Highlands and Lowlands and installed Lowland values and styles of life in a preeminent position.

There were other important preconditions as well: sufficient economic prosperity, adequate institutional support, and an absence of intellectual or religious restrictions. Each of these preconditions came to exist in the urban centers of Lowland Scotland in the middle decades of the eighteenth century. In the 1740s, the Scottish economy began to show signs of the progress that had been predicted of the union—not an industrial takeoff, but significant, if slow, growth. As we have already noted, in widening circles of the Lowlands, agricultural "improvers" were introducing new crops, new farming techniques, and new financial management. Perhaps more important, the urban, commercial economy of the Lowlands developed relatively rapidly. This expansion was most pronounced in Edinburgh and Glasgow, which, however, developed in very different ways.

Edinburgh, the largest city in Britain except for London and Bristol, was no longer the capital of an independent country, but it became the administrative and legal center of "North Britain." Professional people dominated the town, and lawyers were by far the most influential and prosperous professional group. In connection with wealthy Lowland aristocrats and gentry, for whom they did much work, the lawyers generated a lively intellectual life of legal philosophizing, political talk, and social thought. They were also largely responsible for the building of "New Town," the elegantly classical district that made (and still makes) Edinburgh the "Athens of the North," one of the great monuments of eighteenth-century taste.

Glasgow was dominated by its business people. Glasgow had long enjoyed a reputation for architectural elegance (later destroyed by the Industrial Revolution of the nineteenth century). Its commercial people aggressively took advantage of the new market of England and its empire opened to them by the union. Linen manufacturing, sugar refining, and shipping all became important Glasgow trades. The tobacco trade with North America became the most important of all: by 1771, the Scots were importing 47 million pounds of tobacco a year, most of it into Glasgow, and the Scots had won 52 percent of all British trade in tobacco. Wealthy "tobacco lords" inspired much of Glasgow's bustling import/export trade and injected a great amount of liquid capital into the Scottish economy.

Institutional support for the Scottish Enlightenment came from Scotland's reformed universities. Because of the kirk's tradition of establishing a school in every parish, Lowland Scotland had a higher literacy rate than England, and boys from the commercial and professional ranks regularly attended one of the four universities—Edinburgh, Glasgow, St. Andrews, and Aberdeen. In the eighteenth century, the Scottish universities grew in size and (unlike Oxford and Cambridge, which remained shackled to classics and mathematics) expanded the range of subjects taught to include law, medicine, rhetoric, and the natural sciences. In addition the mode of teaching changed, and the Scottish universities became famous for teachers who lectured in English (rather than Latin) in their specialized subjects. The leader in this teaching reform was Francis Hutcheson, professor of moral philosophy at Glasgow from 1729, through whose classes many of the leaders of the Scottish Enlightenment passed.

Finally, developments in the Church of Scotland were crucial to the country's intellectual life. If the kirk had remained the oppressive, puritanical institution of the seventeenth century, then the secular, tolerant thought that was central to the enlightenment would have been stifled. But slowly from the 1690s on, the theological temperature of the kirk went down. Although a minority of ministers in the early eighteenth century insisted on maintaining a repressive militant church, the majority of kirk leaders shared the more moderate tone of English religion and even accepted the principle of the appointment of parish ministers by lay patronage. Indeed, the "Moderate party"—tolerant, reasonable, respectable—came to preeminence in the kirk and the universities. For instance, the last execution for blasphemy in Scotland occurred in 1697 and the last for witchcraft in 1722; the laws against witchcraft were repealed in 1736. Like their brothers in the church of En-

Adam Smith. The great political economist published The Wealth of Nations, *a key document in the Scottish Enlightenment and the foundation of free-market economic theory, in 1776.*

gland, the ministers of the Georgian kirk were mainly interested in not repression but in trying to persuade their flocks to be virtuous and in showing the convergence of virtue and happiness.

The concerns of the "Moderate literati" of the Church of Scotland reflected the main themes of Scottish enlightened thought. Scottish Calvinists had always been preoccupied with individual moral reformation and with the associated social discipline; now, in the more sociable spirit of the eighteenth century, leading Scottish thinkers turned to the issue of the moral improvement of human beings in society. Like Locke and the English moralists, the Scots assumed that human beings are naturally social beings and therefore that moral progress is to be understood in the context of social institutions—legal, political, religious. They were among the first social scientists. Furthermore, the Scottish thinkers all believed that Scotland was emerging from an age of barbarism into an age of civilization; thus, they focused on the *history* of various societies by which they could measure Scotland's progress. Their ideas, then, never were peculiarly "Scottish" in the sense of identifying and celebrating traditions and institutions that made Scotland different. Like all enlightened thinkers, they assumed that human nature is everywhere the same and that the purpose of moral philosophy and history is to discover the universal laws of human behavior. Therefore, philosophical history—history as the record of the fundamental laws of nature—was their characteristic mode of thinking.

Next to David Hume, whose work has already been examined in connection with the British empiricism, the greatest thinker in the Scottish Enlightenment was Adam Smith. Like his close friend Hume, Smith articulated all the main themes of the Scottish Enlightenment; consequently, Smith's work is best understood in the context of *preindustrial* Enlightened thought. Later, his work was taken to be the bible of industrialism, which it emphatically was not, for Smith had little or no experience with factories and steam power; his world was that of Lowland Scottish commerce. Born in 1723 in the small port of Kirkaldy, Smith was the son of a lawyer and customs official. He attended Glasgow University, where he learned much from the lectures of Francis Hutcheson. Later, he studied at Oxford, which he found to be mostly asleep. He read widely in Enlightenment thought and was especially impressed by the works of Locke, Newton, Hutcheson, and Hume. In 1751, he was elected successor to Hutcheson at Glasgow University, where he taught natural theology, ethics, jurisprudence, and political economy. He hoped to do for the whole field of moral philosophy what Newton had done for natural science.

In his first important work, *The Theory of Moral Sentiments* (1759), Smith gave a systematic, "scientific" treatment of human nature. In it he joined the "moral faculty" school of men like Shaftesbury. Smith was well aware that people are motivated by "self-love"—that is, they pursue pleasure and avoid pain. He also reasoned that people are by nature social animals and have a natural faculty of sympathetic behavior. What truly brings pleasure, he said, is the approval of others: "It is not wealth that men desire, but the consideration and good opinion that wait upon riches." Everyone exercises the power of sympathetic imagination and so can know what others approve. A person therefore behaves as if there is an "impartial spectator," or conscience, watching every move. Through the operation of this fundamental quality of human nature, our pursuit of self-interest leads to socially benevolent behavior as if by an "invisible hand."

This was the moral foundation of Smith's *Inquiry into the Nature and Causes of the Wealth of Nations* (1776), one of the most influential works in modern Western history. In it, Smith sets out a theory of self-regulating economics, but his moral theory always stands in the background. *The Wealth of Nations* reflects the Scottish interest in how societies progress. Its basic framework, therefore, is philosophical history. Smith believed that nations go through four stages of development: hunting, pastoral, agricultural, and commercial. In each age, the mode of production shapes the political and social institutions. The division of labor characterizes the commercial stage: according to the principle of self-interest, each person (and each nation) takes up what he or she does best. In this way, production is maximized, provided nothing (such as the state) interferes with the natural operation of the market and the division of labor. Smith thus argued for the *utility* of natural liberty, because any intervention by the state in the economy by definition deflects people from natural behavior and maximum production. For this reason, Smith on the whole condemned mercantilism and advocated laissez-faire domestic policies and free trade between nations. Yet Smith was never the proponent of dog-eat-dog competition, and he expressed concern that the routinization of work resulting from the division of labor would dull the wits and imagination of the laborer. He imagined that the "invisible hand" of benevolence would have to keep the self-regulating economic system he advocated from being vicious and exploitive. In this way, Smith expressed the confidence and reasonableness of Lowland Scotland as it claimed the benefits of joining the prosperous and expansive English society.

The Scottish Enlightenment was a great achievement by Scottish intellectuals, but it contributed to the formation of a British nation. As we saw, the union of 1707 created a British *state* but not an integrated British people. The English in the eighteenth century aggressively eradicated that part of Scottish culture they regarded as dangerous to Britain, but they showed no interest in building an emotional bond between Englishmen and Scots or in blending the two peoples. Still, the long, slow process of integration into Britain did begin for the Scots in the eighteenth century. The incorporation of clansmen into the British army was one major integrative force. Another force was the participation of Scotsmen in the administration of foreign and imperial affairs, an arena in which "Britain" did function as a single unit. A third factor was the long series of wars against the French, which inspired British nationalist emotions. A fourth force was the market economy, which expanded and deepened throughout the century and tied the Scots tightly to English commerce and industry. In addition, there was the common Protestantism that most Scots shared with the English. Finally, and not least important, the Scottish Enlightenment brought Scottish thinkers and writers into intimate relationship with the mainstream of English intellectual life. Enlightened Scottish thinkers like Hume and Smith, along with the books they wrote, moved easily among Edinburgh, Glasgow, and London. Empirical ideas, which were cosmopolitan rather than provincial, became the common property of minds on both sides of the River Tweed. A sphere of intellectual discourse grew up during the 1700s that was genuinely British—a *British* high culture that helped Scottish men and women over the long run develop parallel identities, Scottish and British.

Suggested Reading

Black, Jeremy, *Culloden and the '45* (New York: St. Martin's Press, 1990).

Camic, Charles, *Experience and Enlightenment: Socialization for Cultural Change in Eighteenth Century Scotland* (Chicago: University of Chicago Press, 1983).

Chapman, Malcolm, *The Gaelic Vision in Scottish Culture* (London: Croom Helm, 1978).

Chitnis, Anand C., *The Scottish Enlightenment: A Social History* (London: Croom Helm, 1976).

Clyde, Robert, *From Rebel to Hero: the Image of the Highlander, 1745–1830* (East Lothian: Tuckwell Press, 1995).

Daiches, David, *Charles Edward Stuart: The Life and Times of Bonnie Prince Charlie* (London: Thames & Hudson, 1973).

Devine, T. M., *Clanship to Crofters' War: The Social Transformation of the Scottish Highlands* (Manchester: Manchester University Press, 1994).

———, *The Scottish Nation: A History, 1700–2000* (New York: Viking, 1999).

Ferguson, William, *Scotland: 1689 to the Present* (London: Oliver & Boyd, 1968).

Hill, James Michael, *Celtic Warfare, 1595–1763* (Edinburgh: J. Donald, 1986).

Houston, R. A., *Social Change in the Age of Enlightenment, Edinburgh, 1660–1760* (Oxford: Clarendon Press, 1994).

Lenman, Bruce, *An Economic History of Modern Scotland, 1660–1976* (Hamden, Conn.: Archon Books, 1977).

————, *Integration, Enlightenment, and Industrialization: Scotland, 1746–1832* (Toronto: University of Toronto Press, 1981).

————, *The Jacobite Risings in Britain, 1689–1746* (London: Eyre Methuen, 1980).

Levack, Brian, *The Formation of the British State: England, Scotland, and the Union, 1603–1707* (Oxford: Clarendon Press, 1987).

MacInnes, Allan I., *Clanship, Commerce, and the House of Stuart, 1603–1788* (East Linton: Tuckwell Press, 1994).

McLynn, Frank, *The Jacobites* (London: Routledge & Kegan Paul, 1985).

Mitchison, Rosalind, *Lordship to Patronage: Scotland, 1603–1745* (London: E. Arnold, 1983).

Pittock, Murray G. H., *Inventing and Resisting Britain: Cultural Identities in Britain and Ireland, 1685–1789* (New York: St. Martin's Press, 1997).

————, *The Invention of Scotland: The Stuart Myth and the Scottish Identity, 1638 to the Present* (New York: Routledge, Chapman & Hall, 1991).

————, *Jacobitism* (New York: St. Martin's Press, 1998).

Prebble, John, *Culloden* (New York: Atheneum, 1962).

————, *The Highland Clearances* (London: Secker & Warburg, 1965).

Raphael, D. D., *Adam Smith* (New York: Oxford University Press, 1985).

Richards, Eric, *A History of the Highland Clearances* (London: Croom Helm, 1982).

Roberts, John L., *The Jacobite Wars: Scotland and the Military Campaigns of 1715 and 1745* (Edinburgh: Polygon, 2002).

Sher, Richard B., *Church and University in the Scottish Enlightenment* (Princeton, N.J.: Princeton University Press, 1985).

Smout, T.C., *A History of the Scottish People, 1560–1830* (London: Fontana Press, 1969).

Speck, W. A., *The Butcher: The Duke of Cumberland and the Suppression of The '45* (Oxford: Blackwell, 1981).

Todd, Margot, *The Culture of Protestantism in Early Modern Scotland* (New Haven: Yale University Press, 2002).

Whatley, Christopher, *Scottish Society, 1707–1830: Beyond Jacobitism, Towards Industrialization* (Manchester: Manchester University Press, 2000).

Youngson, A.J., *After the Forty-Five: The Economic Impact on the Highlands* (Edinburgh: Edinburgh University Press, 1973).

Chapter 7

The Expansion of British Power and Empire, 1715–1763

By the end of the War of Spanish Succession (1713), Britain had become a major European power. Between 1715 and 1763, Britain became a genuine world power as well, not only ranking among the half-dozen strongest European states but also holding an empire larger and richer than any other in the Western world. Thus, in the first half of the eighteenth century Britain first emerged from its position as a medium-rank European state and began to assume a global role that it held until the mid-twentieth century. The expansion of British power was to have a great impact on the lives of ordinary Britons—Scots, Welsh, and Irish in addition to the English—and of millions of other peoples around the world as well. The impact—political, constitutional, military, economic, social—has been bewilderingly varied and complex, and whether the overall results have been for good or ill is impossible to say. By any accounting it was a remarkable achievement for such a relatively small group of islands off the shore of Europe.

How did British power in the eighteenth century expand so rapidly? No one could have predicted it in 1550 or even 1650. World-power status was never the goal of any deliberate, unified British plan, at least before the latter 1750s, except in the sense that Britain like all European states of the eighteenth century sought incessantly to aggrandize itself at the expense of others. Britain's position of power on the Continent and overseas came as the by-product of a century-long struggle with France (only half over by 1763) and the expansion of British trade. These two factors were not independent of each other but were mutually reinforcing, and both were rooted in the general economic prosperity and political security of eighteenth-century Britain.

THE EUROPEAN STATE SYSTEM

The British ascended to world power in the context of an extremely competitive system of nation-states. In the first half of the eighteenth century there were five major European powers, not all of equal strength—France, the Hapsburg monarchy, Russia, Prussia, and Britain. Spain's great century of wealth and power had come to an end, and Holland, commercially more advanced even than

England, had been exhausted by its long war with French absolutism. France was the leading state in Europe, no longer dominant as it had been before 1715 but with more than twenty million people still one of the largest, wealthiest, and best-organized nations, capable of supporting an army of 150,000 even in peacetime. The Hapsburg monarchy, a heterogeneous collection of states centered on Austria, was the heir to the Holy Roman Empire. It ruled over impressive resources, but it was afflicted by political, religions, and ethnic divisions. Russia was largest of all, capable of fielding an army of 500,000 men, but was severely weakened by ethnic diversity and had only recently emerged from a barbarous condition.

The up-and-coming states in Europe were Prussia and Britain. Prussia had a population of only 2 1/4 million (less than Ireland), no naturally defensible borders, and meager resources. Yet the relentless ambition of the ruling Hohenzollern family had made Prussia into a considerable force by building an army of enormous size (eighty thousand men in 1750) and by enforcing exemplary training. Practically the entire Prussian state apparatus was devoted to raising and maintaining the army. Britain, on the other hand, had only formally come into existence in 1707 and operated under the handicap of the landowners' fear of a standing army. The British navy, an effective tax-collecting machinery, and the taxable wealth of the country (including now Wales, Scotland, and Ireland) made Britain a power to contend with. The British navy had showed its supremacy in the wars against Louis X1V, and British governments thereafter maintained it fairly consistently. Parliament's ability to tax the whole of the British Isles made it possible for Britain to maintain the navy, which supported the bountifully taxable overseas trade, and to subsidize the armies of Continental allies. Britain could fight for itself on the seas and pay others to fight for it on land.

Different as they were, all of these states conducted their diplomacy and warfare with broadly similar objectives. In all of them, governments took foreign policy as their primary concern, and the people who made foreign policy were a tiny elite consisting of the monarch and his or her aristocratic advisers. This was true even of Britain, although Parliament and public opinion could on occasion make themselves felt in foreign affairs. The mind-set of all the European governing elites held that the *increase of state power itself* was what counted in foreign affairs. The age of religious wars had largely passed, and the age of ideological wars had not yet arrived. What mattered to eighteenth-century policymakers was adding to state power by increases in territory, population, and trade, all of which enabled a state to support a larger army and win yet more resources. Hence the state system of eighteenth-century Europe was a Machiavellian world of rapacious power and violence with no end beyond power itself.

The economic side of this mentality of incessant competition and war was *mercantilism*, which was most fully developed and implemented in France but was shared as a set of assumptions by all Europeans. Mercantilism was an elegant circular theory worthy of the rationalistic age in which it was born: trade engenders wealth; wealth supports armies and navies; armies and navies increase state power; and state power expands trade. European statesmen saw commerce as a means of increasing the strength of the state, and merchants saw state power as a means of increasing commerce. One British merchant put the case clearly in 1745: "Our commerce in general will flourish more under a vigorous and well-managed naval war, than under any peace which should allow an open intercourse with those two nations [France and Spain]."

The objectives of foreign affairs composed one of the two principal factors shaping the nature of warfare. Because the goal was not to obliterate an opposing political or social system, war tended to be limited. (England's wars in Ireland and Scotland, where the existence of the regime itself was at stake, were significant exceptions.) Likewise, it was counterproductive for a state to wage war to the point that its own economic and social systems cracked under the stress. The second factor limiting the conduct of wars was military technology. In the late seventeenth and early eighteenth centuries, firepower by infantry troops carrying flintlock muskets became the dominant force on the battlefield. Especially when used with the newly invented ring bayonet (which turned a musket into a pike), muskets could defeat cavalry troops and were regarded as more important than the artillery, long disdained by aristocratic officers. But muskets were inaccurate and slow to load and fire (three rounds per minute at best); hence they were most effective when used by massed troops to deliver murderous volleys at close range. Such tactics required elaborate maneuvering and iron discipline on the part of the infantry, both acquired only after lengthy training according to rigid drill. As a result, the best armies were *professional* armies rather than feudal levies or militia, because professionals trained full time.

Professional armies, however, became so precious the kings and generals hesitated to commit them to a protracted war. The object of commanders was to conduct campaigns of limited engagements, which were bloody and terrible to the troops involved but meant to gain finite advantages that could be useful at the bargaining table. Pieces of territory, trading stations, fortifications, and colonies were all power resources that made up the coinage of the state system, its warfare, and its treaties.

BRITISH INTERESTS AND POWER

In order to see how British interests operated within the European state system, it is important to understand how British policymakers perceived them. These perceived interests consisted of a collection of inconsistent assumptions and beliefs, some of which were primary and some derivative. First, British statesmen (almost all of them English) assumed that what was good for England was good for the rest of the British Isles; hence they really pursued *English* interests with the resources of all of Britain and Ireland. This assumption meant that the very unity of the new state of Great Britain was *the* fundamental interest. Second, the Whig oligarchs believed that the Hanoverian—that is, Protestant—succession was crucial to British unity, independence, liberty, and prosperity. Because both the state and the Protestant succession came under the pressure of Jacobite risings supported by foreign powers, these mostly elementary domestic issues had vital implications for foreign affairs, among them continual suspicion and hostility toward the Catholic powers Spain and France and alliance in one form or another with Protestant Holland.

Moreover, because George I and II were not only kings of Britain but also electors of Hanover, they insisted that Britain regard as a British interest the independence and integrity of their little German state. This matter was never popular among the British, for it involved them in expensive entanglements that seemed secondary to purely British concerns. Hanover was rightly thought of as a hostage to French or Hapsburg or Prussian power. As Lord Chesterfield wrote in 1742, "Hanover robs us of the Benefit of being an Island, and is actually a pledge for our good Behaviour on the Continent."

The fourth primary British interest—and the one that most often conflicted with concern for Hanover—was overseas commerce. The British government was keenly aware that its power derived in large part from trade; thus, trade bulked even larger in the aggregate of British interests than in other European countries. Britain conducted a growing overseas trade with both the Continent and the British colonies. Trade with the Continent traditionally was the larger portion; consequently, British officials felt particularly sensitive about maintaining access to the Dutch ports, which were the entrepôt for British goods to the Continent, and about sustaining trade in the Baltic, from which Britain imported naval stores, spars, and masts. More will be said about the colonial trade shortly. Suffice it to say two things here: first, British colonial trade was growing rapidly in the early eighteenth century (accounting for more than 50 percent of all imports by the 1750s), therefore the traditional primacy of Continental issues gave way over time to colonial gains and losses; second, the great rival for trade overseas was France.

The two derivative British interests resulted from an unconscious process of promoting strategic means into ends. One was the pursuit of a balance of power in Europe. This strategy, which was to be long honored in British policy, first emerged during the wars against Louis XIV, as William III and Marlborough constructed alliances to counter French might. The notion was that Britain should not seek permanent alliances but should throw its weight into the balance of nations in order to check any one power (usually France) that seemed to be achieving dominance over Europe. By the 1720s and 1730s, many English statesmen regarded this policy as an end in itself. The other derivative interest was simply to oppose France at every turn. By 1713, Britain had been at war with France for twenty-five years, and most Englishmen habitually assumed that this rivalry was somehow natural and that Britain should always range itself against France. Thus, in the eighteenth century, Britons began to equate the French national character with popery, poverty, wooden shoes, unmanly groveling before aristocracy, and frog eating. British patriotism, expressed in stirring songs like "God Save the King," "Rule Britannia," and "Hearts of Oak," all of which date from the decades before 1760, came to mean all the things the French allegedly lacked: honesty, independence, forthrightness, endurance, John Bull (the sturdy cartoon symbol of England), and the roast beef of Old England.

Britannia in Distress (1756). *By showing the dangers of aristocratic corruption and degeneracy, this political cartoon reflects the patriotic fervor of the 1750s.*

In pursuit of these interests Britain could deploy impressive and durable strengths: the army, navy, trade and finance, and colonies. Britain's position as an island enabled it to get maximum effect from a small professional army. The British needed only to commit on the Continent an army large enough to drain French resources away from their own navy. The British did not need conscription for this purpose, even when the army rose to more than fifty thousand men, as it did in the Seven Years War (1756–1763). Younger sons of aristocratic families provided the officers; the dregs of society, recruited by patriotism, poverty, or alcohol, supplied the enlisted ranks. The heaviest expenditures went to the navy, which was the best-led and largest in Europe (normally more than one hundred ships) and backed by a very large merchant marine. Parliament, as we have seen, served as an excellent taxing machine, and British financial institutions were second only to the Dutch in mobilizing private wealth for official purposes. The colonies, like the merchant marine, could be a liability as well as an asset because they had to be protected. Yet in the colonies the British found bold and determined people who were willing and able to provide some, at least, of the material resources to fight Britain's battles—and more important, to advance their own interests and so indirectly contribute to the growth of British power.

THE COLONIES

The British Empire in the first half of the eighteenth century included colonies stretching from the Mediterranean and the Atlantic to North America and the West Indies, and even to Africa and Asia. Some of the colonies were simply military stations or trading posts, whereas others were full-scale settlements with substantial British populations. All told, in 1750 perhaps fifteen million people outside the British Isles lived under the British flag. The empire they peopled had grown up in an unplanned and sporadic process mixing overseas trade, military conquest, colonization for profit or religion, and treaties with other European powers—a process dating back to the sixteenth century.

The three main areas of the British Empire were India, the West Indies, and North America. India would one day be the most fabulous jewel in the imperial crown, but in the early eighteenth century British rule had scarcely penetrated the Indian subcontinent. The British did not "colonize" India at all, in the sense of establishing permanent settlements as home to a significant number of Britons. The British Empire in India was the result of private (though officially sanctioned) commercial initiative. A group of English merchants had formed the East India Company and received a charter in 1600 to trade in the East Indies. They established trading posts ("factories") at Surat and subsequently Bombay, Madras, and Calcutta, where the company merchants bought for export and resale in England pepper and cotton fabrics. The Company also traded for coffee in Arabia and tea in China, and by the late seventeenth century its merchants were doing a big business selling opium in both China and England.

The East India Company found in India the Moghul Empire at its height. The Moghuls were Muslims who ruled the northern two-thirds of India and who in the 1600s were seeking to expand into the South. The Company established normal relations with the Moghuls and negotiated for trading rights. But the Moghul Empire had a feudal structure, and its emperors could not exercise consistent rule over all their vassals; therefore, the Company had to deal with a large number of local rulers and fend off Dutch and Portuguese rivals as well. Company traders, never known for their timidity or moderation, did not hesitate to use force to exploit the weakness of the Moghul Empire, and by the eighteenth century the Company was behaving like a middle-rank Indian vassal, though it as yet "ruled" very little territory. In the early 1700s, the Moghul Empire began to break up, and its power began to slip away to important princes, including those of the Hindu Maratha Confederacy of central India. In this fluid situation, one of irresistible opportunity as well as political complexity, the East India Company eagerly scuffled for juicier trading concessions, but from the 1730s it faced increased competition from a new rival—the French East India Company.

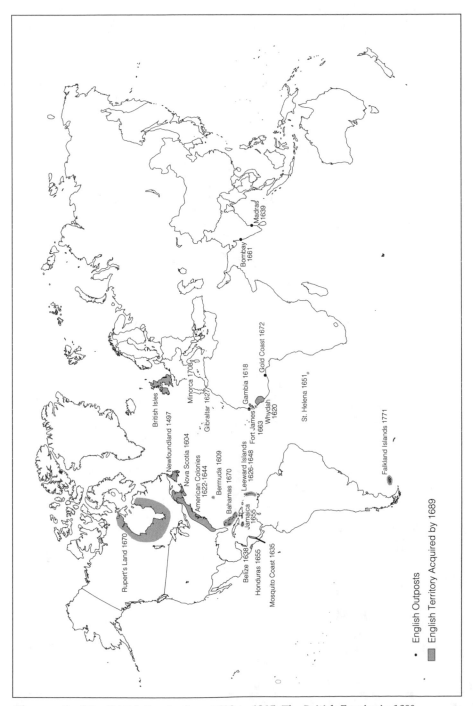

The growth of the British Empire from 1689 to 1815: The British Empire in 1689

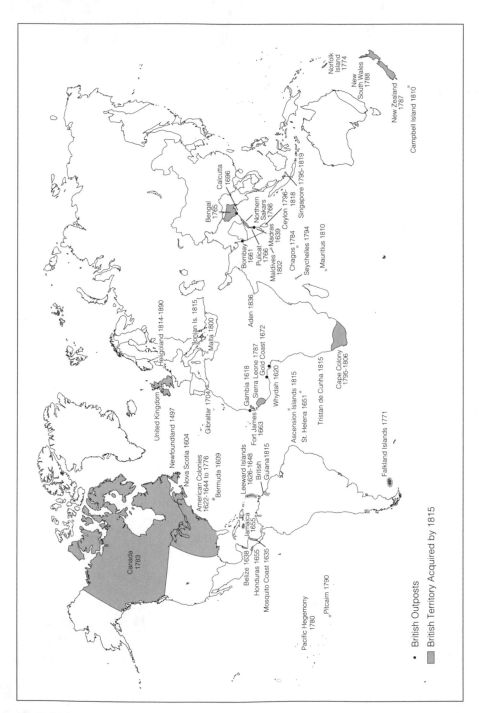

The British Empire in 1815

The West Indian colonies also began as private initiatives in the early seventeenth century. Bermuda and the Bahamas were settled by an enterprise that had separated from a group of adventurers called the Virginia Company. Other islands like St. Kitts, Barbados, Jamaica, and Antigua were colonized by smaller chartered companies. It did not bother these entrepreneurs that the islands they settled were claimed by Spain, but they did have to seize and defend their "plantations" in a long series of clashes not easily distinguishable from piracy. Eventually, English control of colonies in the West Indies was sanctioned by treaties between England and Spain.

Unlike India but like North America, the West Indian islands attracted large numbers of British settlers. The British regarded them as "empty" and there for the taking. Further, the adventurers who went to the West Indies seeking their fortunes found that they could grow tobacco there and sell it for handsome profit in England. Tobacco plantations required labor, so the West Indian landowners began to import from England and Ireland indentured servants, who for the cost of their passage, food, and clothing worked for a period of time (four to seven years) before achieving independence and moving on to their own land. By the 1640s there were twenty-five thousand English and Scots in the West Indies.

The tobacco trade, however, peaked in the mid-1600s, and West Indian plantation owners switched to growing sugar cane instead. Sugar was an immensely profitable crop and made the West Indies the most valuable part of the British Empire in the early eighteenth century. Sugar was harder to grow than tobacco, however, and required a larger and tougher work force. The planters, who were not in the West Indies for philanthropic purposes, found the solution to their labor problem by importing black slaves from Africa. The slave population in the West Indies grew rapidly, forcing many smaller white landowners to sell out and move to North America. By the 1660s, there were more black slaves than white settlers in the British West Indies.

The growth of slavery in the West Indies (and the simultaneous importation of slaves into some North American colonies) constituted a very important and new feature of life for some Britons. In England, where slaves were not needed for labor, slavery existed but was limited almost exclusively to domestic servants. In 1772, Lord Chief Justice Mansfield ruled in effect that slavery was illegal in England. But the British were until then remarkably tolerant of slavery. Slaves for the West Indies and the southern colonies of North America were supplied by chartered companies—the Company of Royal Adventurers and its successor, the Royal African Company—which established forts in West Africa for the purpose. The trade among West Africa, Britain, and the West Indies became enormously profitable, even though thousands of Africans died on the crowded slave ships. Great fortunes were made in eighteenth-century Bristol and Liverpool as merchant captains sent guns, rum, and trinkets to West Africa to trade for slaves, who were exchanged in turn for sugar in the West Indies. In the early 1750s, for instance, fifty-three slave ships a year left Liverpool in this triangular route.

The pattern of colonization in North America was much more varied than in the West Indies. A number of colonies were founded for straightforward purposes of commerce and profit. Virginia, for instance, was colonized by a company of Londoners who wanted to make money any way they could. Tobacco plantations based on slave labor soon proved the answer. Later, New Amsterdam was seized from the Dutch and divided into sections (New York, New Jersey, and Delaware) for great proprietors. Similarly, North and South Carolina were granted as money-making opportunities to court favorites. To the north, in what is now Canada, the Hudson Bay Company was chartered to allow certain English merchants a monopoly of the fur trade west of Hudson Bay. Newfoundland was settled to exploit its rich fishing grounds and formally ceded to Britain in 1713. Other North American colonies were founded by Englishmen seeking to practice without interference their own brands of Christianity: Massachusetts, Rhode Island, and Connecticut by Puritans and other nonconformists; Maryland by Roman Catholics; and Pennsylvania by Quakers. Georgia was established last (1732) by a philanthropic trust as a refuge for Englishmen released from debtors' prison.

By the beginning of the eighteenth century, the British colonies in North America made up a highly variegated patchwork quilt of settlements. They differed from each other in religion, economic activities, and political structures, but they did have some features in common. One was that the colonies—or at least the thirteen strung out along the Atlantic coast—all had some degree of representative self-government. The English, after all, had always allowed people to undertake colonizing enterprises on condition that it cost nothing to the London government; thus colonies were expected to take charge of their own local rule and protection. It would have been impossible for the English to exert direct rule across 3,000 miles of ocean. Hence by the 1700s, a standard form of government had grown up in the colonies from a combination of normal company organization and the model provided by the English constitution. Most had a royal governor, an appointed advisory council, and elected assembly. The assemblies had the right, or rather the responsibility, of legislating and raising taxes to pay the governor and support other local government activities.

A second common feature of the colonies was that their populations grew rapidly. Like their counterparts in the West Indies, the British colonists in North America regarded the land they found as empty and open to their settlement. It seems likely that disease that had come up from Mexico had slashed the Native American population even before the British arrived; hence the Native Americans populated the land thinly and presented the British colonists with no civilization of visible splendor such as the British merchants found in India. In any case, the diseases brought by the English ravaged the Native Americans, killing over 90 percent of some eastern tribes. Thus, what appeared to be open land beckoned to many people of middling ranks in the British Isles, some of whom were willing to risk the hazardous voyage, frontier hardships, and often a period of indentured servitude for a chance to better their lot. Some English emigrants wanted a religious environment more suitable to their liking. Most hoped eventually to set up as small farmers or even as gentlemen. Relatively few of the very top and bottom rank of the English social hierarchy came—few aristocrats on the one hand or landless vagrants or beggars on the other. Highland Scottish clansmen led by their tacksmen came in large numbers after the Battle of Culloden. Scotch-Irish Presbyterians, unhappy in Anglican-dominated Ulster, came in droves—perhaps 250,000 came between 1700 and 1775. By 1700, the white population (overwhelmingly British) stood at a quarter of a million in the thirteen colonies; by 1750 it had grown to almost a million, and there were 250,000 African slaves as well. In 1750, then, there were more Britons in North America than in Wales and almost as many as in Scotland.

These prosperous, enterprising, aggressive people were excellent partners for British trade. This is what made them important to the increase in British power. Even though the British Empire in North America was never as centralized as the French in Canada or the Spanish in Central and South America, British trade with the American colonists was extremely lucrative. The Navigation Acts of the 1660s still provided that all ships trading in the colonies be either British or American and that certain "enumerated" products exported from the colonies had to go first to a British port. Among these were tobacco, sugar, indigo, rice, molasses, and naval stores—either extremely valuable goods not produced in Britain or items vital to the British navy. Further, most goods shipped from anywhere to America had to come through a British port. The Navigation Acts were never rigorously enforced, but they did help channel colonial trade to Britain's advantage. Even as the North American population grew, more than half of its exports went to directly to Britain. By 1760, 15 percent of all British trade was with the North American colonies.

THE WAR OF JENKINS' EAR—KING GEORGE'S WAR (1739–1748)

The acquisitiveness and aggression embodied in the European state system and imperial expansion was bound to produce war. Despite Walpole's preference for peace and quiet in foreign affairs (to keep taxes down and prevent Jacobite invasions), public clamor forced him to declare war on Spain in 1739. The problem was that British colonists in the West Indies were determined to exploit trade opportunities in the Spanish-American Empire in the teeth of efforts by the Spanish coast guard to stop them. Local clashes went on in the Caribbean throughout the 1720s and 1730s. In 1738, one Captain Jenkins displayed to an outraged House of Commons the ear (pickled in a jar) that he had lost to a Spanish cutlass. Regardless of the fact that the incident had happened seven years before, British and West Indian merchants, plus a number of political opportunists in Parliament, would have war.

No doubt this colonial war (known in America as "King George's War") would have involved France soon, because French commercial efforts in India, the West Indies, and North America alike were beginning to rival British interests. In any event, the Anglo-Spanish war was enveloped in 1740 by a general European conflict that erupted over the succession to the Hapsburg monarchy. The combination of military war on the Continent and naval war overseas revived a dispute in Britain over what the best strategy was—to fight France directly by armies on land (the "Continental" strategy) or to take advantage of Britain's naval strength to strike overseas (the "maritime" or "blue-water" strategy). The concern of George II over Hanover and the commitment of the leading British policymakers to the European balance of power swung the debate in this instance toward the Continental approach. Britain sent an army of twelve thousand to Europe, hired thousands of German mercenaries, and subsidized both the Austrian and the Hanoverian armies. The British also pursued an aggressive naval policy, bottling up the French fleet in Brest, attacking numerous points in the West Indies, and preying on French merchant shipping.

King George's War was something of a standoff, and the treaty that ended it (Aix-la-Chapelle) in 1748 was a compromise. On the whole, the French had the best of the fighting in Europe, taking territory in Flanders regarded as vital by the British and Dutch. The French East India Company also took Madras. But the British generally did better overseas, most notably in capturing Louisbourg on Cape Breton Island with colonial troops in 1745. The longer the war on the continent dragged on, the more expensive and unpopular it became, especially among the English country gentry, whose patriotism always burned hot until taxes went up. Pitt expressed the general unhappiness with the Continental war: "The confidence of the people is abused by making unnecessary alliances; then they are pillaged to provide the subsidies. It is now apparent that this great, this powerful, this formidable Kingdom is considered only as a province of a despicable electorate."

By 1747, both Britain and France were weary of war and ready for peace. The treaty they arrived at merely restored the *status quo ante bellum* (the situation before the war): France gave up the Austrian Netherlands (Flanders) and Madras; Britain gave up Louisbourg.

THE SEVEN YEARS' WAR (1756–1763)

The Treaty of Aix-la-Chapelle said nothing about the West Indian issues over which Britain had gone to war. This curious fact suggests that the treaty marked not a genuine settlement but a truce as far as Britain was concerned. The rivalry for empire between Britain and France intensified after 1748. In particular, British colonists in North America clashed with Frenchmen throughout the next seven years. The British colonists along the Atlantic seaboard simply wanted to push to the interior in order to claim land for commercial purposes. Two Virginia land companies, for example, sought to claim large tracts in the Ohio Valley. But, as they had long expected, the colonists ran into French opposition. Though there were only about seventy-five thousand French settlers in North America, they had established forts and trading posts along the St. Lawrence, through the Great Lakes, and down the Mississippi. Now the French sought to extend their lucrative fur trade with the Indians by seizing control of the Ohio Valley. Skirmishes between British and French colonists resulted.

In 1754, several militia companies from Virginia led by George Washington were defeated by the French and their Indian allies near what is now Pittsburgh. In a fateful and unprecedented decision, the British government dispatched regular army troops under General Braddock to aid the Virginians and directed the navy to prevent France from reinforcing their Canadian garrison. The British navy began capturing French merchant vessels, but Braddock's little army was ambushed and defeated in July 1755. The British now felt they could not turn back; in May 1756 they declared war.

The events of 1755 in America sent the British and French scrambling for allies in Europe. The Treaty of Aix-la-Chapelle had not reconciled Prussia and Austria, who had been combatants in the War of Austrian Succession (in which Britain had become involved through the War of Jenkins' Ear with Spain). Britain traditionally supported Austria as a counterweight to France, but this time the British government thought than an alliance with Prussia would best protect Hanover and check the French; meanwhile the Austrians settled into an alliance with France and Russia. The Anglo-French colonial war that broke out in 1755 thus expanded into a general European struggle, and because the war was fought simultaneously in Europe, Asia, and the Americas, it was in fact the first world war.

At first the war went disastrously for the British, and parliamentary and public opinion alike demanded that Pitt, who had caught the imagination of the country with his imperial vision and blue-water strategy (fighting mainly on the oceans) be given control of the government. Horace Walpole wrote:

> Minorca is gone, Oswego gone. The nation is in a ferment. Instructions from counties, boroughs, especially the City of London, in the style of 1642 . . . all these tell Pitt he may command such numbers without doors as may make majorities within the House tremble.

George II loathed Pitt because he believed that Pitt had insulted Hanover by his remarks about that "despicable electorate." But in 1757, George was forced to give way. Pitt came to power on a wave of supreme confidence: "I know that I can save this country and that no one else can."

Once in office, Pitt concentrated all his prodigious energy on the war effort. Recognizing that the nature of the war demanded simultaneous success on the Continent and in the colonies—otherwise, the winnings in one theater would have to be traded to compensate for losses in the other—Pitt gave up his extreme maritime strategy. Britain increased its own army to more than fifty thousand men, subsidized Prussia with £670,000 a year for four years, and paid for large numbers of German mercenaries as well. Largely because of the military genius of the Prussian king, Frederick the Great, the allied armies fought the French and Austrians to a standstill. Pitt in fact claimed that Canada was won for Britain in Germany.

Pitt did not neglect the war overseas, for he was able to see the war effort as a whole. The British navy imposed a close blockade on the French coast, turned the Mediterranean into a "British lake," and fended off French invasion of England by crushing the French fleet at Quiberon Bay in 1759. Combined army and navy forces plundered French islands in the West Indies. In North America, Pitt directed a three-pronged offensive against New France: one force retook Louisbourg and proceeded up the St. Lawrence to Quebec, which fell to General Wolfe in 1759; a

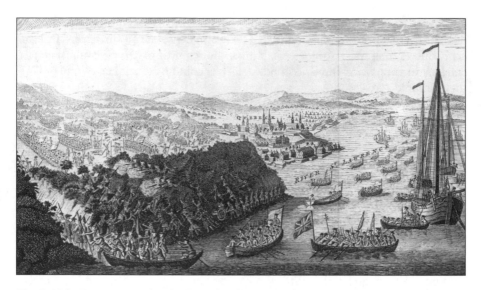

The British Victory at Quebec (1759). *This illustration from the* London Magazine *shows the British troops (Scottish Highlanders) under General Wolfe making their way up a hidden path to the Plains of Abraham above Quebec, where they defeated French forces under General Montcalm. Though Wolfe was mortally wounded, the battle was a key to British supremacy in North America*

second moved north along Lake Champlain to attack Montreal; and a third marched west to take Fort Niagara and Fort Frontenac on Lake Ontario. All three campaigns were successful. By 1760, the British controlled all of North America east of the Mississippi.

Pitt refused to commit regular British forces to the struggle in India. He did increase the size of the British navy in the Indian Ocean so as to equal the French; otherwise, he left the East India Company on its own. "John Company," as it was called, proved equal to the task. Conflict between the East India Company and its French rival had not stopped at the end of the War of Austrian Succession in 1748. The two companies struggled for influence in south-central and southeastern India. In 1749 both put up rival Indian candidates for rule in the Carnatic (the area inland from Madras). The British won, thanks to the heroic efforts of a small Anglo-Indian army led by a twenty-five-year-old clerk named Robert Clive, a man who was like Pitt in many ways—depressive but gifted, ambitious, and energetic. Pitt rightly called him a "heaven-born general."

In the 1750s the British and French East India Companies began to clash in an even wealthier region, Bengal, with its great trading city, Calcutta. The nawab (prince) of Bengal died in 1756 and was succeeded by one Siraj-ud-Daula, who soon marched on the fat British post in Calcutta with a massive army. The nawab's troops plundered Calcutta and imprisoned the British survivors in a miserable cell later called "the Black Hole of Calcutta." About one hundred people died. The Company sent Clive with a force of three thousand men to relieve Calcutta. Siraj-ud-Daula withdrew, but Clive elected to join an Indian conspiracy against him. In June 1757, Clive led his small force of about one thousand Europeans and two thousand Indian sepoys against Siraj-ud-Daula's sixty thousand at the Battle of Plassey. Astonishingly, Clive's minuscule army won, probably because it was well disciplined in the European style of drill. Bengal fell to the Company, which now installed its own puppet as nawab. Indian politicians and bankers showered money on Clive, who returned to England with £234,000 in cash plus rentals worth £27,000 a year. Given the possibilities for riches in India, it was not so much. "By God," Clive later testified, "I stand amazed at my own moderation."

Politics in India thus proved even more profitable to the Company than trade; consequently, the Company made politics its business. Company officials in Bengal made prodigious sums by replacing one nawab after another, for each time they threw out a native governor, hopeful political and commercial Bengalese came forward with magnificent bribes and gifts. Then, in 1760–1761, the Company succeeded in driving the French out of southern India. By 1763, the East India Company, without ever really meaning to, had become a major political power in India, and the Moghul emperors were too weak to stop them.

THE PRIZES OF VICTORY

Given the impressive string of British victories on sea and land in all major theaters of the Seven Years' War, one would think that Pitt could have remained prime minister as long as he wished and that the British would proceed to crush France once and for all. Neither was to be the case. Pitt in fact did want to extend the war in a preemptive strike on the Spanish Empire, but his grandiose plans alarmed the more cautious members of the cabinet. By 1760, the French were already making overtures for peace. Meanwhile, when George II died in 1760, Pitt lost a major pillar of support. In October 1761, Pitt resigned.

Ironically, the war with Spain came anyway, and in 1762 the British took Havana and Manila. The new king, George III, cared less about Hanover than had his predecessors. "I glory in the name of Briton," he declared. Thus he and his favorite, Lord Bute, were willing to stop the subsidy to Prussia and reach an agreement with France. In 1763, the Peace of Paris was signed. In the House of Commons, an ill and shaky Pitt denounced the treaty as a surrender of the fruits of victory, but the Commons (and the public) were weary of taxes and accepted it. In fact, the British did very well out of the treaty, winning back Minorca from France, and retaining Grenada, Domenica, St. Vincent, and Tobago in the West Indies; Canada, Cape Breton Island, Florida, and all of North America east of the Mississippi River; Senegal in Africa; and the East India Company's winnings in Bengal. Britain thus emerged as the most powerful commercial, colonial, and naval country on earth—a startling development from the small, bitterly divided state of the mid-seventeenth century.

Were these prizes worth the cost of seven years (nine, counting the skirmishes of 1754–1755) of war? No one asked the ordinary British and colonial soldiers and sailors who shed their blood in battles around the globe. By custom, the soldiers in a victorious army were allowed to loot the enemy dead and wounded on the battlefield, and sailors were given a share in the spoils of captured "prize" ships, but the surviving evidence does not say whether they regarded these rewards and the simple pleasures of triumph as sufficient recompense for years of weary marching, harsh discipline, and privation, as well as moments of sheer terror and suffering. No doubt colonial North American soldiers, particularly those in the militia, found the removal of danger from the French and Indian forces on the northern and western frontiers very satisfying. Britons of the ruling elite and the mercantile classes not only benefitted from colonial investments but also took pride in Britain's imperial identity. For the common farmer or laborer of the British Isles, however, the war in the short run made little difference. To be sure, excise taxes and land taxes were high (four shillings to the pound for landowners); thus, consumer prices went up and some landlords may have raised their rents as a result. As we saw in Chapter 3, the state apparatus grew because of the need to collect taxes and supply the army and navy. Otherwise, for the vast majority of Britons the most important facts for the short term were that no battles were fought on British soil and that agricultural life went on as usual.

In the long run, however, the Seven Years' War, like all those since 1689, contributed to British economic development. Some economic historians have argued that Britain's entry into industrialization would have occurred sooner had these wars not happened. Britons of the day did not think so. To be sure, many enlightened philosophers like Adam Smith believed that trade and wealth grew best in the soil of peace. But most Britons, landowners and commercial men alike, thought that success in war had increased national prosperity. They were probably right, especially in the case of the Seven Years' War. The war interfered very little with trade, and it stimulated many industries associated with shipbuilding, weapons manufacturing, and military supply. Given the limited nature of eighteenth-century warfare, defeat (or a refusal to fight) would probably not have meant foreign rule in the British Isles. The loss of the American colonies in 1783 was to cause no damage to British trade over the Atlantic. Nevertheless, a loss in the Seven Years' War would have deprived the British of many of the possessions that made Britain a great maritime and colonial power and fueled the commercial sector of the economy. Perhaps that was reward enough.

Suggested Reading

Anderson, Fred, *Crucible of War: The Seven Years' War and the Fate of Empire in British North America, 1754–1766* (London: Faber, 2000).

Bayly, C. A., *Imperial Meridian: The British Empire and the World, 1780–1830* (New York: Longman, 1989).

Bence-Jones, Mark, *Clive of India* (London: Constable, 1974).

Black, Jeremy, *British Foreign Policy in the Age of Walpole* (Edinburgh: J. Donald, 1985).

———, *The British Seaborne Empire* (New Haven: Yale University Press, 2004).

———, *Eighteenth-Century Britain, 1688–1783* (New York: Palgrave, 2001).

Brewer, John, *The Sinews of Power: War, Money, and the English State, 1688–1783* (New York: Knopf, 1989).

Cain, P .J, and A. G. Hopkins, *British Imperialism: Innovation and Expansion* (London: Longman, 1993).

Dalley, Jan, *The Black Hole: Money, Myth and Indian Empire* (New York: Viking, 2006).

Daunton, Martin, and Rick Halpern, eds., *Empire and Others: British Encounters with Indigenous Peoples* (Philadelphia: University of Pennsylvania Press, 1999).

Davis, David Brion, *Inhuman Bondage: The Rise and Fall of Slavery in the New World* (Oxford: Oxford University Press, 2006).

Fischer, David Hackett, *Albion's Seed* (New York: Oxford University Press, 1982).

Gauci, Perry, *The Politics of Trade: The Overseas Merchant in State and Society, 1660–1720* (New York: Oxford University Press, 2001).

Greene, Jack P., and J. R. Pole, eds., *Colonial British America* (Baltimore: Johns Hopkins University Press, 1984).

Howard, Michael, *War in European History* (New York: Oxford University Press, 1976).

Kennedy, Paul M., *The Rise and Fall of British Naval Mastery* (London: A. Lane, 1976).

Lloyd, T. O., *The British Empire, 1558–1995*, 2nd ed. (New York: Oxford University Press, 1996).

Marshall, P. J., ed., *The Oxford History of the British Empire: The Eighteenth Century* (New York: Oxford University Press, 1998).

Mason, Philip, *A Matter of Honour: An Account of the Indian Army: Its Officers and Men* (London: Cape, 1974).

McKay, Derek, and H. M. Scott, *The Rise of the Great Powers, 1648–1815* (New York: Longman, 1983).

Moon, Penderel, *The British Conquest and Dominion of India* (London: Gerald Duckworth, 1989).

Peckham, Howard, *The Colonial Wars, 1689–1762* (Chicago: University of Chicago Press, 1969).

Williams, Basil, *The Life of William Pitt, Earl of Chatham*, 2 vols. (New York: Longman, 1914).

Wilson, Kathleen, *The Island Race: Englishness, Empire and Gender in the Eighteenth Century* (London: Routledge, 2003).

——, *The Sense of the People: Politics, Culture and Imperialism in England, 1715–1785* (New York: Oxford University Press, 1995).

Woloch, Isser, *Eighteenth-Century Europe: Tradition and Progress, 1715–1789* (New York: Norton, 1982).

Part II

The Age of Revolutions

1763–1815

Chapter 8

The Crisis of Empire, 1763–1783

No sooner had the British attained the heights of imperial power than they were beset by a series of major revolutions—colonial, economic, social, and political. Thus the fifty years after 1763 constituted an age of crisis, a time when British industry was transformed, the society restructured, and the nation locked in a colossal struggle against the French Revolution. Even the religious temper and intellectual outlook of Britain were radically altered. It is a tribute to the stability and strength of eighteenth-century foundations—not least the landowners' regime—that Britain was able to weather these shocks without completely collapsing.

The first of these great crises came in the imperial realm. The British lost the American colonies they had fought with such determination to win. In the long discussions leading to the Treaty of Paris (1763), the British government chose to keep all of North America at the expense of advancing British interests in the West Indies. They consciously ranked the American colonies at the very top of their imperial plans. Yet it was precisely these colonies—the "most English" of all British possessions—that broke away. How this happened and how it might have been avoided are questions that have intrigued students of history ever since. In retrospect, two things seem certain: first, the Americans insisted almost to the end that all they wanted were the rights of Englishmen, and second, the British contributed mightily to the outcome, less by asserting despotic authority than by political insensitivity, a failure of imagination, and military blundering.

GEORGE III AND THE POLITICIANS

The failure to retain the American colonies was, therefore, a *political* failure, for which both the British political system itself and the politicians who ran it shared the blame. At the center of the system after 1763 was the king, George III, who played a bigger political role than either of his Hanoverian predecessors. For many years, both patriotic American historians and their liberal British colleagues believed that George III drove the American colonies out of the Empire by trying to make himself a despot—in other words that George III attempted to arrogate all power unto himself and thus to undo the events of 1688 and the Revolution Settlement. More recent and exhaustive research, however, supports a more ironic interpretation of George III and his behavior. Far from being a tyrant, George III

George III in Coronation Robes, *by Allan Ramsay. The famous Scottish portraitist painted George III in his most elegant ceremonial costume, making the king appear rather grander than he actually was.*

was a thoroughgoing Whig in his constitutional views. What he insisted on was the sovereignty of Parliament within a balanced constitution, and his obstinacy on that score constituted his contribution to the rupture with the American colonies.

George III was one of the most pathetic figures in modern British history. He was not up to the massive crises that Britain faced during his long reign (1760–1820), and from 1788 on he periodically suffered from severe mental imbalance caused by the disease porphyria. He spent the last ten years of his life in a state of pitiable madness, often confined in a straitjacket. He was not insane at the time of the American crisis, however. Born in 1738, George III was only twenty-two when he succeeded to the throne, and he was emotionally and intellectually immature. His father, Frederick, the Prince of Wales, loathed King George II, and the feeling was mutual. Frederick and his advisers believed that George II had been duped and reduced to puppet status by wily politicians like Pelham and Newcastle. Although Frederick died in 1751, he passed on these semiconspiratorial views to his son

George. The young prince grew up in a lonely and stifling atmosphere. He was of average intelligence but was diffident, shy, lethargic, and awkward.

The dominant figure in George's early life was the earl of Bute, a Scottish nobleman who was George's tutor and his mother's adviser. Bute clearly became a beloved father figure for the young Prince of Wales. Bute was learned in a bookish way, elegant, polished, and ambitious. That he won the task of teaching George how to be king proved unfortunate, since beneath Bute's arrogant exterior there lay only cleverness but no wisdom. George became completely dependent on Bute, and Bute reinforced the view that George II was caught in the web of the politicians. The Prince of Wales grew up determined to rise above the "corruption" that typified Augustan politics, to free the Crown of political entanglements, and to exemplify virtue and morality. He would rule "above party." There was in these intentions a good deal of priggish self-righteousness but no tyrannical leanings. "The pride," he wrote in a youthful essay, "the glory of Britain and the direct end of its constitution, is political liberty." In short, George accepted fully the Glorious Revolution and the supremacy of Parliament.

When George III became king in 1760, he felt he desperately needed Bute beside him. He hated the cabinet of the moment, including Prime Minister Pitt, whom George suspected of having betrayed his beloved father, the late Frederick. George made it clear that Bute spoke for him and that Bute would stand first among his ministers: "Whoever speaks against My Lord Bute speaks against me." As we have seen, Pitt resigned in 1761, and Bute became first lord of the Treasury (prime minister), though he had no claim to high office other than being the king's favorite.

Disgruntled Whig politicos interpreted the king's support for Bute as evidence that the king and Bute were subverting the constitution by restoring the royal prerogative. Such rhetoric had long been the resort of oppositional politicians of the Tory and Country Whig types. As we will see, the rhetoric found acceptance in America. Now three other factors seemed to give substance to the rhetoric. One was that Bute was not tough or smart enough for the job of prime minister and soon resigned the office; yet he wanted to retain his personal influence with the king and thus to exercise power without responsibility. Many people believed—falsely—that Bute's influence depended on illicit relations with George III's mother.

A second factor was that George III, under Bute's tutelage, did wish to rise above party—indeed, to put an end to party divisions, which he called "faction." Hence George in effect adopted old-fashioned "Country party" ideology and accepted Tories back into the pale of court and office. This meant that George was adopting Whig *theory* but not Whig *practice*, which were two very different things. The Whigs who had run the political machine since Walpole's day claimed that George was in fact restoring Tory/Stuart ideas from before 1688.

Whig propaganda against George and the supposed backstairs illegitimate power of Bute became intense. Various proposals to limit the power of the Crown— to eliminate placemen from the House of Commons, for instance, or to abolish sinecures (jobs without real work attached) in the gift of the Crown—gained fairly widespread approval. The best example of Whig criticism of George III was Edmund Burke's *Thoughts on the Cause of the Present Discontents* (1770). Burke, an emigré Irish intellectual, was the client of a Whig magnate, the marquess of Rockingham. He argued that in trying to rule without party, the king was substituting personal rule and royal influence for the proper supremacy of the House of Commons. To Burke, parties were not mere factions seeking office but bodies of men "united for promoting by their joint endeavours the national interest upon some particular principle in which they are all agreed." This noble idea became the classic definition of political parties in the nineteenth century, but it was not an accurate description of "party" in the eighteenth century. It was only a sublime rationalization of Whig self-interest and quest for office and power. In fact, George III had better claims to constitutionality than did Burke and the Rockingham Whigs. Yet in this case, as in most politics, what people believed was more important than the facts.

JOHN WILKES AND POPULAR POLITICS

The third factor leading people to suspect George III of working to establish royal tyranny was one that had great impact on colonial American political consciousness—the affair of John Wilkes. More than any other individual of eighteenth-century Britain, Wilkes challenged the assumption that the populace should be excluded from the legitimate political system. He was a very unlikely radical hero. The son of a rich London brewer, Wilkes was a debauched spendthrift who got by on his audaciousness, wit, and charm. Though he was startlingly ugly, he could, as he said, talk away his looks in half an hour. He was ambitious to cut a figure in the world of the governing elite. By spending thousands of pounds in the ways customary to Augustan politics, Wilkes got himself elected to Parliament, but soon gambled and drank away the rest of his (and his wife's) fortune. To make ends meet, he became a journalist, dependent on the patronage of the Whig grandee, Lord Temple. Then his political troubles and triumphs began.

Wilkes's paper, the *North Briton*, was a flashy, aggressive critic of Bute's government and that of his successor, George Grenville. In the famous Number 45 of the *North Briton*, Wilkes launched a fierce attack on the king's speech of 1763 (the policy statement of the government of the day that opens the annual session of Parliament) and the terms of the Treaty of Paris. Wilkes not only described the king's ministers as "tools of despotism and corruption" but seemed to call the king a liar. The prime minister of the moment, George Grenville, thought that this was seditious libel and issued a general warrant for the arrest of "the authors, printers, and publishers" of the *North Briton*. Wilkes was arrested, but he fought the charges on grounds that general warrants (which specified no names and therefore could be used to arrest any troublemaker) were illegal. Moreover, Wilkes deliberately identified himself with the ordinary citizen by claiming that his arrest threatened the liberty "of all the middling and inferior sort of people who stand most in need of protection."

John Wilkes, *by William Hogarth (1763). The great caricaturist portrayed Wilkes, the popular political gadfly, in his most devilish aspect.*

Wilkes won his case and became a popular champion of civil liberties as well. But the Wilkes affair had only just begun. In a triumphant mood, he republished Number 45. This enraged the House of Commons, which now expelled him. Wounded in a duel and intimidated by government pressure, Wilkes fled to Paris, but he was prosecuted and outlawed in absentia for having published an indecent satire called *Essay on Woman*. In 1768, however, Wilkes, dogged by his creditors in France, returned to England and stood for Parliament in Middlesex. This constituency in North London was one of the few with a broad electorate. Wilke's candidacy was popular with the artisans and shopkeepers (as well as with the mobs of nonvoters) of London and of the provincial cities as well. He was elected but denied his seat by the House of Commons and then imprisoned on the old charge of seditious libel. Well-to-do merchants and workmen alike rallied to his cause, and while in prison he was reelected by the Middlesex voters two more times, only to be expelled by the House of Commons. Finally, after a third reelection, the Commons simply declared the election of the government-supported candidate, who actually had lost miserably to Wilkes.

By then the radical Wilkesite movement was well under way. Everywhere the slogans "Wilkes and Liberty" or simply "45" were chalked on walls or paraded on banners. Provincial newspapers speaking for the middling and lower ranks still excluded from the vote brimmed over with stories about Wilkes and defenses of his cause. Affluent business and professional men, and even some country gentlemen, in 1769 founded the Society of Supporters of the Bill of Rights. Initially it was chartered to pay Wilkes's debts, but it later advocated a program of reform including both civil liberties and political change. For the first time in England there was a nationwide popular political movement. It was antiaristocratic and civil libertarian in sentiment, for Wilkes had challenged general warrants and asserted freedom of the press. But the Wilkesite movement also advocated parliamentary reform: the right of a constituency to send to Parliament anyone they pleased, the removal of government officeholders from the House of Commons, more frequent elections, and "more equal representation" in the sense of disqualifying rotten boroughs in order to give representation to the large cities. Implicit in all these ideas was a new and different concept of parliamentary membership—that is, that an M.P. ought to *represent* (consciously speak for) his constituents. The enormity of this claim was clear to the elite. As one M.P. complained, "Such is the levelling principle that has gone forth, that the people imagine that they themselves should be judges over us."

Wilkes in 1774 was again elected to Parliament and allowed to take his seat. This helped defuse the radical bomb. Wilkes did not prove to be a vigorous reform M.P. and referred to himself as "an exhausted volcano," although he did insist on the right of newspapers to publish accounts of parliamentary proceedings. George III had once called him "that devil Wilkes" but now was surprised to find him a gentleman. However, the effect of the Wilkes affair on British politics had been profound, partly because it was a transitional movement between the riotous popular politics of eighteenth-century England and the more focused and better-organized mass politics of nineteenth-century Britain, and not least because many American politicians followed the case closely and became enthusiastic Wilkesites.

BRITONS INTO AMERICANS

The sympathy of British colonists in North America for Wilkes was but one of many pieces of evidence indicating that they were, in ways mostly unnoticed, becoming a people less British and more American. The conscious identity of the colonists clearly remained British until July 1776, but the Wilkesite seeds fell onto the soil of a political culture that already was subtly different from the dominant culture in Britain. The slow growth of a new national identity of America was so complex, and the emotional and mental roots of most colonists so firmly planted in Britain, that the discovery of their differentness in the heat of events after 1763 came as a disagreeable surprise to people on both sides of the Atlantic. Unless this growth is understood, the violence of American reaction to post-1763 imperial policies and the rapid growth of the independence movement must remain a mystery.

The growth of American identity was not a steady linear development. Broadly speaking, the earliest English settlers in America retained close personal and economic ties to England. Then, in the course of the seventeenth century, as a result of coping with wilderness conditions in isolation from the Mother Country, colonial cultures in North America began to grow apart from Britain. With the taming of the coastal (or tidewater) areas and the original river valley settlements, however, came an economic and social stability and a relative ease of intercourse with England that tended to anglicize the colonies. The ideas of the Enlightenment, which spread to North America, incorporated colonial high culture into the British world. The great evangelical religious revival of the early eighteenth century, called the "Great Awakening" in the colonies, did the same for popular religion. Perhaps more important, the tremendous sale of English consumer goods in America anglicized colonial material culture. As one historian, T. H. Breen, has put it, "Staffordshire china replaced crude earthenware; imported cloth replaced homespun." In these ways, the colonies were never so English as in the third quarter of the eighteenth century.

Nevertheless, there were some important differences between the colonists in North America and the English at home. For one thing, by the 1760s there were substantial numbers of people in America who were not English by origin or descent. By 1775, probably 20 percent of the 2.5 million people in the colonies were of African origin or descent. Another 10 percent were Scotch-Irish immigrants from Ulster, and another 9 percent were Germans. There were also thousands of Scots, Dutch, French Huguenots, Swedes, and other national groups.

Moreover, it is important to remember that many of the original English colonists were religious refugees who had deliberately rejected England. The Pilgrims, for instance, had sought to found a utopia of pure, simple piety separate from the corrupting power and wealth of England. The Puritans had rejected the English state in order to establish perfect Calvinist communities that would stand as cities of righteousness for all the world to follow. Neither ideal was sustainable over the long haul, but the sense implicit in both, that the colonization of America was the fulfillment of God's plan, sounded chords that would resonate in the emerging American identity. In the eighteenth century, as even today, there was a sense that America had a special place in the unfolding of human events.

There were differences, mostly unremarked, between English and American social structures as well. As has been noted in Chapter 7, the English social hierarchy was not completely replicated in the colonies because the very top and bottom ranks did not cross the ocean. To be sure, colonial elites did form during the 1700s, and most of their members aped English ways. Their efforts to make themselves into English-style aristocrats and gentry were not very successful, however. The colonial "aristocracy" was based on money alone, and most of the families had made their fortunes so recently that the hard work showed. They lacked the polish and time-honored traditions that served as the emblems of social distinction in England. Further, the deference that English landed families enjoyed and that colonial elites desired simply was not forthcoming from the ordinary colonist. The ready availability of land and the rigors of the frontier life bred a sense of independence that fitted poorly into a hierarchical social structure. Even in the southern colonies, where the planters liked to think of themselves as landed gentry, the resemblance to English gentlemen was strained: the planters, after all, were slave-owners and hard-pressed agricultural businessmen who treated their slaves more like industrial workers than tenant farmers or farm laborers protected to a degree by custom and paternalism.

Some recognition of such differences began to be articulated during the colonial wars, when colonial troops came into contact with the British army. Especially during the Seven Years' War (called the French and Indian War in the colonies), feelings of dissimilarity between themselves and the British became widespread among American militiamen. More than twenty thousand colonists served during the war, many of them in operations with regular British army units. Neither side liked what it saw. The British thought the colonials were ill-disciplined, unreliable, and incapable of executing a sustained campaign. The Americans found the British officers to be impenetrably arrogant and inflexible and the troops to be servile and brutalized.

The differences between British and American governmental institutions went largely unrecognized because most colonists believed that colonial political arrangements duplicated in miniature the British constitution. Yet there were differences. The colonial governors had more formal powers than did the king at home—they could, for example, dismiss judges at will and dissolve or delay sessions of the colonial assemblies—but much less informal power in the shape of patronage and influence. More important, the assemblies in the American colonies more directly represented their constituents than did the House of Commons. The colonies had no rotten boroughs. In New England, town meetings customarily instructed their representatives about the policies they should pursue. Because landownership was so widespread in America, the ordinary forty-shilling freehold franchise gave the vote to 50 to 75 percent of the adult male population. The sense of independence characteristic of colonial British American society was thus reflected in colonial politics.

Finally, there developed in the thirteen colonies a distinctive political ideology. The colonial self-image of simplicity and uncorrupted innocence inclined the Americans to accept Lockean political theory in pure form. Hence the "opposition" or "Country" philosophy, the stance of a minority in Britain, became the dominant ideology in America. The colonists believed in natural, unalienable rights; in the concept of an original social contract; in government by consent of the governed; and in the necessity of a balance in the constitution to protect liberty. Like British Country oppositional publicists such as John Trenchard (d. 1723), Thomas Gordon (d. 1750), and Viscount Bolingbroke (d. 1751), Americans thought that a virtuous citizenry was necessary to maintain the constitutional balance. In the 1740s and 1750s, some colonial visitors to Britain began to believe that political corruption was ruining the ideal British constitution, and so threatening liberty. John Dickinson of Pennsylvania wrote of the English election of 1754: "Bribery is so common that it is thought there is not a borough where it is not practiced. . . . It is grown a vice here to be virtuous." It was this prevailing Country ideology that led British Americans to understand imperial events after 1763 as a conspiracy to subvert the British constitution and destroy their liberty.

TIGHTENING THE EMPIRE

It would be a mistake, however, to say that the slow development of a colonial self-identity led inevitably to independence and war. The imperial crisis that began in 1763 and ended in 1776 should have been manageable if the British had shown some imagination and flexibility. An arrangement giving the colonies *some* kind of home rule—provincial autonomy under Parliament and/or the Crown—was a distinct possibility even after the colonials had taken up arms. How different the history of the modern world would have been if some such solution had been found! But the course of events after 1763 led the British government to think that the very foundation of the Empire and the sovereignty of Parliament were being challenged and the colonials to think that their cherished British liberties were being denied. Once locked into these positions, the two sides could find no compromise.

After the Peace of 1763, the British quite reasonably and naturally took up the problem of how to manage their vastly expanded empire. During the first half of the eighteenth century, British policy toward the North American colonies had been one of "benign neglect." Now, however, the king and his ministers believed that a degree of rationalization was in order so that the expense of maintaining the colonies would not cancel their positive value to Britain.

The policies that resulted from this concern bore the imprint of George Grenville, who had succeeded the egregious Bute as the king's chief minister. Grenville was an able man in a plodding sort of way. George III heartily disliked him: "That gentleman's opinions are seldom formed from any other motives than such as may be expected to originate in the mind of a clerk in a counting house." Like most British politicians, Grenville knew little about American attitudes and traditions. He began tightening the lines of imperial rule by ordering customs officials to enforce the various laws regulating colonial trade. Next, by the Proclamation of 1763, Grenville set the western limit of British settlement at the Appalachian mountains, beyond which the Mother Country would not defend American settlers. By this act, he hoped to keep down the cost of the Empire, for he knew that colonial expansion into the vast territory between the Appalachians and the Mississippi would cause endless trouble with the Indians. Defense of the region would require many thousands of regular army troops and expenditures far beyond what the British taxpayer would tolerate.

The British government thought that taxes at home already stretched public support to the limit. The Seven Years' War had increased the national debt to nearly £140 million. Grenville did not seek to have the Americans pay any of the annual debt charge, but he did think it reasonable for them to help pay for their own defense, namely for the ten thousand redcoats now left in America. He might simply have imposed a quota on each colony and let them raise the money as they pleased, but such a "requisition" system had not worked during the war. Thus Grenville chose to treat the colonies as a single unit and tax them directly. By the Sugar Act of 1764, Parliament reduced the duty on foreign molasses imported into the colonies, with the view of actually collecting the smaller duty. By the Stamp Act of 1765, the government imposed fees on legal papers, newspapers, customs documents, diplomas, advertisements, and the like.

Grenville's policies were logical, but they ignored colonial opinion. The colonists erupted in protest to the point that war almost broke out in 1765–1766. The land-hungry colonists were unhappy about the Proclamation Line, and they complained loudly that the Sugar Act took away their property (that is, money) without their consent. They were even angrier about the Stamp Act. Newspapers lashed out in editorials and letters of protest; riots flared all along the Atlantic seaboard. Crowds harassed stamp officials and attacked their homes and offices. In most towns, colonials formed groups called "the Sons of Liberty" to defy the tax. Merchants organized a boycott of British goods.

In their protests, the Americans did not bother with the details of the Stamp Act but went directly to the fundamental issue of constitutional rights. This is what made their defiance of the law so alarming to the British and inspired the official British response to be so inflexible. Against the colonial cries of "no taxation without representation," the British argued that the colonies *were* represented in Parliament, not directly but *virtually*. Just as the people of Manchester or Birmingham, who sent no members to Parliament, were yet represented there, so were the people of America, because each M.P., as one writer put it, "sits in the House not as a Representative of his own Constituents, but as one of that august Assembly by which all the Commons of Great Britain are represented." Moreover, when the colonists rejected the will of Parliament, they denied the most crucial element of the British constitution—the sovereignty of Parliament. Without that principle, British liberties would collapse.

The colonists readily agreed that British *rights* reached across the Atlantic to the New World, but they denied that British *jurisdiction* did. From their beginnings, the Americans contended, the colonies had borne the responsibility and right of legislating for themselves. Parliament might regulate imperial trade for the benefit of the Empire, but to *tax* the colonists denied the principles of 1688 and laid the basis for the destruction of colonial liberty. They dismissed as ridiculous the claims that the colonies enjoyed any kind of representation in Parliament. American traditions of voting and representation were straightforward and direct: all freeholders voted for representatives in the colonial assemblies, which were thereby empowered to tax. But they were not represented in Parliament in any sense, nor did they ask to be. The Americans preferred their own assemblies, which would be more responsive to their needs than a Parliament 3,000 miles away in London and in which the few American M.P.s would be as ineffective as the Scottish representatives after 1707.

Grenville possibly would have backed up the Stamp Act by force, but in 1766 he fell from office after a personal dispute with George III. Into power came a ministry of "old"—that is, mainstream—Whigs led by the marquess of Rockingham. They sought to embarrass Grenville and placate commercial interests in Britain who were hurt by the American boycott by repealing the Stamp Act. They undid much of the good will they thus generated by passing a Declaratory Act, which insisted that Parliament did in fact have the authority of legislating for the colonies. Even Pitt, who had supported the American protests against the Stamp Act, agreed with the Declaratory Act. Such was the limit that even sympathetic British politicians would go: all Britons agreed that the principle of parliamentary sovereignty over every part of the Empire must be defended.

Despite its accomplishments, the Rockingham ministry lacked the confidence of both king and Commons, and it inevitably fell from office later in 1766. It was succeeded by a government formed by Pitt (now elevated to the peerage as earl of Chatham),who could conceivably have constructed a lasting accommodation with the colonies. But Chatham's mental stability gave out in 1767, and the lead was taken by his chancellor of the Exchequer, Charles Townshend, who proceeded to reverse Chatham's policy of reconciliation with America. Townshend, a brilliant but politically obtuse man, wrongly believed that the colonies would not object to external taxation. Thus he sought to relieve Britain's financial troubles, and to free the colonial governors from their dependence on their assemblies at the same time, by laying duties on the importation into the colonies of glass, lead, paints, paper, and tea. The revenue would be used to pay the salaries of the governors and other colonial officials.

Townshend's grievous mistake in judgment roused colonial opposition that was as fierce and effective as the earlier one against the Stamp Act. The Americans revived their arguments about fundamental rights and renewed the boycott of British goods. Worse, the British officials sent to America to collect the Townshend duties behaved little better than rapacious racketeers. Confrontation between bureaucrats and protesters became very intense. Townshend died later in 1767, and because an insignificant amount of revenue was actually collected, Parliament backed away. In 1770, the Townshend duties were repealed, except for one on tea, which was retained as a symbol of British authority.

The repeal of the Townshend duties did little to dissipate the mistrust between Parliament and the colonials. The British government sent troops to Boston to help enforce the Townshend duties, and the colonists interpreted this action as another step in the campaign to deprive them of their liberty. The Wilkesite affair, which the colonists watched closely, confirmed their suspicions. At home, incidents between the army and the citizens of Boston resulted, the worst being the so-called Boston Massacre of 1770, when five colonials were killed. In 1772, after further clashes between American merchants and British revenue collectors, the colonies began to set up "Committees of Correspondence" to coordinate their opposition. In 1773, Parliament made the matter worse by its attempt to help the financially troubled East India Company. The Company was granted the right to sell tea in America at a cut rate and without dealing through colonial merchants. People in all the colonies resisted what they saw as a British conspiracy to establish a monopoly, and in Boston protesters dumped the tea into the harbor. Parliament responded with a number of laws punishing Boston, which only roused the solidarity of other colonies with their Massachusetts neighbor.

By this point, a growing body of Americans was reacting to every move Parliament made in an almost paranoid fear of British "tyranny." Thomas Jefferson, for instance, claimed that the British imperial reforms amounted to "a deliberate, systematical plan of reducing us to slavery." In June 1774, with a ghastly sense of timing, Parliament aggravated these suspicions by passing the Quebec Act. This set up a civil government with only an appointed council, gave special recognition to Roman Catholicism, and extended the boundary of the former French province into the Ohio Valley. The Americans saw the Quebec Act as an obvious attempt to frustrate American expansion to the West, to sponsor the spread of popery, and to establish nonrepresentative colonial institutions to boot. Coupled with the "Coercive Acts" on Boston, the Quebec Act stood as tyranny exposed. Representatives of twelve colonies gathered in Philadelphia to discuss collective efforts to defend colonial rights. Independence was still too extreme a measure for them, but probably a majority agreed with Jefferson that Parliament had no sovereignty over the colonies even though the colonies and Britain were united under the Crown. Hence this Continental Congress rejected a plan suggested by Joseph Galloway, which would have established a united colonial government exercising "home rule" but subordinate in imperial affairs to Parliament. Perhaps something like "dominion status" (colonial authority under the Crown but not under Parliament) probably was still possible, but the British (including George III) were incapable of imagining such a solution. In their view, as the governor of Massachusetts said in 1772, "No line can be drawn between the supreme authority of parliament and the total independence of the colonies."

THE WAR FOR COLONIAL INDEPENDENCE

Given the determination of the king and his ministers to force the colonies to submit to the will of Parliament and given the resolve of many Americans to resist, violence was inevitable. In 1775, General Thomas Gage, governor of Massachusetts and commander of British forces of North America, decided to carry out a preemptive strike on the local militia by seizing the powder and shot they were storing in Concord. On the way, his troops were fired on by Massachusetts "minutemen" at Lexington and then suffered severe losses on the return march to Boston.

The outbreak of fighting radically altered the situation. When the Second Continental Congress gathered in May 1775, they had to conduct a revolution that already had started. Still, the Congress petitioned George III, asking that he redress their grievances and treat the colonial assemblies as co-equal with Parliament. George III, determined to protect the supremacy of Parliament, rejected this "olive branch" petition and declared the colonies to be in rebellion. Colonial opinion now swung sharply against him. In January 1776, colonial animus against the king was articulated and spread by Tom Paine's *Common Sense*, one of the most effective political tracts in the history of the English-speaking world. Paine, who had only emigrated to America from England in 1774, argued with telling simplicity and cogency that the colonies ought to break with Britain completely, and that meant breaking with the king as well as with Parliament. The American faith in monarchy, he wrote, was entirely unjustified, for the Crown itself stood as a principal source of arbitrary government. The law ought to be king in America, not the "royal brute of Britain." Paine's tract was crucial in turning the Americans into Republicans.

Finally, in July 1776, the Continental Congress adopted the Declaration of Independence, ironically one of the greatest documents of the British Enlightenment. It was a thoroughly Lockean piece of reasoning—a statement of natural rights philosophy that explained why the Americans believed that their consent to be governed had been violated and why they therefore dissolved the "original contract" of civil government with Britain. It explored, in short, a contradiction in standard Whig philosophy between the sovereignty of Parliament (which Britain chose) and consent of the governed (which America chose).

George III, his ministers, and a majority in Parliament all resolved to end the rebellion by force. Given this intention, the British should have waged the war with full commitment, energy, and ruthlessness, while holding out a constitutional compromise to woo colonial moderates. But they never understood either the extent of colonial opposition or the kind of war they faced. Moreover, they underestimated the staggering difficulty of coordinating and supplying military operations in hostile territory an ocean away. The British government thought that basically their role was to assist the loyal colonists (whose numbers they overestimated) to overcome the disloyal ones. In fact, though the British army (with German mercenaries) won many battles, colonial opposition sprang up again as soon as the army left a given locality. Thus the British never committed the number of troops necessary, and worse, they eventually lost their accustomed mastery of the seas.

British tactics were adequate, had they been executed with sufficient vigor and resources. At the outset, the British aimed sensibly enough at cutting New England off from the rest of the colonies. General William Howe's forces took New York in 1776, and in the following year, General Burgoyne moved south from Canada along the Hudson toward Albany. Howe should have pushed north from New York to link up with him, but he allowed himself to be diverted by Washington's Continental army and the prospect of capturing Philadelphia. Burgoyne found his army isolated and outnumbered near Saratoga, New York, where he surrendered.

The defeat at Saratoga proved doubly disastrous because it gave the French sufficient confidence in the Americans to ally with them and ended the continuing hope among some Britons that the colonies could ultimately be salvaged. Since 1763, the French had been anxious to restore their own prestige and reduce British power. The American war for independence gave the French a splendid opportunity. From 1778, therefore, the British faced a renewal of world war, struggling with France in the East Indies and in the West Indies as well as in America. In 1779, Spain joined the conflict against Britain, and in 1780 Britain had to declare war on

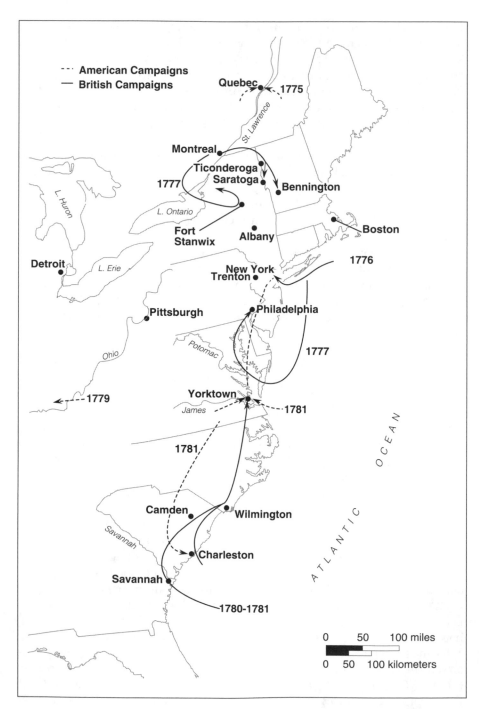

Military campaigns against the American colonists during the American Revolution

the Dutch in order to protect the Baltic trade. These developments drained British resources away from the war in America. The British government feared a French invasion of the British Isles and committed a large number of ships to the English channel. In 1778–1779, the British had to shift army and navy units away from America to the West Indies.

In 1780, the British effort in America fared better, as the army captured Georgia and South Carolina. Had the British commander in the South, earl Cornwallis, been able to launch an effective attack northward, he might have separated the southern colonies from the rest and then put down the rebellion in the mid-Atlantic region. But colonial guerrilla warfare harassed the British and Loyalist detachments in the South, and Cornwallis soon found himself in Virginia without adequate support and besieged by Washington. In 1781, a French fleet in the Chesapeake cut Cornwallis off from relief or retreat by sea, and Cornwallis surrendered.

By then the failure of the British government to conduct the war effectively had stimulated much opposition at home inside and outside Parliament. The chief minister, Lord North, had been in office since 1770 and was the first politician since Bute whom George III trusted. The two thought alike, and North was intelligent, witty, and an able public financier. Yet North was not a strong war minister, for he was indolent and lethargic. He was unable to weld the cabinet into a single unit, and even the two ministers in charge of the army and the navy pulled in different directions. North knew his own weaknesses and frequently begged George III to let him resign. But George III himself was facing the war with stubborn, if dull-witted, courage, and he insisted that North stay on. George's political activism only aggravated the sense among the opposition that he was imposing personal rule on the nation. Independent country gentlemen joined commercial men who were unhappy about the disturbance of trade to form a radical movement devoted to ending financial waste and war profiteering and to "restoring" the balance in the constitution. Certain Whig factions—the Rockingham and Chathamite interests—took up the related issues of peace and parliamentary reform. Finally, in 1782, a sufficient number of independent M.P.s joined the opposition to force North to resign and the king to accept a cabinet committed to peace.

THE AFTERMATH

The Treaty of Versailles (1783) that ended the war granted the American colonies independence and ceded to them all the land between the Appalachians and the Mississippi. This was a grievous loss to Britain—perhaps one-fifth of all the people in the Empire and a territory that was bound to grow in prosperity and trade. Otherwise, the British did fairly well in the treaty making. France was the biggest loser in the war. The British navy had reasserted its preeminence in the West Indies; consequently, the French won only a few West Indian islands, plus Dakar and Senegal in West Africa. Spain got Florida and Minorca, but Britain kept Gibraltar, Canada, and the Newfoundland fisheries. Most important, the British kept the trans-Appalachian west out of French hands. Further, though few expected it in 1783, British trade with America rebounded with amazing speed. By 1790, for instance, British exports to America exceeded prewar levels.

Nevertheless, from the British point of view, it obviously would have been better to keep the American colonies in the Empire. Could they have done this after 1763? Certainly the American colonies were growing and maturing so rapidly that some degree of autonomy would have been necessary by the early nineteenth century. Further, the removal of the French threat to the colonies by 1763 reduced the need for British protection. However, timely and intelligent constitutional concessions might well have attracted moderate colonial opinion and strengthened the Loyalists, who composed between a fourth and a third of the colonial population. Three things seem to have prevented such conciliatory proposals: (1) the near-universal assumption of Britain that colonies existed to serve the home country; (2) the complete agreement of Britons on the principle of parliamentary sovereignty; and (3) the inadequacy of the political system. It is important to remember that the British political structure actually functioned to promote the political interests, narrowly conceived, of the members of various elite factions and not to formulate policies directed to the welfare of the country. Hence it was no accident that the domestic cry for reform and the constitutional claim of the colonists coincided.

As for the war, it was possible for the British to win militarily but impossible to impose direct parliamentary rule on the colonies or even to return to pre-1763 conditions. To win the war would have required the British government to recognize that this was no conventional European campaign wherein holding the battlefield at the end of the day meant victory, and it would have required a huge commitment of money and men—perhaps even in Europe—to draw off the French. Neither requirement ever came close to being met. But blame should not rest too heavily on the shoulders of George III and his hapless ministers: not even the great powers of the twentieth century had much success in fighting against movements for national liberation.

Suggested Reading

Bayly, C. A., *Imperial Meridian: The British Empire and the World, 1780–1830* (New York: Longman, 1989).

Bailyn, Bernard, *The Ideological Origins of the American Revolution* (Cambridge, Mass.: Belknap Press, 1967).

Bradley, James, *Popular Politics and the American Revolution in England* (Macon: Mercer University Press, 1986).

Breen, T. H., *The Marketplace of Revolution: How Consumer Politics Shaped American Independence* (New York: Oxford University Press, 2004).

Breen, T. H., and Timothy Hall, *Colonial America in an Atlantic World* (New York: Longman, 2003).

Brewer, John, *Party Ideology and Popular Politics at the Accession of George III* (Cambridge: Cambridge University Press, 1976).

Brooke, John, *King George III* (London: Constable, 1972).

Cain, P. J., and A. G. Hopkins, *British Imperialism: Innovation and Expansion* (London: Longman, 1993).

Cash, Arthur H., *John Wilkes: The Scandalous Father of Civil Liberty* (New Haven: Yale University Press, 2006).

Christie, Ian, *Crisis of Empire: Great Britain and the American Colonies, 1754–1783* (New York: W. W. Norton, 1966).

———, *Wars and Revolutions: Britain, 1760–1815* (London: Edward Arnold, 1982).

———, *Wilkes, Wyvill, and Reform* (London: Macmillan, 1962).

Conway, Stephen, *The British Isles and the War of American Independence* (Oxford: Oxford University Press, 2000).

Guttridge, George H., *English Whiggism and the American Revolution* (New York: AMS Press, 1979).

Langford, Paul, *A Polite and Commercial People: England, 1727–1783* (Oxford: Clarendon Press, 1989).

Mackesy, Piers, *The War for America, 1775–1783* (Cambridge: Harvard University Press, 1964).

Maier, Pauline, *From Resistance to Revolution: Colonial Radicals and the Development of American Opposition to Great Britain, 1765–1776* (New York: Knopf, 1972).

Morgan, Edmund S., *The Birth of the Republic, 1763–1789* (Chicago: University of Chicago Press, 1977).

Morgan, Edmund S., and Helen M. Morgan, *The Stamp Act Crisis* (New York: Collier Books, 1971).

O'Gorman, Frank, *The Long Eighteenth Century: British Political and Social History, 1688–1832* (London: Arnold, 1997).

Perry, Keith, *British Politics and the American Revolution* (New York: St. Martin's Press, 1990).

Pocock, J. G. A., ed., *Three British Revolutions: 1641, 1688, 1766* (Princeton: Princeton University Press, 1980).

Rudé, George, *Wilkes and Liberty* (Oxford: Clarendon Press, 1962).

Wills, Garry, *Inventing America: Jefferson's Declaration of Independence* (Garden City, N.Y.: Doubleday, 1978).

Chapter 9

The Rise of the Protestant
Nation in Ireland

America was not the only source of colonial troubles in Britain in the eighteenth century. Just across St. George's Channel in Ireland, a patriot movement threatened to lead the Emerald Isle along the trail toward independence blazed by the Americans. In fact, the spirit of independence in America reinforced that in Ireland, and vice versa. There were, however, distinct differences between the two movements. Irish patriotism in the eighteenth century was not the product of the nation as a whole but of the Anglo-Protestant population—that exceptionally narrow landowning elite that had been planted in Ireland as an English garrison. Hence the Irish patriot movement of the eighteenth century had only tenuous links to the mass of the Irish people, Celtic and Catholic as they were. In America, the white population formed a social order heavily weighted toward the middling sorts—small farmers and merchants. In Ireland, there existed two separate cultures, the one standing uneasily on the back of the other. Indeed, the rise of the so-called Protestant nation in Ireland depended on the absolute ascendancy of the Anglo-Protestant landlords over the impoverished native Irish. That relationship of ascendancy and subordination first allowed and then limited the development of the Protestant nation.

THE PROTESTANT LANDLORDS AND THEIR CULTURE

The victory of William III's army in 1689–1691 left the Anglo-Protestant ascendancy firmly in control of Ireland. Although they numbered no more than about 250,000 people (approximately 10 percent of the total Irish population) in 1700, the Anglo-Protestants owned 85 percent of the land. The Catholic aristocracy and gentry had for the most part been reduced to the status of tenant farmers, some of them living sullenly on the edge of estates they had once owned. The Irish Parliament, once more in the hands of the Protestant landlords, ensured the continuation of the Protestant ascendancy by passing the penal laws (see Chapter 2), which, among other things, prevented Catholics from acquiring land and made it difficult for the remaining Catholic owners to hold on to their estates. The penal laws gradually decreased the amount of land held by Catholic landlords. By 1739, one writer could say with some accuracy that "there are not twenty Papists in Ireland who possess each £1,000 a year in land."

The Anglo-Protestant ascendancy sought to exclude even the Protestant nonconformists of Ulster from their monopoly of power and privilege. In the early 1700s, the Irish Parliament passed a Test Act similar to that in England, excluding dissenters from public office. The nonconformists of Ulster, most of them Presbyterians of Scottish origin, amounted to perhaps 9 percent of the total Irish population. Though few were landlords, they were a hardworking and prosperous people who despised the episcopal system of the Church of Ireland. Consequently, the Anglican landlords viewed them with suspicion. This treatment drove many of the Scotch-Irish to emigrate to North America between 1700 and 1775.

The Church of Ireland itself showed little interest in proselytizing either the Ulster nonconformists or the native Irish Catholics. Afflicted by the same diseases of political patronage, plural holdings, and nonresidence of clergy that handicapped the Church of England, the Church of Ireland contented itself with maintaining its position of established privilege, including the requirement that everyone, regardless of religion, had to pay the tithe to the Church of Ireland. The bishops were usually English appointees, and few of them took any interest in their duties. One bishop remarked that "a true Irish bishop had nothing more to do than eat, drink, grow fat, rich and die." Here and there humane Anglican priests brought a note of English-style civilization to their remote Irish parishes, but most of them had little contact with the mass of the population. The Anglican parsons were mostly English educated and spoke only English, whereas the people were illiterate and spoke only Gaelic, a language that most Anglican clergymen and gentry alike regarded as barbaric.

The relationship of the Irish Catholic priest to his flock was totally different. The penal laws did not prohibit the practice of Catholic services, but they banned Catholic bishops and "regular" clergy (that is, members of religious orders) from Ireland, and they prevented priests from coming into Ireland from abroad. Most Irish Catholic clergymen were recruited, therefore, from the impoverished people whom they served. Few were well educated, and many spoke only Gaelic. But their roots in the Irish population and their own poverty made for close relations with their parishoners. Many received payment in kind. As one priest said, "The people give the fruit of their labours liberally to me and I give them my time, my care and my entire soul. . . . Between us there is a ceaseless exchange of feelings of affection." Because of these relations of trust, and because of the absence of a native Catholic gentry, the Catholic clergy in Ireland inherited the leadership of the populace.

That leadership did not contribute to any Catholic revolutionary movement, except at the very end of the century. For most of the eighteenth century, the ascendancy of the Anglo-Protestant landlords was unquestioned. Jacobitism caused no ripples in Ireland in either 1715 or 1745. Agrarian crime, which always expressed an element of religious and political resentment, was never entirely absent, but it stood at a low level through the first half of the century. Neither the

Catholic clergy nor the gentry was in a position to provide leadership of a popular political movement, and a Catholic merchant class developed only slowly. Thus the Protestant landlords for the time being could push to the recesses of their consciousness the natural insecurity that arose from their isolation amid the sea of native Irish.

In the eighteenth century, therefore, the Anglo-Protestant gentry lived in what was for them a time of comparative security and ease. Many of them, however, never felt comfortable in Ireland and spent most of their time in England. Some of the newcomers, whose families had obtained their land only toward the end of the seventeenth century, failed to win acceptance at the top of their local social hierarchy. Others naturally gravitated to the center of their culture—London. These absentee landlords, who often were the butt of English scorn for their Irish brogue and backwoods manners, had a damaging effect on the Irish economy and society. They drained capital away from the country, and they deprived the agricultural sector of much-needed leadership. They also failed to establish the face-to-face relations that might have bridged the enormous gap between rulers and ruled.

Yet the resident landlords were scarcely better. The rate of imprudent, lavish, and riotous living was unusually high among the Irish gentry. They prided themselves so much on their swashbuckling independence that dueling was an important aspect of Irish life. Many Irish landlords had no interests other than field sports and hard drink, and they ruined themselves in the pursuit of both. One critic wrote in the 1770s that the Irish gentry "enjoy their possessions so thoroughly, and in a manner so truly Irish, that they generally become beggars in a few years' time, by dint of hospitality and inadvertence." The Anglo-Protestant landlords possessed conviviality in abundance, but most lacked the sense of paternal responsibility that was the saving grace of many English landowners.

Although the landlords ultimately depended on English power and thought of themselves as part of English culture, they could be quite aggressive in defense of their political interests as Irishmen. This was the inevitable result of the fact that the British tended to treat them as colonials. The Irish Parliament clearly was subordinate to both the British Crown and the British Parliament In this sense, it was more like an American colonial assembly than like the pre-1707 Scottish Parliament. The lord lieutenant, a British official, was the chief executive in Ireland, and he was responsible to the British government, not to the Irish Parliament. His principal task was to ensure that the Irish Parliament regularly passed bills of supply to pay for the administration of Ireland, including approximately twelve thousand troops of the British army kept in Ireland.

Further, the British Parliament at Westminster could and did legislate directly for Ireland. In 1699, for example, the English Parliament responded to complaints of English woolen manufacturers by passing an act prohibiting the export of Irish woolens to any country except England, where they were already subject to prohibitory duties. As a result, the fledgling Irish woolen industry died. In 1719, by a declaratory act called "the Sixth of George I," the British Parliament asserted unequivocally its right to legislate for Ireland.

The Irish Parliament, meanwhile, was limited in its powers. It could not turn out the lord lieutenant, no matter how unpopular his administration. Various Irish M.P.s and publicists claimed that the Irish Parliament was the co-equal of the British Parliament, but the facts spoke otherwise. By Poynings' Law (see Chapter 1), the Irish Parliament technically could initiate no legislation. During the seventeenth century, Parliament had developed some power of initiative through the practice of passing "heads of bills," which were statements of intention to legislate. Heads of bills were forwarded to the lord lieutenant and his privy council and then to the English king and his privy council. Either the lord lieutenant or the king could reject or alter such a bill, and if a bill was so altered, the Irish Parliament could only accept it or reject it in the new form. Finally, the Irish Parliament was even more unrepresentative than was the British. No Catholic could sit in Parliament, and after 1727, no Catholic could vote. The exclusively Anglican electorate was very small, and parliamentary constituencies were even more subject to "influence" and bribery than in England. In Ireland, then, the aim of patriots had to be directed toward making Parliament effective within its own sphere.

ECONOMY, LAND, AND POTATOES

The overriding fact of eighteenth-century Irish social history was that the native populace ruled by the Protestant ascendancy suffered from chronic poverty. Ireland's economic development did not reach the level attained in England or Lowland Scotland, though it was to improve sharply in the last few decades of the century. The market system for the exchange of goods was inadequate and would continue to be so until well past the middle of the nineteenth century. Both coins and paper money were scarce, and barter prevailed in all parts of the island. Agriculture remained relatively backward. Thus the peasantry lived in conditions resembling those of the least advanced Third World nations today, conditions that shocked most foreign visitors to Ireland. The peasants' squalid cabins, hardly more than mud huts, littered the countryside, and beggars crowded the towns. As Jonathan Swift, Anglican dean of St. Patrick's Cathedral in Dublin, wrote in 1726: "The whole country, except the Scottish plantation in the north, is a source of misery and desolation, hardly to be matched this side of Lapland."

Both the British and the Anglo-Protestant garrison in Ireland tended to attribute Irish poverty to Catholicism because of its holidays and alleged superstitions. The fundamental cause of the problem, however, was that Irishmen had no economic resort except the land. There was not enough commercial or economic development to absorb excess rural population or to give peasants some alternative to farming. The lack of commercial growth itself had multiple causes. Ireland had little in the way of mineral resources, and the absentee landlords diverted capital to England. The infrastructure of educational, banking, and transportation facilities was totally inadequate. The great mass of the population had not adopted a consumer orientation, and the landed elite showed little of the English or Lowland Scots' commercial instincts. In sum, the backwardness of the Irish economy itself created an inertia that resisted expansion.

Further, British policy contributed heavily to Ireland's poverty. The export of cattle to England had been cut off in the 1660s, and the export trade in woolens was ruined in 1699. By various acts of the British Parliament in the 1700s, Britain damaged promising growth in brewing and glassmaking. Thus only two economic activities other than farming itself developed to any extent before the 1770s: linen manufacturing and the provision trade. Irish linens did not compete with any major British industry and so were encouraged to grow, especially in Ulster, where French Huguenot settlers brought their skill and capital. The provisioning of ships with beef, butter, hides, and the like was a product of the agricultural sector that could thrive on the colonial trade; hence the provision trade contributed to the prosperity of southern Irish coastal towns like Cork.

The Irish population, over 90 percent of whom lived in rural areas, thus depended almost exclusively on agriculture for a living. Yet Irish agriculture, even by the standards of the traditional segment of English farming, was very backward. The English observer Arthur Young figured in the 1770s that Irish farming in some respects lagged two hundred years behind England's agriculture. Tools were relatively primitive—clumsy wooden plow, the spade, and the sickle were the peasant's main implements. "Drawing by the tail" rather than by harness still was the means by which peasants used horses to pull plows and harrows. Landlords rarely undertook improvements on their estates and usually allowed leases for short periods only. If a tenant made an improvement on his holding, he was likely to find his rent raised accordingly. Living in almost complete ignorance of improved farming methods, and without capital or security of tenure, the peasants themselves rarely made improvements to their land. Yet the landlords were always able to find tenants to bid up the rent and often let holdings by a kind of auction to the highest bidder—a system known as "rackrent." As Lord Chesterfield, a man of no great humanitarian sympathies wrote, "The poor people of Ireland are used worse than negroes" (that is, slaves).

Only in Ulster were these conditions avoided. There, by the so-called Ulster custom, the tenant was thought to have some salable interest in his holding. This custom generally took two forms. First, the tenant's occupancy itself could be sold. Thus if a tenant wished to sell his occupancy to another, he could; or if the landowner wished to evict a tenant, he felt obliged to buy the tenant's right to occupancy. Second, a tenant was entitled, at the time of eviction or the sale of his right to occupancy, to collect the full value of any improvements that he had made. If a tenant built a fence or drained a bog, then the value of that improvement was his. Ulster custom gave the tenant some sense of security and encouraged improvements. Not surprisingly, rents were paid more regularly in Ulster, and farming was more efficient than in the rest of the country.

All over Ireland, unlike in England, tenancies tended to become increasingly subdivided; hence the land was let in ever smaller parcels. In England, the landlords believed that it was in their own interest to honor the customary size of holdings or even to increase them. But in Ireland, where landlords normally were interested *only* in rental income, they leased their land to "middlemen," who then sublet to the tenants. The middlemen—easily the most hated group in Ireland—wanted only immediate profit and so promoted subdivision of holdings. The tenant by custom provided for each of his sons by separating pieces of his holding until there was very little left. The novelist Maria Edgeworth, whose father owned an estate in Longford, wrote:

> Farms, originally sufficient for the comfortable maintenance of a man, his wife and family had, in many cases, been subdivided from generation to generation; the father giving a bit of land to each son to settle him. . . . It was an absolute impossibility that the land should ever be improved, if let in these miserable *lots*.

Pressure on the land in Ireland was heightened by population growth. From 2.5 million in 1700, the Irish population rose to 3 million in 1750 and 4.6 million in 1790. It grew fastest in the poorest areas, the South and West. Why it increased is still something of a mystery. There were no significant breakthroughs in medicine, hospital care, or public sanitation that might have decreased the death rate. Certain killer diseases like the plague seem to have died away, but smallpox still was very common. Inoculation became widespread in Ireland by the end of the century, but it was a dangerous practice. Vaccination was more effective but was available too late in the century to have an impact on population growth. Hence, life expectancy in eighteenth-century Ireland remained static—less than twenty-nine years.

The population growth probably was the result of the increased birth rate. The reason for the increased birth rate seems to have been a combination of social custom and plentiful food supplies. Compared to English men and women, the Irish married young—most of them before they were twenty-five. Because of subdivision, tenancies for new couples to establish households were readily available. Moreover, poverty was so pervasive that a peasant could not lift himself out of it by thrift or by delaying marriage. Why not marry young? According to one observer, "The only solace these miserable mortals have is in matrimony." Apparently, Irish couples did not practice either contraception or abortion, partly because of the teachings of the Catholic church and partly because they saw no reason to. As one writer put it, "A farmer often estimates his riches by the number of sons. . . ." Children contributed to the family economy, and when they were older they could be provided for by subdivision of the parents' holding. For these reasons, every discouragement to early marriage and a large number of children failed to operate in Ireland.

The nature of the plentiful food supply was simple: the potato, which had been introduced into the British Isles in the sixteenth century, now dominated the Irish peasants' diet in the eighteenth century. The average tenant grew grain for rent and potatoes for food. The potato was easily cultivated and required only the simplest tools. It was relatively high in nutritional value; hence, one acre devoted to growing potatoes could support eight people. By the latter 1700s, Irish families consumed on average about 280 pounds of potatoes a week—about 10 pounds a day for each adult! Coupled with buttermilk, some oatmeal, fish (in the coastal areas), and occasionally a little meat, the potato provided an excellent, if monotonous, diet. Travelers in Ireland often remarked on the healthy, strapping appearance of the Irish peasants, as well as their grinding poverty.

Unfortunately, the potato crop sometimes failed, and localized famine was the result. In the years 1727–1730, there were four bad seasons in a row, with much consequent suffering. One observer wrote of the old and ill "dying and rotting by cold and famine and filth and vermin." In 1740–1741, conditions were even worse, and a report was made of "roads spread with dead and dying bodies" and of "corpses being eaten in the fields by dogs for want of people to bury them."

Even in good years, however, the material conditions of life for the Irish peasantry were extremely low. Tenants and "cottiers"—agricultural laborers who held only a few acres and who depended on wages to pay the rent—alike lived in the subsistence level. Possessions were sparse and housing primitive. One observer recorded in 1777 that, "upon the same floor, and frequently without any partition, are lodged the husband and wife, the multitudinous brood of children, all huddled together upon the straw or rushes, with the cow, the calf, the pig, and the horse, if they are rich enough to have one." Amid this riot of smells and noises and a total lack of sanitation or privacy, the Irish peasantry lived in illiteracy and superstition, subject to the whims of weather, disease, and landlords. Yet they were not without the pleasures of hospitality and sociability. Arthur Young has left this indelible picture of Irish peasant life:

> . . . mark the Irishman's potatoe bowl placed on the floor, the whole family on their hams around it, devouring a quantity almost incredible, the beggar seating himself to it has a hearty welcome, the pig taking his share as readily as the wife, the cocks, hens, turkies, geese, the cur, the cat, and perhaps the cow—and all partaking of the same dish. No man can often have been a witness of it without being convinced of the plenty, and I will add the cheerfulness that attends it.

Of course, this cheerfulness disappeared when the potato crop failed, and it masked the violence that bubbled just below the surface of Irish agrarian society. Yet rural violence in Ireland did not usually result from bad growing seasons. It broke out instead when the peasants had reason to feel that the landlords were abusing their power. For instance, in the early part of the century, a well-organized body of men in Connacht killed and mutilated cattle and sheep in protest against the expansion of pasturage. After 1759, when Britain removed its restrictions against the importation of Irish cattle and thus encouraged the spread of pastures, agrarian violence became more serious and widespread. Bands of men known as "Whiteboys" terrorized the countryside, tearing down fences and killing cattle. They also protested the collection of the tithe. Even in Ulster, "Oakboys" and "Steelboys" clashed with landlords over mandatory labor on the roads and over rent increases. Agrarian violence was made a capital crime, and the landlords ferociously combated it. Nevertheless, sporadic rural violence lasted well into the nineteenth century, as much a part of popular culture as Celtic legends, harps, and leprechauns.

RISE OF THE PROTESTANT NATION

In retrospect it is clear that the enormous social and economic gap between the two cultures in Ireland—the settler ascendancy and the native peasantry—created a dangerous fault in Irish society. In the eighteenth century, however, the landlords' disproportionate power allowed them a temporary sense of security within which the seeds of colonial patriotism could take root. The British actually helped fertilize those seeds by frequently antagonizing the Protestant ascendancy. The British habitually dealt with all Irishmen, Protestant and Catholic alike, in ways calculated to promote British (more accurately, English) interests; consequently, they unwittingly goaded the Anglo-Protestant landlords into considering themselves as Irish. In defense of their own interests, the Protestant ascendancy developed a kind of settler-nationalist identity, which grew into a movement for political autonomy. Gradually, the landlords developed a desire to establish a "Protestant nation" in Ireland.

This idea originated late in the seventeenth century, when the English had moved to limit the Irish woolen industry. An Irish M.P. named William Molyneux published in 1698 a pamphlet (*The Case of Ireland's Being Bound by Act of Parliament in England, Stated*) arguing that Ireland was as separate from England as was Scotland. In 1720, the brilliant essayist and satirist Jonathan Swift urged that Irishmen express their grievances with English policy by boycotting English-made clothes. In 1724 Swift voiced the anger of the Protestant landlords at the highhanded and casual way in which the British government had granted a patent to an Englishman to produce coin for Ireland. He asserted that the people of Ireland were connected to the people of England *only* by having a common sovereign. Moreover, as he was to argue in his savage essay, "A Modest Proposal," *all* the people of Ireland, Catholics as well as Protestants, would be better off if Ireland had more autonomy under the Protestant ascendancy.

An Irish Protestant "patriot" movement crystallized in the 1720s and thereafter kept alive the issue of constitutional relations between Ireland and Britain. The British, always concerned to rule Ireland in the interests of England, remained confident that the Protestant landlords in Ireland would be mindful of their ultimate dependence on British power. The lord lieutenant and his political managers, called "undertakers," could normally put together a majority for English purposes in the Irish Parliament. The patriots, however, expressed Irish interests at every turn, and like the Americans habitually leapt from particular issues to constitutional questions. Separation from Britain was never one of their claims. They sought simply the right of the Irish Parliament alone to legislate for Ireland, whether the topic was taxation, surplus revenue, parliamentary elections, or the penal laws.

The Irish patriots were well aware of the relevance of American issues to their claims. Because of emigration, many of the Protestants in Ireland had personal ties with America. Further, they recognized that the American protest against taxation without representation was identical to their own concerns. A Dublin newspaper argued: "By the same authority which the British parliament assumes to tax Amer-

Irish Volunteers Firing a Salute in Lisburn, 1782, *by John Carey. The Volunteers, an almost exclusively Protestant military organization, had become very well armed and trained by 1782. They represented the Irish patriotism of the Protestant ascendancy.*

ica, it may also and with equal justice presume to tax Ireland without the consent or concurrence of the Irish parliament." After the American Revolution began, Irish trade suffered, and the patriots complained loudly about a British embargo on the provisions trade. Irish public opinion sympathized with the Americans. As one Irish Tory declared, "Here there are none but rebels."

Such discontent coalesced into a potent organization in 1778, when the French entered the war and the British government removed most of the regular army from Ireland to fight elsewhere in the Empire. Fearing a French invasion, the Protestant ascendancy established volunteer army units to defend the country. The Volunteers were not under the control of the British armed forces or the lord lieutenant. The Volunteers were almost exclusively Protestant, the officers coming from the gentry, the rank and file from the Protestant merchants and tenant farmers. As one patriot said, they represented "the armed property of the nation." Not content with their defensive role, the Volunteers took an interest in patriotic issues, and especially in "free trade"—that is, removal of British restrictions on Irish trade. They dressed in splendid uniforms made of Irish cloth and paraded menacingly in Dublin and elsewhere. As the sense of crisis grew, Britain's troubles in America proved to be Ireland's opportunity. The Irish Parliament, taking its lead from the Volunteers, demanded free trade and threatened to withhold Irish revenue from the

British until they got it. The British prime minister at the time, Lord North, was in no position to resist, and in 1780, Parliament granted free trade to Ireland.

The patriot movement also accomplished some reform of the penal laws. The liberal spirit of the Enlightenment worked some effect even in Ireland, and the Protestant ascendancy gradually had become agreeable to loosening the penal code, especially after 1745. During the 1770s the Irish Parliament passed a series of acts allowing Catholics to own and inherit property on nearly the same basis as Protestants. The Rockingham government that succeeded Lord North's in 1782 believed in accepting measures of reform so as to stave off social strife and included relief of Irish Catholic grievances in their liberal program. The last of the landholding provisions of the penal laws were abolished, and Catholics were given the right to serve as schoolmasters and teachers. Nevertheless, Catholics still suffered from certain disabilities: Catholics could not vote; Catholic universities were prohibited; and no Catholic could own a horse worth more than five pounds.

In this sense Catholic relief for a time became identical with Irish nationalism, but as the views of the two key leaders of the patriot movement show, it was an issue that had the potential of dividing the Protestant ascendancy. The first great leader of the patriots was Henry Flood (1732–1791), wealthy and well-connected landowner of impressive oratorical ability and genuine patriotism. Flood was one of the few members of the ascendancy to take an interest in Gaelic literature and language. He was, however, unalterably opposed to granting Irish Catholics any *political* power whatsoever. In 1775, Flood accepted office in the Irish administration, and because the administration ruled Ireland in England's interests, he forfeited his standing among the patriots. His successor as leader, Henry Grattan (1746–1820), remarked that Flood stood "with a metaphor in his mouth and a bribe in his pocket." Grattan was a young lawyer of small stature and awkward mannerisms, but he was an inspirational and poetic speaker. He argued that until the penal laws were relaxed, the British could play the Protestants off against the Catholics: "The Irish Protestant could never be free till the Irish Catholic had ceased to be a slave." Despite such rhetoric, Grattan no more than Flood sought to end the Irish Protestant ascendancy; for both of them, an autonomous Ireland was still to be a Protestant nation.

After the crisis and triumph of 1778–1780, the patriots sought to consolidate their victories by establishing the sole right of the Irish Parliament to legislate for Ireland. They realized that Lord North had granted free trade because of the difficulties that plagued the government. In more secure times, the British might take back what they had given. Flood rejoined the patriots, and in 1780–1781 he and Grattan unsuccessfully urged alteration of Poynings' Law. In 1782, a Volunteer convention representing about forty thousand armed men passed a series of resolutions calling for the autonomy of the Irish Parliament in Irish affairs. Irish popular enthusiasm again reached a fever pitch. The new Rockingham ministry in London feared that Ireland might go the way of the American colonies. Therefore, in 1782, the British granted full legislative initiative to Ireland, repealing the "Sixth of George I," and then explicitly surrendered British claims to legislate for Ireland. In 1779–1780, therefore, the Irish Protestant ascendancy had won the same commercial benefits for which Scotland had abandoned its Parliament; now in 1782 they gained without fighting the status that most American patriots had sought as late as 1773 or 1774. This was no small achievement, but it probably would never have occurred if Britain had not faced a general imperial crisis.

GRATTAN'S PARLIAMENT

The period of legislative autonomy in Ireland was to last eighteen years. Because of Grattan's inspirational leadership in winning the rights of the Irish legislature, the period has become known as the time of "Grattan's Parliament." Indeed, Grattan was awarded £50,000 by the Irish Parliament in gratitude for his services. However, Grattan did not become a prime minister, and though he remained a highly influential leader of patriotic opinion, he found that his reputation suffered during the period, not least because of the damaging rivalry of Flood. Hence the period of 1782 to 1800 perhaps is better remembered simply as the time of the flowering of the Protestant nation.

For all their importance, the constitutional arrangements with Britain won in 1782 did not grant full "responsible government" to Ireland. This limitation was to put a serious crimp in Irish national development. The constitution of 1782 gave the Irish Parliament sole authority to legislate for Ireland, but it left the Irish executive in British hands. The lord lieutenant remained the chief executive for Ireland, and he was not responsible to the Irish Parliament but to the British cabinet and Parliament. The British government, which remembered the constitutional difficulties with the Scottish Parliament before 1707 and which had clashed disastrously with the American colonial assemblies after 1763, had no intention of encouraging the development of an independent Irish executive in Ireland. Curiously, the Irish patriots seem never to have realized the importance of developing their own executive system responsible to the Dublin Parliament, though it is very probable that such a development would naturally have occurred if the period of legislative independence had lasted long enough. As it was, a group of parliamentary officials in Ireland emerged to form a kind of "Irish cabinet," but it remained responsible ultimately to the lord lieutenant and thus to the British government. When the British were strong enough to ignore those officials' views, as they generally were after 1784, then the Irish "cabinet" had no choice but to carry out the British government's policy.

Nevertheless, the period of legislative autonomy was one of significant achievement for Ireland. The Irish Parliament received credit for the remarkable blossoming of high culture and economic prosperity. The trade concessions that the patriots had won in 1779–1780 paid off in the mid-1780s. Linen manufacturing tripled in volume, the woolen and brewing industries recovered, and Irish trade in general expanded. In 1784, the Irish Parliament enacted a bounty to encourage the growing of wheat. In combination with an increasing demand for grain, the Irish Corn Law of 1784 caused the expansion of tillage at the expense of pasturage. Moreover, because the Dublin Parliament now really mattered, formerly absentee landlords were more inclined to stay at home. The proportion of rents paid to absentees went down.

Parliament House, Dublin. Parliament House was one of the most imposing examples of the neo-Classical architecture of eighteenth-century Ireland.

Irish prosperity and self-confidence were reflected in the blossoming of Dublin, which took its place as a major capital city in the British Isles. Building in the Classical style flourished, and Dublin became (and remains) a splendid monument to Augustan taste. Country houses had been built in the Classical style throughout the eighteenth century in Ireland—Castletown House in County Kildare (1720) being the grandest example. The late eighteenth century saw the construction of a wonderful collection of public buildings in Dublin: the Royal Exchange (1768), the Custom House (1780s), and the Four Courts (1780s) joined Parliament House (1730s) as noble expressions of the Protestant nation's temperament and outlook—serene, confident, haughty, and masterful.

Unfortunately, the expansion of commerce that followed the winning of free trade and the founding of Grattan's Parliament did little for the peasantry. The Corn Law of 1784 was supposed to aid the tenants by encouraging tillage, but even it could not solve the fundamental problems of Irish agriculture. Nor could it counter the growing pressure exerted on the land by the rapidly increasing population. By the 1780s, competition for tenancies had caused a revival of agrarian violence, especially in County Armagh (Ulster), where the secret terrorist societies took on a sectarian character. Protestant "Peep o'Day Boys" and Catholic "Defenders" fought with each other as well as with the landlords. Poverty, ignorance, and sectarian bitterness remained the chief features of rural Ireland.

The Irish Parliament itself (and the patriot movement generally) became bitterly divided over two issues: parliamentary reform and Catholic emancipation. Parliamentary reform—abolition of rotten boroughs and extension of the franchise—had by the 1780s become as heated an issue in Ireland as in England. The Volunteers eagerly sought reform because their recruits increasingly came from the middling ranks of society—merchants, shopkeepers, petty professional men—who as yet were denied the vote. But the rumbling of rebellion that accompanied the talk of reform frightened the landlords in Parliament, as did Flood's appearance in the Irish House of Commons in the uniform of the Volunteers. One M.P. declared: "I do not think life worth holding at the will of an armed demagogue." Parliament rejected reform and thereby broke with the Volunteers.

Granting political rights to Roman Catholics was an even more emotional issue. Many members of the ascendancy like Flood believe that if the Catholics got the vote, they would destroy the liberties of the Protestants. Others like Grattan thought that if the Catholics were *not* brought into the constitution, they might turn to political extremism and eventually destroy Protestant liberties. Once the French Revolution began in 1789, and democratic ideas radiated from Paris throughout Europe, the need to placate the slowly growing middling ranks of Irish Catholics seemed more pressing. The British prime minister, William Pitt the Younger, thought so. Under his pressure, the Irish Parliament in 1793 granted the franchise to the as-yet small number of Catholics possessing the required property qualifications. But Catholics still were not able to sit in Parliament or hold the highest offices under the Crown.

The French Revolution caused ominous reverberations in Ireland, just as it did in England and Scotland (see Chapter 11). Its ideals of toleration, equality, and democracy won support among many Irishmen of middling rank, particularly among the Presbyterians of Ulster, who still were second-class citizens. Liberal and even Republican principles were advocated publicly in Belfast and Dublin. At least among urban lawyers and journalists, a desire for an alliance between Protestants and Catholics became a potent force. In 1791, a young Anglican barrister from Dublin, Theobald Wolfe Tone, helped found in Belfast the Society of United Irishmen. The society's purpose was to bring about political reform and complete religious equality—in one sense, to form a genuine Irish nation, and in another to bring the French Revolution to Ireland. The United Irishmen wanted to enlist Catholics and Protestants alike, and they recruited effectively among the Protestant professional and mercantile ranks. The Irish executive, with the specter of a peasant rising always numbing their minds, were alarmed.

The atmosphere in Ireland became yet more tense in 1793, when Britain went to war with revolutionary France. Tone and the United Irishmen were not in the least pacified by the extension of the franchise to propertied Catholics. The British government and its Irish Protestant garrison believed that a French invasion and revolution in Ireland were immediate threats. In May 1794, the Irish executive tried to suppress the United Irishmen but only forced them underground. Tone began plotting to convert peasant unrest into political revolution and the United Irishmen began to make contact with the Defenders. The great geological fault running through Irish society began to shift and crack: the two cultures of Ireland became more polarized than ever. As rural sectarian violence between Peep o'Day Boys (Protestants) and Defenders (Catholics) escalated into large-scale riots in 1795, Protestant landlords, many of them Anglicans, founded the "Orange Society" to defend the Protestant ascendancy. By then it was clear that Ireland was caught up in a European-wide struggle, and the question was whether the consequent seismic shocks would thwart the further development of Ireland under the guidance of the Protestant nation or propel forward the development of a united, nonsectarian, democratic Ireland.

Suggested Reading

Bartlett, Thomas, *The Fall and Rise of the Irish Nation: The Catholic Question, 1690–1830* (Savage, Md.: Barnes & Noble, 1992).

Beckett, J. C., *The Making of Modern Ireland, 1603–1923* (Boston: Faber & Faber, 1981).

———, *Protestant Dissent in Ireland, 1689–1780* (London: Faber & Faber, 1948).

Connell, K. H., *The Population of Ireland, 1750–1845* (Westport, Conn.: Greenwood Press, 1975).

Connolly, S. J., *Religion, Law, and Power: The Making of Protestant Ireland, 1660–1760* (New York: Oxford University Press, 1992).

Corkery, Daniel, *The Hidden Ireland: A Study of Gaelic Munster in the Eighteenth Century* (Dublin: Gill, 1967).

Cullen, L. M., *An Economic History of Ireland Since 1660*, 2nd ed. (London: Batsford, 1987).

Fischer, David Hackett, *Albion's Seed: Four British Folkways in America* (Oxford: Oxford University Press, 1991).

Foster, Roy, *Modern Ireland 1600–1972* (New York: Penguin Press, 1988).

Gwynn, Stephen, *Henry Grattan and His Times* (London: Harrap, 1939).

Hachey, Thomas et al., *The Irish Experience* (Englewood Cliffs, N.J.: Prentice-Hall, 1988).

James, F. J., *Ireland in the Empire, 1688–1770* (Cambridge, Mass.: Harvard University Press, 1973).

Johnston, Edith Mary, *Ireland in the Eighteenth Century* (Dublin: Gill & Macmillan, 1974).

Kee, Robert, *The Most Distressful Country*, Vol. 1 of *The Green Flag* (New York: Penguin Press, 1972).

McDowell, R. B., *Ireland in the Age of Imperialism and Revolution, 1760–1801* (New York: Oxford University Press, 1979).

———, *Irish Public Opinion, 1750–1800* (London: Faber & Faber, 1994).

Moody, T. W., and F. X. Martin, eds., *The Course of Irish History* (Cork: Mercier, 1944).

Moody, T. W., and W. E. Vaughan, eds., *A New History of Ireland: IV. Eighteenth-Century Ireland, 1691–1800* (Oxford: Clarendon Press, 1986).

O'Brien, Gerard, *Anglo-Irish Politics in the Age of Grattan and Pitt* (Dublin: Irish Academic Press, 1987).

O'Connell, Maurice R., *Irish Politics and Social Conflict in the Age of the American Revolution* (Philadelphia: University of Pennsylvania Press, 1965).

Pakenham, Thomas, *The Year of Liberty: The History of the Great Irish Rebellion of 1798* (New York: Random House, 1969).

Powell, Martyn J., *Britain and Ireland in the Eighteenth-Century Crisis of Empire* (Houndmills: Palgrave Macmillan, 2003).

Smyth, Jim, *The Making of the United Kingdom, 1660–1800* (New York: Longman, 2001).

———, *The Men of No Property: Irish Radicals and Popular Politics in the Late-Eighteenth Century* (New York: St. Martin's Press, 1992).

York, Neil L., *Neither Kingdom nor Nation: The Irish Quest for Constitutional Rights, 1698–1800* (Washington, D.C.: Catholic University of America Press, 1994).

Chapter 10

The Triple Revolution, 1760–1815

The waves of the French Revolution, as we will see, were to pound the British Isles from the 1790s through 1815. As it happened, the British were already experiencing enormous economic and social change in the form of a "Triple Revolution"—agricultural, demographic, and industrial. This three-pronged revolution caused the greatest alteration of life in the British Isles since the prehistoric invention of agriculture. It destroyed the bulwarks of traditional society and transformed Britain into the first "modern" nation in the world. In a sense, British economic and social history from the late eighteenth century to the present has been the working out of the consequences of the Triple Revolution.

Such a massive change cannot be fitted into convenient chronological boxes, nor can it be easily analyzed. Each element in the Triple Revolution had origins that extended far back in time, and none had completed its course in 1815 or even in 1830. Yet each took off in the second half of the eighteenth century and had important results by 1815 or so. To be sure, the elements did not happen at the same time in all parts of the British Isles. Ireland, for instance, did not experience industrialization at all, except in Ulster, and only in the spread of the potato could it be said to have had an agricultural revolution. But one or another element in the Triple Revolution, and often two or three together, eventually affected practically every locality in the British Isles; hence it is safe to say that because of the Triple Revolution Britain, including Ireland, was a very different place in 1815 than it had been in 1750.

This process of economic and social change is often known simply as "the Industrial Revolution," because the rise of modern, factory-based industry was the most dramatic and visible force in the Triple Revolution. The Industrial Revolution has seized the attention of a great many historians and policymakers alike. However, it is important to remember that the three prongs of economic and social change occurred, roughly speaking, simultaneously and that they were mutually interactive: each had a major influence on the others. For instance, without the Agricultural Revolution, there would have been no population explosion; without population growth at a particular rate, there would have been no Industrial Revolution; and without an Industrial Revolution, there would have been no permanent increase in the population. But such simple statements hardly exhaust the problems of analysis. Why did the Irish population grow if Ireland had no English-style Agricultural Revolution? Why did population growth *not* result in industrialization everywhere in the British Isles? To what extent were the social disorders of the new industrial cities the result of any one of the three forces? Such are the fascinating but difficult issues to which we now turn.

THE AGRICULTURAL REVOLUTION

The Agricultural Revolution began in England and then spread to Wales and Lowland Scotland. Historians used to think that the Agricultural Revolution occurred in a clearly defined period—from 1760 to 1815 or 1830. Research in the last twenty years, however, has shown that agricultural innovation in England began as early as the sixteenth century. All of the elements of the Agricultural Revolution—reorganization of land ownership and tenancies; new crops; new patterns of crop rotation; and systematic improvements of livestock breeds—had been introduced by the late seventeenth century. By the early eighteenth century, traditional English open-field agriculture prevailed mainly in the great Midlands grain belt (see Chapter 3); much of the rest already had either been "improved" or turned into pasturage. Hence the Agricultural Revolution was a long process whereby progressive organization and techniques caught on in different areas at different times. By 1815, it is safe to say, most of the English open-field and the equivalent Scottish systems were gone, and even the Scottish Highlands were yielding to commercial pasturage. If this was not a revolution in the *pace* of change, it was in *results*. By 1800, the agricultural sector of England and Wales was producing at least 60 percent more than in 1700. Almost everywhere in the British Isles a rational, commercial outlook prevailed in agriculture.

The impulse to improvement in England stemmed from a combination of economic, cultural, and political conditions. Landlords in the late seventeenth and early eighteenth centuries felt pressured by the low prices for the grain they grew. Because of overproduction, grain prices in 1760 were probably 30 percent lower than in 1660. For consumers, the low food prices were a great boon, but for landowners they were a source of anxiety—a good reason to increase the efficiency of their farms. The acquisitive, calculating mentality of the English landed elite led to the pursuit of innovation at the expense of custom. Parliament after 1688 was highly responsive to the needs of landlords and put no obstacles in the path of increased farm profits. Parliament, for example, clarified the rights of private property, passed enclosure acts to consolidate landholdings, and until 1750 paid a bounty for the export of grain. In short, English landlords increasingly saw agricultural innovation as the way to earn the money necessary for the Augustan style of life.

Once underway, the spirit of agricultural improvement took on a momentum of its own. Adoption of new crops and new farming techniques became the fashion among English landlords. The Welsh gentry and, later, Scottish aristocrats and lairds emulated the English improvers; thus progressive farming served as an agent of anglicization. English landlords took an active interest in their estates and sponsored local and county fairs to promote new methods of cultivation, new crops, and improved breeds of livestock. They devoured farming journals. Some landowners like Thomas Coke of Holkham in Norfolk worked diligently to spread the gospel of progressive agriculture to their friends and neighbors. Even George III caught on to this public-spirited fad, involving himself thoroughly in the farms at Windsor and welcoming the nickname of "Farmer George."

The fashionable interest in improved farming helped make English landlords into more efficient estate managers. The new techniques available for adoption steadily multiplied. For instance Jethro Tull (1674–1741), a Berkshire squire, advocated the use of sanfoin grass (a good cattle crop that does not exhaust the soil), the seed drill (a tool that provides for greater yield from seed than the traditional "broadcast" sowing), and French vineyard cultivation (cultivation of fields after as well as before planting). Charles "Turnip" Townshend (1674–1738) promoted the planting of clover and turnips, which restore nutrients to the soil and provide winter feed for animals. Townshend also helped popularize the "Norfolk" (or four-field) system, in which wheat, barley or oats, grasses, and turnips were rotated, so that no field ever had to lie fallow. The survival of more animals through the winter allowed for rational experimentation in breeding. The most famous exponent of this practice was Robert Bakewell (1725–1795), who had a capitalist's eye for raising animals for food. A sheep, he said, was simply "a machine for turning grass into mutton." Such innovations paid off in increased output. By the 1790s, the average yield per acre of wheat had risen from 10 to 22 bushels per acre, and much higher numbers of heavier livestock were reaching the markets.

ENCLOSURE

The spread of progressive agricultural techniques was accompanied by a massive reorganization of landholding. This process was known as "enclosure." It was highly controversial in the eighteenth century and remains so among historians today. The objectives of the landowners who promoted enclosure were, first, to consolidate their farms into more efficient units than the scattered strips in the old open fields, and second, to bring under cultivation or pasturage the common or waste lands such as woods, bogs, fens, and moors. Such activity had been going forward since the sixteenth century; consequently, by 1700, about half of the land in England had already been removed from the open-field system.

The enclosure process took different forms. Sometimes a rich proprietor simply bought the land of neighboring small owners and then reorganized it. Another form was "engrossing," whereby a landowner, on the expiration of his tenants' leases, consolidated their holdings into compact farms and let them anew to the highest bidders. A third form was voluntary agreement: in parishes where there was a small number of owners, it was often possible for them to agree to end open-field farming and consolidate their lands into more efficient plots.

The most dramatic form of enclosure, however, was *parliamentary enclosure*. This is the form for which the eighteenth century was famous (or infamous, depending on one's point of view). In parishes where there was opposition among the proprietors to enclosing the land, the proponents of enclosure had to resort to private acts of Parliament. These acts were routinely passed, usually with no real opportunity for opposition, on petition by the owners of a substantial majority of the acreage in the parish, even though the petitioners might constitute only a small minority of the number of owners concerned. An enclosure act nullified all existing leases and customary arrangements in the parish and named several commissioners to survey the land (including common land) and to divide it up as compact farms among the owners. The commissioners (themselves agents of the big owners) usually honored any documented claims to ownership and to the use of common or waste land—the right, for example, to graze a cow or to run a dozen geese on the commons. Such claims were translated into small plots of land, but nondocumented claims were rejected. The commissioners also set aside land for the lord of the manor, for the owner of the tithe (usually but not always a clergyman), and for new roads. Finally, they required proprietors to erect fences or hedges around their new properties and to share the costs of enclosure, including legal fees, surveying charges, roadbuilding expenses, and the like.

Enclosure acts were passed with increasing frequency during the century. There were 189 enclosure acts between 1730 and 1760; 926 between 1760 and 1790; and 1,394 between 1790 and 1820. About 2.8 million acres were added to the cultivated land of England and Wales—about a 10 percent increase. By the 1820s, most of the ancient open fields had been enclosed.

Enclosure affected different social levels in the parish differently. *Large landowners*, who dominated the process whether it was voluntary or by parliamentary act, benefited greatly. Enclosed farms were more efficient than open-field property and much more accessible to the improved farming techniques. Rents went up by about 13 percent overall; thus, expensive as it was, enclosure probably brought big proprietors a return of 20 percent or more on their investment. *Small owners* had a harder time. Although a few of the more aggressive small owners seized the opportunity to farm more efficiently, most had to mortgage their land to pay their share of enclosure costs, and many ended up selling out to their rich neighbors. Many thousands of small owner-occupiers, as well as small *tenant farmers*, were reduced to day laborer status. Similarly, many *cottagers* could not document their claims to use common land and received nothing. Others were awarded plots too small to be of use. *Squatters* on the parish commons typically were evicted and their huts thrown down. Enclosure thus accelerated the tendency in English agriculture toward concentration of ownership into a relatively few hands, with the actual work of farming being done by substantial tenants who hired landless laborers on a wage basis.

The social effects of enclosure, therefore, were ambivalent. Enclosure certainly contributed to the aggregate increase of agricultural output and income during the eighteenth century. It liberated the agricultural entrepreneur from the restrictions of tradition. It altered the English landscape and gave to the English countryside the look of neat, compact farms and well-tended hedges and stone fences that was (and is) attractive. Nevertheless, thousands of small owners, tenants, and cottagers undoubtedly experienced enclosure as a catastrophic and bewildering loss. Not only did they find that enclosure prevented them from tilling particular plots of land that they and their ancestors had worked from time immemorial, but also they lost the communal arrangements of the open-field system. The countryside was *not* depopulated, but the English peasantry *was* "proletarianized," for enclosure abolished the cherished use-rights of the rural poor to common and waste land. The abolition of the commons destroyed one of the main sources of independence for the small holder or cottager. As one observer said in 1780, "Strip the small farms of the benefit of the commons, and they are all at one stroke levelled to the ground." A clergyman in Berkshire said that by enclosure "an amazing number of people have been reduced from a comfortable state of partial independence to the precarious condition of mere hirelings." To put it abstractly, enclosure—and agricultural improvement generally—changed the whole way of life for thousands of people, substituting rationality and contract for tradition and custom. For some, this represented liberation; for others it was misery.

THE POPULATION EXPLOSION

In 1700, one person in the British agricultural sector fed 1.7 people, but in 1800, one person in farming fed 2.5 people. Because the total number of people engaged in agriculture remained about the same, British farming by the latter date obviously was supporting a markedly increased population. Indeed, the British population grew rapidly after 1760; this growth was one of the great social facts of late eighteenth- and early nineteenth-century social history. As Table 10.1 shows, the British and Irish population grew by about 145 percent in 120 years.

Except for Ireland, where there was a terrible setback in the years 1845–1848, the population of the British Isles continued to increase throughout the nineteenth century. Thus the population for the first time broke through the upper limits that had seemed to be set by nature.

The population grew at different rates in different geographical areas. In all parts of the British Isles, population growth was slight between 1700 and 1750 but very marked thereafter. Between 1750 and 1800, the rate of increase in Ireland was clearly greater than in England and two or three times greater than in Scotland.

Table 10.1: British and Irish Population 1700–1820

	1700	1750	1800	1820
England	5,000,000	6,000,000	8,400,000	11,340,000
Wales	400,000	500,000	587,000	660,000
Scotland	1,000,000	1,256,000	1,608,000	2,100,000
Ireland	2,500,000	3,000,000	5,000,000	7,800,000
Total	9,900,000	10,750,000	15,595,000	21,900,000

Source: Chris Cook and John Stevenson, eds., *The Longman Handbook of Modern British History, 1714–1980* (London, Longman, 1983), pp. 96–97.

During the first half of the nineteenth century, the Irish population grew at a rate unequaled in British history. In Ireland, as we have seen, the population grew fastest in the poorest areas (Munster and Connacht). In Scotland, the population growth was concentrated in the comparatively prosperous Lowlands; in Wales, vast numbers settled in the coal fields of the South. In England, the population growth was more evenly distributed but came principally in the more prosperous regions—the South and Southeast, the Midlands, and the industrial North and Northwest.

Why did the population of the British Isles grow? Given the different rates of growth and the spotty nature of the statistical data (the first census did not come until 1801), the answers must remain speculative. It is helpful to remember that a number of obstacles traditionally operated to keep population numbers down. First, the great majority of people before 1700 lived at the subsistence level, therefore a series of poor harvests could cause at least localized starvation and disease. Second, the state of medical knowledge was poor and offered no defenses against killer diseases like the plague, typhus, smallpox, dysentery, and influenza. These periodically swept through the population and caused great peaks in the death rate. Third, the people themselves exerted some control over population growth by delaying marriage and limiting the number of children within marriage, effectively maintaining a rough equilibrium between the numbers of people and material resources. In pre-eighteenth-century Britain, neither the food supply nor the number of "slots" available to people—tenancies, cottages, apprenticeships and so on—was very expandable. Thus in that comparatively static world, both the average age at marriage and the proportion of unmarried women were high.

In the late eighteenth century, in different ways in different places, these obstacles were partially broken down. Whether the resulting increase in the British population was due more to a decreased death rate or to an increased birth rate is hotly disputed by demographers. As in the case of Ireland, it seems reasonable to say that both were involved. In England, for instance, the death rate declined from 26 per 1,000 to 22 per 1,000 between 1750 and 1850. This is not because of any improvements in either medical practice or public sanitation. It is true that inoculation and vaccination were widely adopted in the latter half of the 1700s (earlier in England than elsewhere in the British Isles), but these practices came too late to explain the initial surge of population growth. Likewise, some 150 charitable hospitals were built in Britain between 1700 and 1825, but these were accessible to only a tiny proportion of the population. Moreover, their principal treatments—bleeding, purging, and vomiting—were gruesome and unhelpful. What did happen is that certain killer diseases, most notably the plague, disappeared from the British Isles for reasons not yet understood. Perhaps it was that the plague-carrying fleas did not take to the brown rat, which seems to have replaced the black rat in the early 1700s. Perhaps there was a natural genetic weakening of the plague bacillus, or perhaps the European population had gradually developed antibodies against the disease. Whatever the reason, the last great outbreak of the plague in Britain occurred in 1667, and typhus also gradually disappeared.

Another factor reducing the death rate was improved nutrition. In Ireland the potato, and in England and Scotland agricultural improvement generally, enhanced the diet of ordinary people. The impact of the potato on nutrition and population growth in Ireland has already been discussed in Chapter 9. The potato had much the same benefit in the western Highlands of Scotland and Wales and a lesser effect in England. In England and Lowland Scotland, agricultural progress provided a more diverse and regular diet. Further, because of the improvement there of the transport and market systems, food could be moved more easily from one region to another. Localized famine became less likely because one area could support another. The improvement in nutrition made for a healthier population, one more resistant to disease.

Meanwhile, the birth rate also was increasing in all parts of the British Isles. There was, as far as demographers can tell, no *biological* change—no increase in human fecundity—that might explain the increased birth rate. Rather, as in Ireland, more people married earlier, and because couples were together longer, they had more children. In Ireland, the potato and the subdivision of tenancies encouraged people to marry younger. The same kind of thing happened in England and Lowland Scotland but for different reasons. Here it is important to remember economic and demographic trends before 1760. Between about 1660 and 1760, the population grew slowly, but gradual agricultural improvement kept food prices low. This relatively favorable standard of living seems to have encouraged people to marry younger and have more children.

Likewise, commercial expansion and the growth of domestic manufacturing tended to multiply the number of slots available to young men and women. It slowly became easier for couples to set up households and begin to raise families. Similarly, certain other gradual economic and social changes encouraged comparatively early marriages. The custom of apprenticeship, which delayed marriage for young men, slowly faded in the face of commerce and capitalism. The acceleration of the Agricultural Revolution reduced the number of young people who "lived in" the household of the farmers and correspondingly increased the number who worked for wages. Both trends gave a greater degree of personal freedom to young people and thus contributed to early marriages. For all these reasons, the average age at marriage in England and Scotland declined from twenty-eight years (for men) to twenty-four between 1700 and 1800, and the birth rate rose from 33.8 per 1,000 to 37.5 per 1,000. These trends produced a "bulge" in the demographic curve in the third quarter of the century; in the absence of traditional checks of famine, disease, and utter economic privation, the population represented by this bulge was able to reproduce, thus causing the demographic curve to soar during the early nineteenth century.

The social consequences of the population revolution can hardly be overestimated. However, since the demographic explosion was, in England, Wales and Scotland, so closely associated with industrialization, the consequences can only be touched on here. For one thing, the age structure of the population was altered; thus in England at least the population on average was significantly more youthful in 1815 than in 1760. For another, this expanded and more youthful population contributed to the further erosion of traditional economic and social arrangements because the teeming numbers of people put irresistible pressure on customary rents and on traditional artisanal control over wages, standards of work, and entrance into trades and crafts. A third consequence was to help keep real wages (wages in terms of the cost of living) down. The economy was expanding in terms of commerce and output, but partly because of the rapid growth of the population—which tended to push prices up and wages down—real wages did not increase until after 1820.

Finally, the growth of the population caused severe overcrowding in both rural and urban areas. The total number of people living in the countryside (excluding Ireland) could grow only slightly; therefore, the surplus population settled in the towns and cities, swelling the urban areas and completely overwhelming urban governments and facilities. In 1750, England had only one town with a population of fifty thousand (London); in 1801, there were eight; in 1851, there were twenty-nine. By 1851, a majority of people in mainland Britain lived in urban areas. In the late eighteenth- and early nineteenth-century urban areas, housing was miserable, sanitary conditions shocking, and water supplies polluted and insufficient. Mortality rates in the cities actually went up, and life expectancy went down. Urbanization in Britain was closely associated with industrialization; yet one should remember that because agricultural arrangements (outside Ireland) did not allow for a big increase in the rural population, the historic population increase alone would have accounted for much of the misery of the new urban centers. Seen in this light, the Industrial Revolution was a godsend, for eventually it provided the means by which the burgeoning population could be supported and British cities could be made tolerable.

THE INDUSTRIAL REVOLUTION

The Industrial Revolution in Britain is one of the most intensively researched and hotly disputed subjects in all historiography, and rightly so. It now seems clear that the industrialization process began earlier, was more uneven, and worked its effects over a longer period than historians used to think. Still, Britain industrialized before any other nation, and this headstart was the principal reason for Britain's preeminent position in the nineteenth century. By 1880—earlier for most people—industrialization altered the way that the British led their lives. It was the process by which Britain broke through to levels of output and consumption unparalleled in human history. Hence the questions debated by economic and social historians are of great consequence: What were the causes of industrialization in Britain? Why did the British industrialize first, and why in the eighteenth century? What was its impact on the quantity and quality of life?

Let us first define the term *industrial revolution*. It implies a vast expansion of the economy by means of the substitution of a factory system for domestic manufacturing: the factory system is based on machines that replace human muscle and multiply the productivity of each worker. *Industrial revolution* or *industrialization*, then, denotes not an *event* but a *process*, by which the economy as a whole is transformed and reaches a level of self-sustained growth. Such a revolution took root and flourished in Britain between about 1760 and 1830, though the seeds were sown well before and though it continued to throw out shoots and branches long past the mid-nineteenth century. In 1750, Britain remained a land of farms, pastures, and commercial towns; by 1830, congested industrial cities clustering around factories housing iron machines driven by steam power were common features of the landscape.

A few figures will give a sense of the magnitude of the change. Industrial and commercial output had risen by 50 percent between 1700 and 1750 but increased by more than 160 percent between 1760 and 1800. Between 1750 and 1800, coal production doubled; between 1788 and 1830, iron production increased by more than 600 percent. Between 1760 and 1820, cotton production went up 6,000 percent. Production in all these areas continued to surge upward through the 1800s. Foreign trade also lept ahead, almost tripling between 1750 and 1820. In domestic manufacturing, the average capital invested per worker was between two and three pounds. But in the cotton mills of 1820, it stood at between forty and fifty pounds per worker. According to one estimate, 750 operatives in a cotton mill produced as much yarn as 200,000 domestic spinners. One lace-making machine operated by two workers could produce as much as ten thousand hand weavers. In short, individual and national productivity in 1820 was far beyond what anyone in 1650 or 1700 might have dreamed. Britain was experiencing, one observer said, "the accumulation of property beyond all credibility . . . and [it was] rapid in growth beyond what the most sanguine mind could have conceived."

Yet a note of caution is in order. Industrialization did not affect the whole economy at once. In effect, two different economies—the traditional and the modern—worked side by side during the years between 1760 and 1820 or 1830. The modern economy—including coal mining, iron, engineering, cotton textiles, pottery, and transportation—got rapidly larger, whereas the traditional sector—agriculture, domestic industries, and most trades and crafts—shrank by comparison. Still, by 1815 or 1820, the industrial sector did not encompass half the economy.

KEY INDUSTRIES: IRON, COAL, AND COTTON

Iron, coal, and cotton were the key industries in the early decades of industrialization. Iron had been produced for many centuries before 1760, but most was produced by using charcoal as fuel for smelting iron ore. The resulting pig iron was impure and brittle, and its impurities could be removed only by repeated hammering in the forge. These processes were slow and expensive. They also required proximity to rivers and forests. Water wheels were used to operate the big bellows of the blast furnaces and the huge mechanical forgehammers. The blast furnaces were heated by the burning of charcoal, which in turn comes from the slow burning of wood. By the mid-eighteenth century, this presented a problem, since wood was scarce. Technical obstacles, therefore, inhibited the growth of the iron industry.

The Iron Bridge at Coalbrookdale, *as painted by William Williams. This was the world's first cast iron bridge, a wonderful example of the artistry of the early iron founders.*

Technological breakthroughs opened the way to rapid expansion of iron production. Abraham Darby, a Quaker ironmaster from Coalbrookdale in Shropshire, succeeded in 1709 in substituting coke (from coal) for charcoal in the production of iron. The iron industry slowly adopted the new technique—and thereby put new demands on the transport system for the shipment of coal, stimulating the development of canals and iron barges. Then, in the early 1780s, Henry Cort developed processes for rolling and puddling molten pig iron that removed impurities much more quickly than forging. In the 1770s, John Wilkinson, an ironmaster in the Midlands, applied the steam engine to the blast process, liberating iron manufacturers from the need to be near a source of water power. The iron industry took off.

Coal mining was another old industry, but because of the sheer bulk of coal, the industry was limited either to locations near water transport or to production for a local market. As the earliest pits were used up, new pits were dug farther from the waterways, so systems of wooden-railed wagon ways had been constructed to move the coal from pithead to the rivers and canals. Coal pits could not be sunk very deep because of drainage problems and because of the difficulty of lifting ("winding") the coal from coal face to pithead.

These technical problems began to be overcome by the use of the steam engine early in the eighteenth century. A steam-powered pump had been invented as early as the 1690s, and Thomas Newcomen designed a commercially useful steam pump

Boulton and Watt Steam Engine, late eighteenth century. This kind of engine was perhaps the key machine of the early Industrial Revolution.

in 1709. Newcomen pumps were widely used for winding by midcentury, but the Newcomen engine was too inefficient to allow for big profits. In 1769, a laboratory technician at the University of Glasgow, James Watt, developed a much more efficient engine by adding a separate condensing cylinder. In 1775, Watt and a Birmingham manufacturer, Matthew Boulton, secured a patent and established a firm to produce Boulton and Watt steam engines. These engines revolutionized British coal mining, solving both the winding and pumping problems. Then, in the 1780s, Watt learned how to turn the reciprocal motion of his engine into rotary motion, thereby making it possible to apply the steam engine to many kinds of machinery, including textile spinning and weaving, and to pulling coal wagons on iron rails— that is, the earliest railways.

Cotton textiles proved to be the most rapidly growing and most typical industry in the British Industrial Revolution. To think of British industrialization is to think of cotton mills. England had long been noted for the manufacture of woolen cloth in the domestic system. Until the eighteenth century, cotton could offer little competition to wool, because raw cotton, grown only in India and North Africa, was too expensive. In the 1770s, however, the southern American colonies began to produce cotton in tremendous quantities, and this cotton was readily available to British merchants. Further, a series of technological innovations made it easier and cheaper to spin and weave cotton fiber: for weaving, the flying shuttle (1733), and for spinning, the spinning jenny (1767), the water frame (1769), and the "mule" (1785).

By the latter 1780s, spinning cotton had been revolutionized. In huge spinning mills, machines turned out thousands of threads at once. Handloom weavers using the flying shuttle multiplied by the thousands to keep up with mechanized spinning. Whole villages turned to weaving cotton cloth in the domestic system. The demand for cheap cotton cloth at home and abroad was insatiable; hence the early years of mechanization in the cotton industry also composed a "golden age" for handloom weavers. Steam power was eventually applied to weaving as well as spinning, and this shifted weaving from a domestic to a factory industry. Because weavers were reluctant to give up their independence and go into factories, the spread of power looms was slow until 1815. Thereafter, it accelerated. By 1825,

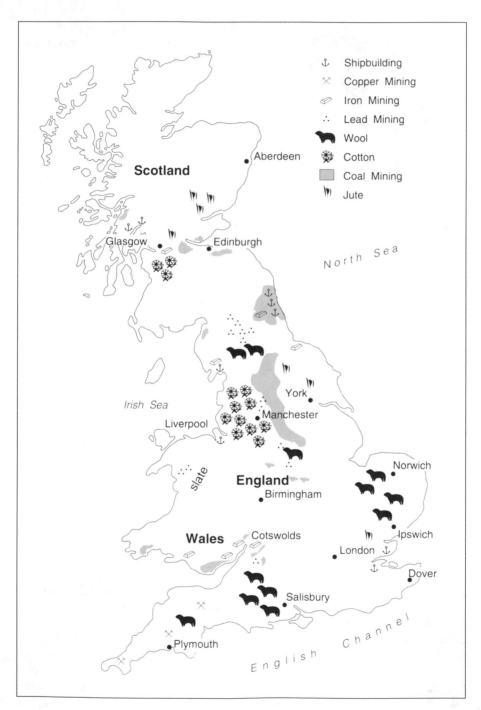

The advance of the Industrial Revolution from 1760 to 1848. Above, the Industrial Revolution in 1760

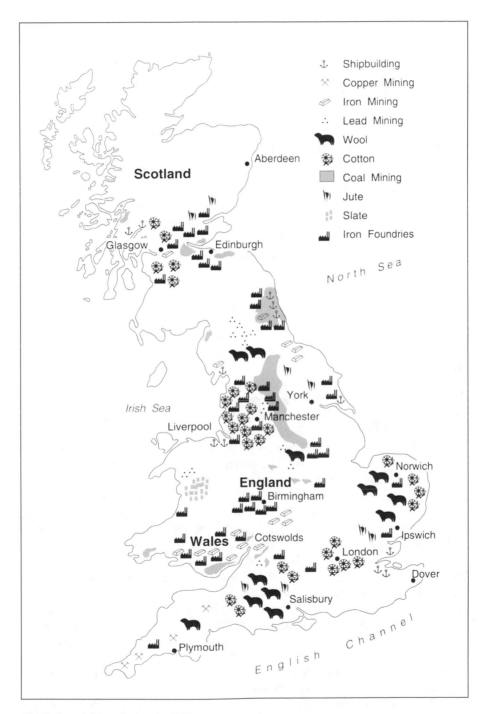

Shipbuilding

Copper Mining

Iron Mining

Lead Mining

Wool

Cotton

Coal Mining

Jute

Slate

Iron Foundries

Scotland

Aberdeen

Glasgow   Edinburgh

North Sea

Irish Sea

York

Liverpool   Manchester

England

Birmingham

Wales   Cotswolds

Norwich

Ipswich

London

Dover

Salisbury

Plymouth

English Channel

The Industrial Revolution in 1848

nearly 100,000 power looms were in use. By the 1850s, most hand weavers of cotton textiles were gone. Cotton production went forward in great clattering mills of two hundred to three hundred workers each, most of them located in the swollen, soot-blackened "cotton towns" of Cheshire, Lancashire, and the Clyde Valley of southwest Scotland—Manchester, Wigan, Bolton, Bury, Preston, Blackburn, Burnley, Glasgow, Paisley, and so on.

GEOGRAPHICAL SPECIALIZATION

The concentration of cotton production in the English and Scottish cotton towns was typical of the geographical specialization that resulted from industrialization. The woolen industry, which was slower than the cotton industry to adopt the factory system, industrialized in the 1830s and 1840s and became concentrated in the West Riding of Yorkshire, where coal was readily available. The older woolen-producing areas—East Anglia, Gloucestershire, Wiltshire, and Devon—faded in importance. The coal industry depended on the location of coal deposits, but it continued to be scattered in rural mining villages in the West Midlands (Shropshire and Staffordshire), Derbyshire, the West Riding of Yorkshire, South Wales, and Lowland Scotland. Iron production had been widely scattered before the advent of coke smelting; afterward, it settled in South Wales, Shropshire, Staffordshire, Derbyshire, and Yorkshire. The South of England remained comparatively unindustrialized.

In Ireland, the only province to experience significant industrialization was Ulster. In the Belfast area, linen manufacturing had prospered during most of the 1700s. When Ireland won free trade in the 1780s, Irish merchants got direct access to North American cotton, and the cotton industry then won a foothold in Ulster. Ulster cotton manufacturers were quick to adopt the new technology: the first power-driven machinery in Ireland was used in 1784 in a cotton mill near Belfast. In the 1790s and early 1800s, cotton rivaled linen in Ulster. In the 1820s, however, certain governmental supports to the Irish cotton industry were removed. Without such assistance, Ulster cotton manufacturers could not compete with the English, and they rapidly faded out. The linen industry expanded again to take the cotton industry's place, once again locating in the Belfast region of eastern Ulster. The linen industry constituted the basis of Ulster's prosperity in the 1830s and 1840s. This industrial base distinguished the northern province sharply from the rest of Ireland, which remained unindustrialized.

Industrialization in Wales took yet a different form. It occurred slightly later in Wales than in England, the key years being 1790–1840. The principal Welsh industry in those decades was iron, as ironworks proliferated in the great South Wales coalfield. This remarkable area included parts of Monmouthshire, Glamorganshire, and Breconshire. Here entrepreneurs (many of them English) found rich iron and coal deposits together in the numerous river valleys that descend from the mountains eastward to the Severn Estuary. By 1839, South Wales was producing over 40 percent of the iron made in England and Wales. The burgeoning iron and coal industries drew in tens of thousands of Welsh peasants as workers, making the population density of the valley communities of South Wales in 1840 as great as anywhere in Britain. This concentration of Welsh-speaking workers played a great part in saving the Welsh language, but it created a situation in which ironmasters and colliery owners spoke English and thought of themselves as part of English life, whereas the vast majority of workers spoke Welsh and remained part of traditional Welsh popular culture.

CAUSES OF INDUSTRIALIZATION

What were the causes of the Industrial Revolution in Britain? Some historians think that the principal cause was technology: innovations in manufacturing drove the whole process. Others believe that the root cause was population growth: the expansion of the population provided cheap labor, which stimulated entrepreneurs to adopt the factory system. Still other historians have cited external trade, or internal trade, or the availability of capital. But the research of the last twenty or thirty years suggests that no one cause was both necessary and sufficient. The Industrial Revolution was a complex process with origins that lay deep in the history of the British economy and society. Therefore, it is useful to think in terms of the *preconditions* for industrialization—factors without which the age-old obstacles to industrial revolution would have remained insurmountable. Yet, even granted the existence of all the preconditions, the Industrial Revolution did not begin automatically, as if by spontaneous combustion. There had to be a significant number of people with the knowledge and the desire to take advantage of the preconditions—entrepreneurs with the right frame of mind to exploit the circumstances.

The preconditions for industrialization can be classified as economic, social, and cultural. In considering the economic preconditions, it is crucial to remember that England and Lowland Scotland had experienced significant economic expansion in the century before 1760. Much of mainland Britain by 1760 had a market economy of a maturity and vitality unmatched in any European nation except Holland. The English had erected a serviceable banking system, including both the Bank of England and protobanks in the provinces. The English and Scots in 1707 had established a large free-trade area, with no internal obstacles like customs duties or political borders to impede the flow of money and goods. By midcentury, the commercial sector of the economy was generating significant amounts of capital that could be mobilized either through the emerging banking system or through networks of personal contacts. The amount of capital required to set up a small spinning mill or forge was not large—perhaps £500 to £1,000. Such amounts could be raised by an entrepreneur, an ironmaster, or a textile merchant, and then magnified by plowing the profits back into the industry.

Another economic precondition was an adequate level of technology in the appropriate areas—steam power, iron metallurgy, mechanical devices for spinning and weaving. In fact, the basic technology was available significantly before the late eighteenth-century revolution As we have seen, the innovations initially required were not very complicated and could be produced without a sophisticated scientific education. Very few of the early inventors were scientists: James Hargreaves, who invented the spinning jenny, was a carpenter; Edmund Cartwright, who developed the power loom, was a preacher; many others—Abraham Darby, Henry Cort, Josiah Wedgwood—were businessmen who learned by doing. British entrepreneurs were quicker to apply scientific and technical developments like the French jacquard loom and the Belgian soda-making process than were their Continental rivals. Nevertheless, scientific knowledge and thought in a general sense were necessary for technological innovation, and here again the British had an advantage. The Scientific Revolution of the seventeenth century, which provided the background knowledge, was a European-wide phenomenon. But British science was, because of the empirical tradition, more practical and less abstract on the whole than Continental science.

Finally, as economic preconditions, there had to be access to raw materials and to potential markets for manufactured articles. Britain was better endowed than Holland with coal and iron but not significantly better endowed than other European countries. However, Britain did have exclusive access to one essential raw material—the cotton grown in the southern United States. Britain's capacity to exploit this resource was not hindered at all by American independence. As for potential markets, historians disagree whether the external market (including the British Empire) or the internal market was more important. Foreign trade unquestionably expanded more rapidly than production after 1760, and in the cotton industry exports accounted for about one-half of all goods produced. This is not to say that exports *caused* British industrialization, though colonial demand for British manufactured goods undoubtedly accelerated technological innovation. About two-thirds of the goods produced in the modern industrial sector were consumed at home. The growth of the population combined with a relatively high degree of commercialization to generate an extremely powerful domestic demand. Foreign trade was important, but all things considered, the domestic market was the essential ingredient in demand.

SOCIAL PRECONDITIONS

The issue of domestic demand is related to the domain of *social* preconditions of industrialization. It is apparent that British (or, more specifically, English, Lowland Scots, and Ulster Irish) society was well suited to nourish revolution in industry. How so? The first factor was the population increase. The case of Ireland shows that population growth by itself could not cause industrialization. The cases of India and Latin America today show that population growth can inhibit industrialization by creating poverty, dampening demand, and discouraging the adoption of labor-saving devices. By good luck, the British population growth hit just the right level to stimulate domestic demand and provide a large surplus of cheap labor.

The population explosion was a European-wide phenomenon; therefore, British society (excluding most of Ireland) seems to have been uniquely equipped to take advantage of the opportunity when other nations could not. The relatively *open* nature of the British social hierarchy (see Chapter 3) explains the difference. In Britain, property brought status, and property could be purchased. This inspired a love of money and a desire to buy the badges of status that went much deeper into the society in Britain than anywhere in Europe except Holland. To some degree, the laboring poor had to be taught to desire consumer goods; capitalists like Richard Arkwright systematically undertook to inculcate acquisitive instincts in their workers. On the whole, however, the desire of each person in Britain to emulate his or her social superiors generated a powerful desire for riches. As Adam Smith said, what drove people to economic activity was in the last analysis "the consideration and good opinion that wait upon riches."

British society also shaped political arrangements in such a way as to encourage economic enterprise and expansion. The landlords, victorious in 1688, established the rule of law. Although they used the law for their own benefit, the rule of law itself supplied a regularity and predictability essential to commercial and industrial initiative. Further, the English landlords established absolute rights of private property because they needed to be able to buy and sell land and exploit their estates. For instance, among the landlords of Western Europe, only the British owned the minerals beneath the soil. This encouraged them if not to lead the process of industrialization then at least to cooperate with it by making capital and mineral resources available (for a price) to entrepreneurs. Moreover, the landlords made sure to limit the state's interference with their liberties, including the liberty to make money. Thus, out of self-interest, the English landlords and their Scottish imitators created the political conditions suitable for industrialization: the rule of law, individual liberty, relatively low and highly predictable taxes, and a bare minimum of state control over internal economic activity. Finally, it is worth remembering that England (and after 1746, Scotland) was free from the destruction and turmoil of war fought on its own soil. The comparative unity and security of Britain encouraged economic growth.

CULTURAL PRECONDITIONS

None of these opportunities would have been exploited had there not existed a body of people with the appropriate values and outlook. As the example of France shows, the state in eighteenth-century Europe was not an effective engine of industrial expansion. But by the 1700s, Britain had an unusual number of people, each acting on individual initiative, with the requisite qualities. The reason had to do in part with Protestantism. The Protestant "ethic" of worldly success within any calling, including commerce and industry; of rational application of means to ends; and of divine sanction for human exploitation of nature helped create an atmosphere favoring hard work in the pursuit of worldly success. Such an explanation can be pushed too far. Many Europeans before the Protestant Reformation had pursued riches. Moreover, from a worldwide perspective, Protestantism and Catholicism do not seem very different in their attitudes toward rationality and the manipulation of the natural environment.

Nevertheless, there was in the eighteenth and early nineteenth centuries a rough correlation between Protestantism and economic advancement. Furthermore, in Britain nonconformist Protestants played a special role in promoting values that were essential to capitalism and economic innovation. They also took a prominent part in organizing the early industries. Nonconformists—Quakers, Baptists, Presbyterians, Congregationalists, and (later) Methodists—made up less than 10 percent of the population but almost 50 percent of the most important industrial entrepreneurs. Their moral code encouraged hard work and self-denial. Moreover, their social position channeled them into business. Because they were not part of Anglican landed society, they were second-class citizens, usually relegated to the towns. Their psychological need for economic success was great, as was their practical need, because a nonconformist could join the elite by making a fortune and buying enough land. Often, a switch to Anglicanism followed a man's purchase of an estate; meanwhile nonconformism had done its work.

To give one example, Jedediah Strutt (1726–1797) was a major entrepreneur in the cotton industry. Strutt was a Unitarian, the son of a small farmer. He was apprenticed to a wheelwright in 1740, but after completing his apprenticeship, he returned to farming. However, because of his mechanical skill, Strutt was able to improve the standard stocking frame so that it could be used to knit ribbed stockings. He was not content to apply his innovation to the local cottage industry. Granted patents in 1758–1759, Strutt set up a factory in Derby that became extremely lucrative. In 1768, he took into partnership the great inventor Richard Arkwright, who had developed the water frame for spinning cotton threads. Their firm rose to even greater levels of profit. When Strutt died, he left a huge fortune and a fine country estate. His grandson became the first Lord Belper. Strutt had provided his own highly appropriate epitaph: "Here lies JS—who, without Fortune, Family or friends rais'd to himself fortune, family & Name in the World."

The point is that men like Strutt could see the opportunities presented by the economic situation, and they had the skills and the motivation to take advantage of them. Britain in the 1700s was producing a substantial number of such people—managers of aristocratic estates, ambitious tradesmen, capitalists in the domestic system of manufactures, and opportunistic commercial captains. They proved to be willing to take the risks necessary not only to expand production but also to expand it by wholly new means. Thus the answer to the questions Why Britain? and Why then? is that the preconditions for industrialization and a set of people capable of exploiting them alike came to exist in eighteenth-century Britain but not elsewhere (at least to the same degree) and not before. Britain's advantages over wealthy nations like France and commercialized nations like Holland were not great, but they were enough to give Britain a headstart, and that headstart was decisive in widening the differential.

SOCIAL CONSEQUENCES OF THE TRIPLE REVOLUTION

The social consequences of the Triple Revolution were both complex and comprehensive. They did not happen overnight and were to reverberate throughout the whole length of the nineteenth century. Here we must restrict our view to the short term, for even by 1815 British society was being strikingly altered. Some of the effects have already been noted: the substitution of contract for custom in agriculture; the reduction of many small owners and tenants to the status of farm laborers; overcrowding in both rural and urban areas; the erosion by pressure of numbers of customary arrangements in trades and crafts; and the general forcing of real wages down. Now we will factor in the short-run consequences of industrialization and then consider the impact of the whole.

No one would deny that because of industrialization, the great majority of Britons enjoyed a higher standard of living in 1880 than in 1750. They earned more, consumed more, and lived longer lives. But it is far from clear that industrialization had worked any such beneficial result by 1815. True, the gross national product (GNP—the total of goods and services produced by a nation) doubled in the period from 1760 to 1815, so that even though the population increased, output per head also increased. Unfortunately, rents and prices also went up markedly—partly because of the war with France from 1793 to 1815—thus it would be only after 1815 that average real wages improved over the levels of the 1750s. Moreover, to estimate standards of living in terms of averages is misleading. For instance, there is good reason to believe that during early industrialization, the distribution of income shifted away from wages and toward profits. In other words, the share of the national income enjoyed by the rich grew at the expense of the share going to the poor. The expansion of economic opportunities caused the middling sorts to proliferate. It must have been cold comfort to an artisan whose wages were falling because of competition with factories to know that statistically the per capita national income was going up or that commercial and industrial captains were prospering.

The improvement or reduction of the actual standard of living for a person depended in large part on the occupation he or she was in. Overcrowding in the countryside kept wages low and work irregular for most farm laborers. Factory workers were relatively well paid because most working men disliked factory work and had to be enticed into it by higher wages. However, women and children recruited to work in the factories were paid less than men. Moreover, by 1815, only about 35 percent of the British labor force worked in industry, and the percentage actually working in factories was much smaller yet. Craftsmen (and women) whose skills were in demand—printers, cabinet makers, cutlers, blacksmiths, engineers, and cotton spinners—benefited from industrial expansion. These, however remained a small minority of the work force. Other craftsmen who had to compete with the machines or who could not protect their trades from the rising tide of population—wool combers, calico printers, wool shearers, and handloom weavers—suffered acutely from falling wages. The handloom weavers constituted the most tragic case. At their peak in the late 1700s, the weavers numbered about 400,000 men, earning an average of twenty-three shillings a week. By the 1830s, the weavers averaged five shillings a week, and their numbers had been cut in half. On balance, in the period from 1760 to 1815, probably more workers suffered in standard of living because of the Industrial Revolution than gained from it.

The Industrial Revolution affected more than material standards of life. The family, for example, was in some ways profoundly changed. It was not that industrialization altered the structure of the family from extended to nuclear; the basic pattern of the family in England, at least, had been nuclear from the earliest times for which there is evidence. Nor did industrialization initiate women's and children's labor. Among the laboring people, they had always worked. But industrialization tended to break up the old pattern of families working cooperatively in the home. For one thing, industrialization caused a "de-skilling" of many traditional occupations, as machines did the work formerly done by human beings, and, in particular, machines tended by women did the work formerly belonging to men. Many artisans under this pressure responded by reemphasizing the male exclusivity of the work—and, all too often, vented their frustration by beating their wives. For another, as industrialization shifted manufacturing work from the home to the factory, it changed the nature of work for many women. Spinning at the wheel, for example, in the preindustrial world had always been women's work. But in the new mills that were devoted to cotton spinning by large spinning machines, men took over spinning, and women and children were relegated to auxiliary tasks like piecing yarn and cleaning the machines. As women lost access to spinning, many took up weaving, formerly reserved to men, so that by 1800 perhaps half of all handloom weavers were women. And in the case of weaving, women retained employment when powerlooms were introduced and gathered into factories. In the early nineteenth-century weaving factories, men usually worked as "tenters" (powerloom mechanics) while women operated the looms. But whatever the change of men's versus women's work, industrialization undermined the traditional family economy.

It can be argued that industrialization helped emancipate women by increasing their opportunities for work outside the patriarchal family; but the facts appear to argue otherwise. Certainly, factory owners recruited women and children whenever possible, both because their hands were more nimble than men's, and because they were more easily disciplined and could be paid less than men. In general, industrial capitalists avoided paying adult males if they could. In 1835, more than 60 percent of all cotton mill workers were women and children. Moreover, women slaved underground in some coal mines and on the surface of most lead mines. The contribution of female workers was crucial if their families were to survive. But the standard pattern was for girls to work in the factories until marriage, after which they were confined to household duties and to such domestic work as sewing or straw plaiting to make ends meet. Only a quarter of all women working in factories in the early nineteenth century were married. At the same time, attitudes among the upper orders, especially in the middling sorts, were hardening about what constituted proper "women's work." Women who worked for a living outside the home gradually came to be regarded as lacking virtue and morality, for, it was increasingly assumed, a woman's proper place was in the home where she would be provided for by an adult male.

All of the workers—men, women, and children—in the early Industrial Revolution were subjected to severe discipline. The laboring poor were used to working

*Woman and child dragging a basket of coal in a mine. From the Report of the Royal
Commission on the Employment of Children in the Mines, 1842.*

at their own (or nature's) pace and rhythms. But in the new industries, the work
force had to be "tamed"—that is, it had to be subjected to the pace of the machines,
which represented too great an investment to stand idle. With the advent of the factory came a culture of time—clocks, steam whistles, and factory bells. Time became
something that was to be *saved* and *spent*, not *passed*. Factory owners adopted a
variety of insistent devices to discipline their preindustrial workers: educational
exhortations and warnings, code books, clocks, fines, corporal punishment, and
dismissals. Rule books of hundreds of precise orders were not unusual. Workers
arose before dawn by the factory whistle; went to work by the whistle; ate breakfast,
lunch, and dinner by the whistle; and at the end of a fifteen-hour day slogged home
in the dark after the final whistle.

The Industrial Revolution—indeed the Triple Revolution as a whole—transformed social relations, the way that people related to each other in the work place
and in society generally. As the sheer number of people grew, as they coagulated in
the dense and harsh new urban environment, as contract replaced custom in the
countryside, and as the factory replaced the household in the manufacturing sector, the face-to-face relations of the preindustrial world crumbled. The "scale of
life," as Professor Perkin calls it, changed: the towns in which an increasing number of people lived and the institutions in which they worked became larger, more
complex, and less manageable. Although some factory owners adopted paternalist
policies in managing their workers, the way that employers and employees related

to each other inexorably became more formal—more rule bound, contractually defined, and bureaucratic. Paternalism, deference, and custom dwindled in importance. Because landed proprietors and factory owners alike were driven by the pressure of competition and the fear of failure, social relations with the work force became harsher. The laboring poor on their part were driven to try to defend their customary rights and independence, as well as their standards of living, from the pressures applied by property owners and the marketplace.

Eventually, the worsening of social relations helped produce a new kind of social structure—namely, a class society. But because the formation of social classes in Britain occurred during the highly politicized atmosphere of war against revolutionary France, that process will be discussed in Chapter 11. What must be emphasized at this point is that the Triple Revolution greatly intensified social conflict. In one locality after another, by efforts that were not at first coordinated or even understood in a national context, working men and women strove to protect their wages, working conditions, and preindustrial community. They petitioned Parliament, formed local combinations, issued threatening letters and manifestoes, and went on strike. Employers, on the other hand, demanded as a condition of hiring that workers forgo strikes and refuse to join workers' combinations. They also resorted to Parliament to obtain laws that would control the laboring poor. In order to ensure that labor was subject to the free market, they got Parliament in 1813–1814 to repeal the remnants of the old Elizabethan law regulating wages and apprenticeships. Moreover, Parliament by 1799 had passed more than forty laws against trade unions, and in 1799–1800, it passed the Combination Laws, which prohibited any industrial combination whatsoever.

The intensity of the social conflict resulting from the Triple Revolution was illustrated by two dramatic sets of events, one in industry and one in farming: the Luddite movement and the Swing Riots. Luddism is the name given to machine-breaking activities that erupted in the Midlands, Lancashire, and the West Riding of Yorkshire in 1811–1812 and again in 1814–1816. Crowds of working men and women who believed that new machines were threatening their traditional crafts and livelihoods conducted secret operations to smash the machines and intimidate the factory owners. Often they issued proclamations signed by "Ned Ludd" or "General Ludd." For instance, shearmen conspired to break shearing machines that deprived them of work, and framework knitters organized to break stocking frames operated by cheap ("dishonorable") labor. Several factories were attacked by Luddites and defended by armed mill owners. Whether there was much cooperation among the Luddite groups is not known, but it seems clear that they were not irrational in their violence. They were people frustrated by the failure of their petitions to Parliament and by the authorities' suppression of their unions. The Luddites wanted restoration of the traditional "moral economy"; thus they were heirs on a wider and more dangerous scale of the food riots of the eighteenth century.

Much the same can be said of the Swing Rioters, who struck at threshing machines, burned hayricks, and issued threatening proclamations throughout the South, Southeast, and Midlands of England. Agrarian change had produced spo-

A threatening letter from General Ludd to the foreman of a Nottingham jury, March 1812. The writer warns: "Remember the time is fast approaching when men of your stamp will be brought to Repentance."

radic riots and machine breaking during the years before 1830. But "Captain Swing," as the rioters named their fictional leader, swept through the countryside like wildfire in 1830–1831. Sometimes the agricultural laborers who rioted were seeking to abolish threshing machines (which deprived them of winter work) and sometimes simply to raise wages to a livable standard. The Swing Rioters were not seeking political or social revolution—though the property owners thought so—but wished to force the landowners to acknowledge once again their traditional paternal obligations. Like the Luddites, they were attempting to stop the erosion of traditional society, and like the Luddites, they failed.

The Luddites and the Swing Rioters can be seen as indices of the social effect of the Triple Revolution. By the early nineteenth century, the agricultural, demographic, and industrial revolutions were transforming life in Britain. Output and productivity were increasing by leaps and bounds, so there existed the potential for an improved standard of living for a rapidly growing population. The Triple Revolution was also causing acute social conflict. Britain in the last years of the eighteenth century and the early years of the nineteenth century was becoming ripe for revolution even if the storm from France had not come ashore at the same moment.

Suggested Reading

Berg, Maxine, *The Age of Manufactures: Industry, Innovation and Work in Britain, 1700–1820,* 2nd ed. (London: Routledge, 1994).

Chambers, J. D., and G. E. Mingay, *The Agricultural Revolution, 1750–1880* (London: Batsford, 1966).

Clark, Anna, *The Struggle for the Breeches: Gender and the Making of the British Working Class* (Berkeley: University of California Press, 1995).

Daunton, M. J., *Progress and Poverty: An Economic and Social History of Britain, 1700–1850* (New York: Oxford University Press, 1995).

Flinn, M. W., *British Population Growth* (London: Macmillan, 1970).

Floud, Roderick, and Donald McCloskey, *Economic History of Britain Since 1700, Vol. I: 1700–1860.* 2nd ed. (New York: Cambridge University Press, 1994).

Habakkuk, H. J., *Population Growth and Economic Development Since 1750* (Leicester: Leicester University Press, 1971).

Hobsbawm, E. J., *Industry and Empire* (Harmondsworth: Penguin Press, 1968).

Hudson, Pat, *The Industrial Revolution* (London: Arnold, 1992).

Jones, Eric L., *The European Miracle* (New York: Cambridge University Press, 1981).

Landes, David, *The Unbound Prometheus* (Cambridge: Cambridge University Press, 1969).

McKeown, Thomas, *The Modern Rise of Population* (New York: Academic Press, 1976).

Mokyr, Joel, ed., *The British Industrial Revolution: An Economic Perspective* (Boulder: Westview Press, 1993).

Morgan, Kenneth, *Slavery, Atlantic Trade and the British Economy, 1660–1800* (New York: Cambridge University Press, 2000).

Perkin, Harold, *The Origins of Modern English Society, 1780–1880* (Toronto: University of Toronto Press, 1969).

Price, Richard, *British Society, 1680–1880* (Cambridge: Cambridge University Press, 1999).

Rule, John, *The Labouring Classes in Early Industrial England, 1750–1850* (London: Longman, 1986).

———, *The Vital Century: England's Developing Economy, 1714–1815* (London: Longman, 1992).

Sharpe, Pamela, *Adapting to Capitalism: Working Women in the English Economy, 1700–1850* (New York: St. Martin's Press, 1996).

Taylor, Barbara, *Eve and the New Jerusalem* (London: Virago, 1983).

Thompson, E. P., *The Making of the English Working Class* (London: V. Gollancz, 1963).

Tranter, N. L., *Population and Society, 1750–1940* (London: Longman, 1985).

Valenze, Deborah, *The First Industrial Woman* (New York: Oxford University Press, 1995).

Voth, Hans-Joachim, *Time and Works in England, 1750–1830* (New York and Oxford: Clarendon Press, 2000).

Williamson, Tom, *The Transformation of Rural England: Farming and the Landscape, 1700–1870* (Exeter: University of Exeter Press, 2002).

Wrigley, E. A., and R. S. Schofield, *The Population History of England, 1541–1871* (Cambridge, Mass.: Harvard University Press, 1981).

Chapter 11

The War Against the French Revolution, 1789–1815

The pressures on the British ruling elite generated by political developments in Ireland and by economic and social change in the United Kingdom were acutely intensified by the French Revolution. This violent transformation, which was to hold all Europe in its toils for a quarter of a century, began in the summer of 1789 and seemed to surge with breathtaking speed from one event to the next: the calling of the Estates General; the formation of a National Assembly; the fall of the Bastille to a Parisian crowd; the rebellion of the peasantry; the issuance of the Declaration of the rights of Man and of the Citizen; the articulation of a radical ideology—liberty, equality, and fraternity; the flight of King Louis XVI; war; the execution of the king; and the Reign of Terror. Almost immediately on its outbreak, the French Revolution began radiating its ideals of democracy and nationalism in waves that threatened to swamp all of the European states of the old regime.

The aristocratic regimes of Europe found their rule shaken by a dual conflict; by war with French armies abroad and by ideological struggle with radical movements at home. Armed conflict between revolutionary France and reactionary states began in April 1792, when France declared war on Austria and Prussia, and it was to go on ferociously if sporadically until Napoleon's final defeat in 1815. Britain stood apart from the war at first but soon aligned itself with the reactionary powers and eventually became the principal and most consistent opponent of the French Revolution. At several times, the struggle of the British ruling elite with the revolution abroad and at home became desperate. Yet the oligarchy survived and was able to bring about the defeat of France. Three important questions arise from these facts: (1) Why did Britain, the most progressive state of Europe, throw its weight with the reactionary powers? (2) Given the dangerous state of affairs in the British Isles, how was the British oligarchy able to survive the challenge? and (3) What were the consequences of the war effort on British society?

WILLIAM PITT THE YOUNGER AND NATIONAL REVIVAL

The answer in part to all three questions had to do with the extraordinary character and ability of William Pitt the Younger, prime minister from 1783 to

Prime Minister William Pitt the Younger addressing the House of Commons on the French Declaration of War, 1793, *by K. A. Hickel. Pitt was thirty-four at the time.*

1801 and again from 1804 to 1806. Pitt, the second son of the great earl of Chatham and heir to many of his father's talents and ideas, was a man easy to respect but hard to love. Born in 1759, Pitt was reared in an atmosphere of worship for Chatham's oratorical genius and statesmanship. Doted on by his parents, the younger Pitt was trained for distinction in public life and was convinced of his own surpassing ability and virtue. He was educated at home and at Cambridge and seems to have skipped adolescence. He emerged from the university with a mature understanding of the classics, mathematics, and modern literature, as well as a unique self-assurance. A boon companion to a small circle of friends, Pitt by age twenty-one displayed icy self-control in his public demeanor. He was an unnaturally mature statesman before most young men have found their way in life.

Pitt was returned to Parliament in 1781 from Appleby, a pocket borough controlled exclusively by a wealthy patron. Despite his position as a client, Pitt rapidly won a reputation as an independent reformer. From his first speeches, he impressed the House of Commons with his mastery of detail, his clarity of mind, and his debating skill. By advocating parliamentary reform, by criticizing the war in America, and by attacking the corruption and incompetency of Lord North's government, Pitt earned a commanding position as a "patriot"—a man working above party for the national interest. In 1782, only eighteen months after first taking his seat, Pitt became chancellor of the Exchequer.

Scarcely a year later, Pitt became prime minister at the age of twenty-four. The events leading to his elevation were among the most controversial in modern

British political history. As we have seen, Lord North's unpopular government was replaced in 1782 by a ministry devoted to peace. The prime minister was the marquess of Rockingham, but its key figure was Charles James Fox, a brilliant orator, urbane leader of fashionable society, and outspoken defender of civil liberty. Fox believed in reducing the patronage of the Crown and in the right of the parliamentary leadership to form their own cabinet, regardless of the king's views. These ideas were contrary to the constitutional arrangements of the day, though they eventually became accepted parliamentary practice. When Rockingham died suddenly in July 1782, Fox asserted his novel constitutional claims, but George III rejected them and Fox resigned. The Chathamite earl of Shelburne formed a government. Fox took his revenge by cynically forming an alliance with his former archenemy, Lord North, which succeeded in toppling Shelburne's government. George III was forced to accept what he and all independent politicians—including Pitt—regarded as a corrupt ministry, the Fox-North Coalition. The monarch looked for an opportunity to throw them out and found one in 1783, when Fox introduced a bill to reform the government of British India. George III let it be known that he would consider as a enemy anyone who supported the bill. That was sufficient to kill it; the bill's rejection overturned the Fox-North Coalition, and George III invited Pitt to form a new cabinet. Whig doggerel commented:

> A sight to make surrounding nations stare;
> A Kingdom entrusted to a school-boy's care.

Both Pitt and George III knew that the new ministry lacked majority support in the House of Commons, but they were content to have the government rely exclusively on the king's confidence, certain that the electorate supported them. The Foxites were outraged at what appeared to be royal tyranny, but Pitt and George III proved to be right. In 1784, confident that he had shown his mettle in parliamentary combat, Pitt called a general election. With the liberal application of funds from the Crown and from the East India Company, but also relying on his reputation as a patriot and reformer, Pitt swept to a big victory. In the process, he earned the abiding hostility of Fox, who regarded himself as the "tribune of the people" and a "martyr" for popular liberty. In truth, the nationalistic mood of the day had shown its unhappiness with the cynicism of the Fox-North Coalition and its support for George III's view of the constitution.

In the next eight years Pitt rebuilt the governmental machinery and finances that had been thrown into disarray by the war against the American colonies. Having at last found a first minister in whom he was confident and who was also effective, George III supplied steady support. For his part, Pitt did not press issues likely to upset the king. He supported bills to abolish slavery and to reform Parliament, but when they were defeated, he let them go. At the same time, Pitt resolutely pursued governmental efficiency. He gradually improved the civil service by appointing competent professional administrators. He also abolished sinecures (functionless state offices); he rationalized administrative departments; he substituted government salaries for private fees; he introduced a system of accounting in government finances; and he opened government financing and contracts to competitive bidding. All this earned Pitt the image of a coldhearted bureaucrat, but it also enabled the British state to withstand the shocks of the war and social change to come.

Pitt also renovated government finances. The American war had driven the national debt to an unprecedented level, and the disruption of trade had cut into government revenues. Pitt had learned from Adam Smith's *Wealth of Nations* that free trade and reduction of governmental encumbrances would actually increase commerce and the state revenue from it. At one public dinner, he declared to Smith himself, "Nay, we will stand until you are seated, for we are all your scholars." Thus he promoted British commerce and negotiated a mutual reduction of duties on trade between Britain and France. He made smuggling unprofitable by cutting import duties drastically—and then aggressively collected the remainder. He concocted a long list of new items to be taxed, including racehorses, carriages, servants, windows, and hair powder. He invented a national lottery, and he established a "sinking fund" to reduce the national debt—an appropriation of £1 million that was allowed to accumulate at compound interest, which in turn was used to repay the debt. By 1792, his measures had restored public confidence, for they had increased governmental income by 50 percent and had decreased the national debt by £10 million. By the time the French Revolution began, the British state had revived from the dangerous ailments of the American war years.

ORIGINS OF THE WAR WITH FRANCE

The outbreak of the French Revolution presented Pitt with a new set of challenges and eventually turned his tenure of office into a nightmare. At first, the British received the news of revolutionary events with complacency. Weren't the French simply trying to accomplish what the English had done in 1688? Fox said the fall of the Bastille was "much the greatest event that ever happened in the history of the world." Pitt himself declared that the convulsions in France would eventually calm down, and then France "will enjoy just the kind of liberty which I venerate." Young poets like William Blake, William Wordsworth, and Samuel Taylor Coleridge greeted the French revolution as if it were the great news of human liberation. As Robert Southey put it, the Revolution meant "the regeneration of the human race."

This complacency, however, soon turned into ferocious controversy. Not only did the events in France rapidly assume a visage frightening to the British oligarchy, but also they inspired the revival of the radical parliamentary reform movement in Britain. In Ireland, as we have seen, the principles of the French Revolution led to the formation of the United Irishmen. In England, the French Revolution reinvigorated and broadened the reform movement that had originated during the Wilkesite controversy of the 1760s and that had applied significant pressure to the government during the war against the American colonies (see Chapter 8). Moreover, because of the rapid social and economic changes of the late eighteenth century—population growth, industrialization, urbanization, and social conflict—

hopes for radical reform of the constitution penetrated more deeply into British society than ever before. Thus, whereas organizations like the Society of the Friends of the People (1792) were aristocratic, most other reform organizations grew from the middling and artisanal ranks. The Revolution Society, for instance, had been founded by urban nonconformists to celebrate the centenary of 1688 and now called for repeal of the Test and Corporation Acts and affirmation of the sovereignty of the people. Similarly, the Society for Constitutional Information, originally established in 1771, and re-formed in 1780 to promote the ideals of popular sovereignty and peace with the American colonies, was revived in 1789 by business and professional people like John Cartwright and John Horne Tooke and included a few artisans and craftsmen. Broadly speaking, the objective of all such societies was moderate parliamentary reform—abolition of "rotten" boroughs, redistribution of seats to provide for more fair and independent representation, and extension of the franchise.

More ominous, from the vantage point of the oligarchy, was that thousands of artisans and shopkeepers in London and the provincial towns began on their own to organize on behalf of radical constitutional change: universal manhood suffrage, annual elections, and constituencies of equal size. Of these groups the most important was the London Corresponding Society (LCS), formed in 1792 by the shoemaker Thomas Hardy. Such societies did not mean to establish a republic, but they did associate themselves with the French Jacobins and criticized the principle of aristocracy. As was typical of British reformers, the radical artisans talked in terms of *restoring* lost liberty, but that restoration would have overturned oligarchical rule; it would mean, the LCS declared, "the press free, the laws simplified, judges unbiased, juries independent, needless places and pensions retrenched, immoderate salaries reduced, the public better served, taxes diminished and the necessaries of life more within the reach of the poor."

The inflow of revolutionary ideas caused a strenuous ideological dispute in Britain. In 1789, the dissenting minister Richard Price celebrated the French Revolution by comparing it to the Glorious Revolution of 1688. His sermon provoked Edmund Burke, the leading Whig intellectual, into writing a sustained attack on the French Revolution—*Reflections on the Revolution in France* (1790). This brilliant polemic became the chief statement of growing counterrevolutionary movement in Britain and has remained a powerful influence in British conservatism to the present day. Burke argued that the events of 1688 and 1789 had nothing in common. Whereas the English in 1688 had revered the past and therefore had taken care that their actions were consistent with tradition, the French in 1789 broke with their past and were renovating their state according to pure reason. History, Burke contended, is a safer guide in human affairs than reason, for the principles of societal arrangements are, "like every other experimental science, not to be taught *a priori*." Experience, as the English knew, teaches better than an abstract "rights of man." The propensity of the French to follow abstract rights must lead to destruction of the monarchy, debasement of the currency, anarchy, and tyranny.

Events in France were to make Burke's argument seem more and more correct. Meanwhile, Tom Paine, who had played such a crucial role in the American independence movement, produced the most sensational of the radical responses to Burke: *The Rights of Man* (1791–1792). Paine argued with unequaled clarity and simplicity for a complete break with the past: "It is the living and not the dead, that are to be accommodated." Reason, not tradition, should form the basis of society and constitution. In truth, he said, the vaunted British constitution merely defends inequality and injustice. Reason says that all people have natural rights, but the British constitution denies natural rights in order to protect a hereditary monarchy and aristocracy, of which the former is useless and the latter degenerate. A "representative democracy" (that is, a republic) would bring real benefits to the people. It would eliminate corruption and waste and install a progressive income tax. These reforms would pay for material improvements like family allowances, education grants, old-age pensions, and funeral expenses. Such arguments made *The Rights of Man* the bible of popular radicalism in Britain; indeed, it helped thousands of people among the laboring poor to understand their common experiences and aspirations and so begin forming a *working class consciousness*. More than 200,000 copies were sold in 1793 alone. Paine gave radicalism a positive program: destruction of the oligarchy, universal manhood suffrage, and the foundations of a welfare state.

The spread of radical societies and the popularity of Paine's tract increasingly worried George III and his government. Radicalism seemed to suggest that the laboring poor might throw off their habits of deference and obedience. In May 1792, the king issued a "Proclamation against Seditious Writings." At the same time, Pitt said that under the circumstances any further effort at parliamentary reform would cause "anarchy and confusion." Nevertheless, Pitt remained more concerned about the traditional balance of power in Europe than about embarking on an ideological crusade against the French Revolution. Even when Austria and Prussia went to war against France in 1792, Pitt did nothing. But French encroachment on the Low Countries, through which the British had their commercial entrepôt to the Continent, dragged him toward war. Already in 1788, Pitt had arranged a triple alliance with Holland and Prussia to defend the Low Countries. When in 1792, France defeated the Austrians, opened the river Scheldt to French commerce, and then annexed the Austrian Netherlands (roughly, modern Belgium), Pitt and his government decided to go to war with France.

WAR WITH FRANCE, 1793–1798

Pitt little anticipated that the war begun in 1793 was to continue almost without interruption until 1815. He thought that the Revolution had so weakened France that the war would not last long, and he viewed the war as a chance to make up for British losses in the New World between 1775 and 1783. Indeed, he saw the war in terms made popular by his father: the British would pick up French colonial holdings around the world by use of their peerless navy, while buying mercenaries from the small German states and paying subsidies to larger allies like Austria and Prussia so as to divert French energy and resources to the Continent. The British regular army in 1789 was, as usual, relatively small, and it remained under the thumb of the aristocracy, who, regardless of any lack of competency, purchased their commissions and raised their own regiments. About twelve thousand of the fifty thousand troops were stationed in Ireland, and eighteen thousand others were in the colonies overseas. But Pitt had done much to refurbish the navy, and it stood capable of fairly rapid expansion. Pitt and his chief strategists thought that as long as the government could raise the funds to maintain the army, subsidize the Continental allies, and keep the navy afloat, Britain could not lose.

The problem was that Pitt's strategy was vulnerable on two points. One was that Britain's main Continental allies—Austria, Prussia, and Russia—as yet understood no better than the British that they were fighting a new kind of opponent. Consequently, they paid too much attention to their individual territorial ambitions, especially in Poland, over which they competed greedily. The first coalition against France (1793–1797) organized by the British was at best a loose collection of headstrong dynastic states, with no common strategy or integrated command.

The other weak point was that France was a new kind of nation conducting a new kind of war against traditional eighteenth-century states. France rapidly became a society mobilized for war—a "nation in arms." The French revolutionary armies were not the comparatively small professional armies of the eighteenth century but the product of the *levée en masse* (conscription) and fervent patriotism. The officer corps, purged of its aristocratic element, became a force organized by merit and courage as opposed to birth and social position; the rank and file became a mass of men motivated by nationalism and democratic ideology. The French armies struck with shocking enthusiasm, and they aimed not at winning prizes to be traded later at the negotiating table but at total defeat of the enemy. Further, the French were assisted by radicals and ethnic nationalists within each of the conservative powers. The French Revolutionary War, therefore, was a struggle between a modern society and a number of traditional societies. The British landed oligarchy almost failed to meet this challenge, but in the end it was able to do so by harnessing the economic power of Britain's own modern sector—industry and commerce.

The war went badly for Britain during the first five years. The French threw the allied forces (including British expeditionary units) out of France, seized Belgium, and moved into the Rhineland and Northern Italy. Then in 1794–1795, they conquered Holland, dealing a severe blow to the British army in the process. The coalition began to break up. Spain and Prussia made their peace with France in 1795, and after defeat in Northern Italy at the hands of the brilliant young French general, Napoleon Bonaparte, the Austrians followed suit in 1797. The coalition collapsed, and the British stood alone against the French. Pitt had focused on taking the French possessions in the West Indies, but that theater turned out to be a sinkhole for the British army and navy, which together lost nearly forty thousand men, mostly to yellow fever.

Only the navy had much to show for its efforts. In naval warfare, the British retained their traditional advantage over the French. A century of war at sea gave the British an impressive backlog of experience in tactics and commanders. To be sure, the British navy remained a traditional aristocratic institution, with the officer ranks a preserve for oligarchy and the enlisted men a mistreated and brutalized segment of the laboring population. Yet naval operations required much knowledge and skill of its officers. The necessity of promoting according to merit had asserted itself and made the Royal Navy into a highly professional service. French revolutionary enthusiasm, so effective in the army, could not make up for the loss of professional skill that resulted from the purging of aristocrats from the French navy. The British navy never lost a major engagement during the twenty-five years of the war, and the French suffered about ten times as many casualties as the British in naval battles. Throughout the war, the British navy showed enthusiasm and aggressiveness in battles and flexibility and opportunism in tactics. In the years from 1793 to 1797, the navy collected French colonies in the West Indies; a fleet under Admiral Richard Howe defeated the French off Brest ("The Glorious First of June," 1794); and Admirals John Jervis and Horatio Nelson destroyed a large Spanish flotilla at Cape St. Vincent (and thus prevented them from joining the French). By 1797, then, the war was a standoff: French victories on land and British victories at sea. The British navy alone stood between Britain and the French army that was making preparations for invasion.

THE WAR AT HOME

Meanwhile, the war at home was intensifying. British trade with France collapsed, and French privateers had some success in preying on British commercial shipping. An economic recession was the result. This was followed by a poor harvest in 1794, which caused serious food shortages, high prices, and food riots. Such economic disruptions were to occur sporadically throughout the war. Combined with high taxes and unpopular recruiting practices by the army and navy, economic troubles contributed to the growth of radicalism among the laboring ranks.

The extent of popular radicalism in the 1790s is very difficult to determine, for the evidence is shadowy at best. Clearly the radical movement was significant and was regarded as dangerous by the government. The LCS had perhaps five thousand members by 1795, and radical societies in other big cities sometimes enrolled half that many. They could rally very large crowds: the LCS, for instance, gathered at least 100,000 in central London on several occasions. These societies corresponded with each other and with the French Jacobins (the most militant revolutionaries), and the government heard rumors of nocturnal drillings on Yorkshire moors. In Scotland, most of the Lowland boroughs produced radical societies, and in 1792–1793, delegates from eighty of them met in a convention in Edinburgh. The Scottish Convention and the massive demonstrations in London were the boldest radical activities of the early 1790s. On the whole, the radicals before 1797 stuck to petitioning and persuasion. Certainly they failed to mobilize the mass of the laboring poor; hence they remained a minority of the population.

In the eyes of the government, however, the radical movement was a grave threat. Beginning in 1793, Pitt's government undertook to suppress the radicals by authoritarian, if legal action. In Scotland, two radicals—a lawyer and a Unitarian preacher—were convicted and sentenced to transportation to Botany Bay in Australia for spreading *The Rights of Man* and an address from the United Irishmen. When the Scottish Convention reconvened in November and December of 1793, the authorities broke it up, arrested the leaders, and sentenced three more of them to transportation. In England, the government adopted an extensive system of spies and paid informants. With secret (and shaky) evidence, Pitt secured from Parliament suspension of habeas corpus in 1794. Shortly after, the government arrested twelve London radicals, including Hardy and Horne Tooke, and tried them for treason. Although the jury refused to convict them, the effect of this pressure on the radical societies was great. Many respectable reformers like Hardy and Horne Tooke withdrew from politics. Then in 1795, following one of the largest demonstrations in London, Pitt got Parliament to pass the "Two Acts," which prohibited meetings of more than fifty people and made speaking or writing against the crown and constitution treasonable.

This repression occurred within the context of a very strong conservative reaction. Burke's *Reflections on the Revolution in France* was the first but far from the last work of conservative propaganda. Conservative writings such as the *Anti-Jacobin*, edited by George Canning, and the *Cheap Repository Tracts*, published by Hannah More, emphasized to rich and poor alike that British liberty depended on maintaining the existing constitution, the "natural" social hierarchy, and the rights of private property. They played very effectively on the nationalist sentiment that had developed during the century of war against France. Revolutionary ideas were portrayed as corrosive of good old English forthrightness and purity. The ideology of the inseparability of church and state was revived, and the "Church and King" mobs rioted against reformers like Joseph Priestley, a Unitarian minister and chemist whose laboratory was sacked in 1791. The government deliberately concocted rituals celebrating loyalty to the Crown. In 1792, men of property founded the Association for the Preservation of Liberty and Property against Republicans and Levellers, with hundreds of branches in both rural and urban areas. Finally, a volunteer force drawn from the gentry and yeomanry was established in 1794; it enlisted over 400,000 men by 1804. The upshot of this potent movement was to identify conservatism with nationalism and reform with disloyalty and to provide the emotional background for the formation of a new Tory party made up of Pittites and conservative Whigs.

THE CRISIS OF 1797–1798

The repression of the years 1793–1797 did not kill the radical movement but drove it underground. Because many of the more cautious reformers dropped out, leadership of the movement fell into the hands of extremists, some of whom had revolutionary intentions. The LCS, for example, now turned into a revolutionary conspiracy. Such revolutionary organizations established close connections with the United Irishmen, who by 1796–1797 were actively plotting to set up an independent republic in Ireland with French help. Agents of the United Irishmen formed United Irish societies among the Irish Catholic immigrants in London, Lancashire, and southwestern Scotland. More ominous, societies of United Englishmen and United Scotsmen were formed. They intended to establish independent republics in England and Scotland as well as in Ireland. The British state itself was to be dismembered.

How serious was the revolutionary movement? Again, the evidence is spotty and often tainted by official paranoia. Probably not every member of the widespread but small revolutionary cells was committed to violence. But the government received reports of drilling and arming among by people in a number of districts. And there is no question that some United Irish agents and English radicals did try to coordinate a revolutionary outbreak. Clearly, the conspirators could not have succeeded by themselves, but with French intervention and a simultaneous mass peasant revolt in Ireland, they might well have brought an end to the British oligarchy in 1798.

The French certainly hoped to invade and only were prevented from doing so by the British navy. In 1797, Napoleon was appointed commander in chief of France's army and began assembling a massive invasion force. Worse, in April 1797 the British Channel fleet at Spithead mutinied, and the North Sea fleet at the Nore followed suit in May. This was the most perilous moment in the history of Great Britain between 1707 and 1940. Undoubtedly, the low pay and miserable conditions of life at sea lay behind the mutinies, but radical ideology also contributed. Over 10 percent of the sailors were Irish, many of them former Defenders or United Irishmen. The LCS spread radical literature among the men. Fortunately for the British regime, the Spithead mutiny was settled by rapid liberal concessions to the mutineers. The Nore mutineers were split by dissension and then put down by force; twenty-eight of the leaders were hanged and nearly a hundred were flogged. By October 1797, the French had missed their great chance. In that month, the Nore fleet was able to smash the Dutch navy at Camperdown. Napoleon gave up his plans to invade and turned to the conquest of Egypt instead. His army was cut off there by Nelson's crushing victory over a French fleet in the Battle of the Nile (Aboukir Bay) in 1798.

The timing of those events was extremely unlucky for the revolutionaries in Britain and Ireland because it deprived the United Irishmen of French assistance just as they rebelled. The United Irishmen had busily prepared for revolution throughout 1796. The Irishman Wolfe Tone went to Paris to seek French assistance. In December 1797, a large French invasion force under General Lazare Hoche and accompanied by Wolfe Tone actually appeared in Bantry Bay in southwestern Ireland. As usual, the weather was Protestant, and the force had to turn back; it was a near miss, however, and the United Irish continued to badger the French for help. Thousands of Irish peasants were mobilized and armed with pikes by the revolutionaries. All through 1797–1798, the British executive in Ireland struggled to break up the rebellion before it started. The British general, Lake, relying on the ill-disciplined Irish militia and yeomanry, set out to disarm the populace by brute force. In their search for weapons, Lake's troops burned cottages and arrested, flogged, and tortured thousands of Catholics. Hideous wooden triangles on which men were tied for flogging blemished the landscape. Then, having penetrated the United Irish organization, the government arrested many of its leaders in March 1798. The remaining conspirators in desperation decided to go ahead with the rebellion even without French help. It began in May 1798.

The rebellion was supposed to break out simultaneously all over Ireland, but the only significant outbursts occurred in Wexford and Ulster. The lack of coordination condemned them to defeat. In Wexford, the insurrectionaries were almost exclusively Catholic. They attacked Protestants indiscriminately, taking revenge for centuries of oppression. But the peasants were badly armed and trained. The Wexford rebellion was beaten, and the Protestant retribution was begun before the Ulster rebellion broke out in June. In Ulster, the rebels were mainly of Protestant origin and reflected the nonsectarian ideals of the French Revolution. They, too, were defeated by the end of June. Only in August did French assistance arrive—too little, too late. The French had dithered and dissembled because they never trusted the United Irishmen's estimates of popular support. Thus the French force that landed in Mayo in August 1798 amounted to only one thousand men. They fought gallantly for a month and then surrendered, while the small band of United Irish enthusiasts and illiterate Catholic peasants who had joined them were cut to pieces by British troops (including Scottish and Welsh regiments). Shortly after, the British navy intercepted a somewhat larger French expedition and captured it—among the captured troops was Wolfe Tone, who was tried and convicted of treason. He cheated the hangman by committing suicide with a razor.

The reprisals taken by British troops, especially by the Irish militia and yeomanry, were savage. But the British government, including Pitt and his lord lieutenant in Ireland, Lord Cornwallis, hoped to prevent further rebellion by more humane means—union between the British and Irish Parliaments plus Catholic emancipation (that is, allowing Catholics the same political rights as Protestants). Unfortunately, George III opposed emancipation: "Mr. Pitt," he wrote, "has in my opinion saved Ireland, and now the new Lord Lieutenant must not lose the present moment of terror for frightening the supporters of the Castle into a Union with this country; and no further indulgences must be granted to the Roman Catholics." Pitt was not the man to press the king on a matter George III felt strongly about, especially since in 1788 George III already had suffered one bout of his debilitating illness from porphyria (thought at the time to be insanity). Thus the bill of union that was presented to both the British and the Irish Parliaments included no measure of Catholic emancipation. The bill passed easily in Britain but met strong opposition in Ireland, especially among Protestant patriots who did not want to give up what they had won in 1782 but also among nervous Protestants who believed that their religion would be more secure from Catholicism under the protection of their own legislators. Gradually, however, some members of the ruling elite became persuaded that their best defense in the long run lay in close connection with the British, and the government meanwhile used all the tools of eighteenth-century corruption to get its way. Though the debate in Ireland was furious, Parliament in Dublin passed the Act of Union in 1800. On January 1, 1801, the Irish Parliament disappeared; Ireland was given one hundred members in the British Parliament at Westminster. Pitt resigned in 1801 because of his failure to carry Catholic emancipation, but he did not press the issue any further. The United Kingdom of Great Britain and Ireland thus came into being; it was to last until 1921, an unhappy and only partly consummated union but one essential to resolve the crisis of 1797–1798.

WAR, 1798–1815

After 1798, the war became a long and drawn out slogging match. Pitt (who died in 1806) and his successors relied on the British navy to stave off a French invasion of the British Isles and to apply economic pressure on France, but not until 1813 could Britain and the allies defeat Napoleon on land. The war went through five main phases: (1) 1798–1802, when Britain organized a second coalition against France, only to see it hammered to pieces by Napoleon; (2) 1802–1803, when by the Peace of Amiens the British and French agreed to a truce in the fighting; (3) 1803–1812, when Napoleon won unparalleled domination over Europe, defeating a third coalition of aristocratic states but losing at the Battle of Trafalgar (1805) his last chance to invade Britain and then suffocating from a British naval blockade; (4) 1812–1813, when Napoleon invaded Russia but was forced to retreat and then suffered a devastating defeat at the hands of the fourth coalition—the first alliance to involve all four anti-French powers: Britain (the organizer and paymaster), Prussia, Austria, and Russia; and (5) 1815, when Napoleon, having escaped from exile in Elba, rallied his army, only to be defeated once and for all at Waterloo.

During the entire period from 1798 to 1815, the British government sustained the war effort by tapping the tremendous economic resources of the nation. Here Pitt's administrative reforms of the 1780s and his wartime financial prowess proved decisive. The increasingly dynamic British economy—whether in cotton textiles, iron, coal mining, or agriculture—suffered repeated temporary dislocations, but each time it bounded back. Pitt sought to use this economic power by both borrowing and taxation. The annual governmental war loans tripled between 1794 and 1797; as the national debt soared, the annual interest charge alone rose to £30 million—more than the entire national budget of 1792! Recognizing the impossibility of financing the war wholly from loans, Pitt turned to heavy tax increases. Eventually, taxes covered about one-half of war expenditures. Customs and excises remained the principal source, but Pitt also invented the income tax in 1799. Although this tax was extremely unpopular, industrialists as well as landowners paid it. In this way, the propertied classes showed their willingness to support the oligarchical state against revolution and French domination.

Napoleon eventually recognized that if he were to win, he had to weaken the

Admiral Horatio Nelson falls mortally wounded aboard HMS Victory *at the Battle of Trafalgar, 1805.*

British economy, consequently, by his Continental System (1806), he sought to exclude British trade from Europe. But this was a game two could play: the British in 1807 responded with their Orders in Council, which blockaded French ports and allowed neutrals to trade with France only if they first shipped their goods through Britain. This was Europe's first major economic war, a kind of struggle for which the British were very much better equipped than the French. Napoleon was unable to stop up all the spigots through which Europeans sought to quench their thirst for British and colonial goods—manufactured articles, textiles, tobacco, tea, sugar, and so on—and his attempt to do so alienated people throughout the Continent. British merchants and manufacturers became extremely unhappy with the Orders in Council, which disrupted their trade, but the French failure to cut off all trade to the Continent for any sustained period gave outlets to their pressure. When the British government (then led by Lord Liverpool) revoked the Orders in Council in 1812, Napoleon was only too glad to abandon the Continental System. "Undoubtedly," he wrote, "it is necessary to harm our foes, but above all we must live."

Napoleon invaded Portugal in 1807 to close off one of the biggest leaks in the Continental System. The British sent an expeditionary force under Arthur Wellesley (later the duke of Wellington) to stop the French in Portugal and to assist the Spanish who were rebelling against French rule. The consequent Peninsular War never absorbed more than forty thousand British troops, but it tied down a quarter of a million Frenchmen. Eventually, Wellington was able to go on the offensive and in 1813 to cross the Pyrenees into France.

The economic war also led Napoleon into the decisive and disastrous invasion of Russia in 1812. By then, Napoleon needed to coerce the Russians into cooperating with his exclusion of British trade. His gigantic army was successful at first, but after taking Moscow it had to withdraw in bitter cold and privation through land destroyed by the Russians themselves. The fourth coalition, again organized and paid for by the British and now including all four anti-French powers, defeated Napoleon and sent its army into Paris in 1814. The French emperor abdicated and retired to Elba.

Meanwhile, the Orders in Council caused war between Britain and the United States (1812–1814). This conflict was a diversion that the British wanted to avoid, but their insistence on stopping and searching American ships for British seamen aggravated American touchiness about freedom of the seas. The French could give the Americans no assistance this time, but the British were unable to deploy enough manpower to defeat and occupy the United States. British troops burned Washington, D.C., but by 1814, the war was a stalemate and both powers were ready for peace. The only outcome from the British point of view was the lesson that to protect Canada in the future, the British must maintain good relations with America.

The final act of the great war between Britain and France was played in the summer of 1815. Napoleon slipped away from Elba, rallied the French army once more, and reclaimed power in France. The allied powers dispatched a huge army under the duke of Wellington to defeat him. The two forces crashed together at Waterloo, near Brussels in Belgium. The battle was, as Wellington said, "the nearest run thing that you ever saw in your life," but the combined British and Prussian armies won the day. Napoleon abdicated again and spent the remainder of his days in exile on the tiny British island of St. Helena.

Now we are ready to understand why the British went to war in 1793 and how the oligarchy was able to survive. Pitt and his sucessors were principally concerned about protecting British interests on the Continent, interests defined as the need to export goods to Europe and to prevent any one power from dominating all the others. Only toward the end did the British government insist on the expulsion of Napoleon, and that was simply because they regarded him as insatiably aggressive. In this way, the British government reflected the concerns of its modern as well as traditional propertied elements.

The regime was able to survive the stress for several reasons. First, Pitt had restored the effectiveness of the government between 1783 and 1793; indeed, he unwittingly had taken important steps toward creating a modern state. Second, he and his successors were able to use parliamentary taxing authority to harness the burgeoning British economy. Third, the British navy kept the French from invading the British Isles in force. Fourth, resolute repressive action by the government—plus a large measure of luck—kept the French, the Irish, and the British revolutionaries from coordinating their efforts. Finally, in the ideological struggle at home, conservative nationalism proved to be marginally stronger than reformism and revolution.

THE PRIZES AND COSTS OF WAR, 1793–1815

It is important to remember that mere survival of the state and security of limited interests on the Continent were all that Britain had fought for; otherwise, one would not think they gained much for their efforts. In the negotiations at Vienna that produced the postwar settlement, the British sought no territory in Europe and not a great deal elsewhere. They kept a few colonial prizes that turned out to be valuable later: Malta in the Mediterranean; Guiana, Tobago, and St. Lucia in the West Indies; the Cape of Good Hope in South Africa; and Mauritius in the Indian Ocean. But the British negotiator, Viscount Castlereagh, was a supreme realist and did obtain what Britain wanted most: security of British interests in Europe. France was not broken up, but its borders were reduced to pre-1792 lines, and the Bourbon monarchy was restored. Holland and the Austrian Netherlands were merged into a stronger state, the United Netherlands, and given British cash to fortify against French intrusion. Further, Castlereagh obtained a balance of power: Britain, Austria, Prussia, and Russia signed an alliance against a recurrence of French might, and Prussia and Austria were made strong enough to block a Russian advance into Central Europe. Finally, Castlereagh persuaded all the powers to meet periodically in congress to settle disputes by discussion.

For these benefits the British had paid dearly. The war had not been distinguished for technological innovations in weaponry; nevertheless; British manpower losses were bad enough—upward of 210,000 died in combat or from disease, or one in every eighty-five people in the British Isles, a more severe loss proportionately than in World War II. Further, the war cost the British about £1.5 billion in direct expenditures, plus untold sums in economic gains forgone because of the diversion of resources into warmaking. But here one has to be careful about cost accounting. First, the propertied few suffered much less than the unpropertied many from the economic burden because the massive loans floated by the government took the form of bonds purchased by the rich. These were redeemed after the war through taxation, now once again customs and excises, which put a disproportionate weight on the poor. Second, British economic growth went ahead during the war, though it was not as great as it would have been if Europe had remained at peace. Because the French economy suffered more than did the British, Britain emerged in 1815 very much ahead of its closest economic rival than it had been in 1793.

Great wars almost inevitably alter the societies of the participating states, including the victors. This was true of British society during the war from 1793 to 1815, even though the regime went to war in part to defend itself from revolutionary social change. It is safe to say that the British ruling elite—the landowners—came out of the war stronger and more secure than any other European aristocracy. This fact would have a great impact on nineteenth-century Britain. Not only did no successful revolution occur in Britain, but also land values and rentals went up. The British landed orders felt sufficiently threatened by domestic agitation and external revolution that they thrust off many of their remaining traditional paternalist obligations. Most notably, they passed the Combination Acts of 1799 and 1800, prohibiting workers from negotiating collectively to regulate wages; they repealed in 1813–1814 the old Tudor legislation regulating wages and entry into crafts; and in 1815 they passed the Corn Law, a duty on the importation of grain for the purpose of keeping prices high on the wheat grown in England. This "abdication of paternalism" is likely to have happened, war or no war, for as we have seen, it was well under way in the general transition from custom to contract. The process was accelerated during the war by the resentment and anxiety the oligarchy felt in the face of popular radicalism. In any case, the abdication of paternalism— and the simultaneous insistence on political repression and social discipline—by the landowners contributed powerfully to a great transformation of the social structure, from social hierarchy to social classes.

By 1815, Britain was well on the way to being a class society—that is, a society organized into three large, self-conscious, and hostile "layers" of people. Each of these horizontal groupings—the landed class, the middle class, and the working class—was becoming aware that its members shared interests and experiences, as opposed to the interests and experiences of the other classes. Everywhere in Europe, this kind of society formed during the first half of the nineteenth century. In Britain, it happened with a special speed and intensity because the tremendous changes accompanying the Triple Revolution (see Chapter 10) coincided with the turmoil of the French revolution and war.

The process of class formation was a matter of *consciousness*. Under pressure from below, the British landed oligarchy between 1793 and 1815 became conscious of the need to stand shoulder to shoulder and protect their power. The commercial and industrial ranks likewise experienced a growing consciousness of their own special interests. They regarded themselves as the people responsible for the commercial and industrial expansion of the nation; hence they considered themselves to be the source of Britain's power and progress. Yet they felt they were denied social and political power equal to their economic accomplishments. Nonconformists especially felt aggrieved by their exclusion from Parliament and municipal office. People of the middling ranks continued during the war years to agitate for parliamentary reform and then objected when the government's suppression of radicalism fell on them as well as laborers. They complained loudly when the Orders in Council and the new Corn Law infringed their interests. Thus in the course of organizing to promote their interests, the British middle class came on the stage of history—self-confident, aggressive, blunt, and feeling aggrieved.

It took the laboring people much longer than the landed orders and the middle class to develop and disseminate widely a consciousness of themselves as a class. In some ways the process was not complete until the late nineteenth century, for obstacles such as illiteracy, poverty, and social dependency were too strong to be overcome easily. How far the working class was formed by 1815 and how much the experience of the war had to do with it is not easy to say. Radicalism spread fairly widely through the British artisan ranks, but it remained a minority movement. Most of the laboring poor seem to have been Loyalist and conservative, or simply ignorant and apathetic, rather than radical or revolutionary. Clearly, the massive social changes of the Triple Revolution had more to do with working-class formation than did democratic parties during the war with France. Nevertheless, the foundations, at least, of the British working-class consciousness were laid by 1815, and radicalism and repression played a part in the shared experience underlying class consciousness. Tom Paine's *Rights of Man*, for instance, became one of the most widely read books in working-class homes.

In the years between 1805 and 1815, artisanal radicalism slowly revived, and popular patriotism began to merge with the movement. The key figure here was William Cobbett, a farmer's son, journalist, and consummate political polemicist. Cobbett was an instinctive Tory, full of nostalgia for traditional rural England, and he criticized the government at first only for its ineffectiveness against the French. But in 1804–1806, his criticism of government inefficiency made him the victim of official prosecution; afterward, he became for many years the leading radical critical of corruption, patronage, the overmighty oligarchy, and the unreformed Parliament. Critics like Cobbett by 1815 were helping the laboring people understand the relations between the abdication of paternalism, the corrupt self-interest of the landowners and London financiers, the abuse of civil rights, and the need for parliamentary reform. This line of thinking proved to be the main connection between the French Revolution and the emerging working-class consciousness in Britain.

Suggested Reading

Ayling, Stanley, *Edmund Burke: His Life and Opinions* (London: Cassell, 1988).

Barrell, John, *Imagining the King's Death: Figurative Treason, Fantasies of Regicide, 1793–1796* (Oxford: Oxford University Press, 2000).

Christie, Ian, *Stress and Stability in Late-Eighteenth-Century Britain* (Oxford: Clarendon Press, 1984).

————, *Wars and Revolutions: Britain, 1760–1815* (Cambridge, Mass.: Harvard University Press, 1982).

Curtin, Nancy J., *The United Irishmen: Popular Politics in Ulster and Dublin, 1791–1798* (New York: Clarendon Press, 1994).

Derry, J. W., *Politics in the Age of Fox, Pitt and Liverpool* (New York: St. Martin's Press, 1992).

Duffy, Michael, *The Younger Pitt* (New York: Longmans, 2000).

Ehrman, John, *The Younger Pitt*, 3 vols. (London: Constable 1969, 1983, 1996).

Elliott, Marianne, *Partners in Revolution: The United Irishmen and France* (New Haven: Yale University Press, 1982).

————, *Wolfe Tone: Prophet of Irish Independence* (New Haven: Yale University Press, 1989).

Emsley, Clive, *British Society and the French Wars, 1793–1815* (London: Macmillan, 1979).

Goodwin, Albert, *The Friends of Liberty: The English Democratic Movement in the Age of the French Revolution* (Cambridge, Mass.: Harvard University Press, 1979).

Hobsbawm, E. J., *The Age of Revolution, 1789–1848* (New York: New American Library, 1962).

Macleod, Emma Vincent, *A War of Ideas: British Attitudes towards the Wars against Revolutionary France, 1792–1802* (Aldershot: Ashgate, 1998).

McFarland, Elaine, *Ireland and Scotland in the Age of Revolution: Planting the Green Bough* (Edinburgh: Edinburgh University Press, 1994).

McKay, Derek, and H. M. Scott, *The Rise of the Great Powers, 1648–1815* (London: Longman, 1983).

Newman, Gerald, *The Rise of English Nationalism: A Cultural History, 1740–1830* (New York: St. Martin's, 1987).

Pakenham, Frank, *The Year of Liberty: The Story of the Great Irish Rebellion of 1798* (London: Hodder & Stoughton, 1969).

Perkin, Harold, *The Origins of Modern English Society, 1780–1880* (Toronto: University of Toronto Press, 1969).

Powell, David, *Charles James Fox: Man of the People* (London: Croom Helm, 1989).

Royle, Edward, *Revolutionary Britannia? Reflections on the Threat of Revolution in Britain, 1789–1848* (Manchester: Manchester University Press, 2000).

Thompson, E. P., *The Making of the English Working Class* (London: Gollancz, 1963).

Wahrman, Dror, *Imagining the Middle Class: The Political Representation of Class in Britain, 1780–1840* (New York: Cambridge University Press, 1995).

Williams, Gwyn A., *Artisans and Sans-Culottes* (London: Arnold, 1968).

Chapter 12

Intellectual and Spiritual Revolutions, 1780–1815

The period from the 1780s to 1815 was one of revolutions in thought as well as in society and politics. Indeed social and political change during these years of crisis set in motion major transformations in the ways that the British people understood themselves, their society, and their place in the universe. Not all of the lines of change went in the same direction, for the society was too complex to call forth only a single set of intellectual and spiritual responses. Thus there emerged in this period two directly opposed strands of thought: one (broadly speaking, the utilitarian) characterized by extreme rationalism and cold calculation, the other (the evangelical and romantic) marked by heightened emotions and otherworldliness. The tension between the two contributed as much as did social and political revolutions to the unique drama of the period. Both strands, however, were alike in that they broke with essential aspects of Augustan ideas and beliefs.

UTILITARIANISM

The utilitarian strand of thought seems in some ways not to break with the main lines of eighteenth-century ideas but to extend them. As we saw in Chapter 5, a form of utilitarianism was a common philosophy of early eighteenth-century moralists. The utilitarianism of the last decades of the century stood firmly in the British empiricist tradition. Yet the leading utilitarian of the late eighteenth and early nineteenth centuries—Jeremy Bentham—extended these earlier lines of thought so radically as to produce something entirely new: not a cheerful philosophy for the landed gentry but a clanking ideology for the new industrial captains.

Jeremy Bentham (1748–1832) was one of the most influential British thinkers of the modern era but a distinctly odd character. Like Adam Smith, whose economic ideas he came to adopt, Bentham was a simple and unworldly man, an empiricist with little experience of the world. His father, a Tory lawyer, was very anxious to climb the ladder of London society. But Jeremy, a weak, shy, painfully awkward youth, found success only in his studies. He became a man of books, almost totally intellectualized. He read Latin and Greek at age six, entered Oxford at thirteen, and took his M. A. at eighteen. Though he studied law, he was not fit for the rough and tumble of practice at the bar. He turned instead to the philosophical criticism of English law and from that to moral and social philosophy in general.

Bentham thought of himself as doing for moral philosophy what Newton had done for physics—reducing all data to one or a few principles. To him the greatest principle was utility. In general, utilitarianism is an ethical philosophy that judges behavior or social action according to its consequences. Bentham was a hedonistic utilitarian—that is, he believed any act is good or bad depending on whether it promotes happiness (or pleasure). To him, this principle was based on the very essence of human nature: that each person behaves so as to pursue pleasure and avoid pain. Bentham totally separated this principle from any concept of a divine plan and set it squarely in a materialistic philosophy. Contemplation of the divine was of no interest to him. Nor was he interested in elevated ideas of beauty and truth. He had no sensitivity to beauty in art or poetry, and he carried empiricism to the extreme. He disparaged words like *society, beauty, good,* or *social contract* as simply abstractions because they stood for no real objects in the world. Use of such words leads people to think that abstract objects do exist and thus to make mistakes in moral and legal philosophy. Bentham believed that all we can know comes through the sensations. Complex ideas of the imagination are nothing but the mechanical manipulation and combination of sensory experience. Indeed, human beings are little more than calculating machines that register sensations and sum up pleasures and pains.

Bentham's first book, published in 1776, was an attack on the orthodox legal thought of the day, best expressed by Sir William Blackstone, the century's most eminent legal philosopher. Blackstone believed that the existing system of English law was natural and reasonable, its basis being the idea of social contract. Bentham, however, regarded the law as an irrational jungle of historical precedent and accident. Further, the social contract was a fiction, a metaphysical mistake. What was needed was a radical simplification and codification of the laws according to the principle of utility. A law (past, present, or future) ought to be judged as to whether it increases or decreases the happiness of the society. Because society, Bentham said, is nothing but the aggregate of individuals who make it up, the happiness of all is just a matter of calculating the total of individual pleasures and pains.

Bentham laid out his system in exhaustive (and exhausting) detail in his *Introduction to the Principles of Morals and Legislation*, first published in 1789. The moral and legal thinking he advocated in it is remarkably mechanical and mathematical. Bentham called his system the "felicific calculus," the process whereby pleasures and pains are analyzed, measured, and summed up. Bentham made no qualitative distinctions between types of pleasures and pains: all are weighted according to the physical sensations they cause. "Pushpin," he was to say, "is as good as poetry." Consequently, he argued that no motive in itself is either good or bad. All actions by individuals or the state are good or bad only according to their consequences—that is, whether on balance the action brings more pleasure or more pain. Lawmaking and governing are simply matters of weighing and counting.

Bentham argued that every government should have as its purpose promoting the greatest happiness of the greatest number of people. This principle would seem to provide the basis for interventionist policies by the government; indeed, some Benthamite civil servants and social scientists in the nineteenth century definitely favored interventionist social engineering. State socialism in Britain looks back to the Benthamite tradition. But Bentham himself adopted Adam Smith's laissez-faire ideas, and so generally opposed state intervention in matters of economic policy. Why? Bentham liked the self-regulating aspect of Smith's free market economic model. It was simple and seemingly scientific. Further, he agreed with Smith that the individual knows best what is good for himself or herself. Because all laws essentially restrict human behavior, they inevitably cause pain; consequently, they should be minimized. The utilitarian philosophy was, therefore, materialist, calculating, and individualistic.

Benthamite philosophy was not necessarily democratic. In theory, every kind of government can pursue the greatest happiness of the greatest number. In his early years, in fact, Bentham was a Tory. He opposed both the American and French Revolutions because of their talk of "natural rights"—to Bentham a clear case of philosophical fiction. After 1800, however, Bentham became a democrat—indeed, one of the leading theoreticians of radical parliamentary reform. He did so because he became disillusioned with the British oligarchy, which refused to accept particular schemes he proposed, notably an elaborate plan for prison reform. By 1810 he reasoned that the only way to make the interests of the rulers coincide with the interests of the ruled was to bring about a more democratic representative government. He and his disciples like James Mill thus combined the ideas of utilitarian legal codification and laissez-faire economics with parliamentary reform. By the time Bentham died in 1832, this package formed a potent program, the dominant political ideology of the new British middle class.

PARSON MALTHUS

There was yet another aspect of the utilitarian package—the population principle of the Reverend Thomas Malthus. This was an odd element in utilitarianism, for the ideas of Bentham and Smith were basically optimistic and progressive, whereas those of Malthus were pessimistic and even reactionary. Nevertheless, many early nineteenth-century Britons believed that these ideas fitted together. Malthus (1766–1834) was the son of an enlightened English country gentleman. His father was a friend of Hume and Rousseau and a believer in the power of reason to improve humankind. In the late 1790s, father and son (who was by then a clergyman in the Church of England) engaged in a profound argument about the fate of humanity. Malthus's father contended that progress was possible and likely. But Malthus himself argued a fundamentally pessimistic position based on his deep concern about the long-term effects of the population explosion. Malthus committed his views to paper in *An Essay on the Principle of Population*, first published in 1798.

Parson Malthus reasoned with great logical force that the population of any country tends to outstrip the food supply. His explanation was that the population tends to increase geometrically—that is, 1, 2, 4, 8, 16, 32, and so on—whereas the food supply can increase only arithmetically—that is, 1, 2, 3, 4, 5, 6, and so on. As any farmer knew, food production could be expanded only by adding increments of land to the already cultivated—increments of less fertile soil, to boot. But the population would double itself in each generation until it was more or less brutally checked. Malthus thought that the only checks on population increase are natural ("vice and misery") and prudential (delay of marriage). Hence, Malthus argued against the paternalism of the Poor Law, which, he said, only spreads poverty and hunger while encouraging the poor to have more children. The Poor Laws, he wrote, "tend to create the poor they maintain."

Malthus was himself a humane and cheerful man. But his gloomy predictions, seemingly based in inexorable facts, appeared to make economics a dismal science. In fact, Malthus became England's first professional economist when he accepted a professorship of political economy at the East India College in 1805. Many utilitarians, who admired his mathematical reasoning and his sticking to hard facts, thought that Malthus was advising against any humanitarian social policy. Thus his ideas strongly reinforced the laissez-faire weapons in the utilitarian arsenal. Moreover, he seemed to blame the poor for their own poverty, for it was their own imprudence that increased the number of mouths to feed. This, of course, was a comfortable doctrine for the wealthy but was not exactly what Malthus meant. His own view was that land reform and a shift of resources to agriculture were necessary to mitigate the harsh facts of life.

JOHN WESLEY AND THE THEOLOGY OF REVIVAL

Parson Malthus's assumption that passion as well as reason determines human behavior forms a bridge to the second great stream of British thought in the age of revolutions. Both evangelicalism and romanticism were intensely emotional movements. The evangelical revival had an enormous impact on the tone and temper of British society. It raised the religious temperature of British Christianity at the same time as it chilled the bawdy and licentious behavior of preindustrial culture. Evangelicalism stood in vigorous opposition to conventional Augustan religion. Whereas eighteenth-century religion (both Anglican and nonconformist) was dry, unemotional, and complacent, evangelicalism was emotional, highly moralistic, and intensely personal. Beginning in the 1730s, the evangelical spark glowed warmly until in the 1780s it burst into flames that swept through the British Isles. It reinvigorated a segment of the Church of England; spawned a dynamic new denomination, Methodism; and revived the fervor of the old nonconformist churches. By 1815, the evangelical revival had transformed the religious life of Britain.

The core of evangelicalism was Methodism, whose principal founder was John Wesley (1703–1791), arguably the most important individual in British history between 1750 and 1850. His own quest for holiness set the pattern for Methodism

John Wesley Preaching in Cornwall, *by Frank Dadd. Here the founder of Methodism preaches one of his outdoor sermons to people of all social orders.*

and the wider evangelical revival that fanned out around it. Born in rural Lincolnshire to an Anglican clergyman and his strong-willed wife, John Wesley inherited from his ancestors the spark of Puritanism. He was the favorite son in a family of nineteen children, but because of his mother's domineering personality he had severe problems in feeling his own worth. At Oxford he shunned the drinking and wenching of most other students, but his real turn to seriousness did not come until he was ordained shortly after graduation. As a young tutor and newly minted priest, Wesley joined a few undergraduates in forming a "holy club" devoted to regular study, prayer, fasting, and charitable work. The methodical activities of this little circle won for its members the derisive label of "Methodists" and became the model for later Methodist cells, but they did not bring Wesley the assurance of holiness he sought.

In the 1730s, Wesley's quest for holiness came to a crisis. He embarked on a missionary expedition to Georgia, hoping to convert the Indians and to learn religious truth himself in the process. Alas, the expedition was a disaster, and Wesley returned to London in 1738, more persuaded than ever of his own unworthiness. But during his service in Georgia he had met some Moravians (German pietists) who deeply impressed him by their simple, calm religiosity even in the face of the terrifying Atlantic storms. They stressed personal salvation in their theology, and they pressed Wesley on the issue. For a time, Wesley could answer their questioning only by saying he knew Christ had died to save people in general. But in May of 1738, in the depths of depression, Wesley finally had a conversion experience and found relief from his agony of self-doubt. One evening at a religious meeting, he reported, "I felt my heart strangely warmed. I felt I did trust in Christ, Christ alone for salvation; and an assurance was given me that He had taken away my sins, even mine, and saved me from the law of sin and death."

Wesley spent the rest of his long life carrying the message of personal salvation to everyone who would listen. He never took a parish but became an itinerant preacher. He preached in churches, homes, village halls, and open fields to high and low, regardless of social rank. He is thought to have traveled some 250,000 miles on horseback and to have preached more than forty thousand sermons. He and his disciples, including his brother Charles and the spellbinding orator George Whitefield (1714–1770), were amazingly effective. Although they rarely were welcomed by the conventional bishops and parish clergymen, and although they frequently had to face hostile mobs inspired by local squires and parsons, Wesley and his team of preachers touched thousands of souls neglected by the Church of England. Their intensely emotional words, and above all their hymns, moved crowds of people to conversion, sometimes causing men and women to gesture uncontrollably, to writhe on the floor, and to groan loudly as they parted company with evil. Moreover, Wesley left behind him in each locality small societies of the converted called "classes," for the purpose of mutual support and exhortation. They were tightly organized, intense groups of people devoted to Bible reading, regular prayer, and mutual confession of sin. By 1780, there were over eighty thousand Wesleyan Methodists in Britain, and in 1815 almost 220,000. These figures show only part of Wesley's influence, for the great revival he inspired affected many thousands of people never organized into Methodist classes as it swept through the nonconformist sects and though one wing, at least, of the Church of England.

What was the theology of the evangelical revival? It was intensely personal and salvation oriented; it put relatively little emphasis on the church as an institution but a great deal on the direct relationship between the individual and his or her God. Wesley and his followers began with a strong sense of original sin: the inherent degradation of human nature tends always to pull the individual into sin and therefore radically to separate him or her from God. Hence Wesley stressed that people are "worms," "corrupt," "diseased," and "enslaved." But God is merciful and sends grace to everyone to save all from the "law of sin and death." In this regard, Wesley rejected the Calvinist doctrine of the elect. His message was that Christ died for *all* sinners. Whitefield and a number of other evangelicals split with Wesley on this point and formed the Calvinistic Methodist branch. But most evangelicals followed Wesley: saving grace is a gift to all, which an individual can do nothing to earn or deserve but which he or she has the free will to accept or reject. Acceptance is made by an act of faith in personal salvation. Thus the essence of the Methodist theology was *salvation by grace through faith*.

Wesley did not believe that a person could remain in that initial state. By accepting grace, one is justified, or forgiven. But he or she would either move forward to sanctification (holiness) or backslide into sin. Wesley set great store by the journey of sanctification; consequently, the Methodists emphasized the practice of good works such as prayer, reading the Scriptures, visiting the sick, and giving to charity. The Methodists and the evangelicals in all the denominations became known for their social action—and above all, as we will see, for their efforts to abolish slavery. Good works, Wesley said, are necessary for holiness. At the last day, each person will stand before the divine throne and receive judgment on the balance of good and evil done in his or her whole life. Everything we have is a gift from God; therefore, we are bound to use it well. Wesley urged his followers to give to the poor not a tenth or a half, "no, not three fourths, but all!"

Methodist theology led believers to philanthropy, but it also tended to make them repressed personalities. They spoke of joyful liberation but often were humorless and censorious toward themselves and others. They regarded life as a struggle toward the final eternal accounting, inevitably a matter of gravity and earnestness. The stakes, after all, were paradise or hellfire. Every little act counted. God had given each person talents and abilities—and in many cases, property—which it was sinful to waste. The stewardship of God's gifts required people to avoid frivolous behavior and to discourage it in others. As the *Methodist Magazine* said in 1807: "If dancing be a waste of time . . . if it be a species of trifling ill suited to a creature on trial for eternity . . . then is dancing a practice utterly opposed to the whole spirit and temper of Christianity." If dancing was wrong, still more so were many of the pastimes in traditional popular culture—gambling, drinking, brawling, cock fighting, bull baiting, and all the rest. Methodism proved to be a primary weapon in the destruction of the preindustrial popular way of life.

THE APPEALS OF METHODISM

Serious and grave though it was, Methodism appealed to people at all levels of the social spectrum except the very highest and lowest. It had little effect on the aristocracy until the nineteenth century, and it failed to draw in the dregs of society. But in between, from the gentry down through the middling sorts to the shopkeepers, artisans, and industrial workers, Methodism made converts. Not all the gentry responded favorably to Methodism, for it plainly aimed to put a damper on their hard-drinking, hard-riding self-indulgence. Many of the ordinary clergymen of the Church of England took their cue from the squirearchy in resisting Methodism; moreover, they believed that Wesleyan preachers violated decorum and church discipline. In some parishes, squire and parson joined to label Methodists as

Jacobites, Jacobins, or revolutionaries. It was common for them to rouse the village roughs against them. One Wesleyan itinerant preacher was stoned to death, and many of the others, including Wesley himself, had to flee from crowds intent on bodily harm. But others among the gentry came to think of Wesleyanism as a bulwark to the social order. They believed rightly that it taught paternalism to the upper ranks on the one hand and orderliness and deference to the laboring poor on the other. Members of the oligarchy found it especially attractive during the French Revolution. They believed that the terrors of the French Revolution were a divine punishment for atheism and infidelity. As one clergyman recalled in 1817: "England was alarmed by the judgements, of which . . . she was a close spectatress, and panted for an opportunity to take the lead in restoring man to his allegiance to his Heavenly Sovereign."

People in the middling ranks responded to the message of evangelical revival practically en masse. Whether they became Methodists or participated in the emotional renovation of one of the old dissenting denominations, they took to evangelicalism enthusiastically. They found it expressed values of duty, work and thrift so important to their lives as directors of commerce and industry. Wesley noticed that Methodism was helpful to people in the market economy and that Methodists often became successful and complacent. He warned his listeners to remember that the purpose of a Christian's labor is "to please God; to do, not his own will, but the will of Him that sent him into the world." Nevertheless, the economic usefulness of evangelicalism was too strong for people in the competitive world of trade to resist. Moreover, industrial entrepreneurs recognized that evangelicalism helped tame the preindustrial laboring poor and turn them into a regular, orderly industrial work force. Evangelicalism, then, served as a weapon for the early industrialists, but one that worked *on* them as well as *for* them.

The attractions of Methodism for the laboring poor were more complex. The social and political message of Methodism plainly was conservative and quietist. Wesley remained a Tory all his life, and he told his listeners among the common people to remember their places in the social hierarchy and to bear their sufferings in this world by concentrating on their rewards in the next. Why then did so many respond favorably? First, the Wesleyans actively reached out to them and offered spiritual solace in a time when life was hard and short and when customary conditions were breaking down. Second, Methodism through its chapels, "love feasts" (quarterly dinners with prayers and singing), and classes offered working people opportunities for community. This was vital because the course of economic and social change was rapidly eroding traditional supports of communal life. Third, whatever Wesley's hierarchical and conservative views, Methodism carried a clear message of equality and independence. There were even female preachers in early Methodism, something not acceptable in the Church of England. The Wesleyan preachers defied the wishes of the elite by preaching to all the people, even outside the parochial system. They gave ordinary people—miners, artisans, blacksmiths, shopkeepers—a chance to express some independence by participating in revival meetings. Methodism gave the laboring poor some means of maintaining their independence by teaching them to read in Sunday schools and by inculcating in them sober and industrious habits. Above all, Methodism taught that all people are equal before God; salvation is equally available to all, not just to the rich. By this message of equality and independence, Methodism was eventually to spawn generations of working-class leaders.

This spirit of equality and independence meant that popular Methodism was subject to repeated splintering. Wesley always regarded himself as a clergyman of the Anglican Church, and he ruled the Wesleyan enthusiasts with an iron hand. In 1784, he was forced to begin ordaining priests in order to supply the revival in North America with clergymen. By this step, he took on the rights of a bishop and in effect separated himself and the Methodists from the church of England. After his death, some groups of working-class Methodists broke away from his organization. In 1797, one Alexander Kilham led a number of northern working men and women out of the Methodist connection because of the orthodox Wesleyan opposition to radicalism. In 1811, two artisan lay preachers founded yet another sect— the Primitive Methodists—because the Wesleyans turned against the revivalist camp meetings that were popular with working people. In the crises of the 1790s, still other laborers turned to various strange forms of millenarian Christianity, such as that led by the mystic Joanna Southcott, a domestic servant from Devon who thought she would give birth to Shiloh, the new divine ruler of the earth. One way or another, all such sectaries hoped for the establishment in England of a New Jerusalem—a new society of purity and justice.

Some historians have argued that Methodism prevented revolution in England. The French liberal Elie Halévy, for instance, said in the early 1900s that social quietism spread by the Methodists was what kept the English from following the French example. To what extent is this Halévy thesis true? As we saw in Chapter 11, revolutionary efforts in Britain failed for a number of different reasons, among them the determination and power of the oligarchy, the strength of the state, the ability of Parliament to tap Britain's burgeoning wealth, and the antirevolutionary influence of nationalist sentiment. Yet it seems certain that Methodism—or, more accurately, the evangelical revival in general—did teach teach people to be patient with their lot in life and to expect their rewards in another world. Thus Methodism did help defuse the revolutionary bomb in Britain. In the long run, Methodism helped the British working people to organize and lead themselves; in the short run, it channeled the enormous energy of popular discontent into safe outlets.

THE EVANGELICALS

Counterrevolution clearly was one of the principal objectives of the people called "Evangelicals," the men and women who were inspired by the message of vital religion but who remained in the Church of England. But combating radicalism was far from their only activity. The Evangelicals (or "Saints") above all wanted to abandon merely nominal Christianity and to make religion count in every way in their lives. They remained a numerical minority in the Anglican Church, but their enthusiasm and their relentless determination to renovate society and reinvigorate the Church gave them influence out of proportion to their numbers. From the 1780s on, the Evangelical insistence on an individual and emotional faith (as opposed to subtle dogma, ecclesiastical privileges, or latitudinarian complacency) made for a formidable Low Church position.

The most famous of the early Evangelicals was a small group of wealthy and well-connected philanthropic activists called the "Clapham Sect"—so named because they lived in the village of Clapham just south of London. The Clapham Sect included Henry Thornton, a banker who owned the estate of Clapham around which they clustered; John Venn, the inspirational vicar of Clapham; Zachary Macaulay, a businessman, former West Indian slave overseer, and colonial governor; Hannah More, a onetime poet and playwright who became the leading popular publicist of evangelical social doctrines; and William Wilberforce, heir to a Yorkshire commercial fortune and a friend of Pitt the Younger. This little group founded a tradition of high-minded but practical public service that characterizes many British intellectual families even to the present day. They involved themselves in a wide variety of philanthropic enterprises: personal charity (Thornton gave away five-sixths of his income until he was married and one third thereafter); Sunday schools and elementary education for the poor; prison reform; Sabbatarianism (banning any nonreligious diversions on Sundays); and the "reformation of manners"—the suppression of what they regarded as immoral activities such as dueling, gambling, drunkenness, prostitution, blasphemy, and traditional blood sports. They also came out strongly against political radicalism after 1793. Hannah More, for instance, wrote a series of *Cheap Repository Tracts* preaching hard work and deference to laborers, the *Tracts* to be distributed to the poor by their betters.

The greatest of all the Evangelical crusades was against slavery and the slave trade. The leader of the Saints' antislavery campaign was Wilberforce, who worked tirelessly against slavery in and out of Parliament for almost fifty years. Wilberforce (1759–1833) converted to Evangelicalism as a young man; thereafter, he devoted himself to the eradication from British life of those practices he saw as sins or as conducive to sin. He organized the Proclamation Society (later the Society for the Suppression of Vice) in 1787. But if he was something of a killjoy, he also led the British parliamentary elite to see what should have been obvious—the cruelty and horror of slavery—and he persuaded them to reject the pleas of the powerful West Indian slavery interest. Parliament finally abolished the slave trade in 1807 and slavery in the British Empire in 1833.

METHODISM IN WALES

The Methodist revival was even more important to Wales than to England. Wesley visited Wales forty-six times, but because of what he called "the heavy curse of the confusion of tongues," native Welsh-speaking revivalists played a greater role than he in converting Wales. The Welsh revivalists began their crusade independent of Wesley. Their efforts were closely associated with the educational work of Griffith Jones. From the 1730s, Jones established a system of schools taught by itinerant masters, who made many thousands of ordinary Welsh children literate in Welsh. At about the same time, revivalism caught fire in southern Wales. The key figures were Howell Harris, a layman of prodigious energy and ego; Daniel Rowland, an Anglican preacher of hypnotic power; and William Williams (known as "Pantycelyn"), another Anglican priest, and one whose hymns became a vital part of Welsh culture. Around the turn of the nineteenth century, Thomas Charles led the expansion of Methodism into northern Wales.

Methodism grew rapidly in Wales between 1750 and 1775, and then from the 1780s it reinvigorated the old dissenting sects—Baptists, Independents, and Presbyterians. The Welsh Methodists cooperated with Wesley, but they preferred Calvinist theology and so sided with Whitefield. Eventually, in 1811, the Welsh Methodists broke with the established church to form a new Welsh sect—Calvinistic Methodism. By then, the Calvinistic Methodists and other dissenters amounted to almost 20 percent of the Welsh population, and dissent continued to grow rapidly. In 1851, dissenters outnumbered Anglicans in Wales by 5 to 1.

The new and old dissenting denominations took the place of the fading Celtic bardic tradition to form the heart and soul of Welsh popular culture. Even before the Methodist revival, there had been a sharp divide between the increasingly anglicized gentry and their Welsh-speaking tenants and laborers. Because the Methodist revival was carried out in Welsh, it added a religious dimension to the great divide: now the gentry were Anglican and English speaking, and the people were dissenters and Welsh speaking. When the Industrial Revolution took hold in South Wales (see Chapter 10), it concentrated there a large number of Welsh-speaking dissenters. There, the church-versus-chapel social division coincided with conflict between upper class and working class.

ROMANTICISM

The equivalent in high culture of Methodist emotionalism was the romantic movement. Between 1780 and 1830, British literature, painting, and architecture experienced a revitalization of emotion and consequently produced a body of work that was miraculous in quantity and quality. The romantics fashioned works that have provided for countless literate men and women an image of what it means to be British—a pastoral, nonindustrial, nostalgic vision. The romantic tradition pitted "nature" against "artifice," the organism against the machine, the past against the present, and so provided the inspiration for continuing and profound critique of urban industrial life.

How is this wonderful flowering of culture to be explained? Despite their claims to be setting out eternal truths, the romantics were deeply engaged with their times, and it is in that engagement—sometimes enthusiastic, sometimes highly critical—that the explanation is to be found. First, there was political revolution. Almost all the British romantic poets at one time or another found the events of France to be exhilarating. The French Revolution seemed to be liberating humanity from ancient bonds and to be drawing all the social and political lines anew. As William Wordsworth wrote:

> But Europe at that time was thrilled with joy,
> France standing on the top of golden hours,
> And human nature seeming born again.

Yet the British romantics were sensitive to a wide variety of political and social changes. Economic expansion, population explosion, and the destruction of traditional social relations all gave them a sense of rapid transformation. Static views of nature would no longer do; dynamic views would have to replace them. Thus the romantics, whether radical or conservative, developed a strong sense of historical change and committed themselves to philosophies emphasizing the living, organic quality of nature. Likewise, the static formulas of classical art no longer seemed appropriate. As Wordsworth put it, the times demanded a new kind of art: a "multitude of causes, unknown to former times" were reducing the mind "to a state of almost savage torpor." Among these causes were "great national events," the "accumulation of men in cities," the "uniformity of occupations," and a "craving for extraordinary incident," all of which required as an antidote poetry that is "the spontaneous overflow of powerful feelings."

Next, the new commercial and industrial society—and the utilitarian philosophy that went with it—seemed to convey a one-dimensional view of human life and to leave no room for the arts. The romantics reacted against this confinement by aggressively asserting the primacy of art and of a life devoted to it. They sharply pitted art against the pursuit of riches—"the God and Mammon of the world." This reaction contributed to the image of the romantic hero, with whom the poets and painters identified, the genius who defies conventional rules and asserts special power and insight into the world. Closely related to economic change was a fourth cause of romanticism—the growth of commercial market for writing. As we saw in chapter 5, art was being commodified during the eighteenth century. As the economy expanded, the middle class grew and generated a demand for literature as well as for instruction and information. The market for fine arts took the place of aristocratic patronage. Many artists reacted against the dictates of this commercial market by insisting on the higher status of art and the independence of individual artistic genius. They claimed that the poet or painter has a special faculty—the imagination—which is superior to reason and offers special insights into nature or the cosmos. The imagination illuminates, or even creates, reality rather than simply mirroring it. It moves in the realm of the strange and finds magic in the commonplace.

THE ENGLISH ROMANTIC POETS

The English romantic poets may be divided into two generations. In the first generation were William Blake (1757–1827), William Wordsworth (1770–1850), and Samuel Taylor Coleridge (1772–1834). Blake was not only the first but also the most unusual of the first generation. He was unique in that he was trained as an artisan. A master engraver, Blake expressed his prophetic vision in highly symbolic poems illustrated by his own magnificent engravings. He was a self-conscious visionary, "the Bard / who Present, Past, & Future sees." The vision revolved around an unorthodox but intense brand of Christianity, his often prophetic poems dealing with the creation, fall, and redemption of humanity. Blake saw the French Revolution as a violent force that foretold the final apocalypse when humanity would overcome its fragmented and isolated existence. That fragmentation, he believed, was in part the result of industrialization, the advent of "dark Satanic Mills," which Blake defied:

> I shall not cease from Mental Fight
> Nor shall my sword sleep in my hand,
> Till we have built Jerusalem
> In England's green and pleasant land.

Wordsworth began his career in a similar enthusiasm for the French Revolution, but he turned eventually to deeply religious and conservative poetry. He became the most English of poets, often celebrating the calming quiet of the English countryside, and was made poet laureate in 1843. Wordsworth and Coleridge as young men published the poetic manifesto of English romanticism in *Lyrical Ballads* (1798). In the "Preface" to *Lyrical Ballads*, Wordsworth announced a new style in poetry, throwing over Augustan decorum in favor of language "really used by men." This was considered radical at the time, but by 1798 Wordsworth had already become disillusioned by the French Revolution. He rejected extreme rationalism and resorted to "the wisdom of the heart." Thereafter, he taught the healing power of nature, especially in particular experiences of everyday life in which a person can enjoy sudden insight into the supernatural:

> There are in our existence spots of time
> Which with distinct pre-eminence retain
> A renovating virtue, whence . . . our minds
> Are nourished and invisibly repaired.

Coleridge was the ablest philosopher among the English romantic poets. As a young man, Coleridge was a radical empiricist in philosophy and religion and even dreamed of establishing a utopian community in America. But in the later 1790s, Coleridge turned away from radicalism to Anglicanism and German Idealist philosophy. As an Idealist, he articulated what is implicit in most romantic poetry: that there is a realm of spirit that suffuses and transcends material objects. That transcendent reality, he said, is not known by the senses but by intuition. The mind participates in creating reality in the process of perception; it makes visible the mind of God. In poetry, the mind repeats "the eternal act of creation in the infinite I AM." Thus to Coleridge, the poetic imagination, not sense perception, is the foundation of all knowledge.

The second generation of English romantic poets—Lord Byron (1788–1824), Percy Bysshe Shelley (1792–1822), and John Keats (1795–1821)—were deeply influenced by Wordsworth and Coleridge, but they remained more radical than these two elder statesmen of the movement. Byron was one of the most famous and notorious figures of the day, a kind of "pop star" of the literary world. He was the classic romantic hero, one who rejected orthodox behavior in both his life and his poetry. His poetic protagonists were moody, disdainful, isolated characters offering ironic criticism of current civilization. Byron died in 1824 in Greece, having taken up the cause of Greek independence from Turkey. Shelley was also an extreme political radical and social nonconformist, and he fought all his life against what he saw as tyranny and oppression. Over time, Shelley became one of the most learned and philosophically abstract of poets. He took as his goal the moral reform of humanity through the power of his art. His masterpiece, *Prometheus Unbound* (1819), concerns the hero of Greek myth who stole fire from the gods on behalf of humanity; in it Shelley showed how tyranny and oppression are the products of morally unreformed humankind. To Shelley, poets should be acknowledged as the "author to others of the highest wisdom, pleasure, virtue and glory," for in modern times it is not knowledge and productive capacity that are needed, but the generous creative faculty—"the poetry of life"—which alone can free people from enslavement to the pursuit of material gain. In his short life as a poet, Keats wanted to re-create sensuous beauty for its own sake and as a symbol for the life of the spirit. It was Keats who gave the most elevated statements of the romantic exhaltation of the aesthetic imagination: "What the imagination seizes as Beauty, must be truth"; " Beauty is truth, truth beauty,—that is all/Ye know on earth, and all ye need to know."

ROMANTICISM IN WALES AND SCOTLAND

The Augustan Age had been a time of integration of provincial cultures into the English cultural mainstream throughout the British Isles. Enlightenment thinkers in the British Isles helped create an arena of public discourse common to Britain as a whole. But the romantic movement, though it crossed national borders, gave rise to cultural nationalist reactions in Wales and Scotland. In both countries, the romantic interest in the strange, the picturesque, and the remote led to delving in the literary and historical past. As early as the 1750s Welsh expatriates in London founded the Cymmrodorion Society to carry out antiquarian studies. A more radical group of London Welsh founded the Society of Gwyneddigion in the 1770s. It published Welsh literature in the Middle Ages, including an edition of the medieval Welsh poet Dafydd ap Gwilym. One of the collaborators on this effort was a stonemason-turned-scholar named Iolo Morganwg, who made a career for himself as the prototype of the Welsh bard while fabricating a number of "ancient" texts. The main result of romanticism in Wales was the revival of the *eisteddfod*—the traditional meeting of the bards and celebration of popular culture, all of which took place in

The Royal Pavilion, Brighton, designed by John Nash. The Royal Pavilion shows English Regency romanticism at its most fanciful.

Welsh. This was accompanied by a renewed affection for druidism, seen by the romantics as an authentic religion of nature. In Wales, then, the fifty years after 1780 were a period of revival for purely Welsh traditions in high culture as well as Methodism in popular culture.

In Scotland, there was similar interest in traditional literature and legends, including those of the Highlands. But the great days of Highland culture were over. The best Gaelic poets had flourished in the mid-eighteenth century, and the Ossian epic, the most famous Highland "medieval" manuscript, was a forgery. Neither of the two Scottish romantic writers—Robert Burns (1759–1796) and Sir Walter Scott (1771–1832)—wrote in Gaelic. Burns composed some poems in elegant English, but he cast his most vivid and memorable work in the Lowland Scots tongue; for this he became the national poet of Scotland. Born the son of a poor tenant farmer in southwestern Scotland, Burns by sheer determination made himself into a well-read man. In his poetry he was able to combine the best of Lowland Scots folk ballads and lyrics with English poetic style His short poems and songs—like "To a Louse," "Scots Wha Hae," "For A' That and A' That," and "Auld Lang Syne"— written in the language of ordinary people with marvelous zest and heartiness, deal with common events and emotions: love, hard drink, friendship, radicalism, and patriotism. Burns was greeted by the English romantics as the primitive plowman-poet. As Byron said of him, Burns was "tenderness and roughness—delicacy, coarseness—sentiment, sensuality—soaring and grovelling, dirt and deity—all mixed up in that one compound of inspired clay."

The Hay-Wain, *by John Constable. Nature and the English countryside depicted by the best-known of the English romantic painters*

Sir Walter Scott was from the Lowland region near the English border, but he assimilated Highland as well as Lowland history and legend. In both his poetry and his fiction he created romantic historical pictures that won enormous popularity—and a great fortune that Scott spent in trying to live in the style of a feudal lord. His "Waverley novels," including *Waverley* (1814), *Rob Roy* (1818), and *The Heart of Midlothian* (1818), provide dramatic historical portraits of Scottish life in the age of the Convenanters and Jacobites. More than anyone else, Scott revived English and Scottish interest in Highland clan culture—a safe thing to do, since the clans by then had been tamed, and besides Scott preached accommodation with Britain, not defiance. Scott was a Tory and made Jacobitism sympathetic, but his message was essentially one of social and political harmony. His role won official recognition. In 1820 he was made a baronet, and in 1822 he acted as the manager of pageantry for King George IV's magnificent state visit to Scotland. By then the Hanoverian line thought it right to wear Highland kilts! During the war against the French Revolution, the British monarchy had been made the focus of patriotic ceremony, and now it served as a device for creating a "union of hearts" between the English and the Scots. As nostalgia for the Highlands became popular, English and Lowland Scottish textile firms did a big business in concocting the whole scheme of clan tartans that prevails in the popular mind even today. Scott, then contributed mightily to Scottish national consciousness, but in the context of a somewhat

A Fire at Sea, c.1835, *by J. M. W. Turner. Turner painted the awesome power of nature with such force that he was said to have painted with "tinted steam."*

bogus and commercialized vision of gallant Highland chiefs and their loyal clan warriors.

BRITISH ROMANTIC ARCHITECTURE AND PAINTING

The romantic interest in the natural, the remote, the picturesque, and the exotic encouraged architects to call on a number of different historical traditions. The parks surrounding the homes of country gentlemen, with their newly constructed temples, "medieval" bridges, and Gothic ruins, showed this sensibility, for they were carefully designed to look natural and unplanned while including items meant to recall the wonders of the past. Many architects continued to draw on the classical tradition, ancient Greece especially being regarded as the epitome of noble simplicity. For example, Sir John Soane rebuilt the Bank of England (1792–1827) as one of London's most imposing edifices with Roman construction methods and Greek decoration. John Nash created imaginative and picturesque city vistas in the classical style, the villas on Regent's Park (around 1810) being the best example. Nash also designed the Royal Pavilion in Brighton (1815–1818) in a bizarre Indian style (cupcake domes, fantasy minarets, and lace doiley interiors) inspired by the "stately pleasure dome" of Coleridge's poem "Kubla Kahn."

The tradition most favored by British romantic architects was the Gothic. To the romantic sensibility, medieval society increasingly seemed attractive because it was "natural" and not reduced to the formulas of pure reason. Gothic architecture, the monuments of which stood in varying states of decay all around the British Isles, represented the historically remote, the sublime, and the mysterious. As early as the mid-1700s, Horace Walpole rebuilt his home, Strawberry Hill, in the Gothic style: plenty of turrets, towers, battlements, and pointed arches over the windows. Although Augustan taste had held that the Gothic was barbarous, the British of the romantic period were drawn to its irregularity, its lack of symmetry, its religious aspirations, and its rustic quality. Most of the Gothic buildings of the romantic period were homes, from thatched-roof cottages to sprawling manors, of which the most imposing was Fonthill Abbey built between 1796 and 1807 by James Wyatt for a millionaire (alas, its 276-foot-high tower collapsed in 1825). The Gothic came to be regarded as the English national style of building, in part no doubt because it recalled past times when the laboring poor stayed in their place.

British painters also reacted against the formalism and artificial qualities of Augustan art in order to express the new taste for the drama and strangeness of life. George Stubbs, for example, besides his graceful portraits of the gentry's favorite animals, occasionally painted so as to express the violent power and drama of nature, as in his "Lion Attacking a Horse" (1770). William Blake's visionary engravings and watercolors created an awesome mythological world. John Henry Fuseli (1741–1825), a Swiss émigré living in London, painted mysterious Gothic nightmares from the darkest regions of the mind. But the two greatest British romantic painters were both landscape artists: John Constable (1776–1837) and J. M. W. Turner (1775–1851). Constable seems to have been the Wordsworth of painting— a careful observer of the familiar localities of the English countryside. Constable's paintings have a calming effect, not because they are sedate but because his landscapes are filled with divine benevolence. This he expressed with free techniques in oil that endowed the landscape with light, life, and movement. Turner, on the other hand, painted nature's violence in powerful canvases that Constable called "airy visions, painted with tinted steam." In his immensely powerful paintings of storms in mountain passes and on the sea, Turner showed nature at its most violent and even catastrophic, a living thing beyond the control of human reason.

Suggested Reading

Abrams, M. H., *The Mirror and the Lamp* (New York: Oxford University Press, 1953).

Andrews, Stuart, *Methodism and Society* (London: Longmans, 1970).

Bebbington, D. W., *Evangelicalism in Modern Britain: A History from the 1730s to the 1980s* (Winchester, N.H.: Unwin Hyman, 1989).

Butler, Marilyn, *Romantics, Rebels, and Reactionaries: English Literature and Its Background, 1760–1830* (New York: Oxford University Press, 1982).

Davies, Rupert E., *Methodism* (London: Epworth Press, 1976).

Dinwiddie, J. R., *Bentham* (Oxford: Oxford University Press, 1989).

Drescher, Seymour, *The Mighty Experiment: Free Labour versus Slavery in British Emancipation* (New York: Oxford University Press, 2002).

Evans, E. D., *A History of Wales, 1660–1815* (Cardiff: University of Wales Press, 1976).

Furneaux, Robin, *William Wilberforce* (London: Hamilton, 1974).

Gaunt, William, *A Concise History of English Painting* (London: Thames and Hudson, 1964).

Halévy, Elie, *The Growth of Philosophic Radicalism* (London: Faber, 1972).

Hempton, David, *Methodism and Politics in British Society, 1750–1850* (Stanford: Stanford University Press, 1984).

Hilton, Boyd, *The Age of Atonement: The Influence of Evangelicalism on Social and Economic Thought, 1785–1865* (New York: Oxford University Press, 1987).

Hobsbawm, E. J., et al., *The Invention of Tradition* (New York: Cambridge University Press, 1985).

Hole, Robert, *Pulpits, Politics and Public Order in England, 1760–1832* (New York: Cambridge University Press, 1989).

Honour, Hugh, *Romanticism* (London: Allen Lane, 1979).

Kidson, Peter, et al., *A History of English Architecture*, 2nd ed. (New York: Penguin Press, 1979).

Kroeber, Karl, *British Romantic Art* (Berkeley: University of California Press, 1986).

Mack, Mary P., *Jeremy Bentham: An Odyssey of Ideas* (New York: Columbia University Press, 1963).

Newman, Gerald, *The Rise of English Nationalism: A Cultural History, 1740–1830* (New York: St. Martin's, 1987).

Rosen, F., *Jeremy Bentham and Representative Democracy: A Study of the Constitutional Code* (New York: Oxford University Press, 1983).

Ryan, Robert M., *The Romantic Reformation: Religious Politics in English Literature, 1789–1824* (New York: Cambridge University Press, 1997).

Schlossberg, Herbert, *The Silent Revolution: Evangelicalism and the Making of Victorian England* (Columbus: Ohio State University Press, 2000).

Semmel, Bernard, *The Methodist Revolution* (New York: Basic Books, 1973).

Taylor, Barbara, *Mary Wollstonecraft and the Feminist Imagination* (New York: Cambridge University Press, 2003).

Thomas, William, *The Philosophic Radicals* (Oxford: Clarendon Press, 1979).

Todd, Janet, *Mary Wollstonecraft: A Revolutionary Life* (London: Weidenfeld and Nicolson, 2000).

Turley, David, *The Culture of English Anti-Slavery, 1780–1860* (New York: Routledge, Chapman & Hall, 1991).

Wearmouth, R. F., *Methodism and the Common People of the Eighteenth Century* (London: Epworth Press, 1945).

Williams, Gwen A., *When Was Wales?* (London: Black Raven Press, 1985).

Wordsworth, Jonathan, et. al., *William Wordsworth and the Age of English Romanticism* (New Brunswick: Rutgers University Press, 1987).

Part **III**

The Rise of Victorian Society

1815–1870

Chapter 13

Class Society, 1815–1850

The British landed oligarchy survived the French Revolution with its status and its hold on the positions of power intact. Yet the incessant forces of the Triple Revolution—agricultural, demographic, and industrial—were too powerful to be confined to the old channels of a hierarchical society, particularly because the landowners set aside their paternalist role during the war against the French. In the half-century after 1815, industrialization accelerated and widened the British lead as the most powerful nation on earth, but it also drew into its vortex ever-widening circles of the traditional economy. Growing numbers of people swarmed into the urban areas. Remnants of the social hierarchy of preindustrial Britain crumbled away, and over time broad, self-conscious, and mutually antagonistic societal layers—landed class, middle class, and working class—formed and hardened. These trends generated severe social tensions and gave Britain in the first half of the nineteenth century an air of crisis; yet in the 1850s and 1860s the tensions eased and the sense of crisis passed. The result was one of the most remarkable civilizations in modern Western history—Victorian society (so named because of the monarch, Queen Victoria, who reigned but did not rule from 1837 to 1901).

The Victorians still have the reputation of being earnest, moralistic, complacent, and hypocritical. This reputation is partly the result of the very strong negative reaction against Victorianism that occurred in the early twentieth century, but it is also partly due to a failure to appreciate the gravity and novelty of the problems the Victorians faced and to an overly narrow focus on one element of Victorian society—the middle-class English male. It is important not to forget the other social classes of Victorian Britain, the people of what came to be called the "Celtic fringe," and women of all social orders and nationalities. But even if one looks at the English middle class alone, contradiction and complexity come into view. They were proud and even arrogant people, but they were also bedeviled by self-doubts and social concerns and divided by gender. They prided themselves on the evolution of parliamentary government, but they liked deferential behavior by the working class. They believed in individualism but were profoundly conformist. They congratulated themselves on progress but were deeply concerned that change was destroying their society. They were very religious but increasingly obsessed with their own religious doubts. Such complexity presents many challenges to historians, above all how to explain the formation of a stable, coherent society out of economic and social change of an unprecedented scope and pace.

BRITISH AND IRISH POPULATIONS, 1815–1850

As we have already noted, one of the most important social facts of early nineteenth-century Britain was the rapid growth of the population. If we take the census of 1821 as the starting point, the British and Irish population grew 31 percent by 1851.

This population was increasingly "English." It is worth remembering that the British nation of 1815—formally entitled "the United Kingdom of Great Britain and Ireland"—was not very old. The union between England and Scotland had occurred only in 1707 and that with Ireland only in 1801. This young nation was dominated by the English. Throughout the nineteenth century and to a degree even until our own times, Britain was commonly called "England" by both the English and foreigners. To an extent, this was justified by the population figures, for the proportion of the British people living in England went up from 54 percent in 1821 to 62 percent in 1851, a fact explained in part by the disastrous effect of the Irish famine and in part by the net inflow of Irish and Scots into England. By 1851, for instance, there were approximately 600,000 people of Irish birth in England and more than 250,000 of Scottish birth.

Of more importance in the "Englishness" of the British was English cultural domination. Because England was the wealthiest and most powerful segment of Britain, its culture exerted steady pressure on the Celtic peoples. If an individual anywhere in the British Isles wanted to succeed in business or cut a figure in fashion or politics, he or she had to be proficient in English. Likewise, English was the official language of government and law, and the British government tended to promote schooling in English in Celtic areas. Thus an increasing majority of the British peoples spoke English and not one of the Celtic languages. In Scotland, the proportion of Gaelic speakers fell as the Highland Clearances took their toll, from about 20 percent in 1801 to 10 percent in 1861. In Ireland, about one-half of the people spoke Irish as their main language in 1801. However, these Irish speakers were concentrated in western Ireland and were the poorest part of the population. The British government ignored the Irish language and conducted its state schools in English. By 1851, only about 23 percent of the Irish spoke Irish. In Wales, the overwhelming majority of people spoke Welsh in 1801, but as Welsh industrial

Table 13.1: British and Irish Population 1821–1851 (in millions)

	1821	1831	1841	1851
England	11.3	13.1	15.0	16.9
Wales	.7	.8	.9	1.0
Scotland	2.1	2.4	2.6	2.9
Ireland	6.8	7.8	8.2	6.6
Total	20.9	24.1	26.7	27.4

Source: Chris Cook and John Stevenson, *Longman Handbook of Modern British History, 1714–1980* (London, Longman, 1983), pp. 96–97.

Over London by Rail, *by Gustave Doré. The artist has here shown the backs of working-class houses in early Victorian London.*

areas were integrated into the English economy and English and Irish workers emigrated to Wales, the percentage of Welsh speakers declined. In 1891, only 54 percent of the Welsh people spoke Welsh.

Urbanization was the other great feature of British population growth in the first half of the nineteenth century. The flood of people into the cities and towns that began in the late eighteenth century continued in the nineteenth. By 1851, for the first time, half of the British population (not counting Ireland) lived in towns, and 34 percent lived in towns of over twenty thousand. By 1851, there were nine cities with more than 100,000 each: London, Liverpool, Manchester, Birmingham, Leeds, Glasgow, Bristol, Sheffield. and Bradford. With 2.4 million people, London was more gigantic than ever; despite the growth of the provincial towns, the capital now was home for a larger portion of the British population (excluding Ireland) than ever—11.5 percent. Outside of London, the population tended to collect in the heavy industrial regions of the Midlands and the North of England, in the Scottish Lowlands (a wide belt from Edinburgh to Glasgow), and in South Wales.

The growth of the new industrial towns was unplanned and unregulated; hence they provided miserable living conditions for their inhabitants. Business and professional people moved to suburbs away from the industrial centers of the towns, into which the laboring masses were packed. In most cases, the working-class districts stood cheek-by-jowl with factories and warehouses. These districts almost invariably became squalid slums with high mortality rates. Such housing as was available was built by private construction contractors, responding to working-class demand in the free market. In their natural drive for profit, the contractors cut corners on space and construction, cramming as many houses into the smallest possible area. Typically, the houses were of the "back-to-back" variety: rows of small two-level houses that were one room deep and that backed up on each other so as to share a common rear wall. Often these rows of houses were laid out around dark, airless "courts," in which were located the common privy and water spigot. Bleak as such housing was, it was far better than the cramped tenements and foul cellars into which hundreds of thousands of the poorest city dwellers swarmed.

Manchester was the greatest of the industrial cities and the prototype of the early urban industrial environment—the "shock city of the Industrial Revolution." It grew from 95,000 to over 300,000 between 1801 and 1851. As the center of Britain's cotton industry, Manchester was busy, productive, and noisy, humming with thousands of spindles in great smoky mills. It was also crowded and largely without paving, sewerage, or water supply for its working-class denizens. Built at the junction of three rivers (the Irwell, the Irk, and the Medlock, all of which had turned oily black from pollution), Manchester became a jungle of narrow, filthy, cramped streets and alleys. The great French political thinker Alexis de Tocqueville visited Manchester in 1835:

> From this foul drain the greatest stream of human industry flows out to fertilize the whole world. From this filthy sewer pure gold flows. Here humanity attains its most complete development and its most brutish; here civilization works its miracles, and civilized man is turned back almost into a savage.

The young German cotton manufacturer (and close friend of Karl Marx) Friedrich Engels was similarly shocked by what he saw in Manchester in the early 1840s: a labyrinthine collection of wretched industrial and working-class slums. The well-to-do had moved outward in order to spare themselves the horrors of the town, but in the inner city, the poor lived amid their own stench and filth. In many crowded districts, he wrote, "the inhabitants can only enter or leave the court by wading through puddles of stale urine and excrement." Everywhere he saw pollution and decay: "filth, ruination and uninhabitableness." In such appalling conditions lived a growing proportion of Britain's industrial population.

THE BRITISH ECONOMY 1815–1850

The British economy in the early Victorian years continued its startling growth, but it was afflicted with alternating short-term cycles of boom and slump. The gross national product (GNP, the annual total of all goods and services produced) went up by more than 300 percent in the forty years between 1810 and 1850.

The annual growth rate of the economy averaged more than 2.5 percent—more than twice as fast as in the early 1700s. Agriculture did well, but it was industry that drove the expansion. Capital invested in productive capacity tripled between 1800 and 1860. Exports streamed out of Britain's workshops, factories, and mines, increasing 400 percent between 1800 and 1850. By today's standards, Britain's industrial growth in the early nineteenth century may have been moderate, but by the standards of the day it was both astonishing and unique.

Even as late as 1850, Britain remained the only industrialized nation in the world; thus it dominated world trade. In 1850, the British enjoyed nearly 25 percent of the world's commerce. In the mechanized production of cotton and woolen textiles, pottery, iron machinery, steam engines, firearms, cutlery, and pots and pans, the British simply faced no competition. This fact shaped Britain's overseas trade patterns. The British typically exchanged manufactured goods (cotton textiles above all) for primary products—that is, foodstuffs and raw materials. This exchange was all in Britain's favor because foreign buyers could obtain manufactured articles from them alone; hence the British needed no elaborate marketing strategies or skills. In addition, the British increased their earnings from "invisible income"—the profits from overseas banking and investment and from trade itself: shipping, insurance, docks, warehouses, and brokerage.

These patterns shaped governmental policies toward trade. The nineteenth century was the era of free trade in British history. British industry and commerce did not need tariff protection; it needed conditions in which British goods had open access to foreign markets and in which foreigners could sell their products in Britain to earn the money with which to buy British industrial goods. Free trade was the obvious policy for Britain, and British industrial captains and their spokesmen, known as the "Manchester School" of economics, vigorously promoted free enterprise and free trade. Though the Corn Law of 1815 remained on the books until 1846, British governments of both parties otherwise moved steadily toward abolition of import duties and other restrictions on trade. William Huskisson, a Tory president of the Board of Trade, abolished a number of restrictive policies in 1822 and at the same time negotiated several reciprocal trade treaties by which Britain and foreign countries mutually reduced import duties. The trading monopolies of most of the old chartered companies such as the Royal African Company and the East India Company were wound up. The Navigation Laws were repealed in 1849. In this context, the Corn Law of 1815 stood out as an anomalous and divisive issue through the early 1840s.

The undeniable success of British capitalism in expanding output was marred by periodic depressions. The state took little role in guiding or regulating economic growth; hence businessmen acted not only in self-interest but also without adequate information in their highly volatile economic environment. Industrial capitalism was as yet such a new phenomenon that speculation and fraud were as common as enterprise, and sudden failure was as frequent as success. Recessions or depressions followed boom periods with bewildering speed. Almost immediately after peace was attained in 1815, for example, demand rapidly deflated and a depression set in until 1821. From that year until 1836 the economy expanded feverishly, but overspeculation and overinvestment broke the fever, causing a severe depression—the worst in the nineteenth century—from 1836 to 1842. Thereafter, the economy began to recover, though times remained very hard through the mid-1840s.

Each of the downturns in the trade cycle threw people out of work. Statistics on unemployment in the period are very unreliable, but one can be certain that substantial numbers of people were unemployed or underemployed at all times and that the so-called reserve army of unemployed went up drastically in bad years. For instance, in Bolton (a cotton town), unemployment among mill workers reached 60 percent in 1842 and stood even higher among construction workers. In general, factory operatives probably enjoyed more regular employment than most others, including skilled crafts-persons, few of whom escaped unemployment for part of each year. This vulnerability to the seemingly uncontrollable trade cycles was one of the gravest psychological pressures shouldered by early nineteenth-century urban workers.

Unemployment and underemployment were two of the reasons why, on the whole, material standards of living did not improve until the 1850s. Average output per capita and income per capita were increasing, and at the same time the long-term trend of prices after 1815 was downward. Yet these promising trends did not improve standards of living for most working people before mid century. In addition to unemployment and underemployment there was the fact that a greater share of the national income went toward profits and rents and away from wages. Moreover, a somewhat higher proportion of the nation's wealth was put to investment rather than to consumption. Furthermore, as we have seen in Chapter 10, some occupational groups like the handloom weavers suffered dramatic reductions in their wages, both because of overcrowding in the trade and because of competition with machine manufacturing. For all these reasons, the material benefits of industrialization for most working people were long delayed. As the great social critic Thomas Carlyle put it, the economy seemed "enchanted." Britain was like Midas with the golden touch: there was work to be done, but people stood unemployed; there was wealth all around, but the poor suffered hunger and degradation.

The industries that led the initial burst of mechanization—cotton, coal, and iron—were joined from the 1820s by a new industry: the railways. Because railways used over 300 tons of iron rails per mile, consumed vast quantities of coal, and employed thousands of unskilled as well as skilled workers in vast feats of civil engineering, their effects reverberated right through the economy. Beginning in 1825, a steam engine was used to pull wagons on iron rails for the twelve miles between Stockton and Darlington. The opportunities for cheap and fast transportation of goods and passengers became obvious to private entrepreneurs. In the next ten years a "railway mania" swept the country (except for Ireland); fifty-four new lines were authorized by Parliament and built by private companies. The depression of 1836–1837 slowed construction, but after 1845, railway building began again. By 1850, more than five hundred railway companies had come into existence and had completed the trunk of the British railway system: more than 6,000 miles of track

Excavation of the Olive Mount on the Liverpool to Manchester Railway, *by Thomas Valentine Roberts. This remarkable painting shows not only an early railway engine but also the huge task of civil engineering required in railway construction.*

stretching from Penzance to Aberdeen. This second burst of railway building pulled Britain out of the "hungry forties."

The railways tied the regions of Britain more tightly together than any force, political or economic, ever had done (or would do, until the world wars and television). Businessmen expanded their markets into all corners of the country. Perishable goods such as milk, beer, and fish could be processed in one place and sold in cities hundreds of miles away. Travel for ordinary middle-class people became a reality, not least because an act of the 1844 Parliament required the railways to run at least one cheap train a day on every line. Commuting by rail was still a thing of the future, but day outings from the cities to the countryside became a common feature of life for bourgeois families as early as the 1840s. By 1850, practically any place in Britain (excluding Ireland, where railways were constructed later) was reachable within a day from any other place. In 1854, for instance, travel time from London to Plymouth was only seven hours; to Manchester, five and one-half hours; and to Edinburgh, eleven hours. London newspapers put on the early morning trains were being read by late afternoon all over the country.

THE LANDED CLASS: ARISTOCRACY AND GENTRY

The nation that was being knitted together by the bonds of iron rails was at the same time sharply divided by social classes. These classes, of course, did not exist as material objects but as cultural constructions—broad layers of people who shared similar experiences, way of life, and values and who understood themselves as having interests conflicting with those of other broad social groups. They were none the less real for that. One might think that the aristocracy and gentry could not flourish in the new world of industries, towns, and class conflict, but in the short run they did. The British landowners enjoyed high rental income in the first half of the nineteenth century, and they also benefited both from their investments in industry and from the vast increase in the price of real estate they owned in and around the big cities. Landowners frequently cooperated with developers to make large profits on new urban housing districts. The dukes of Bedford, Portland, and Westminster, for example, each received more than £50,000 a year (the equivalent of about $7.5 million today) from ground rents in London. As late as the 1880s, more than half of the wealthiest men in Britain got their money from land. Of course, not all the landowners were so wealthy. Nevertheless, the aristocracy—some three hundred families headed by dukes, marquesses, earls, viscounts, and barons—all owned above 10,000 acres and enjoyed at least £10,000 a year. All had palatial country homes and large, elegantly decorated townhouses in London. Most owned hunting lodges as well. The landed gentry, on the other hand, of which there were about three thousand families, owned between 1,000 and 10,000 acres and earned £1,000 to £10,000 a year. Their fine homes dappled the countryside: handsome halls, often in the Gothic style, with upward of twenty rooms. Each was set in a fine park and maintained by a platoon of gardeners, stable boys, grooms, gamekeepers, stewards, scullery girls, cooks, and chambermaids, all arranged in a self-contained social hierarchy.

Life in these country houses was extremely pleasant for the landed gentlemen and their families—less boisterous and more dignified than in the eighteenth century, but a life devoted to leisure activities nonetheless. Aristocrats and country gentlemen alike, as well as their wives and daughters, shunned work as demeaning to high status. Being a gentleman (or lady) meant inheriting the bloodlines of fine families, but it also meant inheriting wealth, most of it based on landed property. Having inherited his income, the landowner could occupy himself in pleasurable pursuits: visiting and entertaining the neighbors; reading in his library; walking and riding in the garden and park; and above all, indulging in field sports. Many landowners spent practically all their waking hours fishing, shooting, horse racing, and fox hunting. Field sports seemed to celebrate the military virtues of courage and prowess that had once been essential to the feudal nobility. Landowners spent vast sums in maintaining hunting preserves and keeping sporting horses and dogs. They also waged incessant war with poachers, who refused to accept that game belonged to landowners alone. The owners used a set of severe statutes called the "game laws" to prosecute anyone outside the gentry who sought to kill game (pheasants, partridges, grouse, rabbits, deer, and so on), even on their own tenancies.

Fox hunting in particular became a well-organized and highly ritualized sport for the Victorian aristocracy and gentry. By custom, the rural districts of Britain were divided into territories (or "countries") hunted by particular groups of landowners. Each hunt country was designated by the pack of foxhounds kept in it: the Belvoir, the Beaufort, the Durham County, and so on. Sometimes the heavy expense of maintaining the hunt servants and pack of hounds was carried by one landowner, but in many places it was sustained by subscription. In either case, the fox hunters claimed the right of access to all land in the area, as well as protection of the foxes for them alone to kill. Tenant farmers sometimes joined the hunt, in which case the hunt meetings expressed the coherence of country life, but often tenants could only stand by to see their crops trampled by the horses and hounds, in which case the hunt revealed the true inequalities of landed society.

When the landed gentleman was not engaged in field sports, he was apt to be involved in public service. Disinterested service to local society as J.P., overseer of the Poor Law, officer of the yeomanry, patron of the parish church, and supporter of village charities was thought to be the privilege and obligation of the landed proprietors. Until the last decade of the century, the landed gentry kept local government in their own hands throughout the rural districts. As one description of a widely admired gentleman shows, the "manly" virtues of hunting and the selfless virtues of public service formed the ideal of the country landlord:

> His character—personal appearance and habits—impetuosity of temper—generosity of disposition—skill in games and sport—kindness to animals and liberality to his servants—his strong sense of justice—high character as Master of Hounds, and as a daring horseman—testimony of his contemporaries.

This notion of the ideal gentleman was part of a revived aristocratic ideology. Although some landowners abandoned paternalism and adopted political economy following the anxiety-ridden years of the French Revolution, others in the landed orders rehabilitated their belief in a hierarchical society and paternal care for the poor. In the interests of patriarchal order and social coherence, they explicitly criticized the individualistic social ideals of utilitarianism and political economy. As one aristocratic writer put it, Tory principles, "while they maintain the due order and proportion of each separate rank in society, maintain also that protection and support are the right of all." This vision inspired, and was inspired by, a romantic nostalgia for medieval England. It set high store by the Church of England as the conscience of the state, a view best expressed by Coleridge in his *On the Constitution of Church and State* (1830). It also revitalized the chivalric idea of the gentleman. One group of Tory paternalists, including the future prime minister, Benjamin Disraeli, went so far as to articulate a new feudalism. This "Young England" movement of the 1840s not only argued on behalf of a natural alliance between aristocracy and poor but also tried to revive medieval pageantry, including jousting in full armor!

In early Victorian Britain, the professions were satellites of the aristocracy and gentry. There were only four recognized professions to begin with: military service, the clergy, law, and medicine. Over time, the number of occupations accepted as professions grew. In each case, the professionals regarded disinterested service rather than personal profit as their social ideal. The older professions, especially the officer corps of the military and the Anglican clergy, were recruited from the younger sons of the landed families. The officer corps thus tended to be arrogant and bold but, at least in the army, not technically proficient. The Anglican clergy closely identified with their landlord patron. Indeed, the Church of England was regarded as "the Tory party at prayer." The squire and the parson often were the dominant figures in rural society.

Yet the Church was changing. Evangelicalism infected "High" and "Low" Churchmen alike with a sense of seriousness and emotional commitment. Indeed, the new vitality of both the High and Low Church positions caused considerable tension in the parishes. Both despised the easygoing, liberal latitudinarians, but Low Churchmen wanted to see more evidence of emotional fervor and personal morality, whereas High Churchmen wanted to revive religiosity by returning to traditional rituals, ceremonies, and vestments. Both sides—Low or High, Evangelical or Tractarian—undoubtedly made the ordinary broad-shouldered, fox-hunting squire very uneasy. Most English gentlemen took religion as a matter of social propriety and habit, an institution to be observed but not to be thought deeply about.

The educational institutions of the aristocracy and gentry were shaped by the fact that these social orders still formed a hereditary ruling elite. Elite schools and universities needed to give no training for an occupation but rather social polish and habits of authority. Most boys from the landed class went to one of the nine famous "public" schools—private boarding schools like Eton, Harrow, and Winchester. ("Public" schools for girls sprang up after mid-century.) The school curriculum consisted almost exclusively of the classics. More practical subjects were despised as "utilitarian," fit only for boys going into trade. Sports like distance running, football, and cricket were as important as scholarship, for they taught character and self-discipline. Studies were not the highest priority. As Thomas Arnold, the most famous public school headmaster, said, "What we must look for . . . is 1st, religious and moral principles; 2ndly, gentlemanly conduct; 3rdly, intellectual ability."

A university education was not necessary for the sons of the landed elite, but it was often thought to be desirable. Oxford and Cambridge were extremely expensive, and they remained the only English universities until the University of London was founded in 1836. Scotland's four universities were more accessible to young men of modest wealth, but Oxford and Cambridge were by far the most prestigious institutions of higher education in Britain by dint of their rich tradition and their connection with the Church of England. They were partly seminaries and partly advanced finishing schools for boys from landed and professional families. Many of the aristocratic youths who attended Oxford or Cambridge never bothered to sit for examinations or take a degree. Of the students who did earn the B.A., a majority went into the clergy. The teaching faculty of the universities—the college tutors— had to be ordained ministers of the Church of England, and most of them expected to have careers not as professional academics but as parish priests. Consequently, the "Oxbridge" atmosphere reflected the lackadaisical attitude of the faculty and the drunken, fox-hunting extravagances of the wealthiest students.

Daughters of the aristocracy and gentry before the 1850s rarely went away to school and never to a university. They were educated at home by private tutors in such polite subjects as music, sewing, literature, and French, in preparation for the day that they would become wives, mothers, and hostesses in landed households. It was unthinkable that a woman from the landed orders have a career. At the same time, custom gave aristocratic women considerable personal freedom. Marriage, of course, was assigned to them as their goal in life, but wealthy daughters usually came into marriage with their own money. This was settled on them by their fathers and did not become the property of the husbands. Because having their own money liberated them from complete dependence on their husbands, aristocratic wives had considerable liberty to conduct themselves as they pleased, provided that they observed the rules of public propriety. Moreover, aristocratic women were less likely than their less well-off sisters to have fallen under the sway of evangelical morality. Hence, they often considered themselves free to travel, speak, and behave as they liked, provided only that they avoided scandal.

THE MIDDLE CLASS

Important as were the aristocracy and gentry, it was the middle class that formed the "soul" of Victorian Britain. "Never in any country beneath the sun," wrote one middle-class newspaper editor, "was an order of men more estimable and valuable, more praised and praiseworthy, than the middle class of society in England." Self-conscious and aggressive, they seemed bent on making Britain over in their own image. Middle-class women were every bit as important, for they shaped the homes and families and inculcated the moral virtues central to Victorianism. The middle class grew as a proportion of the British population, from about 15 percent in 1820 to more than 20 percent in 1850—perhaps one million families—and they exercised influence much greater than their numbers.

The middle class ranged very widely in wealth. The richest bankers and commercial tycoons made as much as the wealthiest aristocrats, and the biggest industrialists only a little less. Hanging onto the bottom rung of the middle-class ladder were clerks, office workers, and shopkeepers, who earned only £100 to £150 a year. In income, these men and women of the "lower middle class" were not much better off than skilled artisans. For them, the struggle to maintain middle-class status was unrelenting, the minimum income for a secure middle-class existence being about £300 a year. Yet if there was a huge income gap between the richest and poorest of the middle class, all of the men shared the qualities of working for a living (but not with their hands), of intense class consciousness, and of aspiration for a "respectable" life-style.

The middle-class style of life required both a house and servants. Clerks and shopkeepers normally had six-room semidetached houses and a maid and could keep their wives from working outside the home. At £300 a year, the middle-class family could have an eight- to ten-room suburban house and a garden, as well as a second maid and perhaps a cook. Three servants were necessary to relieve the mother and daughters of all work in the house; this was assured at £500 a year. The middle class thus was a servant-keeping class, for servants alone made possible the gentility and propriety of home and family cherished by business and professional people.

The better off members of the middle class aspired to the wealth and status of the landed gentry. Men who made large enough fortunes typically bought estates and retired from work. Few, however, made it that far up the economic scale. For most men, work remained central to their lives, and for many of them, that work was fraught with anxiety. The cycles of boom and bust that racked the early industrial economy made them feel that disaster lay just around the next day's trade figures. Moreover, many industrial and commercial men had everything to lose, because most businesses were family firms and because investors were liable for the losses of their firms to the full extent of their personal property. Limited liability companies were not legalized by Parliament until 1862. Given the competitiveness of early capitalism and the desire of middle-class males to rise in society, these business conditions dictated a life of hard work and self-denial. To the early Victorian bourgeois male, life was a battle in which the indecisive, the incompetent, and the unlucky lost out.

Victorian middle-class men and women alike wanted their homes to be a refuge from the harsh economic world. Indeed, they made a cult of the home and family. Where the world of trade and industry was public, competitive, and stressful, the home was to be private, supportive, and restful. Here, in the private sphere, women reigned supreme. Men assigned to their wives the task of ensuring that the household functioned smoothly to aid their daily recuperation from life's struggle. In many cases, wives in less well-off middle-class families contributed significantly to establishing their "family fortunes" by working in the family business. But as soon as possible women were relieved of gainful employment, and their heavy responsibilities in housework or managing a corps of servants were not seen as "work" at all. The fact that the husband, in theory, alone supported the family gave him irresistible authority. A revival of the patriarchal-style family was the inevitable result.

The role of women in the Victorian middle class ideally was restricted to the home and family. "Separate spheres"—the public for men and the private for women—was the generally accepted rule. Gainful employment for middle-class women was out of the question, and few of them brought enough wealth of their own into the marriage to give them any independence. A woman was trapped in marriage even when it failed. Divorce before the Marriage Act of 1857 was impossible except by private act of Parliament. Even after 1857, women had to prove adultery *plus* bigamy, cruelty, desertion, incest, or unnatural sexual offenses to get a divorce. In sexual mores as in marital law, a double standard prevailed: if a man engaged in sex outside marriage, he was thought to have offended respectability but in an understandable and pardonable way; if a woman did likewise, her offense was beyond understanding and unpardonable. A "fallen woman" was ruined forever. Women were to be "undamaged goods" in a marriage; moreover, a woman was supposed to be the perfect guardian of morality—"the angel in the house." Women were regarded as by nature passionless. As the famous nurse and medical reformer Florence Nightingale, who herself dared to remain unmarried, declared in 1851: "Women don't consider themselves as human beings at all, there is absolutely no

Queen Victoria, Prince Albert, and Their First Five Children, *by Franz Winterhalter (1847). The domestic ideal exemplified.*

God, no country, no duty to them at all, except family." To bear children (the average number per family being six), to rear them in morality, and to keep the home an orderly preserve for the male were the functions for which women were thought to be biologically and emotionally suited. As one preacher said, "Woman's strength lies in her essential weakness. She is at this hour what 'in the beginning' the great Creator designed her to be—namely, Man's help . . . accustomed from the first to ministrations of domestic kindness and the sweetest charities of home."

Such remarks revealed the profound religiosity of middle-class life in Victorian Britain. The evangelical revival of the late eighteenth and early nineteenth centuries reinvigorated the nonconformist sects and called the middle class to seriousness. Indeed, evangelicalism played a crucial role in shaping the culture that became identified as "middle class." The values and outlook of evangelical nonconformity became those of the Victorian bourgeoisie. To be sure, not all middle-class people were nonconformists; some were Anglicans. Nor were all nonconformists of the middle class; nonconformity had a hold on certain segments of the working class. Yet the degree of overlap between the middle class and nonconformity—Baptists, Congregationalists, Wesleyan Methodists, Quakers, Presbyterians, and Unitarians—was substantial. And nonconformity was growing: in 1851, about half of the adult population of England and Wales attended church, and almost half of those were nonconformists. Nonconformity contributed to the sturdy individualism, the moralism, and the reformist drive of the middle class. Most nonconformist denominations emphasized the right of the individual to read the Scriptures and establish a personal relationship with God; they also insisted on the right of individual congregations to govern themselves. As evangelicals, most nonconformists believed that sin and the devil were everywhere and that conformity to a strict moral code was necessary to fight them. As one observer put it, in nonconformity "pleasure is distrusted as a wile of the devil." They frowned on drink, dancing, and the theater, and they promoted Sabbatarianism (the policy of prohibiting trade and public recreation on Sundays). The nonconformists also felt aggrieved at the disabilities they suffered at the hands of the established Church: they had to pay rates to the Church of England; they could not be buried in parish churchyards; they had to be baptized and married in Anglican ceremonies; and until 1828, the Test and Corporation Acts made them second-class citizens. In these disabilities they found a substantial agenda for reform.

Education was crucial to middle-class males, both because of their belief in individualism and because of their work in commerce, industry, and, increasingly, the professions. However, being nonconformists, they were excluded from Oxford and Cambridge, and most found the old public schools impractical and expensive. Some found the education they needed—English grammar, arithmetic, history, and foreign languages—at reformed "grammar schools," which were endowed private day schools. Most, however, were educated at various new kinds of private tuition-supported schools that sprang up to meet the demand. Many of these were little more than one-room schools set up by enterprising teachers to give a rudimentary and utilitarian training to lower middle-class boys. Others, the "proprietary schools," were established in fine buildings, often by subscriptions from the parents. Many of them at the outset taught "modern" subjects, but they tended over time to metamorphose into imitations of the ancient public schools. In turn, many of the public schools such as Rugby opened themselves to middle-class youths. The proprietary and public schools eventually had the effect of inculcating in the sons of well-to-do commercial and industrial families something of the values and attitudes of the landed gentry. They tended to lead boys away from middle-class occupations and into the professions; yet at the same time, these same schools helped pass on some of the bourgeois devotion to work and morality to the sons of the landed orders.

It is important not to overestimate the speed at which the expensive private schools diluted the drive and force of the middle class. For one thing, there were few places in such schools; in 1868, fewer than twenty thousand boys were enrolled in all public, grammar, and proprietary schools together. For another, middle-class men had a very firm and resilient set of values and social ideals—an ideology and a sense of masculinity—that they promoted at every turn. These values and ideals were rooted deeply in both the economic role and the religion of the middle class. To begin with, they valued a man by what he achieved rather than by the social stratum he was born into. They set high value to work, especially work of the entrepreneurial sort: active, enterprising, organizing, and directive work. By this measure they found the aristocracy to be idle and parasitic—"double-barreled dilettantes," in Carlyle's memorable phrase. They had a strange love-hate attitude toward the landed orders: they wanted not to destroy the aristocracy and gentry but to take their places. Yet middle-class males admired their own ability to get things done and despised the inherited elegance and patronage of the traditional elite. Middle-class people liked to see a constant increase in the outpouring of material goods, and they valued the entrepreneur who was responsible for it. They valued competition rather than patronage as the society's lubricant because they believed that competition maximized production and efficiency. Competition allowed the strongest individuals, businesses, institutions, and even ideas to thrive, while condemning the weak and outmoded to fall by the wayside.

A set of personal virtues followed from these values and defined "manliness." One was duty. The Victorian middle class had a strong sense of personal responsibilities that each person had a duty to fulfill. The main duty, for males at least, was to be as productive as possible and protective of females. Usefulness was a related virtue: the Victorians believed it was wrong to spend capital or energy on things or activities that were not useful to production and progress. Even art ought to be useful, by instructing, uplifting, or invigorating the mind. Thrift naturally was important because by thrift people avoided the waste of God-given talents and resources and maximized production. Similarly, prudence guided people toward the reasoned and cautious calculation of means and ends. Perhaps the highest of all virtues for men was self-help. Middle-class Victorians idealized the self-made man, the man who independently took responsibility for making something of himself. They assumed that men could rise in life if they only would. Unfortunately, the middle class also tended to create a personal myth about themselves, namely that they *had* made themselves, forgetting, like Charles Dickens' famous character Josiah Bounderby, the contributions that other people and good luck made to their success. They assumed that social misery was the result of personal failings such as intemperance, imprudence, and sloth. Thus their answer to social problems was often simply to exhort the poor to help themselves.

A very powerful political ideology derived from these middle-class values and ideals: liberalism. The specific content of liberalism will be examined in Chapter 14. Suffice it to say here that liberalism was the great political movement of nineteenth-century Britain and that it was essentially the middle class's way of bringing Britain's social and political institutions into line with bourgeois interests and values. Although the Liberal party was not founded until 1859, liberalism was at work from the early years of the century, and it operated within both the Whig and the Tory parties. Liberals often disagreed over particular policies, but generally they believed in individualism and competition. They supported free enterprise, free trade, and free competition among religious sects. They opposed the privileges of the landed orders, though they devoutly upheld private property itself. They sought to create a free market in labor, not least by restricting or prohibiting trade unions; they also sought to spread education so as to make the individual's decisions free from ignorance and superstition. Most important, liberals wanted to reform the parliamentary system in order to make Parliament representative of the nation's reasoning individuals. Here is where Victorian ideas about gender locked liberals into a major inconsistency: women, they believed, must be excluded form the vote because they were like criminals, lunatics, and children in not being independent, self-responsible, and fully rational individuals. Otherwise, the liberals generally favored extension of the franchise and codification of the laws. Individualism, utilitarianism, political economy, and evangelical nonconformity were the taproots of liberal ideology, each growing in rich middle-class soil.

THE WORKING CLASS

The early Victorian laboring population was not nearly as close-knit in experiences or outlook as either the landed orders or the middle class. As Chapter 14 will show, class consciousness spread within the working population only in the process of political agitation. For this reason, *working classes* is at least as good a term as *working class* to denote the laboring poor down to 1850; even then, several large occupational groups like agricultural laborers and domestic servants showed few signs of class identity. Still, it is possible to speak of the "working class" in early Victorian Britain in the sense of denoting all those who worked with their hands— approximately 75 percent to 80 percent of the total population. Some of these people made as much as £100 a year, and others less than £50, but all clearly stood below the ceiling that separated them from the middle class and landed folk. They were distinct from the upper classes by income, clothing, education, accent, and personal bearing, and anyone could spot the differences.

There were three broad categories within the working class: the skilled workers, the semiskilled, and the unskilled. The skilled artisans amounted to 10 to 15 percent of all workers. Most artisans were males who still set high store by the male-bonding rituals of their apprenticeship and journeyman training. Many worked in old crafts like plastering, printing, watchmaking, and cabinetry. Others worked in trades spun off by the new industries: locomotive engineering, machine-tool engineering, and certain special kinds of textile spinning. In all cases, artisans learned their skills through long apprenticeships. They were able to control the quality of their finished products and commanded fairly high wages—perhaps £100 in a good year. Many belonged to more-or-less secret trade unions and despised the "dishonorable" (nonunion) men who degraded their craft. Almost all of the artisans were literate, and they tended to be highly class-conscious and political. Together, they formed an "aristocracy of labor" and the core of the self-conscious working class.

The semiskilled workers composed a largely new group interposed between the artisans and laborers. The Industrial Revolution generated a large number of jobs for both men and women in factories and shops that required a middle level of skill at the same time as it destroyed some traditional crafts such as handloom weaving. Coal miners can be included in this category, for although coal mining was an old industry, it was vastly expanded by industrialization. Mining was a highly differentiated trade, with women and children doing many simple though backbreaking or mind-numbing tasks, and adult males, the hewers above all, doing work that required considerable knowledge as well as courage and stamina. Factory operatives made up the bulk of the semiskilled occupations. Most of them came from the ranks of agricultural labor. They were attracted to the factories by relatively high pay: about thirty shillings a week (£75 a year if fully employed) for seventy-two hours of hard and tedious work, as compared to twenty shillings per sixty-hour week for coal miners. Women were always paid less and generally were relegated to auxiliary tasks. All told, about 40 percent of all workers held semiskilled positions by 1850.

Below the semiskilled workers in status and earnings was the mass of unskilled laborers, about one-half of the entire working class. These were the men, women, and children who did the staggering volume of work that is today done by machines. As Professor J. F. C. Harrison has written,

> A vast amount of wheeling, dragging, hoisting, carrying, lifting, digging, tunneling, draining, trenching, hedging, embanking, blasting, breaking, scouring, sawing, felling, reaping, mowing, picking, sifting, and threshing was done by sheer muscular effort, day in, day out.*

Prominent among the unskilled were the navvies and agricultural laborers. The navvies did the physical work in building the railroads, cutting across hills, tunneling through mountains, and moving enormous amounts of earth and stone. They earned at best one pound a week as well as the reputation of being the roughest and most unruly of all workers—working, drinking, and fighting in prodigious measure. Agricultural laborers like all the unskilled were nonunionized and unable to protect their wages, and they remained the largest single occupational group even in the 1850s, as well as the worst paid. A male agricultural laborer earned on average ten shillings a week for very long hours of hard work in all weather. Sometimes the farm laborer also had a "tied cottage" provided by the farmer as part of his wage, or sometimes a patch of ground to raise vegetables or a pig. In most cases, the life was without variety, physically harsh, and psychologically stultifying. The agricultural laborer, wrote one journalist, "has grown up, and gone to service; and there he is, as simple, as ignorant, and as laborious a creature as one of the wagon-horses he drives."

Domestic service was another major occupation for the unskilled. Because of the demand for servants generated by the middle class, it was a rapidly growing industry, the second largest occupational group and by far the largest for women. About 40 percent of all women in Victorian Britain were employed (not counting unpaid labor, which was the lot of all wives and mothers), and a majority of these were domestic servants—scullery girls, housemaids, nursemaids, cooks, and housekeepers. Only about one-tenth of all servants were males. Because of their

---

*J. F .C. Harrison, *The Early Victorians, 1832–51* (London: Praeger, 171), p. 35

isolation, their direct subordination to their employers, and their conditions of employment, domestic servants were the least class-conscious of workers. Most domestics "lived in"—that is, they lived in the cellars and attics of the homes they worked in. Where a number of servants were employed a strict hierarchy prevailed, with the housekeeper and butler at the top and the scullery girls and chambermaids standing in awe at the bottom. The work was for most of them hard and tedious. The domestics tended the fires, lit the lamps, carried the water, cooked the meals, washed the dishes, cleaned the clothes, and emptied the slops (flush toilets not being common until the 1850s) in bourgeois homes. A butler might make as much as £50 a year, a housemaid £10 to £15, and all received bed and board as well. At all but the highest levels, domestic service was regarded by employer and employee alike as menial. One middle-class advice manual revealed the accepted upper-class attitude toward servants:

> It is better in addressing [servants] to use a higher key of voice, and not to suffer it to fall at the end of a sentence. . . . The perfection in manners in this particular is to indicate by your language that the performance is a favour, and by your tone that it is a matter of course.

Given such a wide variety of occupations and incomes, it is not easy to generalize about the working-class (or classes) life-style in the first half of the nineteenth century. Nevertheless, some aspects of life were common to most workers. One was that in the early 1800s, as in all of the past, hard work was the lot of everyone—men and women alike—except beggars, criminals, and vagrants. Children went to work at age eight or nine and became fully employable as adults at fourteen or fifteen. Everyone worked until illness or death intervened.

Second, almost all working people faced poverty at some point in their lives. Later in the century, when conditions had actually improved, social scientists still found that at least 30 percent of all urban workers lived in poverty. Even for the better-off laboring people, much work was seasonal or part-time. Bouts of unemployment were common, and the highest wages did not allow any margin for families to save for illness and old age. Newly married couples could expect hard times when their children were too young to contribute to the family income. At age fifty, all working people could look forward to a time of declining employment and earnings and of increasing privation.

Third, school was hard to come by through the 1860s. The prejudice of many in the upper classes held that schooling for working people only contributed to discontent and agitation. One scientist declared in 1807:

> However specious in theory the project might be of giving education to the labouring classes of the poor, it would in effect be prejudicial to their morals and happiness: it would teach them to despise their lot in life, instead of making them good servants to agriculture and other laborious employments to which their rank in society had destined them . . . [and] it would enable them to read seditious pamphlets, vicious books and publications against Christianity.

Against such attitudes, people who sought to educate the populace made only slow headway. These reformers were in equal part utilitarians, who promoted the increase of knowledge and the "march of mind," and evangelicals, who wanted to convert the nation. Thus educational reformers sought to make the poor more politically docile, less vice-ridden, and more efficient.

Schooling was available to the working class only on a haphazard basis. There were some private, fee-supported schools, mostly of questionable quality, set up by individual teachers; a few old charity and endowed schools; a slowly growing number of factory schools set up by philanthropic industrial captains; and above all, Sunday schools. By 1851, three-fourths of all children attended Sunday school at some point in their lives. The most important new schools were those erected by rival evangelical organizations. In 1808, nonconformists established the "British and Foreign School Society," and in 1811 the Church of England followed suit with its "National Society." Both organizations adopted the "monotorial system" invented simultaneously by Joseph Lancaster and Andrew Bell, whereby older students taught the younger ones. The first state provision for public education went to these agencies: in 1833, the government granted the two societies £20,000 and increased the amount by 1,000 percent by 1850. Unfortunately, the rivalry between Anglicans and nonconformists led to a great deal of sectarian squabbling over education and severely limited the state's role in providing and regulating schools.

Under the circumstances, it was remarkable that the literacy rate grew at all; yet it did. The early urban environment was destructive of literacy, just as it was of life expectancy. Moreover, economic need forced working-class parents to take children out of school and send them to work, even where there was a school. As late as the 1850s, probably half of all British children attended no school (other than Sunday school), and of those that did, few attended for more than two or three years. Scarcely any attended past age eleven. But the literacy rate by the 1840s probably rose to include two-thirds of all men and one-half of women. Almost all artisans were literate at a fairly high level. Most others who were literate probably could read at only an elementary level; they could sound out a newspaper headline or billboard, or perhaps read a simplified story. Clearly, the British working people were beginning their long march from an oral to a literate culture, but they were as yet not far along the road.

The upper classes in the early nineteenth century tried to take advantage of what literacy there was both by restricting the reading matter available to the working class and by flooding them with cheap literature designed to entertain them and to make them reliable, sober, and moralistic. Generally speaking, the British state did not resort to censorship to control reading materials, though it did prosecute some radicals for blasphemy and sedition. The main instruments of control were a tax of fourpence on each newspaper sheet and taxes on printed advertising. These made newspapers much too expensive for working men. William Cobbett got around these heavy "taxes on knowledge" by publishing his *Political Register* as a pamphlet; however, the taxes remained a significant obstacle until they were repealed in 1854–1855. Meanwhile, the upper classes made "respectable" reading widely available. The old Society for the Propagation of Christian Knowledge published tracts, pamphlets, and penny magazines to evangelize the poor. Middle-class businessmen established Mechanics Institutes in the industrial cities to offer useful knowledge and lessons in self-help to workers. The utilitarians in the 1820s founded the Society for the Diffusion of Useful Knowledge to promote the "march of mind." On the whole, such efforts to indoctrinate working people did not succeed, mainly because the upper classes in their writings failed to show a sympathetic understanding of working-class problems. Working-class men and women preferred their own commercialized literature to the cheap moralistic tracts produced for them by the upper classes. As Professor R. K. Webb has written, the poor preferred "to hammer out their own society, their own culture."*

It is extremely difficult to say how religion fit into this working-class culture. Clearly, the evangelical revival stopped the decline in religious affiliation that was so characteristic of the eighteenth century, and Methodism (particularly Primitive Methodism) won a strong hold on working people, especially the artisanal ranks. The Church of England was unable (or unwilling) to keep up with the growth of the urban working-class population, for it was simply too bound up with the landed social orders. Only the nonconformist denominations and Roman Catholicism grew faster than the population itself. In 1840, probably 60 percent of all nonconformists were from the working class, as were practically all the Catholics, who were by then largely Irish immigrants. But even nonconformity had little luck in attracting semiskilled or unskilled laborers. The new factory workers, for instance, were not recruited successfully by any sect. Nonconformity could express the aspirations of fairly well-off and literate skilled workers; it gave them a measure of community and a legitimate means of rejecting traditional society. Yet it had little appeal for workers of no independence or hope. Of the half of the adult British populace who attended no church at all in 1851, practically all were of the working class.

One of the functions of early nineteenth-century religion was to enter into a widespread campaign against traditional popular pastimes and for the spread of "rational recreation." Evangelicals (and middle-class people in general) strove to put down fairs, animal baiting, and cock fighting because such activities encouraged immoral and irrational behavior. They sought to replace these popular recreations with much more sober and "improving" activities like cricket, choral groups, and brass bands. Above all, the evangelicals waged war on drink. The consumption of alcohol, especially beer, was a principal feature of working-class life, and in the cities the pub and the beerhouse were central institutions of working-class districts. The pubs were often warm and attractive, whereas working-class homes were cold and dismal; moreover, alcohol was "the quickest way out of Manchester." Working-class families frequently spent a third of their incomes on

---

*R. K. Webb, *The British Working Class Reader, 1790–1848* (London: Allen & Unwin, 1955), p. 162.

drink. In the 1870s beer consumption alone amounted to 34 gallons per person per year. Evangelical temperance reformers campaigned against drink, insisting that it was the main social problem of the day. They had some success in establishing temperance clubs and recruiting working-class teetotalers, and in some places they succeeded in polarizing the populace into "church" and "pub" camps. Pubs, however, remained the centers of working-class leisure, providing relaxation, conviviality, handy meeting rooms, and diversions like pub sports, gambling, and popular entertainment.

Finally, the working-class style of life included a variety of attempts to preserve and reconstruct "community"—a pattern of face-to-face relations and mutual support among people with similar interests and experiences. One way was for families to maintain their integrity and their connection with kin-groups even in the move from the country to the city. As village communities were broken down, families sought with limited success to rent housing near each other in town; to find employment for each other; and to lend and borrow in seasons of financial trouble. Another way was to form trade unions. Trade combinations had originated in the early eighteenth century and proliferated during the Triple Revolution, but only among artisans and only on the local level. Many cotton spinners (again, on the local level), the first factory workers to organize, had formed unions by 1815. Though formally outlawed by the Combination Acts of 1799 and 1800, trade unions continued to spread among skilled workers as they acted to protect their wages and status from technological change and "dishonorable" labor. Sometimes, as we have seen in Chapter 10, union activity alternated with Luddism. The unions' struggle to repeal the Combination Laws and to form national organizations we will explore in Chapter 14. Suffice to say here that unions, though they included a very small proportion of the whole working population and almost always excluded women, did offer an expression and a support for artisans' sense of community.

The "friendly societies" such as the Foresters and the Oddfellows also promoted the artisans' sense of community. These mutual-aid clubs, some of which also had trade union functions, collected weekly dues from the members and in return gave sickness and burial benefits. A workingman typically contributed a few pennies a week to buy insurance against pauperdom. As early as 1803, there were some 9,600 friendly societies with 700,000 members; by 1872, there were more than 32,000 societies with over four million members. True, the friendly societies taught to the working class the bourgeois lessons of prudence and self-help, but they also offered working men and women opportunities for conviviality and belonging by their ceremonies and monthly meetings. This was an important prop to community in the otherwise atomizing urban environment.

Suggested Reading

Arnstein, Walter L., *Queen Victoria* (New York: Palgrave Macmillan, 2003).

Beckett, J. V., *The Aristocracy in England, 1660–1914* (Oxford: Blackwell, 1986).

Brown, Stuart J., *The National Churches of England, Ireland, and Scotland, 1801–1846* (New York: Oxford University Press, 2001).

Burnett, John, ed., *Annals of Labour: Autobiographies of British Working-Class People, 1820–1920* (Bloomington: Indiana University Press, 1974).

Cannadine, David, *Lords and Landlords: The Aristocracy and the Towns, 1770–1967* (Leicester: Leicester University Press, 1980).

————, *The Rise and Fall of Class in Britain* (New York: Columbia University Press, 1999).

Davidoff, Leonore, and Catherine Hall, *Family Fortunes: Men and Women of the English Middle Class, 1780–1850* (Chicago: University of Chicago Press, 1987).

Evans, Eric J., *The Forging of the Modern State: Early Industrial Britain, 1783–1870*, 2nd ed. (London: Longman, 1996).

Floud, Roderick, and Donald McCloskey, *The Economic History of Britain since 1700, Vol. I: 1700–1860*, 2nd ed. (New York: Cambridge University Press, 1994).

Gilbert, A. D., *Religion and Society in Industrial England, 1740–1914* (New York: Longman, 1976).

Golby, J. M., and A. W. Purdue, *The Civilisation of the Crowd: Popular Culture in England, 1750–1900* (New York: Schocken Books, 1985).

Harrison, J. F. C., *The Early Victorians, 1832–51* (New York: Praeger, 1971).

Himmelfarb, Gertrude, *The Idea of Poverty: England in the Early Industrial Age* (New York: Knopf, 1984).

Jones, Gareth Stedman, *Languages of Class: Studies in English Working Class History, 1832–1982* (New York: Cambridge University Press, 1984).

Joyce, Patrick, *Visions of the People: Industrial England and the Question of Class, 1840–1914* (Cambridge: Cambridge University Press, 1990).

Koditschek, Theodore, *Class Formation and Urban-Industrial Society: Bradford, 1750–1850* (Cambridge: Cambridge University Press, 1990).

Perkin, Harold, *The Origins of Modern English Society, 1780–1880* (Toronto: University of Toronto Press, 1969).

Peterson, M. Jeanne, *Family, Love, and Work in the Lives of Victorian Gentlewomen* (Bloomington: Indiana University Press, 1989).

Price, Richard, *Labour in British Society: An Interpretive History* (London: Croom Helm, 1986).

Robb, George, *White-Collar Crime in Modern England: Financial Fraud and Business Morality* (New York: Cambridge University Press, 1992).

Rose, Sonya O., *Limited Livelihoods: Gender and Class in Nineteenth-Century England* (Berkeley: University of California Press, 1992).

Rule, John, *The Labouring Classes In Early Industrial England, 1750–1850* (New York: Longman, 1986).

Thompson, E. P., *The Making of the English Working Class* (London: V. Gollancz, 1963).

Thompson, F. M. L., *English Landed Society in the Nineteenth Century* (London: Routledge & Kegan Paul, 1963).

Wahrman, Dror, *Imagining the Middle Class* (Cambridge: Cambridge University Press, 1995).

Webb, R. K., *The British Working Class Reader, 1790–1848* (London: Allen & Unwin, 1955).

Chapter 14

Politics and the State, 1815–1850

The structure of British politics and the nature of the state were remade during the first half of the nineteenth century. A wider franchise, a more equal representation of the people, and a more efficient government service were the results. These developments have given to the period labels like "the Age of Improvement" and "the Age of Progress. " Improvements did not, however, come about by the steady unfolding of a progressive consensus. Instead, the process of change was a matter of conflict and compromise among the three social classes into which British society was hardening.

This is not to say that every issue that arose within the world of parliamentary politics can be understood in terms of class analysis, for Parliament remained largely in the hands of the landed elite. But if "politics" is construed broadly, to include extraparliamentary movements, then the idea of class conflict alone can make sense of it. In fact, political conflict helped form class consciousness. Power was at stake: both the middle class and the emerging working class wanted to remake the political structure and formulate the state agenda according to their own interests, and the landed class sought to retain the oligarchical arrangements inherited from the eighteenth century. The conflict among the classes brought Britain repeatedly to the brink of chaos, and as late as 1848 it was not clear that the nation would successfully address its social and political problems without revolution.

THE STRUCTURE OF POLITICS AND THE SCOPE OF THE STATE IN 1815

The oligarchical constitution remained almost intact in 1815. Despite the waves of war and social change that threatened to engulf the country, Parliament remained an exclusive gathering of property owners returned to Westminster by inheritance and a tiny electorate. The House of Lords consisted of titled nobility—approximately three hundred great landlords. Further, all members of the House of Commons had to meet a steep property qualification, and most faced the expense of elections and the cost of maintaining themselves in London during the parliamentary "season." These expenses restricted membership in the House of Commons to men of wealth and leisure. Almost all M.P.s were therefore landowners, though very rich businessmen could sometimes "buy" a small borough seat, and talented intellectuals occasionally earned nomination by borough patrons.

Defenders of the unreformed constitution saw these features of the political structure as advantages: "It is the very absence of symmetry in our elective franchises which admits of the introduction to this House of classes so various." As one might expect, the cabinets drawn from such a Parliament were predominantly aristocratic.

Both houses of Parliament, as well as the Crown, the judiciary, the military services, and local government, were closely attached to the established Churches of England and Scotland. The Church of England was regarded as an arm of the state, and the state as the protector of the Church. By various laws requiring M.P.s to swear oaths acknowledging allegiance to, and supremacy of, the Crown, Roman Catholics, Jews, and Quakers were excluded from Parliament. Nonconformists could sit as M.P.s, but by the Test and Corporation Acts they were excluded from military, civil, and municipal offices. Though the Test and Corporation Acts were not generally enforced in the early nineteenth century, technically no nonconformist could even vote in a borough where the franchise was restricted to the members of the borough corporation.

The electorate for the House of Commons was very small and irrationally defined. Only in the counties, where forty-shilling freeholders had the vote, was there any regularity. Because many of these freeholders were in fact tenant farmers, they were subject to the influence of their landlords, and because county electoral contests were rare, the freeholder electorate exercised less independence than one might think. In the boroughs, the electorates varied from all male householders in a few places to owners of a handful of particular properties in others. More than half of the English boroughs had fewer than three hundred voters; upward of 250 borough M.P.s were simply named by great property owners. In all, perhaps 500,000 men in England and Wales had the vote—about one in forty-two of the total population. An even smaller proportion in Scotland and Ireland could vote. Moreover, given the ancient and obsolete distribution of seats, most of the new industrial towns went without representation, while a patch of turf like Old Sarum returned two members.

One important set of changes had occurred: the political influence of the Crown had declined since the 1780s. The process of "economical reform" initiated by Pitt the Younger in the 1780s to reduce corruption had eliminated almost all governmental sinecures. During the war against the French Revolution, stricter parliamentary controls over government contracts, revenues, appropriations, and accounting had eroded the Crown's ability to buy support during elections. Only the right to distribute honors such as knighthoods and peerages remained unaltered, but there were not enough "honors" for this to be a politically important privilege. The decline of the power of the Crown entailed a decline in the power of the executive over the House of Commons. Increasingly, cabinets regarded themselves as responsible to Parliament and not to the monarch, but they had little power with which to construct and maintain a majority.

Parliament, therefore, remained an unrepresentative institution. The most significant level of government in the ordinary lives of the people was local, and local government was still in the hands of wealthy landowners and municipal oligarchies. The role of the central government was still limited to external affairs, taxation, and public order, despite the onset of urgent, nationwide social problems. The British state was, compared to those in France, Prussia, or Russia, small and passive. As late as the 1820s, there were fewer than thirty thousand government employees, most of whom worked in the tax-collecting departments. The Home Office had a staff of seventeen, the Colonial Office only fourteen. Moreover, these public officials were often incompetent, chosen as they were for their connections rather than their ability.

TWO DECADES OF REFORM, 1815–1835

This was a structure of politics and government calculated to drive both middle class and working class to distraction. Middle-class men resented their exclusion from local and national government, and they disliked the unsystematic and inefficient character of the legal system, government service, and parliamentary structure. For their part, working-class activists found the government unresponsive to the needs of the common people, because it neither protected customary ways of life nor defended standards of living. Reformers liked to talk in general about the need to make the government more responsible to the people, but in fact, the interests of middle class and working class were not identical. Differing class interests made it difficult for reformers to work together.

Reform-minded people in addition faced the huge problem of how to move an unreformed Parliament to reform itself as well as the other institutions of government. A few radicals believed that revolution was the only way; hence there was an elusive and fragmentary revolutionary impulse that protruded at critical moments right down to 1832 and beyond. Most reformers, however, including practically all those from the middle class, refused to countenance violence. For them, persuasion and pressure by a mobilized "public opinion," expressed mainly by newspapers, petitions, and pressure groups, were the only acceptable tactics.

Fortunately for the moderate reformers, the landed elite were not united in defense of existing institutions. For instance, administrative reform attracted significant support from both Whigs and Tories. Whigs like Sir Samuel Romilly and Sir James Mackintosh joined Benthamites and Tory humanitarians in working for rationalization of the legal code. They focused on the vast number of crimes punishable by death because they wanted to make the law both less savage and more efficient. Tories of the Pittite tradition serving in Lord Liverpool's ministry (1812–1827) were open to this type of liberalizing influence. In particular, the home secretary, Sir Robert Peel (son of a wealthy textile manufacturer), brought to his office a powerful impulse toward high-minded administrative professionalism. He consolidated the criminal code, abolished fees and perquisites for judges, began the reform of prisons, drastically cut the number of criminal offenses, and in 1829 established the London police—the first professional police force in Britain.

Administrative reform was one thing, however, and political reform was another. The Tories, including Liverpool, Peel, and the hero of Waterloo, the duke of Wellington, believed that the British Parliament provided the best government in the world. They believed that Parliament represented all the legitimate interests of the country; that it gave due weight to property owners, who were the most stable and wisest segment of the population; and that reform would lead to "unmanly" subservience of Parliament to an irresponsible electorate that was bent on the pillaging of property.

Advocacy of reform from within the elite was left to the Foxite Whigs, a small faction remaining from the large parliamentary party of the 1770s and early 1780s. These Whigs were loyal to the memory of Charles James Fox and to the defense of liberty established, they believed, in 1688. Largely excluded from office since 1783, the Foxite Whigs insisted that the Crown (and therefore the executive) exerted undue influence over Parliament. Hence the Foxite Whigs sought to reduce government patronage even more than it had been, as well as to defend civil liberties. They also favored granting full citizenship for nonconformists and Catholics, on grounds of religious liberty.

In the first three decades of the nineteenth century, the Foxite Whigs gradually took up the cause of parliamentary reform. As they did so, other Whig factions shifted over to the Tory ranks, leaving the Foxites as custodians of the Whig banner. The Foxite motives were threefold: first, having been out of office for more than thirty years, they came to believe that reform was an issue they could ride into office; second, they realized that reform would strengthen the House of Commons against the executive; and third, they thought that moderate reform could alone head off a dangerous alliance between respectable and radical reformers outside Parliament. They feared revolution as much as the Tories, but as one Whig wrote in 1810, they hoped parliamentary reform would "temper" the extraparliamentary agitation "till it can be guided in safety to the defense, and not to the destruction of our liberties."

The respectable reformers the Whigs had in mind were those of the middle class. For example, Lord John Russell, a leading Whig, recalled that what had converted him to reform in the 1820s was his recognition that "the middle class, as compared with the corresponding body in the previous century, had risen in wealth, and intelligence, and knowledge, and influence." Middle-class people wholeheartedly agreed with this assessment, for it was the view put forward by the powerful new provincial newspapers like the *Manchester Guardian* and the *Leeds Mercury*. "Never in any country beneath the sun [wrote Edward Baines of the *Leeds Mercury*] was an order of men more estimable and valuable, more praised and praiseworthy, than the middle class of society in England." Middle-class nonconformists thought that they deserved a share of power in local government. As men of property, the middle-class reformers believed that their interests should count in national policy. They also believed that the long continuation of the war against Napoleon, the Orders in Council (1812), and above all the Corn Law (1815) discriminated against commerce and industry on behalf of the narrow interests of the landlords. Increasingly, middle-class men agreed with Bentham that the individual knew his own interests better than any oligarchy and therefore that more democratic representation would ensure that Parliament reflected the views of the people.

Radical reform—that is, universal manhood suffrage—was to most middle-class people out of the question. What they wanted was enfranchisement of responsible and independent males. These could best be chosen by a property qualification. As we have seen, they typically believed that women, like children, were either dependent or irresponsible and consequently not eligible for the vote. But all adult males of substantial property, regardless of their religion, should have the right to vote and hold office.

The politically active members of the working class, however, tended to favor more extreme proposals harking back to the radicalism of the early 1790s. Leaders of popular radicalism who themselves were not of working-class origins—men like William Cobbett, Sir Francis Burdett, and Major John Cartwright—agitated for the old program of a household suffrage, annual Parliaments, and equal electoral districts. Working men and women typically went further, taking up the cry of universal manhood suffrage, especially when the end of war in 1815 brought severe economic depression. For them, democracy was the prerequisite to protection from the twin evils of depression and industrial exploitation.

The popular reform movement, therefore, was one part of a broad range of working-class responses to hard times. Luddism and agrarian rioting were, as we have seen, widespread in 1811–1812 and again in 1816. Trade unions proliferated as artisans organized to protect their standards of living and control over their crafts. Union growth was especially rapid after the Combination Laws were repealed in 1824. There were even attempts to form national unions in the late 1820s and early 1830s. Working people also resorted to petitions to Parliament, addresses to magistrates, and strikes against employers, all of which were ominously widespread between 1810 and 1830. Workers tended to oscillate between one or another of these activities and the reform agitation, depending on the immediate circumstances.

Socialist ideas and organizations also began to spread among literate workers between 1815 and 1830. Here the unifying concept was simply that capitalism itself caused the hardships of the working class. A utopian industrialist named Robert Owen, for instance, put forward the view that competition ought to be replaced by cooperation, for competition among workers forced wages down and kept consumption unnaturally low. Owen believed that human nature was malleable and that institutional change could nurture cooperative instincts. Thus he advocated the establishment of utopian cooperative communities. Many Owenites went so far as to advocate ending patriarchal power in marriage and votes for women. Other socialists, like Thomas Hodgskin, emphasized that labor is the source of all value and therefore that profit is unearned and unjustifiable.

All of these popular responses to economic and social hardship tended to raise and spread class consciousness among working people, as did the oppressive reaction of the authorities. The repeal of the Combination Laws had been expected to reduce trade union activity, but when it did not, the government in 1825 imposed strong sanctions against union activities that could be seen as restraining trade. Moreover, as six agricultural laborers in Dorset (the "Tolpuddle martyrs") were to discover in 1833, the government could use against unions old statutes forbidding the taking of oaths. The government also waged war against the "unstamped" popular press in the 1830s. Finally, while Parliament ignored popular petitions, the government broke up mass meetings, sometimes by force. In 1819, for instance, the local magistrates and yeomanry scattered a peaceful gathering of about sixty thousand people in St. Peter's fields, Manchester. In this infamous "Peterloo Massacre," eleven people were killed, and later that same year Parliament passed the "Six Acts" to reinforce magistrates against public meetings and to strengthen the laws against unstamped publications.

The best efforts of the authorities to put down popular agitation only increased the number of working people who associated their troubles with the belief that the government was corrupt. This tradition, dating back to the old Tory and country Whig ideology of the early 1700s, was the key to the popular reform movement. Working people who suffered from industrial and demographic change and from downturns in the business cycle concluded that their difficulties arose because the oligarchy was inefficient and extravagant. On this point, middle-class and working-class radicals could agree, at least in certain localities. In Birmingham and Sheffield, for example, small workshops with close relations between masters and working-class people formed the main pattern in manufacturing. There, political cooperation between middle-class and working-class activists was possible. In cotton towns like Manchester and Leeds, however, where great spinning mills set the pattern for industrial relations, the clash of middle-class and working-class interests made political cooperation impossible.

In any case, pressure on the old constitution was intense by the latter 1820s. The first part of the old system to crumble under the stress was the Anglican monopoly. By 1827, most politicians agreed that the Test and Corporation Acts were of symbolic value only. The Whigs were united in favor of repealing them, and nonconformist pressure from outside Parliament was very strong. The Tory government (now led by Wellington, who cared little about religion) saw no reason to resist. Parliament in 1828 abolished the acts with little dispute.

Giving full political rights to Roman Catholics was more controversial. Repeal of the Test and Corporation Acts left the state in the hands of Protestants, but admitting Catholics to Parliament and other high office was, in orthodox eyes, to reject the very principles of the Reformation and the settlement of 1688–1689. The Whigs favored emancipation of Catholics, but public opinion remained hotly anti-Catholic. In retrospect, it seems clear that if England, Wales, and Scotland alone had been consulted, then Catholics would not have received emancipation until much later in the century. But, as Chapter 15 will show, Ireland was intensely concerned with the issue. Irish Catholics, mobilized by a nationalist leader of unparalleled oratorical power, Daniel O'Connell, were determined to win emancipation. O'Connell, himself a Catholic, won a by-election in 1828 and thereby presented the

Wellington government with a stark choice between Catholic emancipation or civil war in Ireland. Wellington and Peel, both of them hardheaded realists, opted for Catholic emancipation, and it was passed in 1829.

Catholic emancipation, so innocuous to the English-speaking world of the twenty-first century, spelled the end of the Tory government, and thus indirectly it made parliamentary reform immediately possible. Ultra-Protestant Tories did not forgive Wellington and Peel for "betraying" Anglican interests and withdrew their support from the Tory government. A general election in 1830, necessitated by the death of King George IV, coincided with news of fresh revolution in France, and the election intensified discussions of reform. At the same time, another downturn in the economy and a sharp increase in food prices roused public agitation. Finally, in November 1830, the beleaguered Tory government resigned, and a successor was formed by the Whig Lord Grey. This grand Foxite earl had long believed in parliamentary reform, on grounds that the antiquated constitutional machinery had to be brought into line with new economic and social realities if aristocratic rule, which he cherished, was to be saved.

In the circumstances of 1830–1831, Grey believed that the extraparliamentary reform movement was dangerous and could be pacified only by passage of a substantial measure. He and his allies thought that the number of county members, widely regarded as independent and uncorruptible, had to be enlarged; the new towns had to have representation, while pocket boroughs were abolished; and a uniform borough franchise had to replace all the existing irregular franchises. By this combination of provisions, the middle class would be attached to the constitution, Parliament strengthened against the executive, and landed power ultimately preserved. As Grey put it, the middle class had become the "real and efficient mass of public opinion . . . without whom the power of the gentry is nothing."

The bill proposed in 1831 by Grey's ministry was, therefore, bolder than most people had expected. It succeeded in attracting the support of middle-class reformers and even some of the popular radicals. Some working-class democrats argued that the reform bill was a cruel disappointment, since it offered nothing to working men; however, others saw it as a stepping-stone to further reform. This debate within working-class circles was fierce during the spring and summer of 1831, but when the House of Lords rejected the bill in October 1831, radical opinion tended to consolidate behind it. There were spontaneous outbreaks of violence in a number of towns. Even some middle-class radicals, including Benthamites like James Mill and his friend, the radical tailor Francis Place, seemed to countenance armed rebellion. The threat of revolution was probably exaggerated in aristocratic minds, but it was decisive. Wellington was unable to form an alternative government to Grey's, so King William IV had to promise Grey to create enough pro-reform peers to pass the bill through the upper house. The Lords preferred even reform to dilution of their ranks and therefore gave way. The reform bill became law in June 1832.

To complete the account of constitutional reform, it is necessary to jump ahead to 1835, when the Municipal Corporations Act was passed. This act did at the local level what the Reform Act of 1832 did at the national level: it opened the corridors of power to middle-class men, including above all the nonconformists. The Municipal Corporations Act (and a similar one for Scotland) substituted a structure of broadly elected town councils for the old oligarchical borough corporations. The counties continued to be ruled by appointed officials, mainly drawn from the gentry, but the towns were now in the hands of the business and professional people. who swarmed into local office and occupied themselves with making municipal bureaucracies and services more businesslike and efficient. Eventually, their work would have a great effect on the quality of life in the towns.

THE STRUCTURE OF POLITICS, 1832–1850

The structure of politics established by the Reform Act of 1832 (and by similar separate acts for Scotland and Ireland) changed many political practices, but it also left much of the old system in place. The Irish Reform Act retained a very high property qualification established by the Catholic Emancipation Act in 1829. In England, Wales, and Scotland, however, the Reform Acts made essentially two types of changes. First, they abolished many tiny "rotten" boroughs and redistributed those seats to the more populous constituencies, mainly the industrial towns. In England and Wales, for instance, eighty-six boroughs lost all or half their seats, and forty-two new boroughs were created. Second, the acts imposed a uniform property qualification for the vote in all boroughs: any male occupying a household worth ten pounds a year. In the counties the forty-shilling freehold franchise was kept, but farmers who held tenancies worth fifty pounds a year were added as a sop to the landowners, who presumably would be able to browbeat them. Altogether about 800,000 men had the vote after 1832—about a 60 percent increase, though still only about one in thirty of the population (or one-seventh of adult males).

The reforms of 1832, therefore, did not create a democracy. Women still could not vote. A number of boroughs still had fewer than two hundred voters, and perhaps sixty more were small enough to be in the pocket of a big proprietor. The landlords still influenced the way that their tenants voted in the counties. Corruption, in the form of bribery or treating voters to lavish food and drink, remained the style in many constituencies. The ten-pound household franchise was meant to be a rough-and-ready means of including the middle class while excluding the working class, and it accomplished its purpose fairly well. Its precise effect varied from borough to borough, since economic conditions and pay rates differed from one place to another, but only in a few places did the working-class voters amount to a majority of the electorate. In most big cities like Manchester, Birmingham, and Leeds, workers composed no more than 10 to 20 percent of the voters.

In such conditions, deference remained a major factor in determining how a vote was cast. Tenants tended to vote with their landlords; tradesmen with their patrons; and in some cases, industrial workers with their factory owners, especially where the masters adopted paternalist attitudes toward their men. Nor was Parliament flooded with businessmen. The hold of the landed elite was only slowly eroded, and not until the 1880s did the number of middle-class M.P.s approach a majority. Industrial and commercial men, as we will see, made their weight felt in other ways.

Nevertheless, the structural changes worked by the 1832 reforms were extremely important. By both the terms of the acts and the process by which they were passed, the balance in the constitution was shifted toward the House of Commons, and the House of Commons was now clearly attached to public opinion. In the boroughs, public opinion spoke through the voice of middle-class newspapers, journals, and pressure groups. Further, the reduction of "nomination" boroughs and the decline of the influence of the Crown meant that government had less ability than before to command a majority in the House of Commons. If organized, a majority could determine who would form the government. Inevitably, then, stronger party groupings emerged in Parliament, and in terms of enabling a ministry to get its work done, the parties took the place of patronage.

The parties were also strengthened outside Parliament as an unintended consequence of the 1832 reforms. The Reform Acts established a system of voter registration for the first time, and the constituency registers became the key to electoral success. Both Whigs and Tories (or Liberals and Conservatives, as they became) found that they had to employ professionals, usually solicitors, to maximize their own registrations and minimize their opponents'. Local party organizations sprang up to defend party electoral interests. In London, two great political clubs were founded to coordinate national electoral activities: the Carlton Club (1832) for the Tories and the Reform Club (1836) for the Whigs and other reformers. The club secretaries pushed local organizations into action and suggested parliamentary candidates to them. Thus, extraparliamentary party organizations were established for the first time in Britain; though they could not dictate policy to the M.P.s, who cherished their independence, they formed important bridges between the voters and their representatives.

Meanwhile, the fluid alignments of parliamentary politicians called Tories and Whigs began to coalesce into firmer, more broad-based groupings called Conservatives and Liberals. The new alignments reflected the widespread sense among active politicians that because of the new political structures the policies and institutions of society would be questioned in a direct and forceful way. Catholic emancipation and the reforms of 1832 had unsettled the Tory parliamentary faction, and only the clear ascendancy of Sir Robert Peel pulled conservatively minded people together. Peel taught the Tories that they could live with the reformed constitution. Recognizing the renovative tendencies of the times, Peel committed himself to cautious reform of the central institutions of the state so as to save them. In his famous "Tamworth Manifesto" of 1834, Peel called for a "careful review of institutions, civil and ecclesiastical" aiming at "the correction of proved abuses and the redress of real grievances." By then, Peel was acknowledged as the leader of a Conservative party. In 1841 he became prime minister after a general election, the first time that the electorate had turned out one government and installed another.

The touchstones of the early Victorian Conservatives were defense of agricultural interests and defense of the Church of England. The Whigs were as firmly

Sir Robert Peel, *by H. W Pickers-gill. Peel was Conservative prime minister in 1835 and from 1841 to 1846. The model of public spirit and probity, Peel carried repeal of the Corn Law in 1846.*

rooted in the land as the Tories, but in the 1830s landlords and farmers alike drifted to the Conservative party. They did so because they realized that the Whigs were allied with their enemies—middle-class businessmen and radical anti-aristocrats. Preservation of the Corn Law of 1815 became a Conservative preoccupation. As for the Church of England, most Conservatives opposed reform of the institution itself even if they accepted removal of the civil disabilities of nonchurchmen. They feared that the reformed Parliament, now open to Catholics and nonconformists. would destroy the Church. As W. E. Gladstone, the brilliant young Conservative orator, declared in 1836, "The doctrine and the system of the Establishment contain and exhibit the truth in its purest and most effective form." Once again it was the pragmatic Peel who in the 1830s dragged the Conservatives, kicking and grumbling all the way, to administrative reform of the Church, on grounds that if they did not reform it, the radicals would.

The evolution of the Liberal party was more complicated, and in a formal sense, the Liberal party was not founded until 1859. In the 1830s and 1840s, the word *liberal* came to be generally used to refer to an alliance of Whigs, "philosophic radicals" (that is, Benthamites), and Daniel O'Connell's Irish faction. There was no one individual around whom they could rally: Grey was too old; his successor, Lord Melbourne (prime minister in 1834 and 1835–1841), was a kindly friend and mentor to the young Queen Victoria, but he lacked energy and force; and John Russell (prime minister from 1846–1852) showed fiery eloquence but proved ineffective both as administrator and as party leader. Nevertheless, the crystallization of the Conservatives around Peel forced the Whigs, radicals, and Irish M.P.s to compromise their differences. They had to ally in order to maintain power and to move on with the reforms that, to varying degrees, they desired. By the 1840s, ordinary political language referred to this often unhappy alliance of reformers as "the Liberal party."

What did the Liberals stand for? It is convenient to start with the radicals, since they were the group most eager to take the initiative. The radical group included Benthamite intellectuals like the young John Stuart Mill (1806–1873) but also militant nonconformists like Edward Miall (1809–1881). Whether Benthamites or nonconformists, these middle-class radicals wanted to remake the institutions of state and church to conform to the principles of individualism and competition. Aristocratic influence, they believed, had to go. Hence they favored further extension of the franchise, the secret ballot, and shorter Parliaments, all of which would make Parliament more directly representative of the constituencies. They wanted to abolish the Corn Law, which, they believed, gave preference to the agricultural interest over industry and commerce. Furthermore, they wanted to restrict the privileges of the Church of England. Many wished to disestablish it altogether, for which purpose they formed in 1844 a pressure group called the Anti-State Church Association (later renamed the Liberation Society). In the meantime, radicals sought to pare away the excessive wealth of the Church, to abolish compulsory church rates (local taxes), to allow nonconformists to have their own rites for marriage and burials, and to open Oxford and Cambridge to dissenters.

The Whigs displayed a more diffuse range of policies, since Whigs were members of a particular group of aristocratic families rather than ideologues. Generally speaking, they regarded 1832 as final in constitutional reform, but they favored alteration of the Church, both to conciliate middle-class nonconformist opinion and to make the Church less vulnerable to the extremists who wished to disestablish it. Because the Whigs only gradually took up the cause of repealing the Corn Law, the Church issue was what most clearly distinguished them from the Tories. In 1832, the Whig government appointed an ecclesiastical commission to investigate the wealth of the Church, the anomalies in clerical salaries, and the long-standing pluralism and nonresidence of parish clergymen. In 1833, the Whigs abolished ten bishoprics of the Anglican Church of Ireland, an egregiously top-heavy institution. In 1836, they sponsored legislation that legalized nonconformist marriages and set up state (rather than church) registration of births, deaths, and marriages.

The Conservatives and Liberals of early Victorian Britain were not class parties in any rigorous sense. Both of them had aristocratic, middle-class, and even to some extent working-class elements. Yet the center of gravity in the social composition of the one differed from that of the other. The Conservatives increasingly spoke for landed Anglican England, whereas the Liberals voiced the outlook of nonconformist business and commercial men and of Scottish and Irish interests. Such differences did not emerge in connection with every issue, and they would be blurred when Peel accepted repeal of the Corn Law in 1846, but the centrality of religion to the process of class formation in Britain produced a significant degree of class orientation in the two political parties even by midcentury.

THE CONDITION OF ENGLAND, 1832–1850

Whatever their differences, Conservatives and Liberals were men of property and shared a broad consensus about the framework of the society and the constitution. Thus, on many issues that came before them, M.P.s did not divide along party lines. Chief among these nonparty issues were those arising from the massive economic and social problems generated by demographic, industrial, and urban change—the so-called condition of England question.

On such issues, members of both parties felt conflicting impulses. The Liberals generally believed in laissez-faire, the notion that the market economy was self-regulating and would, if left alone, automatically reach maximum production and full employment. However, many Liberals were also utilitarians and believed that the government should intervene in society in order to produce the greatest happiness of the greatest number; hence they admired "scientific" analysis of social problems and expert administration. The Conservatives, on the other hand, often opposed laissez-faire in favor of paternalist policies. But they were also devoted to local interests and the rights of property, both of which attitudes were hostile to centralization and an active government. Both parties were, therefore, pulled in both directions: for and against state intervention in society and economy.

Different aspects of the "condition of England" problem produced results that reflected different mixes of these fundamental attitudes. The first major social issue that Parliament addressed after 1832 was the Poor Law. The existing Poor Law, which dated back to the Elizabethan period, had become by the 1800s a ramshackle system. Worse yet, it was expensive. In 1795, magistrates in Speenhamland, Berkshire, adopted a mechanism of supplying the poor with relief payments that varied with the number of children in the pauper family and the price of bread. It was widely believed by the 1820s that this policy encouraged employers to hold wages down, while total expenditures escalated: in 1831–1832, the Poor Law cost £7 million. Yet the Poor Law did not ensure social peace, as the Swing Riots of 1830 showed. By then, the propertied classes agreed that the Poor Law must be reformed, and the Whigs appointed a royal commission to investigate in 1832.

The Poor Law Commission reported in 1834 and issued a classic monument of middle-class ideology. The commission had been dominated by political economists (most notably, Edwin Chadwick). Chadwick was to become the first great civil servant in British history and also the incarnation of Benthamite relentlessness, narrowness, and intolerance. The commission concluded that the Poor Law itself created poverty by teaching the laboring poor to depend on "outdoor relief"—that is, payments given outside the workhouses. As one witness said, "The system of allowances is most mischievous and ruinous, and till it is abandoned the spirit of industry can never be revived." All relief should be given in workhouses, and the "able-bodied" poor should be forced off the relief rolls. Consequently, conditions in the workhouses should be miserable—"less eligible" than those of the lowest-paying job in the locality. People who really could work would be driven to do so. A central board would set out and implement the new regulations.

The Poor Law was amended along these lines in 1834, with very little opposition. Chadwick was made secretary to the new Poor Law Board, and he proceeded to badger local Poor Law unions incessantly to build workhouses and halt all outdoor relief. The new Poor Law and its "workhouse test" were extremely unpopular with the working class. To them the Poor Law symbolized the heartlessness of the new commercial and industrial men. Moreover, in the industrial North, where large numbers were unemployed during periods of recession, the workhouses simply could not cope, for the new Poor Law had been designed on the false theory that the able-bodied could always find work. It did cut costs, however: by 1840, Poor Law expenditure was down to £4.6 million a year.

Paradoxically, though enacted on laissez-faire principles, the new Poor Law resulted in the growth of government. Factory reforms passed in the 1830s and 1840s did the same, though the motives here were largely paternalist and humanitarian. The principal advocates of factory reform were the workers themselves, especially unions like the Manchester Cotton Spinners, led by John Doherty, and Conservative evangelicals like Richard Oastler and Michael Sadler. The trade unions wanted a reduction of hours of labor in the factories in order to ease the hardship of factory work and create opportunities for unemployed factory hands. They also wanted to monopolize the best jobs for men. The Evangelical reformers were especially moved by child labor in the factories. In 1830, Oastler wrote of "thousands of little children . . . sacrificed at the shrine of avarice, without even the solace of the Negro slave." The general hope of all factory reformers was to restrict the working day of children to ten hours, on the assumption that this would cause adult labor to be restricted as well.

The dispute over the proposed ten-hours policy was heated. Paternalist Conservatives stood for the restriction against Whigs, Liberals, and the majority of manufacturers. Sadler lost his seat in 1832, and parliamentary leadership of the factory reform movement passed to the most remarkable Tory Evangelical of the century, Lord Ashley (later earl of Shaftesbury). The Whigs appointed a commission to study factory reform in 1833; it was led by the ubiquitous Chadwick. In his report, Chadwick refuted many of the humanitarian arguments but admitted that children were not free agents in the labor market and therefore warranted protection. The resulting Factory Act of 1833 prohibited the employment of children under age nine in textile mills and restricted the hours of all those under eighteen. More important, the act established a professional inspectorate to supervise compliance with its regulations.

The inspectorate eventually contributed to further reform. The ten-hours movement continued to agitate inside and outside Parliament for full enactment of their policy, but they had little effect until the factory inspectors uncovered weaknesses in the 1833 act. Their expert testimony, effectively marshaled by Lord Ashley, resulted in additional restrictions of child labor in 1844 and finally in a Ten Hours Act for all textile workers in 1847. Thus a new pattern in the legislative process had emerged: humanitarian reformers brought an issue before Parliament; a royal commission was appointed to gather facts; a law was passed and professional administrators appointed; and thereafter, the professionals provided irresistible impetus for further reform.

Professional expertise also played a crucial role in focusing the power of the state on the great problem of public health in the industrial towns. In this case, many of the experts were doctors who had firsthand experience of the horrors of cholera and typhus in congested urban areas. The key conclusion of such physicians as Sir James Kay (Manchester) and Southwood Smith (London) was based on statistical rather than biological evidence, but it was right nevertheless: filth and disease were closely related. Meanwhile, work on the Poor Law Board turned Chadwick's attention to public health, and in 1842 he issued a Sanitary Report that shocked its readers and became a bestseller. Sheer facts had persuaded him that the unsanitary urban environment caused disease, and disease caused poverty and dependence on the Poor Law. Other royal commissions and parliamentary committees in the 1840s drew the same conclusions.

Yet public health legislation was slow in coming. One reason was that localism—the belief in the rights and authority of borough governments—stoutly opposed centralization. Another was that the institutions that provided water, waste removal, and drainage for the towns were private companies, and they fought effectively to protect their rights. Significant action did not come until 1848, when a breakthrough Public Health Act was passed. It established a central Board of Health (headed by Chadwick) with some power to compel local authorities to undertake sanitary reform. Chadwick alienated many local officials and was dismissed in 1854; the Board of Health was disbanded in 1858, in an apparent victory for localism. But the man who in effect succeeded Chadwick, Sir John Simon, was a much more pragmatic and successful administrator. His Privy Council medical department prepared the ground for effective government intervention, which came in the latter 1860s.

By the 1850s, then, the scope and size of the British state had grown markedly, both because of a humanitarianism largely evangelical and paternalist and because of the development of professional expertise. By 1870, the number of government employees stood at fifty-four thousand. Experts now regulated in varying degrees the Poor Law, the prisons, the railways, and most textile mills; the central government was beginning to take a hand in cleaning up the cities; and the state had become registrar of births, marriages, and deaths as well as regular census-taker.

Not only was the state engaged in activities never dreamed of a century earlier, but also the standard of performance was much higher. Professionalism was making a genuine civil service out of government employees. To advance this process, two businesslike administrators, Sir Charles Trevelyan and Sir Stafford Northcote, issued in 1853 a report calling for a unified civil service based on the principles of appointment by open competitive examination and promotion by merit. This was a bitter pill to swallow for those devoted to aristocratic government, but the scope and complexity of social problems had made the medicine necessary. Civil service exams were introduced in the 1860s, and patronage in most departments ended in

1870. In fact, sons of the aristocracy and gentry continued to monopolize government service, for they had the classical education favored by the examiners. The growth of the British state thus was doubly paradoxical: the state grew during the great era of laissez-faire ideology, and the elite maintained their grip on public office by accepting bourgeois principles of competition and merit.

CLASS POLITICS: ANTI-CORN LAW LEAGUE AND CHARTISM

Class conflict, so evident in the passage of the new Reform Act and the new Poor Law, was not at issue in the other social legislation of the 1830s and 1840s. However, class conflict boiled over ominously in two extraparliamentary movements: the Anti-Corn Law League, the archetype organization of middle-class interests, and Chartism, the first nationwide working-class movement.

The Anti-Corn Law League was founded in Manchester in 1838. It gave voice to the middle-class belief in political economy: the efficiency of the free market and the virtues of free trade. The Corn Law of 1815 had been a key event in the awakening of middle-class consciousness. Businessmen recognized that in its intention of keeping grain prices high, the Corn Law was a blatant attempt by the landlords to protect their own interests at the expense of the rest of the nation. The Corn Law, according to the Anti-Corn Law League, kept food prices high and reduced commercial and industrial profits by forcing employers to pay artificially high wages. Even the introduction by Huskisson of a sliding scale on grain duties did not satisfy the captains of industry and trade. In fact, the Corn Law (now modified) failed to keep grain prices up, but that did not mute the drumfire of criticism coming from the business sector. After 1836, when bad harvests drove food prices up and trade went into a slump, middle-class discontent intensified and then found an organizational outlet in the Anti-Corn Law League.

The leading figures in the Anti-Corn Law agitation were Richard Cobden and John Bright. Both were exemplars of the middle class of Victorian Britain. Cobden, an Anglican owner of calico mills in Manchester, was a self-made man. He preached even to the working class "the love of independence, the privilege of self-respect, the disdain of being patronised . . . the desire to accumulate, and the ambition to rise." He believed that state interference in the economy only promoted privilege and monopoly, which he despised. Further, he reasoned that free trade would strengthen British farming by exposing it to competition, and if adopted around the world it would lead nations into specialization of production and networks of trade that would spell international peace. Cobden recognized that persuasion alone would not win Parliament over; the League had to bring pressure on every candidate, regardless of party, and work for the defeat of Corn Law defenders. He thus created the first modern pressure group.

Bright, a Quaker industrialist from Rochdale, supplemented Cobden's tactical shrewdness with moral passion. He made the campaign against the Corn Law into a moral crusade and became the symbol of the nonconformist in politics: bluff, moralistic, and righteous. To such people, the Anti-Corn Law struggle involved

Dear bread and cheap bread: a membership card of the National Anti-Corn Law League. The elaborate designs served a propagandist purpose when the cards were displayed on a wall or mantelpiece.

much more than economics, for it encompassed a blow at the aristocracy and the Anglican church. As one pro-League newspaper declared in 1841: "The value of tithes and teinds on which they [the Anglican clergy] fatten is vastly enhanced, they know, by the aristocratic restrictions on the food of the community."

The Anti-Corn Law League between 1838 and 1846 held countless meetings; sponsored thousands of tracts, pamphlets, and lectures; and presented many motions in the House of Commons. But they never persuaded a majority to vote for repeal. True, they convinced Peel himself, who as prime minister in 1845 remarked to a colleague after hearing Cobden speak, "You must answer this for I cannot." It was famine in Ireland that brought the Corn Law down. Beginning in 1845, the Irish potato crop failed, and the most terrible famine in modern British history settled on Ireland (see Chapter 15). Peel believed that he had no choice but to seek repeal of the Corn Law in 1846 in order to allow cheap food to be imported into Ireland. He and his personal following joined the Liberals in overturning the Corn Law. Peel gave credit to Cobden, but Cobden himself admitted that without the crisis in Ireland, the League would not have succeeded.

Repeal of the Corn Law did not have the consequences either side had anticipated. It neither saved the Irish people nor undercut the power of the landed class. Nevertheless, it was seen as a great victory for middle-class ideas, though once again enacted by a Parliament of landowners. When stable prosperity blessed Britain in the 1850s and 1860s, free trade got the credit. Britons of the governing classes concluded that free trade was the key to economic success. This would be a difficult lesson to unlearn.

The Anti-Corn Law Leaguers asserted that because the middle and working classes had identical interests, the working class should support the League. But the great majority of politically minded working men and women remained suspicious of the League. They saw it as the rationalization of middle-class interests. They, and especially the Chartists, believed that if repeal of the Corn Law did result in cheaper food, then employers would only reduce wages. Chartists thus sometimes broke up Anti-Corn Law meetings; what *they* wanted was political empowerment.

Chartism was the largest mass movement in Victorian history, so large and dramatic that at times it seemed to threaten revolution. It had roots in the popular radicalism of the eighteenth century—the tradition of the moral economy of the crowd and the radical belief in democracy and a free Parliament. The Chartist program varied widely by region and by social group, but most Chartists were backward-looking in their desire to restore lost independence and community. At the same time, most agreed with the working-class radicals of the 1820s in asserting that social problems were caused by governmental failings. Political reform would in some unspecified way lead to radical social and economic change. Hence Chartism always found its warmest support among artisans. Factory workers in some towns became Chartists, but their activity tended to wax and wane as the economy slumped and boomed. The largest number of Chartists, and the most militant, came from the outworkers, artisans who were suffering because they could not compete with "dishonorable" labor and the factories—handloom weavers, framework knitters, nail makers, and the like. Both men and women were active in the Chartist movement; but many of them had internalized the doctrine of separate spheres for men and women, and others felt that to win the necessary middle-class support they had to accept this conventional ideology and therefore the continued exclusion of women from the electorate.

The founding of Chartism had two immediate causes: first, the frustration of working-class radicals in 1832, and second, the popular hatred of the new Poor Law of 1834. While their former middle-class allies were taking up repeal of the Corn Law, working-class radicals continued to work for a broader franchise. The anti-Poor Law campaign was very widespread in the North of England, especially in the bad years of 1836–1837. Working people thought that the new Poor Law was cruel and degrading, since it forced them to seek relief in "Poor Law Bastilles," where they had to wear prisonlike uniforms, undergo separation of family members, and work at miserable tasks like stone breaking and bone grinding. In 1839, representatives of popular radicalism and the anti-Poor Law campaign met in London to consider possible courses of action. They adopted the six points of the Charter: universal manhood suffrage, equal electoral districts, no property qualification for M.P.s, annual elections, payment of M.P.s, and the secret ballot. All of these but annual Parliaments have since been enacted, but at the time, they were regarded as extremely radical proposals.

From its earliest moments, Chartism was divided by personal clashes among its leaders and by strong disagreements over tactics and ultimate objectives. For example, some militants wanted the first Chartist convention to set itself up as an alternative Parliament. Others sought to intimidate Parliament by means of a national strike. Still others hinted broadly at using physical force. The moderates, however, wanted simply to petition Parliament to enact the six points. Most middle-class radicals in the 1839 convention became alarmed at the loose talk of the militants and withdrew. An attempt in 1841–1842 to patch up the radical alliance between middle- and working-class moderates behind a combined program of repeal of the Corn Law and passage of the six points foundered on the rocks of class antagonism. Thereafter, Chartist leaders followed very different paths: some engaged in conspiracy, arming, and drilling; others organized Christian Chartist or temperance and self-help societies. London Chartists were never in phase with those in the industrial North. Welsh Chartists were moved by old grievances against the local anglicized ruling elite and were therefore as much Welsh nationalist as radical in their motives. Given these divisions, the government's aggressive tactics of spies, informers, and preventive arrests, and Parliament's determination to reject the Chartist petitions out of hand, Chartism faced formidable obstacles.

Chartism went through three phases. In the first (1839–1840), the Chartist convention adopted the six points, argued about tactics, presented the first Chartist petition (which Parliament rejected overwhelmingly), and then dissolved. Scattered violence followed. In Yorkshire and Lancashire some Chartists conspired for rebellion, and in Newport (South Wales), Welsh Chartists marched on the town. These Welsh Chartists were routed by the British army, who killed twenty-four of them, and the conspiracy elsewhere fizzled out. In 1839–1840, the government arrested more than five hundred Chartists, and a general strike fell flat. By midsummer of 1840, the first phase was over.

The second period of Chartist history (1840-1842) was dominated by the Irish-born demagogue, Feargus O'Connor. He was a landowner, a romantic, and an enemy of the machine age. He published in England the greatest Chartist newspaper, *The Northern Star*, and he was a spellbinding orator, though often a victim of his own rhetoric. He spoke boldly of revolution but was temperamentally incapable of planning one, and it is doubtful that he meant what he said. In any case, O'Connor in 1842 gathered a second petition for the six points containing about three million signatures. Parliament abruptly rejected it. T. B. Macaulay, the historian and M.P., spoke for the great majority of the House of Commons when he declared that universal suffrage "would be fatal to the purposes for which government exists," for it was "utterly incompatible with the existence of civilization." In the industrial North, violence broke out as workers engaged in strikes and, in some places, removed the plugs from steam boilers to stop factory operations. O'Connor dithered in his attitude toward this industrial action, and moderate Chartists and trade unionists exerted themselves against it. Agitation for a time was quieted.

The last great Chartist demonstration, 1848. A photograph of the Chartist crowd on Kennington Common, London.

The third phase (1842–1848) included both a back-to-the land scheme and the final Chartist petition. O'Connor dreamed of restoring the people to the land. He established, therefore, a Chartist cooperative to buy land in England and lease it to individual Chartists. Not only would working people return to a kind of yeoman status, but also the oversupply of labor in industry would be reduced. Unfortunately, after some initial success the cooperative soon sank into deep financial trouble. In 1848, when popular revolutions broke out across Europe, O'Connor returned to petitioning and mass demonstrations. A simultaneous rising of the starving tenantry in Ireland would, he hoped, help overawe the government. O'Connor claimed to have gathered five or six million signatures and planned to deliver the petition to Parliament, accompanied by 100,000 Chartists.

The government, however, recognized the seriousness of the situation but did not panic. This time, while the northern provinces were relatively quiet, Chartism caught fire in London. The government summoned four thousand policemen, eight thousand troops, and eighty-five thousand special constables (the great majority of whom were middle-class men) and consulted the duke of Wellington on tactics. Though some 150,000 Chartists gathered on Kennington Common south of the Thames, O'Connor decided not to defy a government ban on a procession across the river to Parliament. Had the Chartists attempted to march on Westminster, a bloodbath would surely have resulted, and possibly a revolutionary conflict would have begun. In the end, O'Connor delivered the petition (which had less than two million signatures, including obvious fakes like the "duke of Wellington," "Robert Peel," and "Victoria Rex") by taxicab. Parliament quickly rejected it. The Irish peasantry did not rise up at the key moment, and during the summer of 1848 the London police mopped up conspiratorial bands of Chartists. Worse yet, a parliamentary investigation found the finances of the land cooperative in chaos. The cooperative was closed, and O'Connor spent the rest of his days in an insane asylum.

Chartism thus failed, whereas the Anti-Corn Law League succeeded. The League was better organized, its single policy less revolutionary, and its social base (the middle class) more powerful than Chartism. Nevertheless, Chartism was of great historical significance. It did more than any other popular movement to spread class consciousness among the working people of Britain and to express their antagonism both to the landed proprietors and to the middle class. At the same time, its failure taught British workers that they must operate within the political and economic system for more limited goals. Furthermore, the Chartist episode contributed to the acceptance of the middle class by the landed orders, because the two upper classes had stood shoulder to shoulder against the Chartist threat. Lady Palmerston, wife of the Whig statesman, expressed this outcome best: "I am sure," she wrote, "that it is very fortunate that the whole thing has occurred, as it has shown the good spirit of our middle classes."

Suggested Reading

Belchem, John, *Popular Radicalism in Nineteenth-Century Britain* (New York: St. Martin's Press, 1996).

Bentley, Michael, *Politics without Democracy, 1815–1914*, 2nd ed. (London: Fontana, 1996).

Brock, Michael, *The Great Reform Act* (London: Hutchinson, 1973).

Brundage, Anthony, *The English Poor Laws, 1700–1930* (New York: Palgrave, 2002).

Burns, Arthur, and Joanna Innis, eds., *Rethinking the Age of Reform: Britain 1780–1850* (Cambridge: Cambridge University Press, 2003).

Cannon, John, *Parliamentary Reform, 1640–1832* (Cambridge: Cambridge University Press, 1973).

Checkland, Sidney, *British Public Policy, 1776–1939* (New York: Cambridge University Press, 1983).

Derry, John W., *Charles, Earl Grey: Aristocratic Reformer* (Oxford: B. Blackwell, 1992).

Dinwiddy, J. R., *From Luddism to the First Reform Bill* (Oxford: Blackwell, 1986).

Eastwood, David, *Governing Rural England; Tradition and Transformation in Local Government, 1780–1840* (Oxford: Clarendon Press, 1994).

Epstein, James, *The Lion of Freedom: Feargus O'Connor and the Chartist Movement, 1832–1842* (London: Croom Helm, 1982).

Evans, D. Gareth, *A History of Wales, 1815–1906* (Cardiff: University of Wales Press, 1990).

Finer, S. E., *The Life and Times of Sir Edwin Chadwick* (London: Methuen, 1980).

Fraser, W. Hamish, and R. J. Morris, eds., *People and Society in Scotland, Volume II: 1830–1914* (Edinburgh: John Donald, 1990).

Gash, Norman, *Politics in the Age of Peel* (London: Longmans, Green, 1953).

———, *Sir Robert Peel* (London: Longman, 1972).

Goodway, David, *London Chartism, 1838–1848* (Cambridge: Cambridge University Press, 1982).

Hanham, H. J., ed., *The Nineteenth-Century Constitution, 1815–1914* (London: Cambridge University Press, 1969).

Hilton, Boyd, *A Mad, Bad, and Dangerous People? England, 1783–1846* (Oxford: Oxford University Press, 2006).

Lees, Lynn Hollen, *The Solidarities of Strangers: The English Poor Law and People, 1700–1948* (New York: Cambridge University Press, 1997).

LoPatin, Nancy D., *Popular Unions, Popular Politics, and the Great Reform Act of 1832* (New York: St. Martin's Press, 1999).

Mather, F. C., ed., *Chartism and Society: An Anthology of Documents* (London: Bell & Hyman, 1980).

McCaffrey, John F., *Scotland in the Nineteenth Century* (New York: St. Martin's Press, 1998).

McCord, Norman, *The Anti-Corn Law League, 1838–1846* (London: Allen & Unwin, 1968).

Palmer, Stanley H., *Police and Protest in England and Ireland, 1780–1850* (New York: Cambridge University Press, 1988).

Parry, Jonathan, *The Rise and Fall of Liberal Government in Victorian Britain* (New Haven: Yale University Press, 1993).

Pickering, Paul, and Alex Tyrell, *The People's Bread: A History of the Anti-Corn Law League* (Leicester: Leicester University Press, 2000).

Roberts, David, *The Social Conscience of the Early Victorians* (Stanford: Stanford University Press, 2002).

———, *Victorian Origins of the British Welfare State* (Hamden, Conn.: Archon Books, 1969).

Sack, James J., *From Jacobite to Conservative: Reaction and Orthodoxy in Britain. c. 1760–1832* (Cambridge: Cambridge University Press, 1993).

Saville, John, *1848: The British State and the Chartist Movement* (New York: Cambridge University Press, 1987).

Schwarzkopf, Julia, *Women in the Chartist Movement* (New York: St. Martin's Press, 1991).

Smith, E. A., *Lord Grey, 1764–1845* (Oxford: Clarendon Press, 1990).

Thompson, Dorothy, *The Chartists* (New York: Pantheon Books, 1984).

Chapter 15

Ireland from the
Union to the Famine

With the Act of Union in 1800, England and Ireland in theory became parts of a single state. Yet the differences between England and Ireland were fundamental, and the United Kingdom of Great Britain and Ireland never really worked. While England (along with South Wales and Lowland Scotland) was industrializing and modernizing, Ireland remained a backward agricultural society. England was, however painfully, becoming the wealthiest and most progressive society in the world, but Ireland stood stagnant, mired in poverty, agrarian violence, and sectarian strife. It is safe to say that England, the predominant partner, never understood Irish problems the way the Irish did—never saw Ireland through Irish eyes. What was called "the Irish Question" thus became an intractable and frustrating set of issues for the English; what might have been called "the English Question" became an alternately maddening and demoralizing brick wall for the Irish. If the new state created in 1800 had worked, the attachment of Ireland to Britain could have been of enormous benefit to the mass of Irish people, but it did not, and the consequence was the greatest catastrophe in Irish history.

THE IRISH QUESTION

The so-called Irish Question of the early nineteenth century had three parts: political, religious, and economic. The political aspect arose from the fact that the Act of Union created a situation in which the great majority of the Irish people were disaffected from their government. The Anglo-Protestant ascendancy, approximately 15 to 20 percent of the Irish population (including the Ulster Presbyterians), thought that the Union was their sole protection, but most of the rest of the Irish regarded the Union as the source and symbol of their oppression. As Arthur Wellesley (later the duke of Wellington) said in 1807, "We have no strength here but our army. Ireland, in a view to military operations, must be viewed as an enemy's country." The Act of Union abolished the Irish Parliament and gave Ireland one hundred M.P.s (out of 658) in Parliament at Westminster. Catholics could vote but could not serve as members of Parliament. From 1801 to 1921, then, all major decisions on Irish policies were made by the British cabinet and Parliament in London, neither of which allowed the Irish much influence.

Likewise, Irish influence—that is, the influence of the Catholic majority of the population—did not propel the administrative machinery in Ireland. The Irish administration was headed by the lord lieutenant, usually a British nobleman who ruled from Dublin Castle, the symbol of Anglo-Protestant power. The main political figure was the chief secretary, a leading British politician who had to defend the government in the House of Commons as well as administer the country on a day-to-day basis. The administrative staff, the legal officers, the magistrates, and the judiciary through whom the lord lieutenant and chief secretary executed policy were all drawn from Irish Protestantism. Local government was carried out by Grand Juries selected by the sheriff of each county and by closed, nonelective corporations in the boroughs; both groups were exclusively Protestant.

The functions of government at first were restricted to preserving law and order. In the 1820s and 1830s, the scope of government in Ireland expanded to include public works, state education, and a Poor Law. In all of its functions, the Irish executive could depend little on the voluntary services of the aristocracy and gentry; hence the administration became more centralized than that in England. This tendency also suited the British attitude toward Ireland, which, despite the Union, held that Ireland was a strange and savage place. As Sir Robert Peel, chief secretary from 1812 to 1818, said, "I believe an honest despotic government would be by far the fittest government for Ireland."

A kind of honest despotism, answerable to the British Parliament, is in fact what prevailed in Ireland. In order to control endemic agrarian violence as well as dangerous political movements, Parliament frequently resorted to "coercion" acts—laws suspending civil liberties from designated periods of time. Rarely was Ireland in the nineteenth century free from coercion. Because execution of the law was in Protestant hands, the Catholics did not trust the judiciary. In order to see that the law was enforced impartially, British administrators like Peel sometimes adopted measures that would have been unacceptable in England. For instance, they often resorted to "stipendiary magistrates"—magistrates employed by the central administration—instead of local J.P.s. Dublin Castle officials also used the army to enforce the law and even to collect tithes and carry out evictions of tenants for nonpayment of rent. The British army in Ireland consistently numbered between twenty thousand and forty thousand men and was backed by a yeomanry of another thirty-five thousand. Ireland thus in theory was part of the United Kingdom; in practice it was an occupied country.

The religious aspect of the Irish Question was clear: the established Church of Ireland, which was Anglican, represented only about 10 percent of the population. Nonconformists (mostly Ulster Presbyterians) composed another 8 to 10 percent; all the rest were Roman Catholics. Further, the Church of Ireland was top-heavy with a huge hierarchy: for 800,000 Anglicans, the Church in 1831 had four archbishops; eighteen bishops; numerous cathedrals, deans, and chapters; plus about 1,400 parish clergymen. Some Anglican parishes had not a single Protestant resident. This lavish establishment was supported by tithes, which all Irishmen, regardless of religion, had to pay. The Catholics hated the tithe, and in the early 1830s resistance to paying the tithe, backed by agrarian secret societies, spread widely through southern Ireland. The government used large numbers of police and army troops to collect the tithe, and the resulting "tithe war" caused much bloodshed and ill-feeling.

Meanwhile, the Catholic church in Ireland was getting its own house in order. Having survived the penal laws, the Catholic church turned its attention to the twin problems of the population explosion and evangelical Protestant missionaries. The Catholic hierarchy undertook organizational reform, building of churches and chapels, renewal of discipline, and parochial education. By the 1830s, the church had a much firmer grip on the people. Moreover, that grip was exercised at the parish level by priests trained in the Catholic seminaries at Maynooth, Carlow, and elsewhere in Ireland. Whereas the older generation (who now held the top positions in the Irish hierarchy) had been trained abroad, the younger parish clergy (who had close daily contact with the people) were educated at home. One Protestant observer said that the Irish priests "displayed the bitterest feelings of the partisan and the grossest habits of the peasant." This is a prejudiced view, no doubt, but the Catholic clergyman, who lived in a small world dominated by the Protestant squire, parson, and the tithe collector, did tend to be highly political. To him, Irish patriotism and Catholicism were one and the same.

The economic dimension of the Irish Question was simply that Ireland was very poor. The Irish in the first half of the nineteenth century were caught in a "poverty trap," in which poverty itself—low incomes, primitive markets, and a low rate of capital formation—defeated every impetus for economic growth. Moreover, the economic obstacles to prosperity were reinforced by seemingly immovable political and social conditions. Politics, society, and economics fed on each other to make a vicious circle of instability, insecurity, and stagnation.

To begin with, there was, as we have seen, no industrialization in Ireland except in Ulster. The Union had envisioned a single free-trade area for the British Isles, but when free trade was actually enacted in 1824, it had severe consequences for the Irish economy. The cotton textile industry centered in Belfast was protected by tariffs until 1824, when Huskisson and the Tory government insisted on free trade within the United Kingdom. Thereafter, the Ulster cotton industry was destroyed by competition from British mills. Belfast was able to switch back to its old staple, linen; however, in the rest of Ireland, British machine-made goods ruined the most important cottage industry, domestic weaving. Given the comparative attractiveness of the burgeoning English and Scottish industrial sector, no one wanted to invest in new industries in Ireland. There was little capital in Ireland, and few English or Scottish investors wanted to transfer their capital into the Emerald Isle. Outside of Ulster, therefore, the great majority of the Irish people became more dependent than ever on agriculture.

Irish farming in the first half of the century was able to increase its production, but it remained inefficient compared to English agriculture, now in the full tide of agricultural revolution. In Ireland, there was a steady shift of land from tillage to pasturage but not much improvement of farming techniques. The problem once again was lack of investment. In order to improve farming, some part of Irish society had to invest in the reorganization of the land, new crops, fertilizer, scientific breeding, and so on. But no one did. Landless laborers and cottiers (cottagers) were too poor to do so, and tenant farmers were either too poor or too insecure of their holdings. Tenants feared that if they made improvements, their rents would go up. Only in Ulster, where "Ulster custom" prevailed, were tenants entitled to compensation for improvements that they made on their land; not surprisingly, in Ulster tenants were more progressive farmers, and landlord-tenant relations were more cooperative than in Leinster, Munster, and Connacht. The Irish landlords had the money to invest, and a few in fact tried to improve their estates, but the results inevitably involved evictions of "excess" tenants and considerable violence. Few landlords viewed improvements as a good bargain. They were alienated from their tenants and laborers by religion, culture, and mutual antagonism. The landlords were understandably fearful of the chronic agrarian terrorism that afflicted the countryside. Many were absentees in England; others opted to spend their incomes on consumer pleasures—fine houses, horses, dogs, entertainment, and drink. What most Irish landlords wanted from their estates was the rent, the collection of which they left to bailiffs and "middlemen." Neither investment nor paternalism had any attraction for them.

The great majority of the Irish people still depended on the land for a living. Upwards of two-thirds of all occupied people worked in farming. They labored on the land but did not own it. In England, the tendency was for landholdings to grow in size, but in Ireland, the rapid increase in the population and the lack of alternative employment put enormous pressure on the land. By subdivision, tenancies became smaller and smaller, as did the plots of land rented by cottiers and wage laborers. A royal commission in 1845 found that to sustain a family of five, a farm in Ireland had to be between 6 and 10 acres, but by the 1840s, 45 percent of all holdings were below 5 acres, and another 37 percent were between 5 and 15 acres.

Meanwhile, competition for holdings and a general decline of agricultural prices were pushing rentals (in terms of tenants' purchasing power) up. Arrears of rent were common, as were evictions for nonpayment of rent. The Irish peasantry tried to defend themselves from rent increases and eviction by forming secret societies, which engaged in intimidation not only of landlords but also of tenants who dared bid for a holding from which a family has been evicted. Whiteboys, Whitefeet, Ribbonmen, Rockites, and the like spread widely, especially from the 1820s. Their tactics consisted of intimidation, mutilation of cattle, and assassination. Most observers thought that the violence did protect the peasantry from predatory landlords, but it also contributed significantly to the vicious circle of poverty and stagnation.

The hard-pressed Irish population became even more dependent on the potato. Generally, the Irish tenants and cottiers produced grain, pigs, and cattle, either on their own holdings or on someone else's, to pay the rent, but they grew potatoes to feed themselves. The poorer the region (mainly in the West) the greater the dependency on the potato. By the 1840s, one-third of all land under tillage was devoted to potatoes, and upwards of half the population ate little else. Travelers in Ireland even noticed fewer pigs living in the peasants' huts, not because standards of hygiene had gone up but because fewer cottiers and laborers could afford them. Cash money had little part to play in the life of the ordinary peasant; hence there was at best a primitive market system and no means of attracting alternative food-stuffs into Ireland. Localized famine was common wherever the potato crop failed. This was a setting for disaster.

DANIEL O'CONNELL AND CATHOLIC EMANCIPATION

It would seem obvious that Ireland in the early nineteenth century was ripe for revolution, or at least a powerful movement against the Union. But in the opening decades of the century, the Irish political scene was quiet. Most Protestants had turned against patriotic politics and looked to the Union as their salvation. The small Catholic middle class had no way to revoke the Act of Union. The demoralized masses were inert, and the horrors of 1798 were fresh in everyone's mind. Thus when the youthful Robert Emmet and the vestiges of the United Irishmen staged a rising in Dublin in 1803, it was abortive. Emmet's rebellion came to nothing except his own execution and the making of another martyr for the revolutionary strain in Irish nationalism. Independence or autonomy for Ireland was out of the question.

Full civil and political rights for Catholics were another matter. The Younger Pitt, it will be remembered, meant to include Catholic emancipation as part of a package with the Union. Many English and Scottish Whigs as well as radicals adopted the issue. In Ireland, middle-class and professional Catholics continued to work for emancipation, partly on principle and partly on the hope that they would benefit directly from public office or the prestige of a seat in Parliament. In the years between 1800 and 1823, however, the Irish Catholic leadership was divided and ineffective. The divisions had to do with the questions of "safeguards" insisted on by the British as the price of emancipation: first, state control over appointments of Catholic bishops; and second, state payment of the Catholic clergy. Presumably, these safeguards would ensure the loyalty of the Catholic church, and many upperclass English and Irish Catholics were content to accept them. Other Irish Catholics, however, including most priests and some bishops, would not; consequently, the movement was paralyzed.

This situation was transformed by Daniel O'Connell, who was to be one of the two great leaders of Irish nationalism in the nineteenth century. O'Connell (1775–1847) was the heir of an old Catholic gentry family of County Kerry. Educated abroad in French Catholic schools, O'Connell read for the bar in London and then became a successful and popular lawyer in Dublin. While studying in London, he became a deist and a Benthamite. The deism he soon abandoned when he returned to Catholicism, but the Benthamism he retained. He was thus one of a certain European type—a liberal Catholic—but one who also was a paternalist landlord, fluent in Gaelic. O'Connell was a passionate Irish patriot and was strongly opposed to the Union. At the same time, his firsthand experience of the French Revolution in 1791–1793 and of the Irish rebellion of 1798 gave him a permanent abhorrence of revolutionary violence. His reaction to the Wexford rising reflected a profound insight: "Good God! What a brute man becomes when ignorant and oppressed! Oh liberty, what horrors are perpetuated in thy name! May every virtuous revolutionary remember the horrors of Wexford."

As a Catholic barrister practicing in the Irish law courts, O'Connell was intensely aware of the civil disabilities suffered by Catholics. Yet he refused to accept emancipation with the "safeguards," on grounds that religious liberty should not be won at the price of shackling the church. His goal was to win emancipation without the safeguards; his strategy was to harness a mass popular agitation to a constitutional parliamentary movement. In 1823 he helped found a new Catholic Association and the next year opened it to ordinary tenant farmers by reducing the membership fee to a penny a month. This was a stroke of genius, for it enabled the Catholic Association to tap the energy of the tenants and to collect thousands of pounds a year for its political fund. Moreover, it mobilized the parish priests, who were held in great esteem in the Catholic communities and who happily urged their parishioners each Sunday to join the Association.

O'Connell's Catholic Association was the first modern political organization in Britain. Why did it succeed in appealing to the Irish peasantry, who, after all, would not personally benefit from Catholic emancipation? One reason was that O'Connell had the gifts of uncanny eloquence and a magical voice. He was a born demagogue, who by his forceful denunciations of British rule acted out the wishes and dreams of his mass audiences. He spoke to the people from within their traditions and appealed to their sense of independence and pride. At the same time, O'Connell made the agitation seem dangerous to the authorities, because, while always eschewing revolution, he deliberately referred to the violence that might occur if Catholic emancipation were not granted. In British eyes, there loomed behind O'Connell the shadowy nightmare of popular revolution.

In 1826, the Catholic Association turned to direct electoral pressure. In the counties, approximately eighty-five thousand Catholic tenants had the vote as forty-shilling freeholders. Traditionally, they yielded to intimidation and voted with their landlords. But the Catholic Association and the parish priests were able to persuade the tenants in Waterford and five other constituencies to defy their landlords and vote for parliamentary candidates supporting Catholic emancipation. In 1828, O'Connell himself dared stand for Parliament in County Clare. He won decisively and thereby presented Wellington and Peel, the leaders of the Tory government, with a hard choice: whether to give in to pressure for emancipation or to reject O'Connell's election (and all the others that were sure to follow) and use military force against the rising that almost everyone expected to be the result. As we saw in Chapter 14, Wellington and Peel gave in. In 1829, they carried Catholic emancipation but exacted a stiff price: the Catholic Emancipation Act allowed Catholics to sit in Parliament and to hold all but a few Crown offices, but it disfranchised the Irish forty-shilling freeholders, about 80 percent of the Irish electorate. O'Connell struggled against the disfranchisement but finally agreed to it because both the English Whigs and the upper-class Irish Catholics supported it and undermined O'Connell's resistance. Otherwise, Catholic emancipation was a great victory for

O'Connell, for the act opened all public offices (except for an insignificant few) and Parliament to Catholics, and it included no "safeguards."

O'Connell took his seat in the House of Commons in 1830 and for some years enjoyed unparalleled popularity—even adulation—in Ireland. Many Irish Protestants gloomily predicted the end of their ascendancy, fearing that democracy, disestablishment, and the confiscation of property would follow; many peasants joyfully expected the same outcome. In the short run both were wrong. Still, O'Connell's triumph in the campaign for Catholic emancipation was of immense significance. For one thing, it taught the Irish people that they could win by demands and agitation what they could not by reason and persuasion. For another, it affirmed the importance of priests in national politics. Most important, O'Connell's strategy welded Irish nationalism to Catholicism. Some later Irish patriots who preferred a nonsectarian nationalism encompassing all Irish men and women regardless of their religious denomination have regretted this feature of O'Connell's legacy. It is ironic that O'Connell, a liberal Catholic devoted to religious toleration, should have been responsible for this step in Irish nationalism, but it is hard to see how he could have acted otherwise. The reality of Ireland under the Union inevitably made unionists of Irish Protestants and Irish patriots of Irish Catholics.

REPEAL AND YOUNG IRELAND

O'Connell had always intended Catholic emancipation to be the first step toward his ultimate objective: repeal of the Act of Union. He was neither a Republican nor a Separatist, thus his constitutional ideal for Ireland and Britain was a dual monarchy: "I desire no social revolution, no social change," he said. "In short, salutary restoration without revolution, an Irish Parliament, British connection, one King, two legislatures." But he faced total opposition form the British Parliament on this issue. Not only were the Conservatives unalterably opposed to repeal, but so also were his former Whig and radical allies. When he first raised the question in Parliament (in 1834), he was defeated by 532 to 39. His support included, besides his own repeal party, only one English M.P., and that one was none other than the future Chartist Feargus O'Connor, who was as much an Irish nationalist as he was a democrat.

Given this blanket opposition, O'Connell thought it wise to win from Parliament whatever help he could for the Irish people. Though the Whigs were as touchy on law and order in Ireland as the most unbending Tories, at least they included Ireland in their program of parliamentary reform. Hence the Irish Reform Act of 1832 restored many leaseholders to the electorate, enfranchised the ten-pound householders in the boroughs, and gave Ireland five extra seats. O'Connell hoped for additional reforms from them. In 1833, the Whig government reorganized the Anglican Irish Church, abolishing ten bishoprics and reducing the income of the others. In 1835, therefore, O'Connell made an alliance with the Whigs in the so-called Lichfield House Compact.

Daniel O'Connell, leader of the movements for Irish Catholic Emancipation and Repeal of the Act of Union.

By this agreement, O'Connell and his repealers acted with the Liberal parliamentary alliance until 1841 and put repeal on the back burner. The Whig alliance was for O'Connell only moderately successful. The Whig government in 1838 tried to solve the problem of Irish tithes, but against ferocious opposition they were able only to convert the tithe into a rent-charge in effect collected by the landlords. In 1839, the Whigs imposed on Ireland the dubious gift of a Poor Law system, complete with workhouses and the "less-eligibility" principle. In 1840, a reform of Irish municipal corporations was passed.

The most beneficial aspect of O'Connell's alliance with the Whigs was a change in the tone of the Dublin Castle administration. The key figure in this administrative reform was Thomas Drummond, undersecretary from 1835 to 1840. He was determined to enforce the law without the usual prejudice in favor of the Protestants, and he opened the Irish civil service and judiciary to Catholics. He even evicted from the bench the more bigoted Protestants. Drummond took strong action against secret terrorist societies, but for once also brought pressure on the Protestant Orange Order and so broke its political power. Drummond understood the economic roots of agrarian crime and admonished the landlords that "property has its duties as well as its rights." In sum, Drummond did more than any other British official before 1870 to win the confidence of the Catholic majority.

O'Connell meanwhile decided to renew the campaign for repeal of the Union. Drummond died in 1840, and the Whig government was on its last legs. There was no prospect of allying with the Conservative leader, known to the Irish as "Orange Peel." In 1840, therefore, O'Connell founded the Loyal National Repeal Association, hoping to win repeal by the same tactics as in 1828–1929: parliamentary pressure backed by a massive popular agitation in Ireland.

The moment seemed ripe for repeal, in part because of the inspired journalism of a small number of romantic journalists called "Young Ireland." In 1842, three young men devoted to the cultural as well as political autonomy of Ireland founded *The Nation* newspaper. They were Thomas Davis (a Protestant barrister), Charles Gavan Duffy (an Ulster Catholic), and John Blake Dillon (a southern Catholic). Their policy was repeal of the Union, but their goal was renewal of the Irish identity based on old Irish cultural traditions and a potent mythology of Irish heroes and martyrs. They wanted the Irish to be more than "West Britain." Their national ideal was nonsectarian, and their propaganda was lofty and effective. By 1843, *The Nation* had a readership of more than 250,000.

O'Connell designated 1843 as "the repeal year." He staged a series of giant open-air gatherings dubbed "monster meetings" to demonstrate the depth of Irish feeling. Some of these monster meetings were attended by more than 100,000 people. O'Connell spoke at the meetings in a crescendo of violent rhetoric. To cautious people in England and Ireland he seemed to be threatening revolution. In June 1843, for example, he warned his audience that "you may have the alternative to live as slaves or die as freemen." By the autumn of 1843, the political temperature of Ireland was at its peak, and the British, already concerned about Chartism, felt embattled.

The problem for O'Connell was that he was deliberately bluffing and had no alternate plan should the British government simply defy him. And defy him they did. Prime minster Peel and his Conservatives, as well as nearly all the Liberals, simply would not countenance repeal of the Union. In 1834 Peel had declared: "I feel and know that the Repeal must lead to dismemberment of this great empire; must make Great Britain a fourth-rate power of Europe, and Ireland a savage wilderness." What repeal ran up against, then, was British nationalism, the deep British mistrust of Catholicism, and British certainty that autonomy for Ireland would destroy the empire. Peel said in 1843: "Deprecating as I do all war, above all, civil war, yet there is no alternative which I do not think preferable to the dismemberment of this empire." In October 1843, Peel banned what was to be the biggest monster meeting and summoned troops to enforce that ban. O'Connell, who had always loathed violence and bloodshed, canceled the meeting. Even so, the government arrested him shortly afterward and convicted him of conspiracy. O'Connell was imprisoned for five months and emerged a more cautious and weary man. The repeal agitation was finished.

THE GREAT FAMINE, 1845–1850

Repeal was in any case soon made irrelevant to the Irish people. Famine became the reality, and suffering was the everyday experience of millions of Irish men, women, and children. In the autumn of 1845, the Irish potato crop was heavily damaged by a fungus now recognized as *phytophthora infestans*. The blight

The Great Famine in Ireland, 1846: starving peasants receiving charity along a roadside.

turned most of the potatoes into a foul mass of putrefying pulp. Dependent as they were on the potato, a large segment of the Irish population suffered grievously through the winter of 1845–1846; and then the crop of 1846 failed utterly. The winter of 1846–1847 brought widespread starvation and disease. Many peasant families ate their seed potatoes; therefore, although the blight did less damage in 1847, the harvest was too small. In 1848, the potato crop failed totally again and only began to improve in 1849. By 1850, the blight had largely disappeared, but in the meantime famine had made a horror of life in Ireland.

The impact of the Great Famine is shown by simple population statistics. In 1841, the Irish population stood at 8.2 million people, and by its natural rate of increase would have risen to about 9 million in 1851. In actuality, the census of 1851 found only 6.5 million, leaving a gap of about 2.5 million between the expected and the actual population. Of these, about 1 million were emigrants; the rest, about 1.5 million people, composed the casualties of the Great Famine. Some died of hunger, but most died of famine-related diseases like typhus, relapsing fever, and dysentery. These 1.5 million dead amounted to nearly 20 percent of the Irish population of 1841. For comparison, it should be noted that Ireland lost more people because of the Famine than all of Britain did in any war between 1688 and the present.

The suffering of the Irish people during the Famine is incalculable. The poorest elements in the society—laborers and cottiers—suffered most, but the small tenant farmers also faced terrible deprivation. None of these classes had any reserves of wealth or possessions with which to buy food. Ireland, ironically, continued to produce food throughout the famine years and indeed to export food (grain, cattle, and dairy products) to England, Scotland and Wales. But the peasants who grew those foodstuffs to pay their rent had nothing left after the rent with which to buy food. Thousands fell into arrears in their rents anyway, and many were evicted. The roads and pathways of the country were crowded with evicted families and beggars; workhouses and hospitals were filled to overflowing. Reports by careful observers of the misery of the people are numerous and heartbreaking: reports of women and children starving; of bodies too numerous to be buried; of dogs eating corpses. Here is a passage from one letter written by a magistrate to the duke of Wellington:

> I accordingly went on the 15th instant [December 1846] to Skibbereen. . . .
> I was surprised to find the wretched hamlet apparently deserted. I entered
> some of the hovels to ascertain the cause, and the scenes which presented
> themselves were such as no tongue or pen can convey the slightest idea of.
> In the first, six famished and ghastly skeletons, to all appearances dead,
> were huddled in a corner on some filthy straw, their sole covering what
> seemed a ragged horsecloth, their wretched legs hanging about, naked
> above the knees. I approached with horror, and found by a low moaning
> they were alive—they were in fever, four children, a woman and what had
> once been a man.

The suffering of the emigrants was scarcely less. Emigration was an old story in Irish history: approximately 1.75 million emigrated between 1780 and 1845, most of them choking the streets and alleys of Britain's worst industrial slums. Now, most went either directly to North America or to Liverpool, where they found passage to Canada or the United States. In both cases, the crossing was hazardous and miserable. Many of the ships that were called into the passenger service were inadequate. Some sank, on others the mortality rate ranged from a third to a half. For instance, the *Agnes* sailed in 1847: of her 427 passengers, only 150 survived. Even when they arrived in the New World, the Irish emigrants faced severe hardships. They were rural people but were forced practically overnight to become urban dwellers, and at the bottom rank of society to boot. They were discriminated against by the Anglo-Saxon (and Protestant) American elite. Over time, the Irish in America learned to protect themselves by building self-sufficiency in their neighborhoods through Catholic parishes, parochial schools, and machine politics. This experience nurtured their Irish identity, and the Irish immigrant communities in America became hotbeds of intensely anti-British Irish nationalism.

The British response to the Famine was horribly inadequate, both because of inability and because of disinclination to help the Irish. Peel, who was prime minister when the Famine began, acted energetically. In November 1845, he had his agents in America buy £100,000 of Indian corn (maize) to be distributed in Ireland. He did not mean to feed the people but to keep food prices down by selling the corn cheaply to local relief organizations. He also helped set up committees of Irish landlords to collect charitable funds and distribute food. He set the Board of Works to constructing roads in Ireland as a means of providing employment. Finally, Peel undertook repeal of the Corn Law, his theory being that if trade were free, cheap grain would flow into Ireland. As we have seen in the previous chapter, this was a costly decision for Peel. It split the Conservative party, and the anti-Peel malcontents joined the Whigs in voting Peel out of office. As far as Ireland was concerned, free trade in grain did not work: the impoverished Irish people could not generate any economic demand for food. Whether Peel could or would have done more than the Whigs for Ireland when the Famine worsened, one will never know, for Peel never returned to office and died in 1850.

Peel's successor as prime minister was Lord John Russell, scion of one of the grandest Whig families and a hero of 1832. Unfortunately for the Irish, Russell and his principal administrators were committed to a narrow version of private enterprise, which in the case of Ireland could not work. The actual day-to-day execution of British governmental policy was assumed by Sir Charles Trevelyan, assistant secretary to the Treasury, who was even more doctrinaire than Russell. Russell and Trevelyan were forced by events into intervening in Ireland, but they struggled incessantly to minimize the government's role. Their actions thus were severely limited by a fourfold policy: (1) the Irish people must not be "demoralized" by receiving too much assistance; (2) Irish poverty must be supported by Irish property; (3) no public works must be carried out that might benefit private individuals; and (4) the government must not sell food below market prices.

This policy was cruelly irrational in view of the Irish realities, but British officials in London understood little of what was really happening in Ireland. One government agent in Ireland wrote Trevelyan: "You cannot answer the cry of want by a quotation from political economy." But the government stuck to its theories. "It must be thoroughly understood," Russell wrote in 1846, "that we cannot feed the people." At first, the Russell government put its faith in public works; then, in early 1847, it shifted to direct outdoor relief through soup kitchens; and finally, from mid-1847, it resorted to the Poor Law. At one point in 1847, the soup kitchens were feeding three million people a day, but the government's best efforts were always too little too late. Each phase of the official policy was overwhelmed by the sheer numbers of starving and diseased people and undermined by the inability of the debt-ridden Irish property owners to pay the necessary taxes. What was needed was a massive mobilization of the wealth of Britain as if it were wartime, but the effort was never made.

Voluntary charitable efforts by the British were, however, impressive, if necessarily inadequate by themselves for the task at hand. Various relief organizations were set up, most notably the British Relief Association. They raised funds in England and Ireland for soup kitchens and infirmaries. The Quakers distinguished themselves in this voluntary effort, not least by sending many Friends to Ireland, where they not only set up the first soup kitchens but also reported back to England about the true state of affairs in Ireland. The established Church of Ireland also did what it could to relieve distress, though some Anglican clergymen demanded conversion as the price of food. The actions of this minority in the Church of Ireland left a legacy of bitterness in the Catholic peasants that lasted long after the Famine was over.

Increased bitterness between the Irish and English was in fact one of the important consequences of the Great Famine. The Irish could not help feeling that the British had let them starve even though Britain was the wealthiest nation on earth, and that the British would never have let a million Englishmen or Scotsmen perish when food was available. (In fact, the potato crop in the western Highlands and islands of Scotland also failed, and Highland crofters suffered as grievously as the Irish tenants.) The Irish survivors of the Famine at home and abroad repeatedly expressed their bitterness toward England in violence and bloodshed as well as in song and verse. The English, on the other hand, in many cases tended to blame the victims for their troubles, concluding that the Irish were an incompetent, irresponsible, and even a racially inferior people. Trevelyan, for example, decided that "the great evil" in Ireland was not famine but "the selfish, perverse, and turbulent character of the people." The Conservative *Quarterly Review* put it this way: ". . . all of the civilization, arts, comfort, wealth that Ireland enjoys she owes exclusively to England . . . all her absurdities, errors, misery she owes herself."

The famine was the great watershed in Irish economic and social history. The immediate demographic consequence we have already seen; the Irish population never recovered to its pre-1845 level. Moreover, the Famine began to roll back the subdivision of land. In 1841, 45 percent of all agricultural holdings in Ireland were between 1 and 5 acres; in 1851, only 16 percent were. The total number of holdings declined. As consolidation of holdings slowly went forward, so also did cereal farming and cattle grazing. Small family farms worked by tenants became the norm; furthermore, the new but profound concern of the tenants with protecting the family farm caused a rise in the average age at marriage and a corresponding decline in the birth rate. Unfortunately, "landlordism" (the predatory and unimproving attitude of Irish landlords) itself survived. Many of the old landowners lost their estates to savvy investors and middlemen during the Famine. These new owners, however, proved to be just as devoted as their predecessors to collecting rents without providing agricultural leadership. Here were the roots of rural tension and violence in Ireland for the next fifty years.

YOUNG IRELAND AND 1848

The relations between O'Connell and Young Ireland, which were never very close, cracked under the stress of the Famine. Part of the problem was generational: by 1845, O'Connell was seventy years old, whereas the Young Irelanders were in their twenties and thirties. Part of the problem also was temperamental: O'Connell was a seasoned and wily politician, whereas they were romantic intellectuals. Finally, part of the problem was tactical. After the failure of repeal in 1843 and the return of the Whigs to office in 1846, O'Connell thought it best to work with the Whigs in order to get what he could for Ireland. The Young Irelanders, however, preferred to stick defiantly to repeal. As early as 1845, O'Connell and Young Ireland had disagreed over a proposal by Peel to establish three nondenominational colleges in Ireland. In the interests of Catholicism, O'Connell denounced the colleges as "Godless," but the Young Irelanders accepted them in the interests of a nonsectarian Ireland. By mid-1846, the repeal movement had split wide open.

This dispute was aggravated by the failure of the Whigs to deal adequately with the Famine. The final break of July 1846 came, nominally at least, over the issue of whether Irish nationalists were ever justified in using force in their struggle. *The Nation* had become more militant because of the Famine. One editorial declared: "Better a little blood-letting to show that there is blood, than a patient dragging of chains and pining beneath them slowly for generations leading to the belief that all spirit is fled." O'Connell responded firmly that "the greatest political advantages are not worth one drop of blood." The Young Irelanders at that point were not aiming at revolution any more than were the O'Connellites, but the Young Irelanders as romantics would not give up the Irish revolutionary tradition. Early in 1847, they withdrew from the Repeal Association and founded their own organization, the Irish Confederation.

From that moment on, some Young Irelanders slipped hesitantly into a revolutionary posture. O'Connell, by then fatally ill, made one last pathetic appeal to Parliament for help against the Famine and then died on the way to Rome. Young Ireland became more radical. One of the radicalizing influences was James Fintan Lalor, who joined Young Ireland in 1847. He emphasized the rights of the tenants against those of the landlords and urged that "the national movement" temporarily be put aside for a tenant-right agitation. Everyone recognized that in Ireland tenant-right was a socially explosive issue. Another Young Irelander, John Mitchel, took up Lalor's ideas and began to combine them with advocacy of physical force. He wrote, "It is indeed full time that we cease to whine and begin to act . . . Good heavens, to think that we should go down without a struggle."

Despite the advent of such views within the Young Ireland movement, there was no overt action toward a rising until early 1848. The event that precipitated the Young Ireland conspiracy was the outbreak of the European revolutions of 1848, first in France and then in Austria, Prussia, and Hungary. Mitchel and some other Young Irelanders seized the moment to call for an Irish republic—a step far beyond repeal of the Union. These Young Irelanders sent a deputation to Paris and established relations with the British Chartists. Once again, as in 1796–1798, the British government faced a dangerous combination of British radicals and Irish nationalists.

Unfortunately for them, the Young Irelanders made poor revolutionaries. Government spies penetrated their organization. The Irish leaders failed utterly to coordinate their rising with the Chartists. Mitchel was arrested and convicted of sedition in March of 1848, and in July Parliament suspended habeas corpus in Ireland. Aware that the government would soon arrest them, a few Young Irelanders set out to raise the peasantry of south-central Ireland in revolt. The leader was William Smith O'Brien, a chivalrous Protestant landlord who completely lacked the ruthlessness required of a successful revolutionary. The peasants were much too beaten down by the Famine to respond; they had no arms and no organization, and their priests urged them not to rebel. The "rising" of 1848 thus ended in a miserable scuffle in a cabbage patch in County Tipperary. The leaders were arrested, convicted, and transported to Australia.

Tragic-comic as it was, the Young Ireland rising of 1848 nevertheless had considerable significance. The Young Irelanders' romantic and nonsectarian brand of nationalism and their refusal to renounce the revolutionary heritage inspired many later nationalists. Their defiant gesture in 1848 helped emphasize to Irish nationalists the notion that revolutionary acts, no matter how hopeless, can be morally elevating. The connection made by Young Ireland between tenant rights and nationalism, like their rejection of English utilitarian and laissez-faire principles, tended to radicalize subsequent Irish nationalist movements. Irish politicians after 1848 turned for a time to conventional parliamentary tactics, but the idealistic and extremist strain typified by Young Ireland did not die out.

Suggested Reading

Black, R. D. Collison, *Economic Thought and the Irish Question, 1817–1870* (Cambridge: Cambridge University Press, 1960).

Connell, K. H., *The Population of Ireland, 1750–1845* (Oxford: Clarendon Press, 1950).

Cullen, L. M., *An Economic History of Ireland Since 1660* (New York: Barnes & Noble, 1972).

Davis, Richard, *The Young Ireland Movement* (Dublin: Gill & Macmillan, 1987).

De Nie, Michael, *The Eternal Paddy: Irish Identity and the British Press, 1798–1882* (Madison: University of Wisconsin Press, 2004).

Devine, T. M., *The Great Highland Famine: Hunger, Emigration and the Scottish Highlands in the Nineteenth Century* (Edinburgh: J. Donald, 1988).

Donnelly, James S., *The Great Irish Potato Famine* (Phoenix Mill: Sutton Publishing, 2001).

———, *The Land and People of Nineteenth-Century Cork* (London: Routledge & Kegan Paul, 1975).

Edwards, R. Dudley, and T. Desmond Williams, eds., *The Great Famine* (Dublin: Browne & Nolan, 1956).

Foster, Roy, *Modern Ireland, 1600–1972* (London: A. Lane, 1988).

Gray, Peter, *Famine, Land and Politics: British Government and Irish Society, 1843–1850* (Dublin: Irish Academic Press, 1999).

Hoppen, K. T., *Elections, Politics, and Society in Ireland, 1832–1885* (Oxford: Clarendon Press, 1984).

Kee, Robert, *The Green Flag* (New York: Delacorte Press, 1972).

Kerr, Donal A., *"A Nation of Beggars?" Priest, People, and Parties in Famine Ireland* (Oxford: Clarendon Press, 1994).

Kinealy, Christine, *The Great Irish Famine: Impact, Ideology and Rebellion* (New York: Palgrave, 2002).

Lees, Lynn H., *Exiles of Erin: Irish Migrants in Victorian London* (Ithaca, N.Y.: Cornell University Press, 1979).

Lengel, Edward, *The Irish through British Eyes: Perceptions of Ireland in the Famine Era* (Westport, CT: Praeger, 2002).

MacDonagh, Oliver, *Ireland: The Union and Its Aftermath* (London: Allen & Unwin, 1977).

———, *The Hereditary Bondsman: Daniel O'Connell, 1775–1829* (New York: St. Martin's 1988).

———, *The Emancipist: Daniel O'Connell, 1830–47* (New York: St. Martin's, 1989).

McCaffrey, Lawrence, *Ireland from Colony to Nation State* (Englewood Cliffs, N.J.: Prentice-Hall, 1979).

Miller, Kerby A., *Emigrants and Exiles: Ireland and the Irish Exodus to North America* (New York: Oxford University Press, 1985).

Mokyr, Joel, *Why Ireland Starved* (London: Allen & Unwin, 1983).

Neal, Frank, *Black '47: Britain and the Famine Irish* (New York: St. Martin's Press, 1998).

Nowlan, Kevin, *The Politics of Repeal* (London: Routledge & Kegan Paul, 1965).

O'Faolain, Sean, *King of the Beggars: A Life of Daniel O'Connell* (London: T. Nelson & Sons, 1970).

O'Ferrall, Fergus, *Catholic Emancipation: Daniel O'Connell and the Birth of Irish Democracy, 1820–1830* (Dublin: Gill & Macmillan, 1985).

O'Grada, Cormac, *Black '47 and Beyond: The Great Irish Famine in History, Economy and Memory* (Princeton: Princeton University Press, 1999).

———, *Ireland: A New Economic History* (New York: Clarendon Press, 1994).

O'Tuathaigh, Gearoid, *Ireland Before the Famine, 1798–1848* (Dublin: Gill & Macmillan, 1972).

Palmer, Stanley, *Police and Protest in England and Ireland, 1780–1850* (New York: Cambridge University Press, 1988).

Salaman, R. N., *The History and Social Influence of the Potato* (Cambridge: Cambridge University Press, 1949).

Vaughan, W. E., *Landlords and Tenants in Mid-Victorian Ireland* (Oxford: Clarendon Press, 1994).

———, ed., *Ireland Under the Union. Part I: 1801–1870* (Oxford: Clarendon Press, 1989).

Woodham-Smith, Cecil, *The Great Hunger* (London: Hamilton, 1962).

Wright, Frank, *Two Lands on One Soil: Ulster Politics before Home Rule* (New York: St. Martin's Press, 1996).

Chapter 16

Mid-Victorian Society and Culture, 1850–1870

The disintegration of Chartism, the end of the Famine, and the collapse of Young Ireland—all of which occurred in 1848—marked the end of more than a half-century of social and political turmoil. In Britain there followed a period of relative prosperity and social harmony. Poverty, urban misery, and class divisions did not disappear, but economic conditions improved compared to what had gone before, and social conflict was channeled into workable institutions. An atmosphere of confidence bathed the society. This atmosphere was reinforced by English preeminence within the British Isles and by British preeminence on the seas and in the world markets. The result was what Professor E. L. Burn has called "the Age of Equipoise"—the two decades of the 1850s and 1860s, when social and cultural forces came into balance, when forces of continuity seemed to balance those of change, and when forces of conservatism seemed to balance those of progress.

The mid-Victorian years from 1850 to 1870 were the high noon of Victorianism. On the basis of relative security, prosperity, and social harmony, the high culture of Victorianism flourished and blossomed. Later, Modernists of the twentieth century were to react strongly against Victorian culture, and "Victorianism" still carries negative connotations of bourgeois complacency and hypocrisy. This hostility toward Victorian culture fails to give credit to the Victorians either for their achievements or for the sincerity of their attempts to deal with difficult problems. In culture, as in society, Victorianism was a balance of dynamic forces—conservative and progressive, believing and doubting, romantic and utilitarian. Victorian culture was in fact one of the high points of modern society.

ECONOMIC STABILITY

Prosperity, or at least the illusion of it, was the foundation of the mid-Victorian equipoise. Britain in the 1850s and 1860s was the greatest nation on earth because of its economic power. The British headstart in commercial and industrial expansion put them for a time far in advance of other countries. In 1850, for example, the British produced about 28 percent of the world's industrial output, including

60 percent of the coal, 50 percent of the iron, 70 percent of the steel, and nearly 50 percent of the cotton textiles. By the 1860s, the British controlled 25 percent of the world's trade, and an even greater percentage of international trade in manufactured goods. Britain had become "the workshop of the world."

Even the agricultural sector of the economy prospered. The repeal of the Corn Law in 1846 did not result in any decline of farm prices or rents. As a result of the Agricultural Revolution, British farming by 1850 was among the most advanced in the world, and in the 1850s and 1860s British farmers adopted even more productive techniques. The consequent highly intensive and capitalized method was called "high farming." It included the use of steam engines for plowing and harvesting and systematic fertilization to increase crop yields. At midcentury, therefore, the British could still produce about half of the wheat and six-sevenths of the meat they consumed. The mid-Victorian years were a "golden age" for British agriculture as well as for British industry.

The productive power of the British industrial sector gave Britain an unusual position in the world economy. The British sold manufactured goods abroad and in turn imported vast quantities of primary products (food and raw materials). Foreign trade had always been important to the process of industrialization in Britain, but now it became more so, rising to 25 percent of the GNP. Britain sat like a spider at the center of a web of worldwide trade. In the mid-Victorian years, more than one-fourth of all international trade passed through British ports. This fact allowed the British to enjoy very healthy "invisible earnings"—that is, profits from the transactions of trade itself, such as finance, insurance, brokerage, and shipping, plus capital investment abroad. The British owned perhaps one-third of all the merchant ships in the world, and by the 1870s they were earning £50 million a year as a return on their foreign investments. This invisible income was crucial to the British economy because it made up a substantial deficit between imports and exports. Britain was not only the workshop but also the banker and creditor of the world.

The mid-Victorian decades also brought conditions of stability and growth that contributed to an expansive attitude among businessmen. After a slowing of the rate of growth in the early 1840s, the British enjoyed a fresh bout of economic growth from the early 1850s through the mid-1860s, mainly due to the rapid construction of railways. Moreover, because of the rapid accumulation of capital, the banks were able to keep interest rates low, which made additional investments in industry relatively cheap. More important yet for the middle-class mood was a mild inflation: the mid-Victorian years saw an increase of prices, not enough to dampen demand but sufficient to bring commercial and industrial men the sense of ever-improving earnings. Prices generally ran ahead of wages paid to working people; hence businessmen enjoyed improvement of their profit margins. For this reason, British businessmen of the 1850s and 1860s were somewhat less anxiety ridden and somewhat more open-handed in granting wage increases to their workers than they had been in the first half of the century.

MUTING OF SOCIAL CONFLICT

The expansive attitude of mid-Victorian commercial and industrial men contributed to a muting of social conflict. Social tensions eased despite the fact that trends in the economy led to an increase in inequality. Wages continued to do less well than profits and rents. In 1803, for instance, the richest 2 percent of families in Britain enjoyed one-fifth of the national income; in 1867, the richest 2 percent had two-fifths. True, wages did go up, but not as fast as prices or profits. Moreover, as Victorian firms matured, there were fewer opportunities for working men to go from rags to riches than in the early days of industrial triumph. Nevertheless, there was some upward social mobility in the mid-Victorian years, mainly in the form of a general movement of working people from lower-paid to higher-paid jobs. This movement was made possible by the broad expansion of the economy and the consequent multiplication of semiskilled, skilled, and clerical positions.

More important than actual social mobility was the myth of social mobility. As we have seen in Chapter 13, the middle class preached to the working class the ideas of self-help and the self-made individual. By self-help, the message went, any person could rise in the world. Britain enjoyed, wrote Walter Bagehot, "a system of removable inequalities." In the words of Lord Palmerston:

> We have shown the example of a nation in which every class of society accepts with cheerfulness that lot which Providence has assigned to it, while at the same time each individual of each class is constantly trying to raise himself in the social scale not by injustices and wrong, not by violence and illegality, but by persevering good conduct and by the steady and energetic exertion of moral and intellectual faculties with which the Creator had endowed him.

The fact that a viscount could mouth such bourgeois sentiments is proof conclusive of the triumph of middle-class ideas. Of particular importance as the propagandist for these middle-class social ideals was Samuel Smiles, a doctor, journalist, and railway executive who wrote a number of best-sellers in the years between 1850 and 1880: *Self-Help; Thrift; Lives of the Engineers; Character;* and *Duty*. His view was that neither political radicalism nor socialism could help the working class; instead, individual moral reform was required. His message was simple and clear: "Thrift is the basis of Self-Help and the foundation of much that is excellent in character." Illustrated by inspirational biographies, this message had a strong impact at a time when, because of the failure of Chartism and the pressures of survival, many British working men and women were inclined to accept their place in the industrial capitalist system.

Furthermore, the doctrines of self-help and the self-made individual were part of a package of "softened" middle-class attitudes and social policies. As Chapter 14 showed, by the 1850s evangelicalism and paternalism were merging with utilitarian expertise to produce genuine social improvements such as the factory acts and public health reform. Temperance reform and "rational recreation," both preached by the middle-class to the working-class, were genuinely meant to help working men and women rise in material well-being and social status. These bourgeois virtues in part were supposed to make the working class tame and orderly, but they were also an invitation to join the bourgeoisie in respectability. Whereas Hannah More and other upper-class propagandists of the early nineteenth century sought to keep the laboring poor in their proper place, intellectual leaders of the mid-Victorian middle-class stressed the unity rather than the differences between middle-class and working-class folk. They insisted that, given the appropriate education and charitable treatment, individual members of the working class could achieve the independence and morally reliable behavior characteristic of all respectable people. John Stuart Mill, for example, wrote in his great textbook, *Principles of Political Economy* (first published in 1848), that working people were advancing "in mental cultivation, and in the virtues dependent upon it."

Respectability and progress thus were key mid-Victorian concepts. They arose from the middle class but served to encourage class reconciliation. "Respectability" became a cult word in the mid-Victorian years. It implied behavior that displayed acceptance of conventional Christian morality—independence, orderliness, cleanliness, and propriety. Anyone in any class could become respectable by individual choice. On the one hand, respectability was the means by which a commercial or industrial captain and his wife showed that they were worthy of being called a "gentleman" and a "lady," terms that increasingly connoted a moral quality rather than the old notion of bloodlines; on the other hand, respectability was the means by which working men and women demonstrated that they accepted the values of the middle class and still asserted their independence. Hardly anything warmed the heart of Victorian reformers more than the sight of a "respectable" working-class family—sober, scrubbed, and clothed in their Sunday best, on the way to church or chapel—but respectability did not mean deference.

By "progress" the Victorians meant not only the increase in technology and material production of modern society but also the perception that ever greater numbers of people were choosing respectable life-styles. The obvious accomplishments of industry and commerce, and the fortunate turn of Britain away from revolution in favor of reform, led the British into vigorous nationalism by midcentury. Pride in their legal, constitutional, commercial, and industrial institutions led many mid-Victorians into belief in the intrinsic, even biological, excellence of what they called "the British (or English) race." It also led the British to think that progress is automatic, that it is identical to change, and that it is a central theme in human history. Many Victorian historians like T. B. Macaulay celebrated progress in English history and thereby created a magnificent and useful, though somewhat inaccurate, myth of the English past. The "scientific" historian H. T. Buckle (the son of a shipowner) put it best: English history, he said, is "the progress from barbarism to civilization"; indeed, "history is the living scroll of human progress."

Progress was a concept that the better-off members of the working class could share, and many members of the "aristocracy" of labor—the skilled craftspersons—met the middle class halfway along the road to respectability. As one former

Chartist said, "It is in the very nature of the intelligent and virtuous to feel self-respect, and the claims of manhood as a man." Now that Chartism and sweeping attempts to form revolutionary national unions had failed, these working men stood ready to accept inequality of wealth, but they insisted on recognition of their equality in moral virtue and mental capacity. Working-class people realized that middle-class propagandists were trying to brainwash them, but they also accepted that capitalism and industry had arrived to stay, and that through temperance, prudence, hard work, and self-education, the top stratum at least of the working class could improve themselves. As one working man put it, through working-class organizations such as cooperative societies, workers "become independent, and feel morally as well as socially elevated."

Once Chartism had failed, the main institutions of the working class all represented efforts by working people to come to terms with capitalism and industry. First, there were friendly societies—voluntary associations of workers for the purpose of providing social security, such as unemployment, sickness, and old-age benefits. By 1872, the friendly societies, which were institutions of collective thrift, enrolled approximately four million members. Second, there were cooperative societies, which were no longer utopian socialist communities but practical voluntary associations for cooperative production and shopkeeping. They were an effective way of securing a place for the traditional concern for community inside a market economy.

Finally, there were "new model" trade unions. These were not revolutionary organizations but cautious and businesslike craft unions devoted to protecting their members within the industrial system. These unions—the Amalgamated Society of Engineers, the Amalgamated Society of Carpenters and Joiners, and so on—all had relatively high subscription fees because they set unemployment benefits as a high priority. For these reasons, the craft unions of the mid-Victorian years never enrolled more than about 10 percent of adult laborers, nor did they adopt an aggressive strike strategy. Their objective was simply "a fair day's wage for a fair day's work," and they succeeded because they could keep the skills of their members exclusive. Their prudent behavior slowly won not only benefits for the working-class elite but also the approval of a section of the liberal middle class. Eventually, in the 1870s, the "new model" trade unions earned from Parliament legal recognition of trade unions and of peaceful methods of pursuing trades disputes.

THE CRYSTAL PALACE, 1851

The Great Exhibition of 1851 symbolized the prosperity, the faith in progress, and the social reconciliation of mid-Victorian Britain. The Great Exhibition, the brainchild of Queen Victoria's beloved husband, Prince Albert, was the first world's fair. Albert was a tireless promoter of science and technology as well as head of the thoroughly bourgeois royal family. His dream was to invite all the nations to put on display the material evidence of the advance of civilization. In fact, the Great

The Crystal Palace, 1851. The huge but graceful building was constructed from prefabricated iron and glass panels. It symbolized science, technology, and progress to the Victorians.

Exhibition boosted British pride, for the exhibits in manufactures, machinery, and fine arts demonstrated Britain's industrial and commercial preeminence. Speaking in effect for the nation, Queen Victoria wrote, "I never remember anything before that everyone was so pleased with, as is the case with this Exhibition."

The building that housed the Exhibition was one of the principal reasons for satisfaction. Known appropriately as "the Crystal Palace," the exhibition hall was a perfect symbol for the age—a splendid hall over 1800 feet long and 108 feet high at the peak of its great arched transept and made of prefabricated iron columns, girders, and glass panels. The Crystal Palace was designed by Joseph Paxton, himself a symbolic figure: formerly a gardener employed by the duke of Devonshire, Paxton by 1850 was a self-made engineer and railway director. His design—in effect a giant greenhouse—took less than a year to plan and build, yet it expressed in its beautiful functionalism the industrial miracle of the British economy. It was a cathedral devoted to material progress. (Eventually, the Crystal Palace was moved from Hyde Park to Sydenham and lasted until 1936.)

The Crystal Palace proved to be a meeting-ground for Britons of all social classes. Although the upper-class promoters of the Great Exhibition feared at first that members of the working class—Chartists and other radicals—might cause embarrassing trouble at the Crystal Palace, the working people who came were well-behaved and respectable. Huge numbers came: more than six million tickets were sold in less than a year. Railway companies ran cheap trains for ordinary people to take day-long excursions to the Exhibition. At the Crystal Palace, working-class folk rubbed elbows amicably with the rich. Who would have thought, mused the *Times*, that such events "should have taken place not only without disorder, but also without crime." The events of 1848 seemed to have receded into the distant past.

HIGH CULTURE OF THE VICTORIAN PERIOD

The social consensus of the mid-Victorian period was both promoted by and reflected by Victorian intellectuals. Victorian writers were a major force behind the softening of attitudes and the "meliorism" (reformism) of the ruling elite. Intellectuals typically urged charity and social harmony on their middle-class readers even as they preached bourgeois values to the working class. In the mid-Victorian years, British intellectuals generally reflected the optimism of the period, not blindly or complacently but with faith that social relations and cultural values could be improved. They were often very critical of particular institutions and attitudes—the churches, the schools, and the judicial system; or the greed, the self-interest, and the utilitarianism of the commercial and industrial men—but always with the view that progress and reconciliation were possible. Not surprisingly, mid-Victorian intellectuals expressed a balance between the two great streams of thought that they inherited: the romantic and the utilitarian.

In the Victorian years, intellectuals in Britain were called "men of letters," a term that indicated a particular kind of writer standing in a special relationship to the public. The men of letters were neither alienated intellectuals nor academic specialists. "Men of letters" was a label applied to a wide variety of writers—novelists, poets, social critics, historians, political economists, philosophers, and so on—who were tied directly to the general reading public by the sale of books and articles in a market system. Men of letters thus included writers of fiction like Charles Dickens, William Makepeace Thackeray, and Anthony Trollope; poets like Alfred Tennyson and Robert Browning; and social critics like Thomas Carlyle, John Ruskin, and John Stuart Mill.

The audience for the men of letters exerted great influence on their work. By the early Victorian years, a general reading public buying reading matter in great quantities had replaced patronage as the means by which writers earned their living. The lack of an educational system for the working class and the relatively high price of books and magazines limited this general reading public to the well-off. The middle class was by far the larger of the two upper classes; thus the middle class dominated the reading public. Middle-class people hungered for entertainment, information, social instruction, and moral guidance. As members of a new social order, middle-class men and women lacked the traditional breeding that satisfied such needs among the aristocracy and gentry. They looked instead to formal education and to reading matter of all kinds—newspapers, magazines, books, manuals of etiquette, encyclopedias, and the like. Thus the middle class created a demand for writing and called into being the men of letters as a social type.

The men of letters themselves came overwhelmingly from the middle class. Many young men—and, as we will see, women—found the opportunity to make money as writers irresistibly attractive. As Trollope wrote, the profession of literature required "no capital, no special education . . . no apprenticeship." Many of the men of letters depended wholly on the sale of their work for their livelihood, and some with great success. Dickens made a fortune on his novels, selling some of them to publishers for as much as £4,000 apiece; Trollope ascended from the ranks of the lower civil service to the status of landed gentlemen by dint of his novels, which he turned out with businesslike routine; and Macaulay made more than £20,000 on the third and fourth volumes alone of his monumental *History of England*. In short, a young man (or woman) of energy but no connections might make a comfortable living as a professional writer, combining in his work journalism, criticism, and fiction. This success helped keep the men of letters from becoming angry and alienated.

Their influence also worked against alienation. The Victorian men of letters were not prohibited by official censorship (except in regard to blasphemy and libel) from saying what they wanted to. Further, the reading public was relatively compact and accessible, and it included practically all the people who made Britain's political, social, and economic decisions. The men of letters knew that serious works of fiction, history, or social criticism would reach nearly everyone who counted. Moreover, the men of letters were connected with the public both by the market system and by bonds of sympathy. Authors and their reading public understood and trusted each other. The men of letters on the whole did not simply mouth middle-class interests, but they knew the middle class intimately and tended to share its fundamental values—order, progress, work, self-help, and a more-or-less orthodox Christian morality.

One result of the close bonds between serious Victorian writers and their public was that all agreed on the proper function of intellectuals. The public expected men of letters to be useful as entertainers, as instructors, or as moral guides. The men of letters were expected to help their readers through the troublesome times of economic and social change and shore up religious belief and/or rational inquiry against doubt. The Victorians felt strongly the gravity and newness of the problems they encountered, and they turned not only to the churches but also to the men of letters for mental and moral help. The public in effect asked the authors to serve as teachers, preachers, and prophets—sages for a secular society. The men of letters for their part accepted this didactic function, even though they were sometimes uncomfortable with narrow utilitarian or moralistic standards for judging intellectual or artistic work. They realized that the didactic function gave them high status. What England needed, Carlyle wrote, was a heroic "Prophet or Poet to teach us."

EXEMPLARS: CARLYLE, DICKENS, TENNYSON, AND MILL

We can see examples of the different ways of fulfilling that function adopted by Victorian men of letters by looking at four of the greatest writers of the nineteenth century. For Thomas Carlyle, perhaps the prime example of the men of letters, the way was secular prophecy. In a long career of rumbling and thundering, Carlyle (1795–1881) incessantly warned Britain about what he saw as its loss of spirituality. Carlyle's prophetic essays and histories (most notably *The French Revolution, On Heroes and Hero Worship, Sartor Resartus*, and *Past and Present*) arose from an unusual outlook—namely, a volcanic combination of Scottish Calvinism and German Idealist philosophy. From these sources, Carlyle drew his ideas that the material world is only the clothing for the true spiritual reality and that the world's history is the irresistible unfolding of God's will. The individual, he believed, stands at the turning point between the past and the future and therefore can choose to be either the defender of materialism and obsolete institutions or the agent of divine destiny. All work, no matter how lowly, embodies God's will. According to Carlyle, Britain's problem was that people, caught up as they were in a philosophy of utilitarianism and self-interest, failed to see the underlying spiritual nature of reality. Consequently, they confused means and ends, and their society lacked the coherence of medieval culture. What is needed, he claimed, was a devotion to "Heroes" (those who have insight into God's will) and to work (the agency of divine purpose).

By the end of his life, Carlyle was known as "the sage of Chelsea," for his message appealed to the religiosity, the seriousness, and the dutifulness of the Victorians. One of the many men of letters deeply influenced by Carlyle's warnings of a social catastrophe like the French Revolution was Charles Dickens (1812–1870). In a time when novels were the dominant literary form, simultaneously providing entertainment, social observation, and moral instruction, Dickens was the most imaginative of all Victorian writers of fiction. He was the author of a series of sprawling best-sellers through which he established an intimate connection to his audience: *Pickwick Papers, Oliver Twist, A Tale of Two Cities, David Copperfield, Bleak House, Hard Times,* and *Little Dorritt,* to name only a few. In these novels, Dickens displayed an ability to be at once a great comic writer and a serious social critic and reformer. His works provided a miraculously rich panorama of portraits taken from industrial capitalist society. He did more than any other person, whether in public office or in intellectual life, to help his fellow Victorians *see* what was actually all around them—the suffering of the "Hungry Forties," the misery of urban life for most of the working class, the harshness of utilitarian philosophy, the blindness and hypocrisy of many middle-class people, and the need for a renewal of simple human charity and sympathy. Thus Dickens took upon himself as a man of letters the role he assigned to his autobiographical character, David Copperfield: "As the endurance of my childhood days had done its part to make me what I was, so greater calamities would nerve me on, to be yet better than I was, and so, as they had taught me, would I teach others."

The reading public that consumed the fat "three-decker" (three-volume) novels by Dickens, Thackeray, Trollope, and others found in them just the kind of information and guidance that it needed. Fiction was the perfect art form for the Victorian middle class. That same audience tended to be resistant to poetry, at least poetry of all but a certain kind. Victorian readers valued poetry when it was useful to them in some way, especially in stating truths in a poignant manner or in providing moral uplift. Many poets found this situation uncomfortable. As heirs to the romantics, they naturally felt a desire to make art a refuge from the hurly-burly of industrialization, a realm of "higher" values such as beauty, contemplation, and spirit. Yet Victorian poets were also drawn by the urgency of social and cultural change to keep in touch with the main themes of the times and to speak to the concerns of the broad spectrum of literate people. Thus most Victorian poets were divided as to their purpose and were profoundly concerned with defining a poetic role for themselves. No one exemplified these tensions or found solutions more agreeable to the reading public than the greatest of the Victorian poets, Alfred, Lord Tennyson.

Tennyson (1809–1892) was a poet of wonderful virtuosity as well as the writer who best expressed the concerns of Victorian readers, including Queen Victoria, who appointed him poet laureate in 1850. He grew up in the heyday of the romantic poets and seemed destined by his poetic gifts to be their heir. Deeply affected by an unstable home life, Tennyson developed a powerful melancholy streak and found relief only in the discipline of writing verse. At Cambridge University in the late 1820s, however, Tennyson was urged by fellow members of a secret society of undergraduate intellectuals to assume in his poetry moral leadership of the nation. As his closest friend said, "Poems are good things, but flesh and blood is better." Most of Tennyson's early poetry reflects the rival attractions of poetic isolation and public teaching and takes the dilemma of writing poetry in unpoetic times as a main theme. Tennyson also read modern science, including the emerging evolutionary geology and biology, which threw doubt on conventional religious belief. These issues came to a crisis for Tennyson in 1833, when his closest undergraduate friend and moral guide died. *In Memoriam* (1850), written by Tennyson over ten years as a verse diary of psychological recovery, raises and resolves fundamental questions: What is the use of poetry in times of great national change? Is there life after death? Can one believe in a benevolent God, when the death of individuals and the struggle for survival in nature seem to prove otherwise? To all these questions, Tennyson was able to give ringing affirmative answers but only after profound struggle. His ability to adopt a positive outlook and to affirm belief in progress attracted his readers. Without intending to, Tennyson spoke for all literate Victorians.

Tennyson had learned from both science and religion, and in so doing he had forged a balance from the two rival lines of thought in the Victorian period. Such a balance was characteristic of the mid-Victorian decades. Another great man of letters who learned from both streams of thought was John Stuart Mill (1806–1873), by far the preeminent Victorian philosopher and liberal thinker. Mill labeled the two streams of nineteenth-century thought the "Benthamite" (empiricist, scientific, liberal) and the "Coleridgean" (romantic, idealist, conservative), and with characteristic fairness, he gave both credit for Victorian progress. The son of James Mill, who was a close friend of Jeremy Bentham, J. S. Mill was raised as a complete

THE LADIES' ADVOCATE.

Mrs. Bull. "LOR, MR. MILL! WHAT A LOVELY SPEECH YOU *DID* MAKE. ⁞ I DO DECLARE I HADN'T THE SLIGHTEST NOTION WE WERE SUCH MISERABLE CREATURES. NO ONE CAN SAY IT WAS *YOUR* FAULT THAT THE CASE BROKE DOWN."

The Ladies' Advocate. *A Punch* cartoon of the great Liberal philosopher, John Stuart Mill, who was one of the few Victorian political thinkers to advocate equality for women.

utilitarian philosopher—"a logic-chopping engine," as Carlyle called him. He took as his life's work the elaboration of utilitarianism, its philosophical bases, and its political and economic policies. With nearly inhuman efficiency, Mill singlehandedly produced a compendium of nineteenth-century liberal and empiricist philosophy: *A System of Logic, Principles of Political Economy, On Liberty, Representative Government,* and *Utilitarianism.* These works of his mature years significantly modified the narrow and insensitive philosophy of Bentham. When Mill was twenty, he had a nervous breakdown, which he attributed to the failure of his upbringing in developing his emotions. He turned to the romantic poets and the whole Coleridgean type of thought in order to cultivate his feelings. Thereafter, his utilitarian philosophy and liberal politics showed a flexibility lacking in Bentham's work. Mill's brand of utilitarianism acknowledged that mental and spiritual pleasures are higher than the physical; his political economy advocated capitalism but leaned toward socialist values; and his political philosophy tempered democracy with concerns about majority rule. Mill was an individualist, but he interpreted individualism in terms of maximum moral self-development.

WOMEN WRITERS IN THE VICTORIAN PERIOD

One of the most ironic facts about the Victorian "men" of letters is that so many of them were women. Especially in the genre of fiction, women writers emerged in large numbers in the Victorian period; thus, though women novelists probably remained in the minority between 1830 and 1870, writing became one of the main outlets for middle-class female talent and energy. Women did not find that becoming a professional writer was easy, for the Victorian period was not liberated. Not only did women lack opportunities for education, but also they were severely limited by the image of the "proper lady." Victorians assumed that women were suited by the Creator for domesticity: they were supposed by nature to be protectors of morality in the home and suppliers of warmth and consolation to children and husbands. The proper lady was never to put herself forward. Yet some middle-class women had to find a way to earn income, either because they were unmarried or because the financial burdens of the family fell on them. Others, like Charlotte Brontë, simply found that they had to express their creative impulses. Whatever their motives, women found it easier to enter the world of writing than those of the professions or business.

Women of talent adopted striking devices to mask or compensate for the "improper" activity of writing for publication. A few, accepting the convention that women's work was work for others, refused to accept any pay. Most went out of their way to celebrate domestic virtues and to parade antifeminist attitudes. Jane Austen (1775–1817), a keen observer of gentry life in the early nineteenth century, had found a way to write within the norms of landed society while adopting an amusing, ironic criticism of it. Others adopted pseudonyms in order to hide their identity—and to get a fair hearing from the reviewers: Emily Brontë published as "Ellis Bell"; Charlotte Brontë as "Currer Bell"; and Marian Evans as "George Eliot."

Despite these handicaps, some Victorian women writers achieved a literary and intellectual level at least as great as any of the males. Elizabeth Gaskell, for instance, wrote social novels that depicted working-class life in industrial England better than any other works of fiction. In particular, her novel *North and South* explores with wonderful balance and perceptiveness the social and cultural differences between industrial and rural England. George Eliot (Marian Evans) was a writer of unparalleled intellectual power. In novels such as *Adam Bede, The Mill on the Floss*, and above all, *Middlemarch*, she painted the psychological landscape, the egoism, and the moral weaknesses of the Victorians. A thorough rationalist and freethinker, Eliot had given up her Evangelical religion but not her moral imperative, which she translated into the simple desire to help her fellow human beings: "Heaven help us! said the old religion; the new one, from its very lack of that faith, will teach us all the more to help one another." For her, as for most Victorian novelists, realism was the necessary style of fiction because only a realistic depiction of society could supply the needed information about social structure and social relations or about new kinds of moral and intellectual problems. This combination of realism with moral teaching made her the perfect example of the Victorian novelist.

Past and Present, Number One, *by Augustus Egg (1858). This moralistic Victorian paint-ing shows an adulterous woman being banished from her home by her husband. Note the impending collapse of the children's house of cards.*

VICTORIAN PAINTING AND ARCHITECTURE

The visual arts of the Victorian period, dominated by the interests of the new industrial and commercial middle class, displayed the same themes of realism (or "truth to nature") and moralism. In painting, the two most notable developments after Constable and Turner were "genre" or "history" painting and the Pre-Raphaelite movement. In genre painting, the impulse to be instructive was domi-nant, and the result was paintings that were like narratives in that they told a story. William Frith, for instance, painted large canvases giving realistic panoramic views of society, on Derby Day, in a train station, or at the post office. Augustus Egg painted with technical skill but cloying sentimentality little moral lessons, such as the value of female chastity. The Victorian cult of domesticity and the moralistic aesthetics often trapped painters in sentimentality, and this sentimentality under-mined the realistic style. A good example is the work of Edwin Landseer, who made technically exact paintings of animals but gave them human emotions.

The Pre-Raphaelites—Dante Gabriel Rossetti, William Holman Hunt, and John Everett Millais—were self-conscious aesthetes (lovers of beauty) and rebels against

The Houses of Parliament, by A. W. Pugin and Charles Barry. The most famous example of Victorian Gothic architecture; designed 1836–1837 and built 1840–1860.

the orthodox painting favored by the Royal Academy. Influenced by the critic John Ruskin, they took inspiration from the Middle Ages and rejected what they regarded as the "unnatural" painting from Raphael on. Like Ruskin and other advocates of the Gothic, they believed in "truth to nature," and so painted in minute, realistic detail. Yet they also sought to paint in glowing colors like a medieval manuscript and refused to use earth tones. Moreover, while they created an ideal world of medieval myth, beauty, and religiosity, which was plainly a rejection of industrial Britain, they also accepted the moral and narrative standards desired by the middle class. Their confusion of beauty with religiosity and their rejection of the ordinary world were important steps toward the substitution of art for religion that became characteristic of twentieth-century high culture.

In Victorian architecture, the moralistic and "truth to nature" impulses were not easily compatible. Because of their burgeoning wealth and expanding population, the Victorians built a huge number of structures of all kinds, but they had trouble developing an original and authentic style. In fact, the Victorians built in two different modes: one, industrial building, tended to be purely functional, with relatively straightforward materials and designs; the other, the obviously "architectural" building, tended to be extremely ornate, with lavish decorations drawn from some past historical epoch and endowed with heavy moral overtones.

Industrial building was not thought of as truly "architectural" in the day, and only later has it been recognized as distinguished in its own way. Iron and brick were the cheapest building materials; thus factories, warehouses, and dockyards were constructed on iron frames and with brick facades. Many of these were elegantly simple. Others, particularly bridges and viaducts, were strikingly innovative, for the Victorian engineers could span distances and carry weights not even the Romans could imagine. Beginning with Abraham Darby's Iron Bridge at Coalbrookdale (1780), industrial engineers built a series of amazing iron structures, including I. K. Brunel's Royal Albert Bridge at Saltash (1859), Robert Stephenson's Britannia Bridge over the Menai Strait (1850), and Sir John Fowler's Forth Bridge (1890). The greatest example of engineering design was, as we have seen, Joseph Paxton's Crystal Palace, which showed that iron pillars and frames could be graceful and beautiful as well as utilitarian.

In buildings that Victorians regarded as properly architectural, they imitated either the classical or the Gothic style. The best classical examples are the British Museum and the Town Hall in Leeds; the Gothic is exemplified in the Houses of Parliament, the Royal Courts of Justice (London), the Manchester Town Hall, and countless churches everywhere. Gradually, the "battle of the styles" was won by the Gothic, largely because the Victorians associated it with the coherent Christian culture of England's past. The leading theorists of the Gothic were A. W. Pugin and John Ruskin, both of whom were strong critics of industrial society. Pugin (1812–1852), who with Charles Barry rebuilt the Houses of Parliament (1840–1860), regarded the Gothic as "the Christian style," harking back to an idealized hierarchical and devout society. Ruskin (1819–1900) argued that only a morally great society can produce great art; he found his ideal in the Venice of the Middle Ages. Under his influence, Victorian Gothic began to reflect the Byzantine influence on Venice, with multicolored brickwork and vivid, ornate decorations. In All Saints Church (Margaret Street, London) and Keble College (Oxford), both designed by William Butterfield, this riotous Victorian Gothic reached its peak.

Perhaps the finest of Victorian architectural achievements occurred when the industrial and Gothic styles were joined. One of the best examples of this combination was St. Pancras railway station and hotel. The station is a huge, gracefully arched iron and glass train shed, and the attached hotel is an extreme version of the Gothic, massive but with countless pointed arches, gables, and steeples. Another splendid example is the Oxford University Science Museum (1851), which has a lovely, restrained exterior derived directly from Ruskin's Venetian Gothic, and an exhilarating interior based on slim iron pillars vaulting up to an iron and glass roof.

THE RISE OF SCIENCE

The Oxford Science Museum is symbolic of the advent of science in nineteenth-century Britain. If natural science could penetrate the tradition-bound walls of Oxford, it could do anything. Indeed, science by any measure "rose" in the 1800s to take a dominant position in the culture. By the late Victorian years, science had struggled with orthodox theology and won; it had extended its jurisdiction to almost every area of human understanding, including social behavior and cosmology; it had won a place in the British universities and had helped turn them into more modern institutions; and scientists had formed well-organized and aggressive institutions to put forward their claims. Fundamental scientific discoveries—in electricity, in historical geology, in organic chemistry, and in evolutionary biology—proliferated on all sides.

Yet British scientists in the first half of the century liked to complain that science in Britain was "declining" and that scientists abroad were better supported and thereby enabled to be more productive. Such claims were misleading. True, the prevailing ideology of laissez-faire limited government support for science, and industry as yet was not so sophisticated as to require research laboratories. In other words, the free market did not by itself provide for either research in pure science or careers for scientists. It was very difficult for British scientists without independent income to devote their lives to science. The great English universities, Oxford and Cambridge, devoted as they were to classics, mathematics, and theology, made small provision for science. Even the Royal Society, founded in the seventeenth century, had come under the control of aristocratic amateurs.

Nevertheless, natural science in the early 1800s already played an increasingly important part in British society and culture. For one thing, science had been significant in industrialization. Many early industrialists had taken an active interest in science, and they had based some of their technical innovations (most notably, in steam power and iron metallurgy) on scientific discoveries. The Victorian public attributed much of their industrial growth to science. In many industrial cities, scientific institutions, such as "literary and philosophical societies," provided opportunities for business people to participate in "the march of mind" and polite scientific inquiry. Most important, scientific knowledge was regarded as part of the accepted view of the world. Early Victorians normally did not see science as opposed to religion but as a vital source of knowledge of the will of God. The natural world was another book of revelation, and science was the key to reading it.

The fact that scientists felt left out of landed society, and especially left out of Oxford and Cambridge, gave them an urge to advance the claims of science. Their real position of strength made their claims irresistible. The scientists of the first half of the century felt very strong professional aspirations. In 1831, they had founded the British Association for the Advancement of Science (BAAS), which satisfied some of their professional objectives but not others. Many wanted to win places for themselves and for science at Oxford and Cambridge. This urge put the scientists among the forces seeking to reform the ancient universities. The allies of science were, first, the nonconformists, who wanted to open the universities to non-Anglicans; second, the utilitarians and other liberals, who wanted to connect the universities with industrial and commercial life; the third, some of the younger "Oxbridge" tutors, who wanted for themselves careers within the universities as professional teachers and scholars.

Beginning in the 1850s, the reformers broke through the universities' defenses. Parliament appointed Royal Commissions to investigate Oxford and Cambridge and then passed laws opening them to nonconformists and endorsing "modern" courses of study, including natural science. The tutors won careers as teachers with expertise in their own fields. (In the 1870s, nonconformists were allowed to take advanced degrees, and tutors were allowed to marry.) Under the influence of science, research became a much more important activity, and the old-style generalist approach to knowledge gave way to specialized study. New disciplines such as history, anthropology, and economics were founded, each of them on the model of science. Provincial universities began to be established in the major industrial cities—the beginnings of the University of Manchester coming first in 1851. By the late nineteenth century, then, natural science (though not industrial technology) had secured a high place for itself in British culture.

NATURAL SCIENCE AND THE DECLINE OF RELIGION

As science rose, religion seemed to decline. The simultaneity of these two events, dramatized by the highly publicized clash between science and religion over Darwinian biology, made it seem that science *caused* the decline of religion. In fact, what is often called "the decline of religion" was an extremely complex phenomenon occurring over more than one century, of which science was only one cause.

The decline of religion—or to put it more positively, the secularization of culture—began long before the nineteenth century. Over time from the Renaissance onward, the world view of literate Europeans had slowly become secularized. By the end of the seventeenth century the view of nature most Britons held had been "desacralized"—that is, few literate people in Britain by 1700 believed that trees, stones, and rivers were inhabited by spirits. The Scientific Revolution had made even the revolutions of the planets accessible to reason. In the eighteenth century, polite society had raised reason to be a court of appeal even higher than revelation. In the work of some Enlightenment thinkers, miracle stories fell before the test of reason.

If one looks to *popular* religious belief in the nineteenth century, then the obvious historical development was a decline in working-class church membership from the peak reached during the evangelical revival of the early nineteenth century. The explanation for this decline must in large part be social. Substantial numbers of working-class people became nonbelievers (or "free thinkers") because they saw the churches and their teachings as instruments of social control. Moreover, as we have seen in Chapter 5, the Church of England had failed to maintain contact with the laboring poor in the eighteenth century. Both the established Churches of England and Scotland and the nonconformist denominations in the first half of the nineteenth century made some attempts to build churches and chapels in working-class districts, but on the whole these efforts were too little too late. Not the least of their problems was that they alienated the poor by the practice of renting pews to the well-to-do and by preaching the upper-class doctrine of respectability. Some working people in Britain perceived church membership as simply not for their sort of people, though there is evidence that many working-class families retained a much-diluted, nonchurchgoing form of Christian belief.

The upper classes of Victorian Britain themselves experienced various causes of doubt. One was the heritage of eighteenth-century reason, which cast doubt on miracle stories and revealed contradictions in the Gospels. Liberal theologians in the early Victorian years were able to accommodate reason, partly by not insisting on doctrinal purity and partly by urging reform of the ecclesiastical structure of the established Church of England. However, as liberals pressed their reforms, many conservative Anglicans resisted both the expansive claims of reason and alteration of clerical institutions. In 1833 this conservative reaction gave birth to the "Oxford Movement," which for some thirty years roused great theological and political controversy within the Anglican church. The Oxford Movement defended the autonomy and privileges of the Church against liberal reform and insisted on dogma and authority within the Church. John Henry Newman, the leader of the Oxford (or "Tractarian") Movement, regarded liberalism as "false liberty of thought," the application of reason where it has no proper jurisdiction. The Oxford Movement rejuvenated the old "High Church" position and articulated the professional claims of the Anglican clergy. It also appealed to many young men and women by emphasizing the aesthetic aspects of elaborate religious rituals, vestments, and architecture. The Oxford Movement eventually revitalized Anglican liturgy, but it also frightened conventional Victorian Protestants about a possible recovery of Roman Catholicism, fear of which Newman reinforced when he converted to Rome in 1845. More seriously, the Oxford Movement hardened the arteries of the Church and Oxford University against reform and set up a conflict between religion on the one hand and modern science and scholarship on the other.

Another cause of doubt among upper-class Victorians was an ethical reaction against the harshness of certain Christian teachings. Here evangelicalism was crucial because it heightened the intensity of the individual conscience and the drive for personal morality. Evangelicalism also taught the infinite mercy of God in offering salvation to anyone who would accept it. This doctrine, plus the related one of good works as necessary for saintliness and the growing material capacity of the nation to do real social good, created a powerful meliorism, indeed an impulse toward perfectibilism—the notion that people and social institutions are capable of perfection. By the 1840s and 1850s many Victorians were finding their meliorist attitude inconsistent with orthodox doctrines of hell and everlasting punishment. Surely, they thought, a loving God could not condemn millions of souls to eternal torment. This being the case, certain conventional Christian teachings were wrong.

Meanwhile, historical criticism of the Bible led to doubts about the literal truth of either the Old or New Testament. German scholars had led the development of biblical criticism, and in the 1830s these advances were imported into Britain. Slowly, this so-called higher criticism undermined orthodox belief by arguing that the Scriptures should be understood as the works of real men in historical circumstances. It was possible, liberal theologians contended, to separate legend from historical fact in the Scriptures, and historical assertions from allegorical statements of belief. But that admission was heretical to those who clung to the Bible as the literal word of God, and it seemed to make the Bible understandable only by a committee of academic experts. Most Victorians were deeply imbued with a historical frame of mind because they needed history to domesticate change for them; consequently, they could not reject the historical approach to the Bible even though it held such dangers for conventional doctrine.

Likewise, many Victorians were drawn to naturalistic accounts of worldly events. It was in this connection that science played its main part in the decline of religion. Middle-class Victorians were so impressed with the material progress made possible by technology that they were inclined to accept naturalistic explanations of phenomena even when they clashed with supernatural explanations. The conquest of nature by industrialization—not yet seen as dangerous to the environment—made scientific law seem correct, and scientific law assumes the uniform action of unbreakable natural formulae. Any account of the world that relied on divine interventions or creations—the creation of species, for example—seemed hard to believe.

More specifically, science in the early and mid-Victorian years delivered a number of blows to natural theology. Darwin's was the most decisive. Charles Darwin (1809–1882) was an unassuming man who did not go out of his way to attack religion; however, as an early professional scientist he was very devoted to the claims of science. As a naturalist aboard H.M.S. *Beagle* in the 1830s, Darwin had two convergent experiences: first, he read Charles Lyell's *Principles of Geology*, which persuaded him that all geological data must be explained by reference to the operation of uniform natural laws; second, he observed the complex distribution of natural life in South America (and particularly in the Galapagos Islands), which showed him that all creatures are specially adapted to their environment.

Back in England, Darwin struggled to understand *how* the uniform working of natural law modified species to fit their environment. Malthus's *Essay on Population* gave him his answer. Malthus had shown that all living things struggle ceaselessly for limited resources and that only the "fittest" survive. In 1859 Darwin published his *Origin of Species*, in which he summoned a wide variety of evidence to make three points: (1) species *had* varied—they were not created in immutable forms; (2) each species had evolved from antecedent species and ultimately from one or a few forms; and (3) the mechanism of change was *natural selection*, which was nature's automatic process of picking the "fittest" to survive. Then in *The Descent of Man* (1871) Darwin made explicit what was implicit in the *Origin of Species*: humanity fit the same pattern of evolution.

Darwinism immediately became the subject of heated controversy. It was attractive to some Victorians and repulsive to others. It was attractive because it brought vast realms of phenomena under the grasp of the human mind. It asserted the power of science, the marvels of which stood all around the Victorians. Darwinism was also attractive because it coincided with the doctrine of competition, which was such a cherished principle of the middle class. Competition and evolution seemed to justify inequality: the fittest *had* risen to the top. In a sense, then, Darwinism was free enterprise biology.

Darwinism seemed repulsive in part because it appeared to refute the Book of Genesis, which said that God had created the world in six days. However, only the rigid biblicists held this literal view by 1859. Most British theologians already had accepted metaphorical interpretations of Genesis. Darwinism was more disturbing because it seemed to show that nature was *not* harmonious, that it was in fact a vicious struggle for survival—"red in tooth and claw," as Tennyson put it. Darwinism also showed that the human being was nothing special, simply the most complex organism yet evolved, and this seemed a profound blow to Christianity. Finally, Darwinism knocked the pillars out from under natural theology because it appeared to destroy the idea that nature was "providentially designed"—that all things were created by a benevolent God for human benefit. Nature seemed without purpose.

Nevertheless, Darwinism would not have had such a devastating impact on religion had the churches (or part of them) not resisted the way they did. Within two or three decades after 1859, most British theologians had made their peace with Darwinism, either by taking evolution as God's way of creation or by simply declaring that science and religion belonged to separate spheres of discourse and could never come to conflict. But the initial reaction of many leaders in the churches was negative. At Oxford in 1860, for example, Bishop Samuel Wilberforce debated Darwinism's chief propagandist, T. H. Huxley, by asking in a supercilious tone whether Huxley claimed descent from monkeys through his grandmother or his grandfather. That kind of reaction enabled Huxley to claim that Wilberforce (and by implication, all orthodox Christianity) was being obscurantist. Thus the resistance of orthodox Christians to Darwinism made science seem the agent of liberty of thought and progress, and theology the agent of authoritarianism and obscurantism. On these grounds, in Victorian Britain, Darwinism and science were bound to win, and religion in Britain has never fully recovered. Darwinism, therefore, shook the mid-Victorian balance; it proved to be the first but not the only event to do so.

Suggested Reading

Best, Geoffrey, *Mid-Victorian Britain, 1851–1875* (New York: Schocken Books, 1972).
Briggs, Asa, *Victorian People* (Chicago: University of Chicago Press, 1955).
Burn, W. L., *Age of Equipoise* (New York: Norton, 1964).
Clark, Kenneth, *The Gothic Revival* (New York: Harper & Row, 1974).
Daunton, Martin, ed., *The Organisation of Knowledge in Victorian Britain* (Oxford: Oxford University Press, 2005).
Finn, Margot C., *After Chartism: Class and Nation in English Radical Politics, 1848–1874* (New York: Cambridge University Press, 1993).
Flanders, Judith, *Inside the Victorian Home: A Portrait of Domestic Life in Victorian England* (New York: W. W. Norton, 2003).
Floud, Roderick, and Donald McCloskey, eds., *The Economic History of Britain Since 1700.* 2 vols. 2nd ed. (New York: Cambridge University Press, 1994).
Gaunt, William, *A Concise History of English Painting* (London: Thames & Hudson, 1964).
Girouard, Mark, *The Return to Camelot* (New Haven: Yale University Press, 1981).

Goldman, Lawrence, *Science, Reform, and Politics in Victorian Britain: The Social Science Association, 1857–1886* (New York: Cambridge University Press, 2002).

Gray, Robert, *The Factory Question and Industrial England, 1830–1860* (New York: Cambridge University Press, 1996).

Gross, John, *The Rise and Fall of the Man of Letters* (New York: Macmillan, 1969).

Heyck, T. W., *The Transformation of Intellectual Life in Victorian England* (New York: St. Martin's, 1982).

Holloway, John, *The Victorian Sage* (New York: Norton, 1965).

Hoppen, K. T., *The Mid-Victorian Generation, 1846–1886* (New York: Oxford University Press, 1997).

Jordan, Robert Furneaux, *Victorian Architecture* (Harmondsworth: Penguin, 1966).

Kirk, Neville, *The Growth of Working-Class Reformism in Mid-Victorian England* (Urbana: University of Illinois Press, 1985).

Knights, Ben, *The Idea of the Clerisy in the Nineteenth Century* (Cambridge: Cambridge University Press, 1978).

Mason, Michael, *The Making of Victorian Sexuality* (New York: Oxford University Press, 1994).

Morgan, Marjorie, *National Identities and Travel in Victorian Britain* (New York: Palgrave Macmillan, 2001).

Newsome, David, *The Victorian World Picture* (New Brunswick, N.J.: Rutgers University Press, 1997).

Perkin, Harold, *The Origins of Modern English Society, 1780–1880* (Toronto: University of Toronto Press, 1969).

Perkin, Joan, *Victorian Women* (New York: New York University Press, 1993).

———, *Woman and Marriage in Nineteenth-Century England* (Chicago: Lyceum Books, 1989).

Poovey, Mary, *Making a Social Body: British Cultural Formation, 1830–1864* (Chicago: University of Chicago Press, 1995).

———, *The Proper Lady and the Woman Writer* (Chicago: University of Chicago Press, 1984).

———, *Uneven Developments: The Ideological Work of Gender in Mid-Victorian England* (Chicago: University of Chicago Press, 1988).

Robbins, Keith, *Nineteenth-Century Britain: Integration and Diversity* (Oxford: Clarendon Press, 1988).

Ruse, Michael, *The Darwinian Revolution* (Chicago: University of Chicago Press, 1979).

Showalter, Elaine, *A Literature of Their Own* (Princeton, N.J.: Princeton University Press, 1977).

Thompson, F. M. L., *The Rise of Respectable Society: A Social History of Victorian Britain, 1830–1900* (London: Fontana Press, 1988).

Tucker, Herbert, ed., *A Companion to Victorian Literature and Culture* (Oxford: B. Blackwell, 1999).

Chapter 17

The Overflow of Power: British Empire and Foreign Policy, 1815–1870

Britain dominated the global system of international relations in the first half of the nineteenth century. Drained by the dangers and costs of the revolutionary wars from 1793 to 1815, the European powers were inclined toward stability and peace. Meanwhile, the Industrial Revolution opened a great gap between Western Europe and the rest of the world, so that throughout the nineteenth century Europe had its way around the globe. These conditions favored Britain even more than the other European states. In the eighteenth century, Britain had become a great power first in Europe and then in the world. Now Britain's industrial and commercial headstart gave the British preeminence in world-power relationships. British power overflowed the shores of the British Isles and rippled out in ever-larger waves to touch practically every island and continent on earth. These conditions made the Empire a key feature of nineteenth-century Britain.

BRITISH POWER AND INTERESTS

This is not to say that Britain was the same sort of aggressive, buccaneering, mercantilist power as in the eighteenth century. Britain in the first three-quarters of the nineteenth century was a commercial and industrial nation, whose interests lay in trade and not in war and conquest—at least not in Europe. Even though the British Foreign Office, diplomatic service, and imperial government remained in aristocratic hands, external policy reflected the outlook of the middle class. Peace and free trade were the themes because the British knew that they could usually get their profits without force. It is true that British forces were engaged in a series of little wars almost continuously throughout the first half of Queen Victoria's reign—wars in India, China, Afghanistan, South Africa, Burma, and elsewhere. By British standards these were normally little more than skirmishes; between 1815 and 1854, the British took no part in any major war.

British power was real and enormous, but it was economic, not military.

Distrustful as always of a large standing army, Britain cut back on military spending after Waterloo. The army before the 1850s never numbered more then 140,000 regulars, of whom about a quarter were stationed in the British Isles and another quarter in India. The British spent less than 2 percent of the gross national product on the army—far less than in either the eighteenth or the twentieth century. With an army this small, Britain could not think of territorial acquisitions in Europe, or even major interventions for diplomatic purposes in Europe.

British interests were rooted in trade. The British regarded the rest of the world as their market and their warehouse of raw materials. In the 1850s, Europe as a whole produced more than 50 percent of the total manufacturing output of the world. As Professor Bernard Porter has written, Britain "had more factories, consumed more coal and iron and raw cotton, and employed more men and women in manufacturing industry than the rest of Europe put together." About 40 percent of British trade was with the Continent, but the other 60 percent was with the non-European world: North America, Asia (including India), South America, Africa, and Australia, in descending order of importance. Furthermore, as we saw in Chapter 13, the British invested an increasing amount of capital abroad each year.

To protect this all-important trade, Britain had to have a navy. The British naturally let the navy dwindle after 1815 and only built it back up in the 1850s and 1860s. Nevertheless, throughout the whole period from 1815 to 1870, no country could challenge British sea power. Indeed, the British navy was generally more powerful than the next three or four largest navies put together. Naval squadrons could be (and were) dispatched to assert British interests in the Atlantic, the Mediterranean, the Indian Ocean, and the Pacific. British ships were active around the world in putting down piracy and slavery and in protecting British merchant shipping. As ironclad, steampowered gunboats were adopted beginning in the 1840s, the navy could (and did) inject British powers inland by controlling rivers and coastal waters.

THE FREE TRADE EMPIRE

The British Empire in the first half of the nineteenth century was by far the largest in the world and quite unlike any empire that had ever existed. It was different in that it was decentralized and nonmercantilist. It was an empire built on and around free trade. In mercantilist empires, the colonies existed to serve the Mother Country by supplying raw materials and buying its manufactured goods; thus in such empires the colonies were prohibited from trading with other nations and from competing with the Mother Country. Because Britain had such an industrial and commercial advantage over the other Western nations in the years before 1870, a mercantilist empire was not necessary. The British needed neither to exclude other nations from trading with British colonies nor to establish formal control over all of the territories that British commerce penetrated.

British imperial influence resulted from its industrial and commercial predominance. For this reason, it is useful to think of British overseas power in terms of "informal" as well as "formal" empire. In their informal empire, the British dominated many regions without establishing formal governmental control over them. As we have seen, the British industrial sector of the early nineteenth century established satellite economies all around the world—economies of primary producers that were dependent on Britain. Much of Central and South America, for instance, was part of Britain's informal empire, though the British actually governed only the Miskito Coast (now Belize and part of Nicaragua) and British Guiana (now Guyana). Similarly, the cotton-producing states in the southern United States were tied to Britain, and in a sense New Orleans was as much a part of the Empire as Calcutta or Montreal.

Given their economic advantage, the Victorians preferred to expand their influence without taking formal control whenever they could, because it was cheaper. No soldiers or governors or judges were required. Nevertheless, the formal British Empire grew steadily throughout the years from 1815 to 1870—and the Empire had been huge to start with. The British in 1815 held a vast and variegated collection of colonies around the world. India was the biggest, richest, and most important part of the formal Empire; it will be discussed in the next section. The rest of the colonies formed a curious collection of territories, some having value as settlements for British emigrants, some as trading posts or naval bases, and some having no value at all. The British islands in the West Indies—Jamaica, Barbados, Trinidad, and many others—had once been the richest part of the Empire, but the sugar boom on which they depended faded in the nineteenth century, and their economies received a heavy blow when slavery was abolished in 1833. The West Indies by midcentury were the slums of the Empire. Canada had value as a partner in trade, supplying Britain with furs and timber in return for manufactured goods, but Canada was more important as a home for thousands of emigrants from the British Isles, especially Scottish clansmen fleeing the Highland Clearances and Irish peasants fleeing poverty and oppression. Australia, claimed in the 1770s by the Royal Navy, was used as a dumping ground for convicts between 1788 and 1840. When transportation of convicts to New South Wales (the main colony in Australia) ended, more than fifty thousand convicts were working off their sentences there. The Cape Colony in South Africa was acquired in 1815 as a convenient port on the long sea route between Britain and India, and the British had other naval stations in the Indian Ocean for the same purpose. Gibraltar (1713) and Malta (1814) had been won in wars against Spain and France and were kept as naval stations to control the Mediterranean. Altogether, the British Empire in 1815 included about 2 million square miles and approximately twenty-five million people.

What to do with this huge formal Empire caused much discussion in the early nineteenth century. A few "little Englanders," like the free trader Richard Cobden, regarded the colonies as useless and expensive. Cobden and his free-trade allies believed that if the colonies were simply let go, Britain would retain their trade anyway. But a majority of the British governing elite found them useful. Strategically, the colonies provided ready-made allies for the British; economically, they offered secure harbors and naval stations essential for trade. For Benthamites like Edward Gibbon Wakefield, the colonies served as markets for British goods and as safety valves for Britain's excess population. Indeed, emigration in the early nineteenth century was one of the few constructive social policies that won general consent. In the 1820s, the British government expended £65,000 to aid emigration, and between 1840 and 1873, the government-sponsored Colonial Emigration Committee assisted 6.5 million people to emigrate, most of them to the United States but many to Canada and Australia.

Mainly, however, the British retained the colonies because they believed it their duty to do so. Because Britain—so the Victorians thought—was the most advanced nation on earth, the British had a responsibility to spread civilization to the less progressive peoples under their control. As one Colonial Secretary put it:

> The authority of the British Crown is at this moment the most powerful instrument, under Providence, of maintaining peace and order in many extensive regions of the earth, and thereby assists in diffusing amongst millions of the human race, the blessings of Christianity and civilization.

Not surprisingly, evangelical missionaries actively worked to spread these blessings. Evangelicals in the Church of England and in the nonconformist denominations alike established numerous missionary societies, such as the British and Foreign Bible Society (1804), to support the proselytizing effort. The number of British missionaries, most of them evangelicals, grew throughout the nineteenth century; by 1900 there were some 10,000 scattered through the Empire. These remarkably energetic and self-assured folk tended to ignore the virtues and complexities of native cultures, but they nevertheless injected a humanitarian note in the imperial march. Many missionaries became the sole advocates for the welfare of indigenous populations (though not of indigenous cultures) as well as tireless opponents of the slave trade.

The period from 1815 to 1870 was not one of aggressive, concerted belief in the expansion of the British Empire, but imperial growth went on nonetheless. This "creeping colonialism" was in part the by-product of free trade. The British did not insist on exclusive rights to trade within their empire or in other parts of the world, but they did believe that any country, sheikdom, or tribe ought to cooperate in the regular rules of free trade and to provide security of person and property for British merchants. When an indigenous government across the sea, as for instance happened repeatedly in West Africa, refused to accept trade on British terms, or was unable to provide security for British commercial establishments, or insisted on collecting tribute from British merchants, then the British government was prepared to use force. Merchants, like missionaries, inevitably caused trouble with traditional societies on the imperial frontiers, and this "frontier turbulence" frequently drew the British army and navy into action and the government into exerting formal control. As Lord Palmerston, the plainspoken and patriotic prime minister, said in 1860: "It may be true that in one sense that trade ought not be enforced with cannon balls, but on the other hand trade cannot flourish without security, and that security may often be unattainable without the exhibition of physical force."

One of the most blatant examples of the British use of force to secure adherence to free trade occurred in China. The antique and ineffectual imperial Chinese

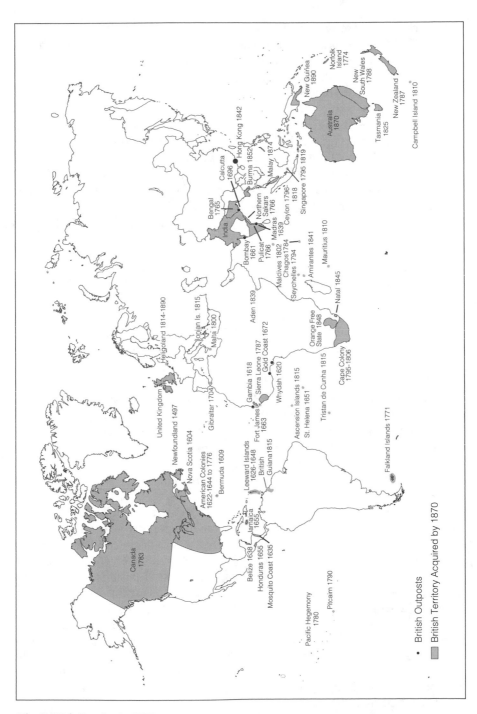

The British Empire in 1870

Labels on map:

Norfolk Island 1774
New Guinea 1890
New South Wales 1788
New Zealand 1787
Campbell Island 1810
Australia 1870
Tasmania 1825
Hong Kong 1842
Burma 1852
Malay 1874
Calcutta 1696
Northern Sakars
Singapore 1795 1819
Bengal 1765
India
Madras 1639
Ceylon 1796-1818
Amirantes 1841
Bombay 1661
Pulicat 1766
Madras 1766
Chagos 1784
Maldives 1802
Seychelles 1794
Mauritius 1810
Aden 1839
Natal 1845
Heligoland 1814-1890
Ionian Is. 1815
Malta 1800
Gambia 1618
Sierra Leone 1787
Gold Coast 1672
Orange Free State 1848
Cape Colony 1795-1806
United Kingdom
Gibraltar 1704
Whydah 1620
Tristan de Cunha 1815
Newfoundland 1497
Nova Scotia 1604
Bermuda 1609
Fort James 1663
Ascension Islands 1815
St. Helena 1651
Falkland Islands 1771
American Colonies 1622-1644 to 1776
Leeward Islands 1626-1648
British Guiana 1815
Canada 1783
Jamaica 1655
Belize 1638
Honduras 1655
Mosquito Coast 1635
Pacific Hegemony 1780
Pitcairn 1790

• British Outposts
■ British Territory Acquired by 1870

government wished to avoid contact with what they regarded as the inferior peoples of the West and therefore restricted trade to a few Chinese ports. The British East India Company developed a lucrative commerce with China, however, exchanging Indian opium for Chinese tea, which was exported to the West. The Chinese government repeatedly attempted to stop the opium traffic and in 1839 declared the sale and distribution of opium to be a capital crime. At the same time, the government attempted to collect tribute from the British merchants. Conflict between Chinese officials and British traders followed. In 1840–1842, British steam gunboats shattered the Chinese navy and a number of fortresses, forcing the Chinese to cede Hong Kong to Britain and opening five "treaty ports" to British trade. Shanghai in effect became a British-governed city. Then, in 1856, the British forced the reopening of Canton to trade, and in 1860 British and French troops fought their way into Peking in order to exact further trade rights from the Chinese. This time the British won the Kowloon Peninsula on the Chinese mainland across from Hong Kong, as well as the right to have a legation in Peking. Gunboat "diplomacy" had opened China to the West even as it protected the British rights to sell opium to China's addicts.

Creeping colonialism was also driven forward by the expansionist impulses of the dynamic colonists themselves. This process of "internal expansion" often involved the mistreatment or even destruction of indigenous peoples. There were four prominent cases of internal expansionism: Canada, Australia, New Zealand, and South Africa. Beginning with several thousand Loyalists from the thirteen colonies in 1783, the population of Canada grew rapidly, reaching 350,000 in 1815 and four million in 1870. Led at first by fur traders and then by farmers, the Canadian people expanded into the Great Plains north of the 49th parallel to the Rocky Mountains and claimed the Columbia River basin in the Pacific. These people, almost entirely of British extraction, simply pushed the Native Americans aside.

In Australia, the convicts and their keepers were accompanied by free immigrants from the British Isles. As the New South Wales colony grew, it threw out new shoots in Victoria and Queensland and pushed inland from the southeast coast to develop extensive cattle-grazing ranches. Edward Gibbon Wakefield sponsored partially successful colonies in South Australia and Western Australia. As the British population pushed into the interior, they came into conflict with the indigenous Australian Aborigines, a seminomadic, Stone Age people. Inspired by humanitarian sentiment, the governor of New South Wales attempted to control the expansion of the colonists and protect the Aborigines, but his effort failed to stop the land-hungry colonists. The Aboriginal population could not resist the firearms and diseases of the settlers, and by 1860 their numbers had been reduced by two-thirds. In New Zealand, traders followed hard on the heels of whaling captains, and in the 1830s, another of Wakefield's projects brought colonists from Britain. These colonists, eager for pasturage for their sheep, fought a series of bloody wars with the indigenous Maoris between 1843 and 1872. By the end of the wars, the Maori population had been reduced by half, and their social structure and land tenure system had been destroyed.

In South Africa, British colonists faced not only indigenous African peoples (Bushmen, Hottentots, and Bantus) but also approximately twenty-five thousand cantankerous Dutch ("Boer") farmers who had settled the Cape Colony in the seventeenth century. The Boer farmers regarded themselves as a racially superior people elected by God to dominate the blacks of Africa. They held Hottentots as slaves. The British, who arrived in 1815, sought to control the Cape Colony for strategic reasons, but also sought to protect the Hottentots and control the land-hungry Boers, who reacted against British pressure by looking for fresh grazing lands to the east and north of the Cape Colony. That expansionism brought them into conflict with the Bantus, who for some time had been migrating south and west, into the path of the Boers. When Britain in 1833 abolished slavery in the Empire, Boer restlessness increased; wars between Boer farmers and Bantus followed. Finally, in 1836, thousands of Boers sought to escape British control and "trekked" east and north, setting up Boer republics in Natal, the Transvaal, and the Orange Free State. The British had no desire to annex territory but found the spillover from the incessant frontier wars between Boer and Bantu intolerable. In 1843, Britain annexed Natal and then in 1848 took over the other two Boer colonies. In the 1850s, however, Britain recognized the independence of the Transvaal and Orange Free State: the Boers were, for the time being, too difficult a meal to swallow.

Meanwhile, an important development occurred in colonial government. Most of the colonies were ruled autocratically by Britain as if they were conquered territories. These were the "Crown Colonies," theoretically under the control of the Colonial Office, but because of the distance involved, they were actually run by local British governors, few of whom knew much about their subject peoples. The colonies with large numbers of white settlers were allowed—indeed, encouraged—to rule themselves through representative institutions. Largely because they had learned from their experience with the American colonies that the old adversarial relationship between colonial governors and their legislatures had to not worked, the British developed over time a new system of "responsible government." By this system, the local executive became responsible to the colonial legislature and not to the governor, who increasingly played the role of constitutional monarch in his colony.

The initial development of responsible government came in Canada. In 1791, to keep the French and British colonists apart, the British had created Upper and Lower Canada. Governed as they were by the old system, neither province succeeded, and in 1837 rebellions broke out in both provinces. The Whig government sent to Canada a new governor-general to solve the problems. This was Lord Durham, a radical aristocrat who believed in cabinet government. In 1839, Durham submitted an extremely influential report, which called for union of Upper and Lower Canada (in which the French colonists would be outnumbered) but also for cabinet government, according to which the colonial executive would be responsible to the colonial legislature. Upper and Lower Canada were joined in 1840, and responsible government was established in 1848.

Responsible government was extended to other colonies as soon as their British (white) population had grown large enough to fend for itself. The Australian colonies received responsible government in the 1850s, and New Zealand in 1856. Jamaica and the other West Indian colonies never developed responsible government because the white population was so much smaller than the population of ex-slaves; indeed, they reverted back to Crown Colony status. In South Africa, the settlers in Cape Colony were finally persuaded in 1872 to accept responsible government, including responsibility for paying for the wars against the Bantus. Responsible government was government as cheap as possible for Britain, the ideal of the free-trade Empire.

INDIA

India was the most highly valued part of the Victorian Empire, and throughout the nineteenth century the British treated it differently from any other colony. India's exotic splendor caught the Victorian imagination. Strange as it may seem, thousands of Indian travelers came to England before the 1850s—some of them impoverished sailors, but others were well-to-do merchants and aristocrats. They did much to teach the British about India and the Indians, and the Indians in India about the British. But India had practical value as well. It was valuable because of its trade, which became even more important when the cotton mills of Lancashire began to export textiles to clothe millions of Indian peasants. To promote British trade in India, the British crushed local Indian industries such as textiles and steel. But India was most valuable because possessing India made Britain a great power in Asia. The Indian army attained the Victorian ideal for empire: it gave power for very little expenditure. The Indian army, numbering about 200,000 men, including the British officers and a few British regiments, was larger than the regular army of Britain, yet it was entirely paid for by Indian taxes. The British administration in India, which was still in the hands of the East India Company until 1858, was largely a tax-collecting institution. It collected the taxes by which the Indian masses paid for their own subjection.

This strange situation had come about as the East India Company flowed into the power vacuum left by the collapse of the old Moghul Empire. By the 1790s, as we saw in Chapter 7, the Company ruled Bengal and was one of the half-dozen strongest powers in India. For a time, the Company did not seek to expand because trade and profits were its concerns. But beginning in 1798, when Richard Wellesley (the brother of the duke of Wellington) became governor-general, the Company adopted an aggressive policy. Wellesley wanted to stop certain Indian states from allying with the French and to secure the Company's trade and property by imposing political order in the territories surrounding the Company's holdings. In its desire to bring order and stability, the Company received the support of many Indian leaders, who could see no alternative to British rule among the petty and corrupt Indian states. Long after the French threat was gone, Wellesley and his successors inexorably extended British rule and influence to reduce turbulence on the

Company's frontiers. Some large states in southern India fell first, followed by several of the Maratha states in central India. By 1805, the Company controlled Delhi and the Moghul emperor himself. By 1813, when the Company's charter came up for renewal, it was in fact the paramount power in India. The British government recognized the Company's true function by ending its commercial monopoly over Indian trade, except for the China trade, which the Company had found to be a fabulous market for opium.

The final wave of British expansion in India began in 1839. By then, only the Punjab, Sind and Afghanistan in the northwest of the subcontinent were truly independent states. The British government was concerned about Russian expansion into the area through Persia and Afghanistan. To preempt Russian designs on India, the British deposed the Afghan rulers and put their own favorite on the throne. The fiercely independent Afghans revolted, and in a furious war from 1839 to 1842, they fought the British to a stalemate. Next, in a pair of wars (1845–1846 and 1848–1849), the British managed to subdue the warlike Sikh state of Punjab (now Pakistan). In 1845, the British annexed the route into Afghanistan, the Sind. Sir Charles Napier expressed the British role with disarming honesty: "We have no right to seize Sind, but we shall do so, and a very advantageous, useful, humane piece of rascality it will be."

Burma was taken in two gulps (1823–1826 and 1852). Thereafter, the British annexed a number of Indian states by insisting on the privileges of "paramountcy." Whenever an Indian prince died without a legitimate heir, the British could, by the doctrine of "lapse," annex the state; they did this a number of times under the governor-generalcy of Lord Dalhousie. The British under Dalhousie also claimed the right to annex a state if they regarded it as badly governed. By this privilege of paramountcy, the British annexed Oudh, the last big independent Muslim state in northern India.

As British power in India grew, so did the British inclination to reform traditional Indian customs and social structure. In the previous century, the Company had been content to leave Indian society and institutions alone, for Company officials recognized Indian civilization to be a splendid if exotic creation. The Company officially prohibited Christian missionaries to work in British India. However, the British desire to westernize India became irresistible as the moral foundations of Victorianism hardened. Evangelicals saw magnificent opportunities for gaining converts in the subcontinent. In 1813, missionaries were allowed in. Certain Indian customs were put down as criminal. One was suttee, whereby a "true" Hindu widow was supposed to burn herself on her husband's funeral pyre. The British made this illegal in 1829, though the practice held on sporadically until the 1860s. In the 1830s, the British banned thuggee, a practice of a Hindu subcaste, whereby they murdered and robbed travelers.

In addition, the British replaced Delhi with Calcutta as the capital of India and deposed the Moghul emperor in 1833. The British introduced new civil and criminal law codes and imposed on India a British-style land system, complete with individual ownership and a free market in land. They also set up a new educational

An imperial scene: blowing sepoy mutineers from the muzzles of cannons. Indian Mutiny, 1857.

system, including university-level education in Western science and literature. This educational system was meant to train a new, westernized ruling elite for India; it also confirmed English as the official language for the country.

The new Western-style elite never won the allegiance of the mass of Indians, and the Indian people deeply resented many of the other reforms. In 1857 a violent reaction changed the tone and texture of British India. This outburst, the Indian Mutiny (1857–1858), proved to be a traumatic event for the British because it threatened to smash the jewel in the imperial crown, because it shook Victorian self-assurance, and because it unleashed demons of racial hatred that could never be penned up again. The mutiny—regarded by many Indians as the first war of Indian national liberation—began among Indian troops ("sepoys") near Delhi. Their British officers issued them cartridges that were greased with beef and pork fat. The Hindu sepoys regarded cows as sacred, and the Muslims thought pigs unclean. The mutineers killed their officers and took Delhi; thereafter, mutinies and civilian rebellions broke out in perhaps one-fifth of India, mostly in the central and northern regions.

The mutiny/rebellion was finally put down but only after strenuous efforts by the British and loyal Indian troops amid scenes of appalling bloodshed. Mutineers slaughtered all the Europeans they could find, and the British responded with savage counterattacks and brutal retributions. Fortunately for the British, the rebels never had a concerted plan, and most of the sepoys in Bengal remained loyal. The British governor-general was also able to deploy just enough British regular regiments to retake Delhi and the other rebel strongholds. After eighteen months, it was all over, but British India, which lasted until 1947, was never the same.

In the aftermath of the mutiny, the British had to reconsider their role in India. They recognized that the rebellion had been a reaction against British (and especially evangelical) interference with India's traditional customs, institutions, and rulers. The British, therefore, after 1858 became much more conservative in propounding westernizing reforms; yet they acclimated themselves to the idea that they would have to rule India for a long time. Christian missionaries were more strictly controlled after 1858, and the traditional princely rulers and great landowners were strengthened. The new westernized elite was left unsupported. The British now directed "progress" toward material development—railways above all, but also irrigation systems, roads, and public works. By 1881, India had almost 10,000 miles of railways and 30 million acres of irrigated land.

In addition, the British government took the rule of India away from "John Company" and put it under the British cabinet and Parliament. The governor-general now became "viceroy," responsible in theory to a cabinet officer—the secretary of state for India—who was in turn responsible to Parliament. The viceroy ruled the annexed parts of British India directly and the nonannexed states indirectly. The Indian army received a higher proportion of British troops, though the majority of soldiers still were Indian. The Indian Civil Service, long a professional service that was exclusively British, now formally became British government employees. They ruled India with extraordinarily high standards of competence and incorruptibility, but they distanced themselves from the Indian people. As the British in India—the "Anglo-Indians"—increasingly brought wives and families out to India, they became more and more a self-conscious, provincial clique; they ruled the 200 million Indians in a spirit of aloof, elitist fatalism.

FOREIGN POLICY, 1815–1850

The other side of Britain's imperial power was the fact that, regarding Europe, Britain was a satiated state. Protected from Europe by the navy's control of the English Channel and the North Sea and preoccupied with economic growth, Britain had no aggressive ambitions on the Continent. British public opinion often expressed sympathy for liberalism and constitutionalism wherever they emerged in Europe, but the British were in no mood to go to war over ideology. The one overriding British interest in Europe was to keep the Continent from being dominated by one power. Such a condition would threaten Britain economically and strategically. Hence the British, as in the eighteenth century, pursued a balance of power in Europe. The British of the nineteenth century differed from their predecessors in practicing balance of power tactics without committing themselves to alliances. They preferred the flexibility of independent action, whereby they could shift their influence as the states of Europe grouped and regrouped. Such a strategy, though it seemed to follow no principles, gave consistency to British policy through a succession of governments and foreign secretaries.

Lord Palmerston (photo taken about 1860). Palmerston, popular because of his British nationalism, was Liberal prime minister from 1855 to 1858 and 1859 to 1865.

The foreign secretaries of the day exercised much stronger personal control over European affairs than would later be possible. The first great foreign secretary of the nineteenth century was Viscount Castlereagh (foreign secretary from 1812 to 1822). Castlereagh was a hardworking, direct, rather secretive man, a master of diplomatic maneuvering but a poor orator and wary of public opinion. He won the unjustified reputation among liberals of favoring reactionary regimes. In fact, however, while Castlereagh supported stability in Europe, he refused to commit Britain to the Holy Alliance, a reactionary alliance of Austria, Prussia, and Russia created to preserve autocratic regimes by active intervention. Castlereagh had hoped to maintain the European balance of power by holding periodic congresses of the great powers, but the movement of the other states toward a general commitment to intervene on behalf of autocracy warned him off.

Castlereagh's successor, George Canning (foreign secretary from 1822 to 1827), followed the same general policies as his predecessor but with a flair for public relations that made him seem much more liberal. Canning gave up on Castlereagh's idea of congresses ("the Concert of Europe"), but he pursued the balance of power by traditional means. In Portugal, where British trade interests were very strong and where the Royal Navy could be effective, Canning intervened to maintain stability and independence. In Spain, however, Canning recognized that the British could not have their way without war, which the nation would not have supported. In 1823, French troops intervened in Spain against British wishes. Canning responded by encouraging the independence of Spain's colonies in America: "I resolved that, if France had Spain, it should not be 'Spain with the Indies.' I called the New World into existence to redress the balance of the Old." This declaration, no doubt, was an exaggeration, but Britain undeniably dominated Latin American trade for the rest of the century.

Like all nineteenth-century British statesmen, Canning found the affairs of the Middle East (Greece, Turkey, the Black Sea, Persia, and so on) more complicated. In that region of the world, the British had constant concerns about the expansion of Russian power to the west and south of the Russian border. British diplomats and imperial governors feared that Russia might damage British interests in the eastern Mediterranean by controlling the Straits of the Bosporus and Dardanelles and might threaten the security of India by pushing through Persia and Afghanistan. In the 1820s, Greek patriots revolted against their Turkish rulers, and British sympathy was all for the Greeks. Lord Byron fought and died for Greek independence. Canning feared, however, that Turkey might collapse, which would open the way for Russian expansion. Canning's policy was to try to win for the Greeks some autonomy under reformed Turkish rule. This policy was a failure; the Turks refused British help, mediation, or bullying. Even after a combined British and Russian fleet destroyed the Turkish navy at Navarino in 1827, the British refused to force the Turks' hand. Finally, in 1830, Greece became independent.

The third great foreign secretary of nineteenth-century Britain was Viscount Palmerston (Henry John Temple), who dominated British foreign affairs for nearly thirty years (foreign secretary 1830–1834, 1835–1841, and 1846–1851; prime minister, 1855–1858 and 1859–1865). Palmerston shared Canning's talent for appealing to public opinion and outdid him in manipulating the press, but in his diplomatic dealings he was notoriously abrasive and impatient. Palmerston was a roguish aristocrat who made himself the spokesman of the self-confident and brassy British middle class. Above all he was a patriot and an opportunist. As a Whig, Palmerston regarded the Reform Act of 1832 as the best possible constitution for Britain and often spoke in favor of liberal regimes abroad: "I consider the constitutional states to be the natural allies of this country. . . . No English ministry will be performing its duty if it is inattentive to their interests." Yet Palmerston in fact was a pragmatist and never sacrificed British strategic or commercial interests for ideology.

Palmerston's diplomatic style and intentions can be seen in the three main foreign areas. First, in 1830, liberal revolutions broke out across Western Europe. Palmerston enthusiastically greeted the French Revolution of 1830 and its new constitutional monarchy. But he resisted the expansion of France's new regime into the Low Countries, where British trade interests were vital. In 1830, the Belgians revolted against the Dutch, to whom they had been joined in 1815. This revolt seemed to open the way for French intervention. Palmerston achieved his goal of keeping the ports of the Low Countries open to British trade by sponsoring Belgian independence, achieved finally in 1839.

Second, in the years from 1839 to 1841, Palmerston came to the support of Turkey, even though his action caused a rift with the French. In those years, the ruler of Egypt, who was nominally a vassal of the Turkish sultan, rebelled against Turkish authority. This Egyptian pasha, Mehemet Ali, had French support. Palmerston feared that if Turkey collapsed, Russia would flow into the vacuum. He managed to bring about an agreement with the Austrians and Russians against Mehemet Ali, the defeat of Ali's forces, and the bombardment of Beirut. In 1841, Palmerston got all the interested powers (including Turkey and Russia) to sign "the Convention of the Straits," which declared that the Straits between the Black Sea and the Mediterranean would be closed to foreign warships as long as Turkey was at peace. In this way, Russian naval influence in the eastern Mediterranean was blocked.

Finally, during the European revolutions of 1848, Palmerston publicly approved of the liberal-nationalist revolutionaries but did little to support them. Poles, Hungarians, and Italians all revolted against Austrian rule, and Palmerston on his own hook gave them verbal support. His policy seemed anti-Austrian, especially when he encouraged the Italian independence and unification movement. Actually, however, Palmerston wanted to maintain the balance of power under the new conditions, and that goal required the continued existence of a strong Austria. Palmerston simply believed that the Austrian Empire would be stronger without the recalcitrant Italian provinces. Thus he accepted Austrian suppression of the revolt in Hungary, even though he publicly criticized its brutality. Palmerston was independent and vocal—these qualities got him dismissed from office in 1851—but he was a pragmatic agent of British interests all the same.

THE CRIMEAN WAR

Several key concerns of the British converged in the 1850s to lead Britain into its only European war between 1815 and 1914. The British concern for the security of India and for the route to India through the Mediterranean and the Middle East had committed them to the defense of Turkey, chronically the "sick man of Europe." At the same time, the traditional British concern about the balance of power in Europe made the British statesmen and public opinion alike highly suspicious of Russia, which seemed potentially the dominant power on the Continent. The British believed, as we have seen, that Turkey stood as a bulwark against Russian expansion into both Eastern Europe and Asia Minor. Unfortunately for the British, the Ottoman Empire in Turkey was a tottering dinosaur, whose weakness was a constant temptation to the Russians and an anxiety to the British. By the 1850s, the menace to Turkey by the Russian bear was rousing the British lion to fight.

In this awakening of British belligerence, another Victorian theme had strong influence: British self-confidence. By the 1850s, Britain's prosperity and progress had bred a pride in British "civilization" that swelled easily into bumptious nationalism. Palmerston had given voice to this attitude in 1850, when, in defense of a British citizen in Athens, he had declared that, "as the Roman in days of old had held himself free from indignity when he could say *civis Romanus sum* [I am a Roman citizen], so also a British subject, in whatever land he may be, shall feel confident that the watchful eye and the strong arm of England will protect him against injustice and wrong." This arrogant British pride by the 1850s was directed at Russia, for in the eyes of the liberal Victorian middle class the Czarist state stood as the very symbol of oppression and reaction.

The Czarist regime in fact had brought some of British Russophobia on itself. The Russian army of 800,000 men was much larger than any other in nineteenth-century Europe. Czar Alexander I (1777–1825) had dreamed up the reactionary

Holy Alliance of 1815, and Czar Nicholas I (1825–1855) was an aggressive autocrat. His armies had put down with great brutality the revolutions of 1848 in Poland and Hungary. Moreover, although the Russians did not seek to destroy Turkey, they were certainly pleased to pick up some pieces as it destroyed itself. By 1853, Nicholas I believed the time had come to carve up the Ottoman Empire. In that year, the Russians claimed the status of protectors of Christians living in Turkey and then occupied two Danubian provinces of Turkey. In October 1853, the Turks went to war with Russia.

The British government dithered during the events leading to the Russo-Turkish war and then stumbled into hostilities on the side of the Turks. Given their influence in the region, the British might have been able to prevent the war, either by warning the Turks that they would get no help from the British or by warning the Russians that Britain would help Turkey. Perhaps if Lord Palmerston had been in charge of foreign affairs, he would have acted with the necessary decisiveness. But Palmerston at the time had been demoted to home secretary, and the prime minister was Lord Aberdeen, who was a Peelite (a former Tory who left the party with Peel after the split over free trade in 1846) presiding over an essentially Whig government. Aberdeen's cabinet could not face down popular enthusiasm for war, nor could it force the Turks to give in to Russian demands. As Aberdeen frequently and pathetically noted, "We are drifting helplessly to war." After reaching an alliance with the French, who had their own grievances with Russia, as well as a need for a dose of *la gloire*, Britain went to war against Russia in March of 1854.

The ineptitude of British diplomacy leading up to the war was exceeded by the incompetence of their war effort. The Crimean War was a throwback to eighteenth-century wars of maneuver: the British did not mean to conquer Russia or overthrow the Czarist regime but to carry out an expedition to the Crimean Peninsula, there to punish the Russians enough to exact concessions from them. The specific target in the Crimea was the Russian naval base on the Black Sea, Sebastapol, to which the British and French laid seige. The beseiging armies were themselves pressured by the massive, if ill-armed and ill-trained, Russian forces that descended on them from the north.

Furthermore, the British army was still operating on aristocratic lines left over from the Napoleonic wars. During the long peace after 1815, the army had ossified. Its logistical arm proved incapable of supplying the initial expeditionary force of thirty thousand men some 4,000 miles from Britain. Many supply ships were destroyed by a storm in the fall of 1854, leaving the British troops to suffer horribly from a lack of food, warm clothing, and dry shelter in the winter of 1854–1855. Thousands died of cholera and dysentery, medical care being backward and haphazard at best. The army bureaucracy was so impenetrable that it took a superhuman effort by Florence Nightingale, the self-appointed autocrat of nursing, to improve the army hospital at Scutari (across the Bosporus Strait from Constantinople).

To make matters worse, the military leadership was spectacularly inept. The commander of the expeditionary army, Lord Raglan, had fought at Waterloo but had never commanded troops in the field. A staff officer to the core, Raglan issued orders in terms of requests and habitually spoke of the enemy as "the French." His ranking officers held their commissions by "purchase" rather than by merit. Two of them, Lord Cardigan (commander of the Light Brigade of cavalry) and Lord Lucan (commander of the Heavy Brigade) were brothers-in-law who had long engaged in a personal feud and who now distinguished themselves as arrogant nitwits. Their aristocratic stupidity resulted in the most glorious event of the war, the magnificent but futile charge of the Light Brigade directly into the Russian artillery at Balaclava. Lord Cardigan survived the charge, but his brigade was destroyed.

The incompetence of the war effort roused a frenzy of frustrated nationalism at home. The leading newspapers were vehemently anti-Russian and pro-Turk. The *Times's* correspondent in Crimea, W. H. Russell, sent home by telegraph (a first in the history of war) vivid reports of the army's bungling. Radical politicians blamed aristocratic government for the inefficiency of the war effort; obviously, they thought, Britain's businessmen could run the war better. Pacifist radicals like John Bright and Richard Cobden were scorned by public opinion, while war-hawk radicals like J. A. Roebuck became wildly popular. Palmerston emerged as the people's choice to reinvigorate the war effort, which public opinion demanded of the Aberdeen government. In 1855, Roebuck carried in the House of Commons a motion calling for an inquiry into the conduct of the war. The cabinet resigned, and Palmerston ("Lord Pumicestone") formed a government.

Palmerston displayed his usual energy and decisiveness, but in fact the Franco-British forces had already turned the corner in the Crimea. The logistical and medical branches in the Crimea became effective and supplies flowed ashore. At home the War Office was reorganized. The Russian army showed the effects of its own antiquated systems of supply, training, and weaponry. Sebastapol fell in September 1855, bringing an end to the fighting. The Treaty of Paris (1856) gave the British what the diplomats (if not the public) had sought: a Russian guarantee of Turkish independence, autonomy for the Danubian provinces (later to become Rumania), an end to Russian claims to be protectors of Turkish Christians, and neutralization of the Black Sea.

SPLENDID ISOLATION AND AN IMPERIAL CULTURE

By 1860 or so, the overflow of power had put the British in a paradoxical position. The Crimean War may have ended in victory for the British, but it gave a powerful blow to British self-esteem. Yet at the same time, the Empire had become a source of immense pride and an important element in national identity for most Britons.

One result of the Crimean War was the public's acceptance of a larger standing army, whose numbers now rose to about 225,000 men. Another result was the reform of the military services; this had begun during the war and continued slowly during the next decade. Ability and merit gradually replaced connection and wealth as the means for advancement in the army. Finally, in 1871, the purchase system itself was abolished. In the navy, technological advances went forward more rapidly, as armored ships, breech-loading cannons, and steam power replaced the old wood-and-sail fleets in the 1860s.

At least as important, in terms of military power, was that the British from the 1860s could call upon a reorganized and more tightly controlled Indian army. The East India Company's army of about a quarter of a million men, led by some 21,000 British officers and noncommissioned officers, was restructured after the Indian Mutiny of 1857. Once the East India Company was abolished and responsibility for India assumed by the British government, the Indian army was manned at a ratio of 1:2, British to Indians—roughly 60,000 British soldiers and 120,000 Indians. This army, paid for by Indian taxpayers but acting on directives from London, made Britain a great power in Asia and the Middle East down through the early twentieth century.

Meanwhile, despite the military reforms of the 1860s, the Crimean War had damaged British prestige and influence in Europe. To be sure, the "Eastern Question"—the problems of Turkish decline and Russian expansion in the Middle East—was put on the back burner for twenty years. Britain played no significant role in the great dramas of Italian and German reunification, which redrew the map of Europe in the 1850s and 1860s. In the case of Italy, the British were torn between sympathy for Italian nationalism, the commitment to keep Austria strong as part of the balance of power, and the belief that Austria would be better off without its troublesome holdings in Italy. In the case of Germany, the British were caught unaware, for in focusing on Austria, they failed to notice the effectiveness of Bismarck's campaign to unify Germany around the steel core of Prussian power. The British stood by in their "splendid isolation" when Prussia defeated Austria in 1866 and France in 1870–71.

At home, the Empire was increasingly influencing British culture and identity and proving to be a source of national pride. Policy makers were certain that the Empire was crucial to British prosperity; colonial goods such as products of native crafts, foodstuffs not grown in Europe, and raw materials for British manufactures penetrated the British market. Two happy examples were India rubber, a latex produced in the tropics that allowed for improvement of waterproof clothing, tires, and toys—not to mention tennis balls, which in turn allowed the development of lawn tennis—and gutta percha, a latex from Malayan trees, from which the first inexpensive golf balls were made. Lawn tennis and golf were among the Victorian recreations that were exported to the colonies and, indeed, the rest of the world. Museums as well as commercial and industrial exhibitions, beginning with the Crystal Palace of 1851, increasingly put imperial products on display. Likewise, commercial panoramas, melodramas, music hall productions, and popular publications all advertised the splendors of Empire. Especially popular were depictions of heroic imperial military events. True, historians disagree about the depth of this "imperial culture," but it seems certain that by the mid-nineteenth century various goods and expressions of Empire pervaded British culture, and that Britishness—particularly among the ruling classes—had become substantially imperial.

By 1870, then, the British stood in a paradox: Tremendously prosperous at home and economically powerful abroad, Britain formally and informally had a gigantic empire, but Britain was standoffish and ineffectual on the Continent. It may be that these apparently contradictory facts were actually mutually re-enforcing. In any case, the British policy of "splendid isolation"—technically the policy of avoiding treaties that specified the conditions under which Britain would go to war—had enabled them to play the role of independent makeweight in the balance scales of European power. Now that policy was beginning to look less splendid and more isolated. British confidence, so characteristic of the mid-Victorian decades, became more dependent on possession and expansion of the Empire. The question for the decades to come would be whether the Empire would continue to be, or seem to be, a source of strength, or whether the Empire itself would become a source of foreign rivalry and a drain on British resources.

Suggested Reading

Bourne, Kenneth, *The Foreign Policy of Victorian England, 1830–1902* (Oxford: Clarendon Press, 1970).

Brown, David, *Palmerston and the Politics of Foreign Policy, 1846–55* (Manchester: Manchester University Press, 2002).

Bridge, F. R., and R. Bullen, *The Great Powers and the European States System, 1815–1914* (London: Longman, 1980).

Dalrymple, William, *The Last Mughal: The Fall of a Dynasty, 1857* (London: Bloomsbury, 2006).

Farwell, Byron, *Queen Victoria's Little Wars* (London: Allen Lane, 1973).

Fieldhouse, D. K., *The Colonial Empires: A Comparative Survey from the Eighteenth Century* (London: Weidenfeld & Nicolson, 1986).

Fisher, Michael, *Counterflows to Colonialism: Indian Travellers and Settlers in Britain, 1600–1857* (New Delhi: Permanent Black, 2005).

Halstead, John P., *The Second British Empire: Trade, Philanthropy, and Good Government, 1820–1890* (Westport, Conn.: Greenwood Press, 1983).

Hall, Catherine, *Civilising Subjects: Metropole and Colony in the English Imagination, 1830–1867* (Chicago: University of Chicago Press, 2002).

Headrick, Daniel R., *The Tools of Empire* (New York: Oxford University Press, 1981).

Hibbert, Christopher, *The Great Mutiny: India, 1857* (London: Allen Lane, 1978).

Hyam, Ronald, *Britain's Imperial Century, 1815–1914* (London: Batsford, 1976).

Judd, Denis, *Palmerston* (London: Weidenfeld & Nicolson, 1975).

Kennedy, Paul, *The Rise and Fall of British Naval Mastery* (London: Allen Lane, 1976).

———, *The Rise and Fall of the Great Powers* (New York: Random House, 1987).

Lloyd, Trevor, *The British Empire, 1558–1983* (New York: Oxford University Press, 1986).

Palmer, Alan, *The Banner of Battle: The Story of the Crimean War* (New York: St. Martin's, 1987).

Porter, Andrew, ed., *Oxford History of the British Empire: The Nineteenth Century* (Oxford: Oxford University Press, 1999).

Porter, Bernard, *The Absent-Minded Imperialists: What the British Really Thought about Empire* (London: Oxford University Press, 2005).

———, *Britain, Europe and the World, 1850–1982* (London: Allen & Unwin, 1983).

———, *The Lion's Share: A Short History of British Imperialism, 1850–1970, 2nd ed.,* (London: Longman, 1984).

Spear, Percival, *The Oxford History of Modern India, 1740–1947* (Oxford: Clarendon Press, 1965).

Woodham-Smith, Cecil, *Florence Nightingale, 1810–1910* (New York: McGraw-Hill, 1951).

———, *The Reason Why* (New York: McGraw-Hill, 1954).

Kings and Queens of Great Britain, 1685–1901

Monarch	House	Reign
James II (of England and James VII of Scotland)	Stuart	1685–1688
William III and Mary II	Stuart	William: 1688–1702; Mary: 1688–1694
Anne I (of the United Kingdom)	Stuart	1702–1714
George I	Hanover	1714–1727
George II	Hanover	1727–1760
George III	Hanover	1760–1820
George IV	Hanover	1820–1830
William IV	Hanover	1830–1837
Victoria I	Hanover	1837–1901

Appendix B

Chief Cabinet Ministers, 1721–1874

The modern party system is not regarded as having come into existence until the late eighteenth century. Hence party affiliations in this list are given from William Pitt the Younger (1783). Before that time, all of the King's ministers were of the Whig persuasion.

Minster	Post	Dates	Party
Sir Robert Walpole	First Lord of the Treasury	1721–1742*	
John Carteret	Secretary of State, Northern Department	1742–1744	
Henry Pelham	First Lord of Treasury	1744–1754	
Duke of Newcastle	First Lord of Treasury	1754–1756	
William Pitt (the Elder)	Secretary of State, Southern Department	1756–1757	
Duke of Newcastle	First Lord of the Treasury	1757–1761	
William Pitt (the Elder)	Secretary of State, Southern Department		
Duke of Newcastle	First Lord of the Treasury	1761–1762	
Earl of Bute	Secretary of State, Northern Department		
Earl of Bute	First Lord of the Treasury	1762–1763	
George Grenville	First Lord of the Treasury	1763–1765	
Marquis of Rockingham	First Lord of the Treasury	1765–1766	
William Pitt (the Elder), Earl of Chatham	Lord Privy Seal	1766–1768	
Duke of Grafton	First Lord of the Treasury	1767–1770	
Lord North	First Lord of the Treasury	1770–1782	

Minster	Post	Dates	Party
Marquis of Rockingham Charles James Fox	First Lord of the Treasury Secretary of State for Foreign Affairs	1782	
Earl of Shelburne William Pitt (the Younger)	First Lord of the Treasury Chancellor of the Exchequer	1782–1783	

Charles James Fox
 	
Lord North
	Secretary of State
	  for Foreign Affairs
	Secretary of State
	  for Home Affairs
		1783	

William Pitt
  (the Younger)
	Prime Minister and First
	  Lord of the Treasury
		1783–1801	Tory

Henry Addington	Prime Minister and First Lord of the Treasury	1801–1804	Tory

William Pitt
  (the Younger)
	Prime Minister and First
	  Lord of the Treasury
		1804–1806	Tory

Lord Grenville Charles James Fox	Prime Minister and First Lord of the Treasury Foreign Secretary	1806–1807	Whig
Duke of Portland	Prime Minister and First Lord of the Treasury	1807–1809	Tory
Spencer Perceval	Prime Minister and First Lord of the Treasury	1809–1812	Tory
Earl of Liverpool Viscount Castlereagh	Prime Minister and First Lord of the Treasury Foreign Secretary	1812–1827	Tory
George Canning	Prime Minister	1827	Tory
Viscount Goderich	Prime Minister	1827	Tory
Duke of Wellington Sir Robert Peel	Prime Minister Home Secretary	1828–1830	Tory
Earl Grey Lord Brougham	Prime Minister Lord Chancellor	1830–1834	Whig
Viscount Melbourne	Prime Minister	1834	Whig
Sir Robert Peel	Prime Minister	1834–1835	Conservative
Viscount Melbourne Viscount Palmerston	Prime Minister Foreign Secretary	1835–1841	Whig
Sir Robert Peel	Prime Minister	1841–1846	Conservative

Minster	Post	Dates	Party
Lord John Russell Viscount Palmerston	Prime Minister Foreign Secretary	1846–1852	Whig
Earl of Derby Benjamin Disraeli	Prime Minister Chancellor of the Exchequer	1852	Conservative
Earl of Aberdeen William E. Gladstone	Prime Minister Chancellor of the Exchequer	1852–1855	Peelite/Whig
Viscount Palmerston	Prime Minister	1855–1858	Whig
Earl of Derby Benjamin Disraeli	Prime Minister Chancellor of the Exchequer	1858–1859	Conservative
Viscount Palmerston William E. Gladstone	Prime Minister Chancellor of the Exchequer	1859–1865	Liberal
Lord John Russell William E. Gladstone	Prime Minister Chancellor of the Exchequer	1865–1866	Liberal
Earl of Derby Benjamin Disraeli	Prime Minister Chancellor of the Exchequer	1866–1868	Conservative
William E. Gladstone	Prime Minister	1868–1874	Liberal

*The title "Prime Minister" was used occasionally in the early eighteenth century and one can argue plausibly that Sir Robert Walpole (1721–1742) was the first "Prime Minister." However, some historians contend that the first of the genuine Prime Ministers, with complete control over choice of ministers for this cabinet, was William Pitt the Younger (1783–1801). By the early nineteenth century, the title of "Prime Minister" was in common use.

Index

Aberdeen, George Hamilton Gordon, fourth earl of, 343
Aberdeen, Scotland, 15
Aborigines, 324
Adam, Robert, 115
Adam, William, 115
Addington, Henry, 342
Addison, Joseph, 51
Afghanistan, 327
Agricultural laborers, 49, 253
Agriculture, 8. *See also* Corn Laws (1815); Industrial Revolution; Science
  in Augustan Age, 57–59
  Conservative Party defense of, 267
  in 1815–1850, 241
  enclosure process in, 175–177
  high farming and, 298
  in Ireland, 21, 163, 283–285
  in mid-Victorian period, 298
  Norfolk system, 175
  revolution in, 174–175
  in Scotland, 16, 17
  in Scottish Highlands, 113–114
  in seventeenth-century England, 5–6
  in seventeenth-century Wales, 13
  social consequences of revolution in, 190–196
Aix-la-Chapelle, Treaty of (1748), 132
Albert, Prince, 301
Alexander I, Czar of Russia, 332
All Saints Church, London, England, 311
American Revolution, 152–155
  events leading to, 149–152
  military campaigns of, *154*
  Treaty of Versailles and, 155–156
Amusements. *See* Recreations and games
Anglicanism. *See* Church of England
Anne, queen of England (1702–1714), 36, 42, 339
Anti-Corn Law League, 273–275

Anti-State Church Association, 269
Architecture, 94–98
  country houses, 94–96, 244
  ecclesiastical buildings, 94
  in eighteenth-century Ireland, 170
  Gothic, 232, 311
  industrial building, 310–311
  Palladian style of, 95–96, *96*
  Romanticism and, 231–232
  Victorian, 310–311
Argyll, Archibald Campbell, ninth earl of, 29, 109
Aristocracy, 243–247. *See also* Gentry; Landowners
  in Augustan Age, 48–51
  educational institutions of, 246–247
  marriage and, 247
  privileges of, 50
  in seventeenth century, 6
Arkwright, Richard, 189, 190
Army, 123, 125
Arnold, Thomas, 246
Art. *See* Literature; Painting
Artisans, 50. *See also* Skilled workers
Ashley, Lord. *See* Shaftesbury, Anthony Ashley Cooper, seventh earl of
Asiento, 43–44
Association for the Preservation of Liberty and Property, 205
Aughrim, Battle of (1690), 38
Augustan Age, 47. *See also* Seventeenth century
  agriculture in, 57–59
  British Empire in, 126–131
  capitalism in, 59–62
  children in, 56–57
  cities and towns in, 53
  commerce in, 59–62
  custom in, 62–63
  education in, 56

Augustan Age (*continued*)
  literacy in, 78, 100–101, 255
  manufacturing in, 61
  patronage and deference in, 51–53
  population explosion in, 177–180
  role of property in, 51
  shipping in, 60
  social mobility in, 50–51
  social relationships in, 51–53
  status hierarchy in, 47–51
  trade in, 60–62
  writers in, 90–91
Austen, Jane, 308
Australia, 324, 326
Austria, 122, 331
Austrian Succession, War of, 75
Authors. *See* Literature; Men of letters;
  Writers

Bagehot, Walter, 299
Bakewell, Robert, 175
Balance of power, 124
Bank of England, 42, 60
Banks, Sir Joseph, 102
Baroque style of architecture, 95
Barry, Charles, *310, 311*
Beaconsfield, Benjamin Disraeli, first earl
  of, 66, 245, 343
Belgium, 331
Beliefs, 101
Bell, Andrew, 255
Bell, Ellis (Emily Brontë), 380
Bentham, Jeremy, 88, 215–217, 262, 306
Bentinck, William Henry Cavendish. *See*
  Portland, William Henry Cavendish
  Bentinck, third duke of
Berkeley, George, 86
Bill of Rights (1689), 35
Bingham, George Charles. *See* Lucan,
  George Charles Bingham, third earl of
Birmingham, England, 239
Birth rates, eighteenth century, 179
Black, Joseph, 115
Black Hole of Calcutta, 134
Blackstone, Sir William, 56, 216
Black Watch Regiment, 109, 111
Blake, William, 200, 226–227, 232
Bleinheim Palace, 94

Bloody Assizes, 30
Bolingbroke, Henry St. John, Viscount, 43,
  44, 68, 88, 148
Bonaparte, Napoleon. *See* Napoleon I
Book of Common Prayer, 10
Boroughs, 70
Boston Massacre (1770), 151
Boulton, Matthew, 183
Boyne, Battle of (1690), 38
Bradford, England, 239
Brewing industry, 9
Bridges, 311
Bright, John, 273, 334
Bristol, England, 60, 239
Britain. *See* Great Britain
Britannia Bridge (Menai Strait), 311
British and Foreign Bible Society, 322
British and Foreign School Society, 255
British Association for the Advancement
  of Science (BAAS), 312
British Empire
  in 1689 (map), *127*
  in 1815 (map), *128*
  in 1870 (map), *323*
  in eighteenth century, 126–131
  emigration to, 321–322
  expansion of, 322
  formal, 321–322
  informal, 320–321
  missionaries and, 322
British empiricism, 84–87
British Isles. *See* Great Britain
British Museum, Leeds, England, 311
British Relief Association, 292
Brontë, Charlotte, 308
Brontë, Emily (Ellis Bell), 308
Brougham, Henry Peter Brogham, first
  Baron, 342
Brown, Capability, 95
Browning, Robert, 303
Brudenell, James Thomas. *See* Cardigan,
  James Thomas Brudenell, seventh
  earl of
Brunel, I. K., 311
Buckle, H. T., 300
Burdett, Sir Francis, 263
Burgoyne, John, 153
Burke, Edmund, 144, 201, 260

Burlington, Lord, 95
Burma, 327
Burn, E. L., 297
Burnet, Gilbert, 32, 35
Burney, Fanny, 91
Burns, Robert, 229
Bute, John Stuart, third earl of, 135, 143, 341
Butler, Bishop Joseph, 84, 88
Butler, James. *See* Ormond, James Butler, first duke of
Butterfield, William, 311
Byron, George Gordon Byron, 6th Baron, 229, 331

Cabinet system, 72, 325
Calvinistic Methodists, 225
Cambridge University, 100, 246
Cameronians, 39
Campbell, Archibald. *See* Argyll, Archibald Campbell, ninth earl of
Campbell, Colen, 95–96, *96*
Canada, 324, 325
Canning, George, 205, 330–331, 342
Capitalism, 61
   in Augustan Age, 59–62
   depressions and, 241–242
Capital punishment, 70–71
Cardigan, James Thomas Brudenell, seventh earl of, 334
Carey, John, *167*
Carlton Club, 267
Carlyle, Thomas, 242, 251, 303, 305, 307
Caroline of Ansbach, queen of England, 75
Carter, Elizabeth, 91
Carteret, John, 341
Cartwright, Edmund, 188
Cartwright, John, 201, 263
Castlehouse, Irleland, 170
Castlereagh, Robert Stewart, Viscount, 211, 329–330, 342
Catholic Association, 286
Catholic Church. *See* Roman Catholic Church
Catholic Emancipation, 171, 264–265, 266, 285–287, 286
Celts, 4, 15
Chadwick, Edwin, 270–271, 272

Chapone, Hester, 91
Charity schools, 10
Charles, Thomas, 225
Charles Edward (Young Pretender), 108, 110–112
Charles II, king of England (1660–1685), 21, 25–28
Chartism, 275–278
Chatham, William Pitt, earl of, 51, 73, 76–77, *77*, 133–135, 143, 151, 341
Chesterfield, Philip Dormer Stanhope, fourth earl of, 88–89, 112, 124
Child, Sir Josiah, 51
Child labor, 271
Children, in eighteenth century, 56–57
China, 322–324
Churchill, John. *See* Marlborough, John Churchill, first duke of
Churchill, Sarah. *See* Marlborough, Sarah Churchill, first duchess of
Church of England, 4, 10, 91, 245–246. *See also* Religion
   Conservative Party defense of, 267–268
   Evangelicalism and, 223–224, 246
   James II and, 30–32
   Oxford Movement and, 314
   Parliament and, 260
   political orientation of, 91–93
   schools and role of, 100–101
   working classes and, 256
Church of Ireland, 160, 269, 282, 287
   Great Famine and, 292
Church of Scotland, 18, 39, 110, 116–117
   Parliament and, 260
Cities and towns
   in Augustan Age, 53
   growth of industrial, 239–240
Civil service, professionalism and, 272–273
Civil War, in Ireland, 20
Clapham Sect, 224
Clarendon Code, 12, 26, 27, 31
Class society, 3, 243–247. *See also* Aristocracy; Middling (middle) sort; Social mobility; Working classes
   formation of, 194, 212–213
   politics of, 273–278
Clergy, 93. *See also* Church of England; Roman Catholic Church

Clive, Robert, 134–135
Clubs
  mutual-aid, 257
  political, 267
Coal mining industry, 182–183
  geographical specialization of, 186–187
  laborers, 252–253
  women in, 253
Cobbett, William, 213, 255, 263
Cobden, Richard, 273, 321, 334
Coercive Acts, 152
Coffeehouses, 78
Coke, Thomas, 175
Coleridge, Samuel Taylor, 200, 227, 231, 245
Collective responsibility of cabinet, 72
Colonial government, 325
Colonial governors, 148
Colonization
  in India, 134–135, 326–329
  of North America, 129–130
Combination Acts (1799), 194, 212, 257, 263–264
Commerce. *See also* Trade, foreign
  in Augustan Age, 59–62
  in seventeenth century, 9
Common Law, 4
Common rights, 57–58
Common Sense (Paine), 152–153
Communication, in Georgian England, 78
Company of Royal Adventurers, 129
Congregationalists, 10. *See also* Noncon-
  formists
Conservative Party. *See also* Political par-
  ties; Tory Party
  agriculture and, 267
  Church of England and, 267–268
  defense of Corn Laws, 268
  early Victorian tenets of, 267–268
Constable, John, 230, 232
Consumerism, 59
Continental System, 209
Convention Parliament, 34
Cooper, Anthony Ashley. *See* Shaftesbury,
  Anthony Ashley Cooper, seventh earl of
Cope, Sir John, 111
Cornish language, 4
Corn Law of 1784 (Ireland), 170

Corn Laws (1815), 212, 241, 262, 269, 273–275
  Conservative Party's defense of, 268
Cornwallis, Charles, first marquis, 155, 207
Corporation Act, 67, 260, 264
Corruption, 264, 266. *See also* Patronage,
  political
Cort, Henry, 182, 188
Cottagers, 49
Cotton industry, 183–186, 241
Country houses, 94–95, 244
Craftsman (Tory newspaper), 74
Craft unions, 301. *See also* Trade unions
Crimean War, 332–334
Cromwell, Oliver, 20
Cromwell, Thomas, 13
Crystal Palace, *302,* 302–303, 311
Culloden, Battle of (1746), *111,* 112, 131
Cumberland, William Augustus, duke of,
  112
Custom House, Dublin, Ireland, 170
Cymmrodorion Society, 228

Dadd, Frank, *219*
Dahl, M., 85
Dalhousie, James Andrew Broun Ramsay,
  tenth earl and first marquis of, 327
Dalrymple, Sir John (earl of Stair), 40–41
Darby, Abraham, 182, 188, 311
Darien, 105–106
Darwin, Charles, 315–316
Dashwood, Sir George, 51
Davis, Thomas, 289
Declaration of Independence (1776), 163
Declaration of Indulgence (1672), 26, 30, 31
Declaration of Rights. *See* Bill of Rights
  (1689)
Declaratory Act, 151
Decline and Fall of the Roman Empire
  (Gibbon), 90–91
Deference, patronage and, 51–53. *See also*
  Patronage
Defoe, Daniel, 49, 51, 90, 107
Deism, 87–88
Dent, Abraham, 61
Depressions, in Victorian era, 241–242
Derby, Edward George Geoffrey Smith
  Stanley, fourteenth earl of, 343

Derry, Ireland, 37
The Descent of Man (Darwin), 315
Dickens, Charles, 303, 304, 305
Dickinson, John, 148–149
Diderot, Denis, 88
Dillon, John Blake, 289
Disarming Act, 113
Disraeli, Benjamin, first earl of Beacons-
    field, 66, 245, 343
Dissenters. *See* Nonconformists
Divine right, 27
Divorce, 99, 248
Doherty, John, 271
Domestic services, 247, 253–254
Domestic system of manufacturing,
    61–62
Doré, Gustave, *239*
Drummond, Thomas, 288
Drunkenness, 256–257
Dublin, Ireland, 170
Duffy, Gavan, 289
Dundee, John Graham, Viscount, 40
Dundee, Scotland, 15
Durham, John George Lambton, first earl
    of, 325
Dutch Wars, 26

East India Company, 60, 126, 134–135,
    151, 241, 324, 326
Ecclesiastical buildings, 94
Edgeworth, Maria, 164
Edinburgh, Scotland, 15, 111, 115–116
Education
    in Augustan Age, 56
    Church of England and, 100–101
    in England, 100–101
    in Scotland, 101, 116
    of Victorian middle classes, 250–251
    of women, 254–255
    of working classes, 254–255
Egg, Augustus, 309, *309*
Egypt, 331
Eighteenth century. *See* Augustan Age
Elections, 65–66
    of 1841, 267
    patronage and, 73
Eliot, George (Marian Evans), 308
Eliot, Sir John, 9

Elizabeth I, queen of England (1558–
    1603), 20
Emigration, 322
Emmet, Robert, 285
Empiricism, British, 84–87
Enclosure process
    effects of, 176–177
    forms of, 175–176
Engels, Friedrich, 240
England, 4. *See also* Great Britain; Ireland;
    Scotland; Wales
    agricultural revolution in, 174–175
    climate of, 5
    eighteenth-century population explosion
        in, 177–180
    Enlightenment in, 84
    geography of, 5
    industry and manufacturing in, 8–9
    population growth, 1815–1850, 238
    population in seventeenth century, 6–7
    religion in, 9–10
    social orders in, 7
    standards of living in, 7–8
English Common Law, 4
English language, 4, 238
Engrossing form of enclosure, 175
Enlightenment
    in England, 84
    in Scotland, 115–119
Entailment, principle of, 54
Epiquoise, Age of, 297
Erastian view, 92
Erskine, John. *See* Mar, John Erskine,
    earl of
Eton, 100, 246
European state system, 121–123
    British interests and, 123–126
Evangelicalism, 218–221. *See also* Method-
    ism; Nonconformists
    Church of England and, 223–224, 246
    doubt among Victorians and, 314
    in India, 327, 329
    missionaries and, 322
    traditional pastimes and, 256–257
Evans, Marian (George Eliot), 308
Excavation of the Olive Mount on the
    Liverpool to Manchester Railway
    (painting), *243*

Exclusion Bill (1680), 27
Exclusion Crisis, 29

Factory Act of 1833, 271
Factory reform, 271
Family life, 98–99. *See also* Women
  in Augustan Age, 56
  Industrial Revolution and, 192
  Puritanism and, 56–57
Famine. *See* Great Famine
Farming. *See* Agriculture
Farm laborers, 49, 253
Ferguson, Adam, 115
Fiction writing, 305
Fielding, Henry, 53, 55, 90
Flood, Henry, 168
Food riots, 79
Foreign affairs, 123–126, 329–332
Foreign trade. *See* Trade, foreign
Forth Bridge, 311
Four Courts, Dublin, Ireland, 170
Fowler, Sir John, 311
Fox, Charles James, 199, 262, 342
Fox hunting, 244–245
Foxite Whigs, 262
France, 124, 331
  war with England (1793–1798), 202–204
  war with England (1798–1815), 208–211
Franklin, Benjamin, 78, 88
Fraser, Simon, 108
Frederick, Prince of Wales, 142
Freeholders, 49
Free trade, 241
French and Indian War. *See* Seven Years
  War (1756-1763)
French Revolution, 173
  effects of, in Ireland, 171–172
French Revolutionary War, 203
Friendly societies, 257, 301
Friends of the People, Society of the, 201
Frith, William, 309
Fuseli, John Henry, 232

Gaelic, 238
  in Scotland, 15
Gage, Thomas, 152
Gainsborough, Thomas, 48, 96–97
Galloway, Joseph, 152

Game laws, 244
Games and recreations, 101–102
  evangelicalism and, 256–257
Gaskell, Elizabeth, 308
General elections, 65–66
Gentleman's Magazine, 90
Gentry, 7, 243–247. *See also* Aristocracy;
  Landowners
George I, king of England (1714–1727), 44,
  71–72, 74, 108, 124, 339
George II, king of England (1727–1760),
  71–72, 112, 124, 133, 135, 339
George III, king of England (1760–1820),
  135, 141–144, 146, 175, 199, 207
  American Revolution and, 152–153
  George Grenville and, 149
  William Pitt and, 77
George IV, king of England (1820–1830),
  230, 339
Georgian England. *See* Augustan Age
Gibbon, Edward, 90–91
Gibbs, Sir James, 94, *95*
Gladstone, William Ewart, 268, 343
Glasgow, Scotland, 15, 60, 115, 116, 239
Glendower, Owen, 13
Glorious Revolution. *See* Revolution of
  1688; Revolution Settlement
Goderich, Viscount, 342
Gordon, George Hamilton. *See* Aberdeen,
  George Hamilton Gordon, fourth
  earl of
Gordon, Thomas, 148
Gothic style of architecture, 232, 311
Government, national, 80–81
Grafton, duke of, 341
Graham, John. *See* Dundee, John Graham,
  Viscount
Grammar schools, 100, 250
Grand Style of painting, 96
Grattan, Henry, 168
Grattan's Parliament, 169–172
Great Awakening, 147
Great Britain. *See also* England; Ireland;
  Scotland; Wales
  economic stability of, in mid-Victorian
  period, 297–298
  eighteenth century population explosion
  in, 177–180

ethnic groups in, 4
European state system and, 123–126
French Revolution and, 200
historic counties of, *2*
in late seventeenth century, 3–5
as political entity, 4
power and interests of, 319–320
topography of, *11*
united with Ireland, 206–207
war with France (1793–1798), 202–204
war with France (1798–1815), 208–211
war with United States (1812–1814),
210
Great Exhibition (1851), 301–303, 311
Great Famine, 274, 284–285, 289–293, *290*
Great Fire of 1666, 6
Grenville, George, 144, 149, 341, 342
Grey, Charles, second earl, 265, 268, 342
Gwilym, Dafydd ap, 228
Gwyneddigion, Society of, 228

Halévy, Elie, 223
Hanoverian dynasty, 44, 124. *See also* indi-
vidual monarch
Hardy, Thomas, 201, 204
Hargreaves, James, 188
Harley, Robert. *See* Oxford, Robert Harley,
earl of
Harris, Howell, 225
Harrow, 100, 246
Hay-Wain (painting), 230
Heads of bills, 162
Henry VII, king of England (1485–1509), 13
Henry VIII, king of England (1509–1547), 4
High Churchmen, 92
High farming, 298
Highland clans, 15–16, *16*, 108, 131
destruction of, 112–115
Highland Clearances, 114, 238
Highlands, of Scotland, 14–15
last stand of, 109–112
society in, 16–17
William III and, 40
Hoadly, Bishop, 92
Hoche, Lazare, 206
Hodgskin, Thomas, 263
Hogarth, William, *55,* 67, 97, *145*
Holland, 32, 41–42, 125

Holy Roman Empire, 33
Horne Tooke, John, 201, 204
Hospitals, 178
House of Commons, 72, 259. *See also*
Parliament
electorate for, 260
rise political parties in, 267–269
House of Lords, 72, 259. *See also*
Parliament
Housing
in Scotland, 17
in Wales, 13
Howe, Richard, earl of, 204
Howe, Sir William, 153
Huguenots, 9, 30
Hume, David, 86–87, 115, 117
Hunt, William Holman, 309–310
Huskisson, William, 241, 273, 283
Hutcheson, Francis, 115, 116
Huxley, T. H., 316

Income tax, 208
India, 126
East India Company in, 134–135
missionaries in, 327, 329
Victorian Empire and, 326–329
Indian Mutiny (1857), 327–328, *328*
Individualism, 251
Industrial building, 310–311
Industrial Revolution, 180–181. *See also*
Agriculture; Science
in 1815–1850, 240–243
cultural preconditions for, 189–190
economic preconditions for, 187–188
geographical specialization and, 186–
187
growth of cities and towns in, 239–240
in Ireland, 186, 283
in 1760 (map), *184*
in 1848 (map), *185*
rule of law and, 189
social consequences of, 190–196
social preconditions for, 188–189
in Wales, 186–187
Industry, 8–9
Infant mortality, 98
Inoculation, 178
Intellectuals. *See* Men of letters

Ireland, 206. *See also* England; Great
    Britain; Scotland; Wales
  agriculture in, 21, 163–164, 283–284
  architecture in eighteenth-century, 170
  British conquest of, 4
  Catholic emancipation in, 285–287
  Civil War in, 20
  cultivation of potato in, 164–165
  economic development in eighteenth
    century, 162–163
  effects of French Revolution in, 171–172
  French Revolution and, 200
  geography of, 18–19
  Grattan's Parliament, 169–172
  Great Famine and, 274, 284–285, 289–
    293, *290*
  historic counties of, *2*
  Industrial Revolution in, 186
  Irish language in, 238
  Irish Question and, 281–285
  movement to repeal Act of Union in,
    287–289
  plantation policy in, 20, 21
  population of, 19, 164–165, 177–178
  poverty in, 162–163
  Protestant ascendancy in, 166–169
  Protestant landlords and, 159–162
  religion in, 4, 19–20
  Revolution Settlement in (1688–1691),
    36–39
  united with Britain, 206–207
  Young Ireland and, 293–295
Irish Parliament, 38, 159–160, 160, 162,
    166. *See also* Parliament
  Catholic emancipation and, 171
  constitution of 1782 and, 169–170
  Grattan's Parliament, 169–172
  parliamentary reform and, 171
  Patriot Parliament, 38
Irish Question
  economic aspect of, 283–285
  political aspect of, 281–282
  religious aspect of, 282–283
Irish Reform Act (1832), 266, 287
Irish Volunteers, 167, *167*
Iron Bridge at Coalbrookdale (painting),
    182, 311
Iron industries, 181–182, 186

Jacobitism
  in Ireland, 160
  in Scotland, 39–40, 107–109
  Tories and, 67–68
Jamaica, 326
James Edward (the Old Pretender), 42, 68,
    108–109
James I, king of England (1603–1625), 4, 20
James II, king of England (1685–1688),
    26–27, 28–32, 39, 108, 339
  Church of England and, 30–32
  death of, 42
  revolt against, 33–34
  Scotland and, 39–40
James VI, king of Scotland (1567–1625),
    4, 20
James VII, king of Scotland. *See* James II,
    king of England (1685–1688)
Jefferson, Thomas, 152
Jeffreys, George, 30
Jenkins' Ear, War of (1739–1748), 75,
    131–132
Jenkinson, Robert Banks. *See* Liverpool,
    Robert Banks Jenkinson, second
    earl of
Jenyns, Soames, 87
Jervis, John, 204
Johnson, Samuel, 48, 59, 91, 114
Joint-stock companies, 60
Jones, Griffith, 225
Justices of the peace, 7, 70

Kay, Sir James, 272
Keble College, Oxford, England, 311
Kent, William, 96
Kilham, Alexander, 223
Killiecrankie, Battle of (1689), 40
King George's War (1739–1748), 75,
    131–132

Laboring poor, 49
Laissez-faire, 118
Lake, Gerard, Viscount, 207
Lalor, James Fintan, 294
Lamb, William. *See* Melbourne, William
    Lamb, second viscount
Lambton, John George. *See* Durham, John
    George Lambton, first earl of

Lancaster, Joseph, 255
Land. *See* Property
Landowners, 243–247. *See also* Aristocracy; Gentry
French Revolution and, 237
Industrial Revolution and, 189
privileges of, 50
1793–1815 war with France and, 211–212
Landscape architecture, 95
Landseer, Edwin, 309
Laslett, Peter, 53
Latitudinarianism, 93–94
Law, rule of, 70–71
Industrial Revolution and, 189
Law, rule of, and utilitarianism, 216
Law, William, 87
League of Augsburg, War of the (1689–1697), 41–42
Leeds, England, 239, 311
Lennox, Charlotte, 91
Letters of Fire and Sword, 17
Liberalism, 251
Liberal Party, 251, 267. *See also* Political parties; Whig Party
evolution of, 268–269
Victorian tenets of, 269
Liberation Society, 269
Lichfield House Compact, 287
Life expectancy
in eighteenth century, 98
in seventeenth century, 3
Limerick, Treaty of (1691), 38
Limited liability companies, 248
Linen industry, 186
Literacy, 100–101, 255
in Georgian England, 78
Literature
in Augustan Age, 90–91
fiction writing and, 305
men of letters and, 303–304
novel in, 90
poetry, 89–90, 226–228, 305–306
Victorian women and, 308
Liverpool, England, 60, 239
Liverpool, Robert Banks Jenkinson, second earl of, 261, 262, 342
Living conditions, 98

Local government, 68–71
Locke, John, 34, 51, 84, *85,* 85–86, 86, 94
London, England, 311
police force of, 261
population of, 239
riots in, 78–79
in seventeenth century, *6,* 6–7
shipping and, 60
London Corresponding Society (LCS), 201, 204–205, 206
Louis XIV, king of France, 26, 27, 30, 41
War of the Spanish Succession and, 42–43
William III and, 32–33
Low Churchmen, 92
Lowlands, of Scotland, 17
Loyal National Repeal Association, 288–289
Lucan, George Charles Bingham, third earl of, 334
Luddite movement, 194–196, 263
Lyell, Charles, 315

Macaulay, Thomas Babington, 276, 300, 304
Macaulay, Zachary, 224
Mackintosh, Sir James, 261
Malthus, Thomas Robert, 217–218, 315
Manchester, England, 93, 239, 240, 311
Manchester, University of, 313
Manchester Cotton Spinners, 271
Manchester School of Economics, 241
Manley, Mary Delariviere, 91
Manufacturing, 8–9, 61–62
Maoris, 324
Mar, John Erskine, earl of, 108
Marlborough, John Churchill, first duke of, 42–43, *43*
Marlborough, Sarah Churchill, first duchess of, 42, *43*
Marriage, 98
aristocracy and, 247
divorce and, 99
increase in early, 179
landowning classes and, 54–56
Victorian middle class and, 248
Marriage Act (1857), 248
Marriage à-la-Mode (Hogarth), *55*
Mary of Modena, queen of England, 31

Mechanics Institutes, 256
Mehemet Ali, 331
Melbourne, William Lamb, second vis-
  count, 268, 342
Men of letters, 303–304. *See also* Literature; Writers
Mercantilism, 118, 122–123
Merchants, 9–10, 50
Merewerth Castle, Kent, England, 96, *96*
Methodism, 256. *See also* Evangelicalism;
  Nonconformists
  attractions of, 221–223
  origins of, 218–221
  in Wales, 224–225
Miall, Edward, 269
Middling (middle) sort, 49–50
  corruption and, 264
  education of, 250–251
  housing and, 247–248
  income ranges of, 247
  men of letters and, 303–304
  Parliamentary reform and, 262–263
  personal virtues of, 251
  political ideology of, 251–252
  reading and, 303
  religion and, 249–250
  role of women in, 248
  servants and, 247
  voting qualifications for, 266
Mill, James, 217, 265
Mill, John Stuart, 269, 300, 303, 306–307,
  307
Millais, John Everett, 309–310
Missionaries
  evangelicalism and, 322
  in India, 327, 329
Mitchel, John, 294
Molyneux, William, 166
Monarchy, divine right and, 27
Monea Castle, County Femanagh, Ireland,
  22
Monmouth, James Scott, duke of, 29–30
Monotorial system, 255
Montagu, Elizabeth, 91
Montagu, Lady Mary Wortley, 91
Montcalm de Saint-Véran, Marquis de,
  133–134
More, Hannah, 205, 224, 300

Morganwg, Iolo, 228
Morier, D., *111*
Morland, George, *58*
Mortality rates, 98. *See also* Life
  expectancy
Mr and Mrs Andrews (painting), *48*
Mrs. Siddons as the Tragic Muse (painting),
  97
Municipal Corporations Act, 265–266
Mutiny Act (1689), 35
Mutual-aid clubs, 257

Nantes, Edict of, 30
Napier, Charles, 327
Napoleon I, emperor of the French, 203,
  206, 208–210
Nash, John, *229*, 231
National Society, 255
The Nation (Irish newspaper), 289
Natural theology, religion and, 87–89
Navigation Acts, 60, 131, 241
Navvies, 253
Navy, 122, 125, 320
  Spithead mutiny, 206
Nelson, Sir Horatio, 204, *209*
Netherlands. *See* Belgium; Holland
Newcastle, Thomas Pelham, duke of, 76,
  77, 92, 142, 341
Newcomen, Thomas, 182–183
Newman, John Henry, 314
New model trade unions, 301
Newspapers, 78, 255–256
Newton, Sir Isaac, 84–85, 94
Newton, Thomas, 92
New Zealand, 324, 326
Nicholas I, czar of Russia, 332
Nightingale, Florence, 248–249
Nile, Battle of the (1798), 206
Nobility. *See* Aristocracy
Nomination boroughs, 267
Nonconformists, 9–12, 91. *See also* Evan-
  gelicalism; Methodism; Religion
  as allies of science, 312–313
  education and, 250–251
  Industrial Revolution and, 190
  in Ireland, 160, 282
  James II and, 31
  Parliament and, 260

Parliament of 1689 and, 36
Victorian middle class and, 249–250
in Wales, 14
working classes and, 256
Norfolk system of agriculture, 175
Norm language, 15
North, Frederick, Lord, 155, 168, 199, 341, 342
North America, colonization of, 129–130.
See also American Revolution
North Briton, 144
Northcote, Sir Stafford, 272
Novel, 90
Nutrition, 179

Oastler, Richard, 271
O'Brien, William Smith, 294
O'Connell, Daniel, 264–265, 268, 285–289, *288*
Young Irelanders and, 293–295
O'Connor, Feargus, 276–278, 287
Old Pretender (James Edward), 42, 68, 108–109
Open-field system, 8, 57
Opium, 324
Orange Society, 171
Orders in Council (1812), 262
Organized labor. *See* Trade unions
Origin of Species (Darwin), 315
Ormond, James Butler, first duke of, 37
Over London by Rail (painting), *239*
Owen, Robert, 263
Oxford, Robert Harley, earl of, 43
Oxford Movement, 314
Oxford University, 100, 246
Oxford University Science Museum, 311

Paine, Tom, 152–153, 201, 213
Painting, 94–98, 309
Grand Style of, 96
portraiture, 96–97
Pre-Raphaelites, 309–310
Romanticism and, 232
Victorian, 309–310
Palladian style of architecture, 95–96, *96*
Palladio, Andrea, 96
Palmerston, Henry John Temple, Viscount, 299, 322, *330,* 331–332, 342, 343

Paris, Treaty of (1763), 135, 149
Paris, Treaty of (1856), 334
Parish unit of government, 69
Parliament, 72, *310,* 311. *See also* House of Commons; House of Lords; Irish Parliament; Scottish Parliament
Bill of Rights and, 35
Church of England and, 260
Church of Scotland and, 260
Convention, 34
reform of (1815–1835), 261–266
unrepresentativeness of, 259–261
Parliamentary enclosure, 175–176
Parliament House, Dublin, Ireland, 170, *170*
Past and Present, Number One (painting), *309*
Patriot Parliament (Ireland), 38
Patronage, political
in Augustan Age, 51–52, 54
concentration of government and, 66
elections and, 73
members of Parliament and, 72–73
Paxton, Sir Joseph, 302, 311
Peel, Sir Robert, 261, 265, 267, *268,* 269, 273, 282, 289, 291, 342
Peers. *See* Aristocracy
Pelham, Henry, 76, 341
Pelham, Thomas. *See* Newcastle, Thomas Pelham, duke of
Penal codes, 70–71
Perceval, Spencer, 342
Periodicals, 90
Perkin, Harold, 53
Peterloo Massacre, 264
Petty, Sir William, 7
Petty, William. *See* Shelburne, William Petty, second earl of
Philosophy
British Empiricism, 84–87
of John Locke, 86
Pickersgill, H. W., *268*
Pitt, Thomas "Diamond," 51, 76
Pitt, William, earl of Chatham, 51, 73, 76–77, *77,* 133–135, 143, 151, 341
Pitt, William, the Younger, 197–200, *198,* 202, 208, 285, 342
Place, Francis, 265

Plague, 178
Plantation policy, 20, 21
Plassey, Battle of (1757), 135
Plumb, J. H., 65
Poetry, 89–90
  mid-Victorian, 305–306
  Romanticism and, 226–228
Political clubs, 267
Political parties. *See also* Conservative
    Party; Liberal Party; Tory Party; Whig
    Party
  Burke's definition of, 144
  formation of, 27
The Polling (painting), *67*
Poor, treatment of, 69–70
Poor Laws, 218, 245
  of 1834, 270–271
Pope, Alexander, 84, 89, 91
Popular politics, 78–80
Population
  growth of, 178–180, 238–240
  of Ireland, 19, 164–165, 177–178
  in seventeenth century Scotland, 15
Porter, Roy, 59
Portland, WIlliam Henry Cavendish
    Bentinck, third duke of, 342
Portraiture painting, 96–97
Postal service, 78
Potato cultivation, in Ireland, 164–165
Potato famine, 284–285, 289–293
Poynings Law, 162, 168
Pre-Raphaelites, 309–310
Presbyterians, 10, 39. *See also* Noncon-
    formists
Press, the, in Georgian England, 78
Price, Richard, 201
Priestly, Joseph, 205
Prime Ministers, 66, 339–341
Primitive Methodism, 256
Primogeniture, 53
Principia Mathematica (Newton), 85
Professional people, 50, 245
Property, 51
  primogeniture and, 53
  strict settlements and, 53–54
Proprietary schools, 251
Protestant Ascendancy, 38–39
Protestant ethic, 189–190

Prussia, 122
Public education, 255
Public health, 272
Public Health Act of 1848, 272
Public opinion, 78, 267
Public schools, 100, 246
  middle classes and, 250
Pubs, 256–257
Pugin, A. W., *310,* 311
Punjab, 327
Puritanism, 10
  family life and, 56–57
  in North America, 147
Putting out system of manufacturing,
    61–62

Quakers, Great Famine and, 292
Quebec, conquest of, 133–134, *134*
Quebec Act (1774), 152

Radical movement, 204–205, 213
Raeburn, Henry, 115
Raglan, Fitzroy James Henry Somerset,
    Baron, 333–334
Railways, 242–243
Ramsay, Allan, 115
Recreations and games, 101–102
  evangelicalism and, 256–257
Reform Act of 1832, 265, 266–267, 331
Reform Club, 267
Religion. *See also* Church of England;
    Church of Ireland; Church of Scot-
    land; Nonconformists; Roman
    Catholic Church
  natural theology and, 87–89
  science and decline of, 313–316
  in Scotland, 17–18
  traditional pastimes and, 256–257
  working classes and, 256–257
Responsible government, in British
    colonies, 325–326
Revolution of 1688, 25
  in Ireland, 36–39
  in Scotland, 39–41
Revolution Settlement, 25, 35
  in Ireland, 36–39
  in Scotland, 39–41
Reynolds, Sir Joshua, 96, *97*

Richardson, Samuel, 90
The Rights of Man (Paine), 201, 213
Riots, 78–79, 195
  agrarian, 263
  Swing Riots, 270
Roads, 78
Roberts, Thomas Valentine, *243*
Rockingham, Charles Watson-Wentworth,
  marquis of, 151, 168, 199, 341, 342
Roebuck, J. A., 334
Roman Catholic Church, 10, 91. *See also*
  Religion
  in Ireland, 4, 19–20, 22, 160–161, 282–
  283
  James II and, 29–31
  political rights and, 264–265
  working classes and, 256
Romanticism, 225–226
  architecture and, 231–232
  first generation poets, 226–227
  painting and, 232
  poetry and, 226–228
  in Scotland, 229–231
  second generation poets, 228
  in Wales, 228–229, 238–239
Romilly, Sir Samuel, 261
Rossetti, Dante Gabriel, 309–310
Rotten boroughs, 266
Rough music, 79–80
Rowland, Daniel, 225
Royal Academy, 97–98
Royal African Company, 129, 241
Royal Albert Bridge, Saltash, England, 311
Royal Courts of Justice, London, England,
  311
Royal Exchange, Dublin, Ireland, 170
Royal Pavilion, Brighton, England, *229,* 231
Royal Society, 312
Rugby public school, 250
Rule of law. *See* Law, rule of
Ruskin, John, 303, 310, 311
Russell, Lord John, 262, 268, 292, 343
Russell, W. H., 334
Russia, 332–333
Ryswick, Peace of (1697), 41–42

Sabbatarianism, 250
Sacheverell, Henry, 78

Sadler, Michael, 271
St. John, Henry. *See* Bolingbroke, Henry
  St. John, Viscount
St. Martin's-in-the-Fields church, London,
  England, 94, *95*
St. Pancras railway station and hotel, Lon-
  don, England, 311
St. Paul's Cathedral, London, England, *6*
Sanitation, 178
Sarsfield, Patrick, 38
Schools. *See also* Education; Universities
  charity, 10
  Church of England and, 100–101
  grammar, 100, 250
  for nonconformists, 250
  proprietary, 251
  public, 100, 246
  Sunday, 100, 255
  for working classes, 254–255
Science. *See also* Agriculture; Industrial
  Revolution
  decline of religion and, 313–316
  revolution in, 188
  rise of, 311–313
Scotland, 4. *See also* England; Great
  Britain; Ireland; Wales
  agricultural revolution in, 174–175
  agriculture in, 16, 17, 113–114
  Celts in, 15
  education in, 101, 116
  eighteenth century population explosion
  in, 177–178
  Enlightenment Age of, 115–119
  geography in, 14
  Highland clans of, 15–16, *16,* 108, 112–
  115, 131
  Highlands of, 14–17, 40, 109–112
  Jacobite rebellion of 1715, 107–109
  radical societies in, 204
  rebellion lead by earl of Argyll, 29
  religion in, 4, 17–18
  revolt of 1745, 109–112
  Revolution Settlement in, 39–41
  Romanticism in, 229–231
  Union of 1707, 105–107
Scott, James. *See* Monmouth, James Scott,
  duke of
Scott, Sir Walter, 229–230

Scottish Convention, 204–205
Scottish Parliament, 105–106. *See also*
Parliament
Scottish Society for the Propagation of
Christian Knowledge (SSPCK), 110
Security, Act of (1696), 105
Semiskilled workers, 252–253
Septennial Act (1715), 66
Servants, 253–254
middle class and, 247
Settlement, Act of (1701), 36
Seventeenth century. *See also* Augustan
Age
agriculture in, 5–6
life expectancy in, 3
London in, *6*
standards of living in, 7–8
Seven Years War (1756–1763), 132–135,
145
consequences of, 135–136
Shaftesbury, Anthony Ashley Cooper,
seventh earl of, 241
Sheffield, England, 239
Shelburne, William Petty, second earl of,
342
Sheriffmuir, Battle of (1715), 109
Shipping, in Augustan Age, 60
Simon, Sir John, 272
Sind, 327
Sinecures, 260
Siraj-ud-Daula, 134–135
Six Acts, 264
Skilled workers, 252
Skimmingtons, 79–80
Slavery, 224
in England, 129
in West Indies, 129
Smiles, Samuel, 299
Smith, Adam, 115, *117,* 117–118, 200
Smith, Southwood, 272
Smollett, Tobias, 58–59
Soane, Sir John, 231
Soap making, 9
Social classes, 3, 243–247. *See also* Aris-
tocracy; Middling (middle) sort; Social
mobility; Working classes
formation of, 194, 212–213
politics of, 273–278

Social mobility, 54. *See also* Class society
in Augustan Age, 50–51
in mid-Victorian period, 299–301
Society for Constitutional Information,
201
Society for the Diffusion of Useful Knowl-
edge, 256
Society for the Propagation of Christian
Knowledge, 26
Society of Friends, Great Famine and, 292
Somerset, Fitzroy James Henry. *See*
Raglan, Fitzroy James Henry Somer-
set, Baron
Sons of Liberty, 150
Sophia of Hanover, Electress, 36
South Africa, 325, 326
Southcott, Joanna, 223
Southey, Robert, 200
South Sea Bubble, 60, 74
South Sea Company, 60, 74
Spanish Succession, War of, 42–44
The Spectator, 90
Spithead, mutiny at (1797), 206
Sports, 101–102
SSPCK (Scottish Society for the Propaga-
tion of Christian Knowledge), 110
Stair, earl of (Dalrymple, Sir John), 40–41
Stamp Act (1675), 150
Stamp Tax, 78
Stanhope, Philip Dormer. *See* Chester-
field, Philip Dormer Stanhope, fourth
earl of
Stanley, Edward. *See* Derby, Edward
George Geoffrey Smith Stanley, four-
teenth earl of
State socialism, 217
State system, European, 121–123
British interests and, 123–126
Status hierarchy, 47–51
Steam engines, 182–183
Stephenson, Robert, 311
Stewart, Robert. *See* Castlereagh, Robert
Stewart, Viscount
Storming the closet, 73
Strict settlements, 53–54
Strutt, Jedediah, 190
Stuart dynasty, attempt to regain Scotland
in 1715 by, 107–109

Stuart, John. *See* Bute, John Stuart, third
 earl of
Stubbs, George, 232
Suffrage, Universal manhood, 263
Sugar Act (1764), 150
Sunday schools, 100, 255
Superstition, 101
Suttee, 327
Swift, Jonathan, 166
Swing Riots, 194–196, 270

Tacksmen, 108
Talbot, Richard. *See* Tyrconnel, Richard
 Talbot, earl of
Tamworth Manifesto, 267
Taxation, 81
 for Napoleonic wars, 208
 William III and, 42
Temple, Henry John. *See* Palmerston,
 Henry John Temple, Viscount
Ten Hours Act of 1847, 271
Ten-hours movement, 271
Tenneyson, Alfred Lord, 303, 306
Test Act (1673), 26, 29, 31, 67, 250, 260,
 264
Textile industry, 183–186, 240
Thackeray, William Makepeace, 303
Thirty-Nine Articles, 10–12
Thompson, E.P., 62
Thornton, Henry, 224
Thuggee, 327
Tocqueville, Alexis de, 240
Toland, John, 88
Tolpuddle martyrs, 264
Tories (Ireland), 21
Tory Party, 65–66, 67–68, 267. *See also*
 Conservative Party; Political parties
 formation of, 27, 205
 George I and, 44
 as opposition party, 68
 support of High Churchmen, 92
 William III and, 34–35
Town Hall, Leeds, England, 311
Town Hall, Manchester, England, 311
Towns. *See* Cities and towns
Townshend, Charles Townshend, second
 viscount, 75
Townshend, Charles "Turnip," 151, 175

Tractarian Movement. *See* Oxford Move-
 ment
Trade, foreign. *See also* Commerce
 in Augustan Age, 60–62
 British interests and, 319–320
 creeping colonialism and, 322
 foreign affairs and, 124
 with North American colonies, 131
Trade unions, 252, 257, 263, 271
 new model, 301
Transportation, in Augustan Age, 60–61
Trenchard, John, 148
Trevelyan, Sir Charles, 272, 292, 293
Triennial Act, 35
Triple Revolution. *See* Agriculture, revolu-
 tion in; French Revolution; Industrial
 Revolution
Trollope, Anthony, 303, 304
Tull, Jethro, 175
Turkey, 331, 332–333
Turner, J. M. W., *231,* 232
Two Treatises of Government (Locke), 23
Tyrconnel, Richard Talbot, earl of, 30, 37

Ulster, Ireland, 19, 20, 21, 163, 186, 207,
 284
Unemployment, 242
Uniformity, Act of (1662), 10–12
Union, Act of (1800), 208, 281–282
Union, Acts of, 13
Union, Treaty of (1707), 106–107
Unions. *See* Trade unions
United Irishmen, Society of, 171, 200, 205,
 206
United Kingdom. *See* Great Britain
United States
 American Revolution, 149–156
 war with Great Britain (1812–1814), 21
Universal manhood suffrage, 263
Universities. *See also* Education; Schools
 establishment of provincial, 313
 reform of, 312–313
 in Scotland, 116
Unskilled workers, 252, 253
Urbanization, 239–240
Utilitarianism, 88, 215–217, 307
Utopianism, 263
Utrecht, Treaty of (1713), 43–44

Vaccination, 178
Venetian Oligarchy, 65–66
Venn, John, 224
Versailles, Treaty of (1783), 155
Victoria, queen of England (1837–1901), *249*, 268, 306, 339
Victorian architecture, 310–311
Victorian Gothic architecture, 311
Victorians, complexity of, 237
Villages. *See* Cities and towns
Virginia, 130
Virginia Company, 129
Voltaire, François Marie Arouet de, 88
Voluntary agreement form of enclosure, 175
Volunteer army (Ireland), 167–168
Voting qualifications, 263, 266

Wade, George, 109, 113
Wakefield, Edward Gibbon, 321–322, 324
Wales, 4, 12–14. *See also* Great Britain; Ireland; Scotland
    agricultural revolution in, 174–175
    eighteenth century population explosion in, 178
    Industrial Revolution in, 186–187
    Methodism in, 224–225
    religion in, 14
    Romanticism in, 228–229
    Welsh language in, 238–239
Walpole, Horace, 71, 133, 232
Walpole, Sir Robert, 52, 56, 66, 67, 68, 71, 73–75, *74*, 92, 95, 341
Waltham Black Act, 62, 63
Warfare, 123
War of 1812, 210
The Warrener (painting), 58
Washington, George, 132
Watt, James, 183
The Wealth of Nations (Smith), 118–119, 200
Webb, R. K., 256
Wedgwood, Josiah, 188
Wellesley, Arthur. *See* Wellington, Arthur Wellesley, first duke of
Wellesley, Richard, 326
Wellington, Arthur Wellesley, first duke of, 209–210, 262, 265, 281, 342

Welsh language, 4, 13–14, 238–239
Wesley, Charles, 219
Wesley, John, 91, 218–221, *219*
West Indies, 129, 326
Whig Party, 65–66, 67, 68. *See also* Liberal Party; Political parties
    Church of England and, 92
    formation of, 27
    Foxite, 262
    O'Connell's alliance with, 288
    policies, 269
    Victorians and, 267
    William III and, 34
Whitefield, George, 220
Wife sale, 99
Wilberforce, Bishop Samuel, 316
Wilberforce, William, 224
Wilkes, John, 144–146, *145*, 200
Wilkinson, John, 182
William III, king of England (1688–1702) and Mary I, queen of England (1688–1694), 32–36, *33*, 339
    Parliament and, 34–35
    Scotland and, 40–41, 105
William IV, king of England (1830–1837), 265, 339
Williams, William, *182*, 225
Wilson, Charles, 9
Winchester, 246
Winterhalter, Franz, *249*
Wolfe, James, 133–134
Wolfe Tone, Theobald, 171, 206
Wombwell, Sir George, 51
Women. *See also* Family life; Marriage
    in coal mining industry, 253
    in domestic service, 253–254
    education of, before 1850, 246–247
    as eighteenth century writers, 91
    Industrial Revolution and, 192
    marriage arrangements and, 54–56
    middle-class, 247
    owning property and, 54
    as readers, 89–90
    role of, 99
    role of Victorian middle class, 248
    Victorian writers, 308
    wife sale and, 99
Woolen industry, 8, 183, 186

Wootton, John, 74
Wordsworth, William, 200, 226–227
Work, 99–100
Workhouses, 271
Working classes, 252–257
   attempts to preserve community of, 257
   attitude towards corruption by, 264
   categories of, 252
   Church of England and, 256
   common aspects of, 254–255
   drinking and, 256–257
   Parliamentary reform and, 263–264
   poverty and, 254
   schooling of, 254–255
   voting qualifications and, 266

The Wreck of a Transport Ship (painting),
   231
Wren, Sir Christopher, *6,* 94
Writers. *See also* Literature; Men of letters
   eighteenth century, 90–91
   Victorian women, 308
Wyatt, James, 232

York, James Stuart, duke of. *See* James II,
   King of England (1685–1688)
Young, Arthur, 163, 165
Young Ireland, 289, 293–295
Young Pretender (Charles Edward), 108,
   110–112

Credits

Page 6, London in the late-seventeenth century: Hulton Archive by Getty Images. Page 16, Highland clansmen: By kind permission of Blandford Press. From *The English Civil War*, by P. Haythornthwaite. Page 22, Monea Castle, Ireland: Crown Copyright. Reproduced with the permission of the Controller of Her Majesty's Stationery Office. Page 33, William of Orange landing at Torbay in 1688: A. C. Cooper photo. Reproduced by gracious permission of Her Majesty the Queen. Page 43, *The First Duke of Marlborough and His Family*: Corbis/Bettmann. By permission of the Duke of Marlborough. Page 48, *Mr. and Mrs. Andrews*: National Gallery, London. Page 55, *Marriage-à-la-Mode*: Dover Publications, Inc. Page 58, *The Warrener*: Dick Laurie. Page 67, *The Polling*: Dover Publications, Inc. Page 74, *Sir Robert Walpole as Ranger of Richmond Park*: Marquess of Cholmondeley. Page 77, *William Pitt, First Earl of Chatham*: National Portrait Gallery, London. Page 85, *John Locke*: National Portrait Gallery, London. Page 95, St. Martin's-in-the-Field: Northwestern University Slide Library. Page 96, Mereworth Castle, Kent: A. F. Kersting. Page 97, *Mrs. Siddons as the Tragic Muse*: Huntington Library. Page 111, *The Battle of Culloden*: A. C. Cooper photo. Reproduced by gracious permission of Her Majesty the Queen. Page 117, Adam Smith: National Portrait Gallery, London. Page 125, *Britannia in Distress*: Courtesy of the Print Collection, the Lewis Walpole Library, Yale University. Page 134, *The British Victory at Quebec*: Library of Congress. Page 142, *George III in Coronation Robes*: A. C. Cooper photo. Reproduced by gracious permission of Her Majesty the Queen. Page 145, *John Wilkes*: British Museum. Page 167, *Irish Volunteers Firing a Salute in Lisburn, 1782*: Ulster Museum. Page 170, Parliament House, Dublin: The Irish Picture Library. Page 182, *The Iron Bridge at Coalbrookdale*: Ironbridge Gorge Museum. Page 183, Boulton and Watt Steam Engine: Science Museum, London. Page 193, Woman and child dragging a basket of coal: Mansell/TimePix. Page 195, Luddite letter: Malcolm Thomis. Crown Copyright. Page 198, Prime Minister William Pitt the Younger: National Portrait Gallery, London. Page 209, Admiral Horatio Nelson at the Battle of Trafalger: Corbis/Bettmann. Page 219, *John Wesley Preaching in Cornwall*: Mansell/TimePix. Page 229, The Royal Pavilion, Brighton: Northwestern University Slide Library. Page 230, *The Hay-Wain*: The National Gallery, London. Page 231, A Fire At Sea, c. 1835: ©Glore Collection/Tate Gallery, London/Art Resource, NY. Page 239, *Over London by Rail*: Mary Evans Picture Library. Page 243, *Excavation of the Olive Mount on the Liverpool to Manchester Railway*: Ironbridge Gorge Museum. Page 249, *Queen Victoria, Prince Albert, and Their First Five Children*: Corbis/Bettmann. Page 268, *Sir Robert Peel*: National Portrait Gallery, London. Page 274, Dear bread and cheap bread: Gower Publishing Co. Page 277, The last great Chartist demonstration, 1848: Copyright reserved. Reproduced by gracious permission of Her Majesty the Queen. Page 288, Daniel O'Connell: The Reform Club. Page 290, Irish Famine Victims Receiving Help: Corbis/Bettmann. Page 302, The Crystal Palace, 1851: Victoria & Albert Museum. Page 307, *The Ladies' Advocate*: University Microfilms, Inc. Page 309, *Past and Present, Number One*: The Tate Gallery, London. Page 310, The Houses of Parliament: National Buildings Record, Crown Copyright. Page 328, An imperial scene of the Indian Mutiny, 1857: Mansell/TimePix. Page 330, Lord Palmerston: Corbis/Bettmann.